D1345698

Muslim Women and Shari'ah Councils

Muslim Women and Shari'ah Councils

Transcending the Boundaries of Community and Law

Samia Bano
Lecturer in Family Law, University of Reading, UK

palgrave
macmillan

First published 2012 by
PALGRAVE MACMILLAN

Palgrave Macmillan in the UK is an imprint of Macmillan Publishers Limited, registered in England, company number 785998, of Houndmills, Basingstoke, Hampshire RG21 6XS.

Palgrave Macmillan in the US is a division of St Martin's Press LLC, 175 Fifth Avenue, New York, NY 10010.

Palgrave Macmillan is the global academic imprint of the above companies and has companies and representatives throughout the world.

Palgrave® and Macmillan® are registered trademarks in the United States, the United Kingdom, Europe and other countries.

ISBN 978–0–230–22148–2

This book is printed on paper suitable for recycling and made from fully managed and sustained forest sources. Logging, pulping and manufacturing processes are expected to conform to the environmental regulations of the country of origin.

A catalogue record for this book is available from the British Library.

A catalog record for this book is available from the Library of Congress.

10 9 8 7 6 5 4 3 2 1
21 20 19 18 17 16 15 14 13 12

Printed and bound in Great Britain by
CPI Antony Rowe, Chippenham and Eastbourne

To Adil and our boys
Umar, Zaki and Qais,
with love

Contents

List of Figures

Acknowledgements

This book began its journey as my Ph.D. thesis at the University of Warwick, School of Law, and since its completion in 2005 has, over the years, evolved into a book. Along the way it as been influenced by numerous scholars and friends who have provided invaluable insights for which I am immensely grateful.

I would like to thank Professor Davina Cooper who supported my initial application for a doctorate and who encouraged me to begin this study. A special thanks to my supervisor Professor Abdul Paliwala for creating the intellectual space for me to develop my work, and for his patience, enthusiasm and unflinching support. Without his generosity this book could not have been. I extend my gratitude to ESRC (Economic and Social Research Council) for providing me with a scholarship while at the University of Warwick and to Faye Emery for excellent support in all matters administrative. I would also like to thank Professor Shaheen Ali Sardar for her guidance and advice during my time at Warwick.

I am deeply indebted to all those who contributed to the study, in particular the female interviewees for their faith, inspiration and strength in sharing personal narratives. I would also like to thank the *religious scholars* at the Shari'ah councils for their time, assistance and effort in providing materials.

I am also thankful to Professors Floya Anthias and Nira Yuval-Davis. The work of both Nira and Floya has been critical to my work, helping to better understand the value of developing critical feminist and intersectional analyses and the social/lived experiences of minority ethnic women in Britain. This pioneering scholarship continues to be an important and invaluable influence upon my work and I thank them both for supporting my early work and for their continued friendship and advice. A huge thanks also to my dearest friend Professor Jennifer L. Pierce, who is both an inspiration to me and who provides me with invaluable guidance and support.

Thanks to Professor Werner Menski for his pioneering work on Muslim Family Law that first provided the impetus for my research and whose work continues to provide invaluable insights.

I would like to thank the scholars Professor Salman Sayyid and Abdool Karim for inviting me to take part in debates on Islam and Critical Muslim thinking and for opening up a new terrain of thinking for me of a high intellectual rigour.

I am grateful to all my friends who have been steadfast and supportive during the write up of the book. In particular my friends Alison Morris,

Selma Dabbagh, Rabia Malik, Brenna Bhandar, Sarra Adams, Hina Rahman, Tina Akoto, Cassandra Balchin and Ashika Thanki, and also to Nicos Trimikliniotis who encouraged me to begin this study. I am indebted to Hilary Todd for her invaluable help with editing; her expert advice and assistance helped make this book possible.

I would like to thank my colleagues and friends at the University of Reading. Professor Carl Stychin and Dr Martha-Marie Kleinhams for their continuing friendship and guidance and Professors Chris Hilson and Sandy Ghandi for critical feedback and support.

Writing this book has at times been a long and arduous journey. Along the way have arrived our children, my absences for maternity leave and dealing with various family issues. The book therefore is also a culmination of an important part of my life; and for all the patience, support, advice and guidance I am truly indebted to my editors Amber Galilee-Stone and Liz Howell at Palgrave Macmillan. Thank you both for staying the course with me. And to Andrew Bird for his continued advice and assistance.

As always I am grateful to my family, and I would like to thank my mother; my sisters, Fareeda and Nabila; sister-in-law Ruby; brothers, Wasim, Haroon and Baber; and brothers-in-law Rod George for their love, support and encouragement. To my nieces, Sayra, Amber and Imaan, and nephews, Aran and Zain, who are a huge credit and inspiration to our family. Sadly my father passed away during the completion of this book; I very much miss our conversations but I take strength from my father's love, hard work and commitment to his family.

Finally I would like to thank my husband, Adil, and our three young children. It is hard to know where to begin with Adil, for I am indebted to his unwavering love, support and commitment without which this book could not have been completed. I dedicate this book to him and our boys Umar, Zaki and Qais, who bring so much joy, love and laughter into our lives.

Part I
Background and Context

1
Multiculturalism and Secularism in the British Context

This book investigates the experience of South Asian British Muslim women using Shari'ah councils as unofficial dispute resolution mechanisms to resolve matrimonial disputes in England. It analyses the experiences of these women as part of the wider context of 'community' demands for formal recognition of Shari'ah councils as state-recognized tribunal bodies to resolve matrimonial disputes in accordance with Muslim family law principles and Muslim jurisprudence.

The increasing moves towards implementing a non-adversarial approach to resolving matrimonial disputes have been extensively discussed by English family law scholars but the extent to which this space is increasingly occupied by a new kind of faith-based approach to reconciliation and mediation within minority diasporic communities warrants further scrutiny. This book draws upon the experiences of Muslim women using Shari'ah councils as part of current debates on the limits of the multicultural accommodation of religious practices in Britain. Framed as sites upon which family law matters are resolved according to the principles of Muslim family law, these bodies have emerged within the 'private' sphere of local community and developed frameworks that are characterized by specific cultural and religious norms and values. Self-governing religious bodies that act as unofficial tribunal bodies in matters of family law challenge not only the assumed centrality of state-law mechanisms in resolving matrimonial disputes but also open up the question of relationality in law and developing policies to resolve matrimonial disputes in multicultural Britain via a cross-cultural setting.

In recent years the renewed visibility of Muslim communities in Britain has led to increased discussions on questions of identity, belonging and citizenship in multicultural societies. Following the September 11, 2001, attacks in the US ('9/11'), relations between Muslims and the British state and their position in British society have come to the forefront during debates on integration and are often contextualized as part of a 'crisis of multiculturalism' in Western democratic societies. This book contributes to such ongoing debates on multiculturalism, family law, minority rights and Muslim claims for greater autonomy in matters of family law. The book contends that, by living their lives across multiple social, legal and political identities, Muslims *are* able to utilize Islamic systems of family law as part of their fabric of everyday life. However, there is little empirical research to date which explores *how* Shari'ah councils provide unofficial dispute-resolution mechanisms (within the wider context of alternative dispute resolution (ADR) initiatives in family law) and the experience of female users. Existing scholarship demonstrates that Shari'ah councils have developed frameworks of 'governance' and administrative processes that are characterized by specific and localized cultural and religious norms and values through which we can see in evidence a new form of 'Muslim family justice' emerging within Muslim communities in Britain.

Crucially the book considers in depth the experiences of British Muslim women who choose to resolve matrimonial disputes within the framework of Islamic dispute resolution. The renewed interest in Muslim family law practices within Muslim diasporic communities living in Western European societies has yet revealed very little empirical evidence on this type of 'law-making'. In the post-9/11 environment, the words 'Islamic law', 'Shari'ah' and 'Shari'ah law' can immediately point to all kinds of assumptions and caricatures. Since most thinking about Islam and human rights continues to focus on the perceived Islamic control and subordination of Muslim women, the tendency to present the uniformity and superiority of Islamic law over other forms of social and legal relations reinforces the idea that Muslim women have little if any choice when utilizing such mechanisms of dispute resolution. Subsequently the arguments that favour the formal recognition of Shari'ah councils as opposed to formalization are often positioned in terms of the ideological struggle surrounding the representation of Muslim women. For example, Razack (2007) explains that it is evident that the ongoing 'war on terror' adopts the terminology and draws upon a historical context in order to reproduce a specific Western imaginary of Muslims and Muslim women that leads to forms of 'real life justice' based upon common stereotypes and caricatures. This is not only based upon highly subjective and culture-specific normative underpinnings of what it means to be a Muslim woman but also overlooks the fact that universal human values are contested in all communities. In this way, Razack explains, 'The body of the Muslim woman, a body fixed in the Western imaginary as confined, mutilated and sometimes murdered in the name of culture, serves to reinforce the threat that the Muslim man is said to pose to the West, and is used to justify the extraordinary measures of violence and surveillance required to discipline him and Muslim communities' (2007, p. 105).

Drawing upon original empirical data, this book challenges the language of community rights versus individual rights and questions the basis upon which claims for legal autonomy in matters of family law are made. In doing so it draws upon critiques of power, dialogue and the position of women within the family, home and community to explore how multiple spaces in law, community and identity both empower and restrict women at different times and in different contexts. It also opens up the conceptual space in which we can see evidence of the multiple legal and social realities in operation, within the larger context of state-law, liberal multiculturalism and the human rights discourse. In this way the book provides an important contribution to current debates on the increasing use of ADR in family law disputes within Muslim communities and the significance of understanding the dynamics of relationality and cultural diversity in new forms of ADR practices. In a wider context the book raises some key questions on the conceptual challenges that the rise of a faith-based dispute resolution process poses to secular/liberal notions of law, human rights and gender equality.

Postcolonial migrations have been described as new migrations (Hall, 1992, p. 310) which have led to the creation of diasporic identities that cut across fixed and bounded categories of 'home' and 'belonging' (Brah, 2005). The migration patterns of Muslim communities to Britain have been extensively documented in anthropological and sociological research. The largest groups of South Asian Muslim migrants emerged from Pakistan in the 1950s and 1960s from rural farming areas of the Mirpur district and some parts of Punjab,[1] to satisfy the acute shortage of labour following the post-war boom in Britain. According to Ballard, the notion of *desh pardesh* encapsulates how South Asian Muslims reconstruct a 'home away from home' to maintain cultural and religious links with original homelands and to keep 'customs and culture alive in Britain' (1996, p. 4). In her study of Pakistanis in Oxford, Shaw (1994, p. 37) outlines the continuation of cultural traditions such as *biraderi* membership, kinship migration and informal networks such as the tradition of *lena-dena*. And Werbner points out that one of the early aims of South Asian communities migrating to Britain was to sustain a cultural identity and, 'as a culturally enclaved minority in the West, many are having to come to terms with an experienced, everyday loss of autonomy and cultural control which permanent settlement in Britain entails' (2000).

Today there is growing literature which seeks to understand identities as multiple, fluid, dynamic and partial and which can only be understood in interaction with other identities, ethnicities and social structures. This understanding of identity as fluid and changing has led many commentators to conclude that, at specific times, a particular aspect of the group identity will emerge as more important than at other times (Modood, 2000). In Britain empirical research suggests the emergence of a 'renewed' Muslim religious identity within South Asian Muslim communities (Werbner, 2000; Modood, 2006). In this way the Pakistani diaspora has been transformed as part of the 'Muslim diaspora' or Muslim *umma* (Castells, 1997). In particular, the role of the family takes precedence in debates on identity, belonging and decision-making.

It is now well documented that the current 'war on terror' in Western Europe and North America has created both a difficult and strained relationship with government for many Muslims living in the West, while raising important questions for legal and political scholars on the role of liberal legality in regulating minority ethnic and religious communities. Against this backdrop we have an emerging body of scholarship which explores the relationship between religion and multicultural citizenship both in Britain and Europe (see Levey and Modood, 2009). This literature conceptualizes our understanding of notions of equality, difference and belonging while seeking to provide a clearer conceptual framework on the relationship between diverse systems of belief, religious activity and state-law relations. In Britain scholars continue to document and explore the tensions inherent in much of Western liberal political and feminist theory on the normative values that underpin the liberal political state, with the social and legal regulation of minority communities and conflicts generated by claims for the recognition of cultural and religious practices. For many it seems blindingly obvious that Western states are unable to cope with the pluralism generated by diverse migration patterns in the 1950s and 1960s and the emergence of plural and heterogeneous societies. In Britain, for example, efforts to ensure the successful integration of minority groups into mainstream society (described more generally as multiculturalism) have been accompanied by ill-defined conceptions of what is understood as British identity, most vividly illustrated by the various commissions on integration and citizenship tests introduced to define national identity (Hall, 1996a; Jacobson, 1997; Bhandar, 2009).[2] Yet it remains unclear what values definitions of nationality should include. While the state's demands for explicit expressions of loyalty and commitment sit uncomfortably with the implicit assumptions of a 'cultural clash', this contradiction also forms the backdrop to the creation of specific legal scenarios and state-law relations with minority communities (see Parekh, 2002). As Banakar (2008, p. 38) questions, 'To what extent is the acceptance or rejection of the legal culture of the 'other' a function of an assessment of the actual compatibility of the cultures in question, that they can or cannot coexist in the same social space, and to what extent is it the outcome of legal ideologies and transient socio-political interests?'

In Western European societies the aftermath of the 9/11 attacks has led to an intellectual rethinking of what is understood as secularism and what precisely it means to be secular. In the opening to his seminal work *A Secular Age* Charles Taylor (2007, p. 2) asks, 'What does it mean to say that we live in a secular age?' Over the next 800 pages or so he attempts to answer this question while tracing the historical and contemporary influence of religion that underpins our ideas of modernity, secularism and the types of contemporary secularity emerging in twenty-first century Western democratic societies.

The significance of the shift towards the renewed assertion of a religious identity in Western societies raises the question of what 'should be the relation between religion and the state in liberal democracies today' (Levey, 2009, p. 1). The commonly held ideas that the spread of modernity, globalization and consumerism will inevitably lead to the decline of religion and religiosity in Western societies have largely been proven to be incorrect. As Inglehart and Norris (2004, p. 16) report, 'The world as a whole now has more people with traditional religious views than ever before – and they constitute a growing proportion of the world's population.' Does religion, therefore, act as a source of discrimination and disadvantage for its followers and adherents?

Such questions can also include the role of religious faith in the public spheres and forms of religious behaviours that may violate the principles of liberal democracies (namely, liberty, tolerance, human rights and freedom of choice). Perhaps, unsurprisingly, the role of Islam and what it means to be a Muslim living in the West underpin much of these discussions. Subsequently over the past decade much scholarly attention has been paid to Muslim integration in the West around the themes of loyalty, citizenship and social cohesion. In Britain the debates have evolved from the policies of assimilation in the 1970s to the integration of ethnic minority communities in the 1980s and 1990s to the contemporary rethinking of multiculturalism as promoting a renewed form of integrated communities (Hall, 1996b). As Levey points out, such concerns are evident across Europe:

> How should liberal democracies respond to their growing Muslim communities? What is the appropriate liberal response to a girl wearing a headscarf to a French school, or to an Islamic organization's request for public funding in the UK, or to a request that images of the Prophet Muhammad not be published in newspapers? Should these cases be seen as instances of 'multiculturalism' and 'diversity' which contemporary liberalism should defend and celebrate? Or are they rather examples of a dangerously theocratic impulse, which threatens the social peace and the liberal separation of religion and the state?
>
> Levey (2009, p. 3)

Central to many of the arguments is the perceived inability of Muslims to successfully integrate into Western societies, premised on the idea of the 'overwhelming, often negative influence of religious tradition upon women' (Purkayastha, 2009a, p. 9). It is this focus on gender equality and the presentation of Islam as anti-West, in conflict and in denial about its own abuse of human rights (mostly presented as the abuse of Muslim women's human rights) that form the core of responses to affording rights to Muslims in general. This discourse of 'Muslim otherness' as Taylor (2009, p. xv) remarks is based upon ideas of cultural difference which seek to highlight Muslim *difference* from Western democratic values of equality and human rights.

Why do demands by schoolgirls to wear headscarves provoke such a disproportionate reaction? The feeling often is: this simple-seeming proposal is really part of a package. The package is 'Islam', and it includes such terrible things as we can read of in the press daily, happening in Nigeria or Saudi Arabia. If you reply that the girls in question aren't living in Nigeria or Saudi Arabia, and almost certainly don't share, say, extreme Wahabi views, people in Europe may look at you with that kind of almost indulgent pity reserved for the terminally naïve; or they will tell you stories about how imams are twisting the girls' arms, making them into unwilling stalking horses for 'Islam'.

Taylor (2009, p. xv)

In this way we see that what remains at the heart of such ideas is the commonly accepted argument that Muslim women who belong to and practise their Islamic faith as part of Muslim communities are effectively disempowered and somehow denied their basic human rights. What remains puzzling for many Muslim women, as discussed later in this book, is that such ideas rarely reflect the social and lived realities of their lives.

Multiculturalism is not a singular doctrine and has been described as embodying three different forms: conservative multiculturalism that insists upon assimilation; liberal multiculturalism which focuses upon integration in mainstream society while tolerating certain cultural practices in private; and pluralist multiculturalism which affords groups rights for cultural communities under a communitarian political order. Hall (2000, p. 210–11) engages in an interesting discussion on whether multiculturalism has any epistemological value when it has been appropriated and critiqued in so many different disciplines. Along with critiques on the failure of multiculturalism to promote positive integration and social cohesion between and among all communities in the UK, the rise of Islamophobia across the UK and Europe has led to an increasing scholarship on the ways in which this concept has been used and conceptually deployed in both academic literature and the media discourse on Muslims and Islam in the West (see Sayyid and Vakil, 2010). The term was first used in a public policy forum with the publication of the Runnymede report, titled *Islamophobia: A Challenge for Us All*, in 1997. Anand (2010, p. 265) describes Islamophobia as 'a coherent and identifiable set of prejudices and stereotypes that generates fear of Islam and fuels a reaction to counter it'. As Sayyid (2010, p. 6) explains, 'Islamophobia is widely deployed, hotly disputed and frequently disavowed. It has entered the general field of debate but it cannot establish an isomorphic relationship between itself and the phenomenon that it is supposed to marshal, and there seems to be some confusion as to what kinds of experiences Islamophobia is supposed to delimit.'

The problem of Islamophobia as critiqued by Sayyid and Vakil and others has led modern democratic societies to grapple with the question of how to regulate the relations between state and religion. Historically the separation of state and religion can be described as the key component of secularism or the emergence of the secular state. At its simplest, secularism can be described as seeking to create a public space that promotes mutual coexistence and respect between all believing and non-believing members of the community at large. Consigning religious identity to the private sphere, it is argued, achieves less religious conflict and increased toleration. It seems that for some declaring oneself a secularist has taken a greater urgency. For example, Bilgrami (2004, p. 174; quoted in Sayyid, 2009, p. 186) writes, 'It seems more and more urgent to declare oneself a secularist (and I hereby do so) in a time when wars are waged by a government dominated by the thinking of the Christian Right, terror is perpetuated in the name of Islam, occupation of territories of continuously displaced population is perpetuated by a state constituted in explicitly Jewish terms and a beleaguered minority is killed in planned riots by majoritarian mobilization reviving an imagined Hindu glory.'

In this way the historical relationship between religion and secularism underpins the current calls to clearly define and put into practice the principles of contemporary secularism in Western liberal societies. However, Sayyid (2009, p. 186) questions why secularism is so often deployed specifically in relation to Muslims and Islam and is critical of easily drawing together wide and disparate movements as part of a historical and contemporary lineage of state relations and religious practice. Responding to Bilgrami's claim on the urgency of declaring oneself a secularist, he points out, 'It is this logic that allows statements belonging to contemporary secularism to be produced, distributed and consumed even though it would be possible to point to many elisions and inconsistencies by which these statements and practices are put together in the first place' (Sayyid, 2009, p. 186). Despite the problems in defining secularism, current debates have led to the argument that Islam is a public religion where its presence in the public sphere is seen to challenge the very foundations upon which liberal multicultural states are built. This representation of Islam and Muslims acts as a mechanism to reinforce liberal values that are deemed to be under threat. As Sayyid (2009, p. 186) goes on, 'Muslims come to represent anti-secularism simply because the designation of Muslim is interpreted as referring to a religious subject position. The emergence of this subject position within the public spaces of Western plutocracies, therefore, seems to erode the divide that secularism seeks to institutionalise.' The lack of secularism in Islamic societies is therefore contrasted with the presence of secularism in the West, where this contrast then helps to confirm the necessity and importance of secularism if a civilization is to prosper. These ideas are further developed in the work of Talal Asad (2003, p. 1) with his critique of Western secularism and the connection between 'the secular' as an epistemic category and 'secularism' as a political doctrine. For him, 'Secularism is not simply an intellectual answer to a question about enduring social peace and toleration. It is an enactment by which a political medium (representation of citizenship) redefines and transcends particular and differentiating practices of the self that are articulated through class, gender and religion' (2003, p. 5). Bhandar (2009) traces the deployment of secularism and multiculturalism in Britain as techniques to manage and govern 'difference'. She points out that the increasing Muslim presence in Europe has reopened debates on several issues: the place of religion in public life, social tolerance in Europe, secularism as the only path open to modernity and Europe's very identity. The framing of these debates in very specific ways, however, underlies the creation of a 'citizen-subject' that is defined according to Anglo-European norms of culture. In effect what we see are the ways in which European countries respond to this 'Muslim issue' by effectively attempting to secularize forms of Islam. The issues of security and of regarding national borders only in security terms can underpin such discussions (Savage, 2004). Secularism is deployed therefore not to ensure civic peace or epistemological advances, but rather to maintain Western political hegemony and, by establishing the boundary between the religious and the political, also becomes another means of policing the boundary between the pre-modern and modern and the Western and non-Western (Bhandar 2009). The problem with the claims made on behalf of secularism is that they are very often conducted through Western historical experience and developments that are seen as having universal relevance, in effect the rise of what Asad refers to as the 'secular imaginary' and explains, 'Secularism can therefore be understood as a process that does not in itself as a principle guarantee toleration but simply puts into play different structures of ambition and fear and toleration and justice. In this way the law never seeks to eliminate violence since its object is always to regulate and control it' (2003, p. 8).

More recently the relationship between secularism and multiculturalism has come under close critique. In social and political theory 'multiculturalism' is a relatively new concept that can be traced to the mid-twentieth century with the deployment of state strategies to manage ethnic difference generated by increased migration. Hesse points out that it has now become 'a contested frame of reference for thinking about the quotidian cohesion of Western civil societies uncertain about their national and ethnic futures' (2000, p. 1). Bhabha describes it as a 'floating signifier' where 'differentiation and condensation seem to happen almost synchronically' (1998, p. 45). Indeed the conflation of 'multiculturalism' with the related terms 'identity', 'race', 'ethnicity' and 'diaspora' has led to epistemological questioning over its precise meaning.[3] Despite problems over its meaning and epistemological use, the term remains useful in understanding the different strategies and policies employed by the state in its attempts to 'govern' and 'manage' ethnic and cultural diversity (Hall, 2000).

The perceived necessity for the promotion of 'integration', 'shared values' and 'social cohesion' has been part of an important discourse in modern liberal politics with input from government, policymakers and academics[4] and has more recently been associated with anxiety about Muslim assimilation. In the UK, the 2001 disturbances in northern towns and the attacks of July 7th 2005 (herein referred to as 7/7) have led to the rejection within mainstream political opinion of multiculturalist policies (see McGoldrick, 2005; Ballard, 2008). The subject of integration formed the basis of the 2001 Cantle Report which drew attention to the segregated communities within towns where disturbances had taken place. This coupled with the Goldsmith Citizenship Review of 2008 emphasized the need to enhance a 'common bond', a 'sense of shared belonging'. The result was a Green Paper, *The Path to Citizenship*, published in February 2008 which proposed an increased substantive content to the naturalization process, incentives to naturalize and the marginalization or even removal of those who fail to 'integrate'. This presumption is most strongly associated with the predominantly Muslim communities identified by Cantle. This is particularly so given that, parallel to the debate about public questions of citizenship and cohesion, there has been an increasing focus on problematic aspects of their private lives. Saeed (2009, p. 212) outlines four types of Muslim settlement in Britain: isolationist, semi-isolationist, non-ideological isolationist and participant, and each responds differently to questions of identity, settlement and citizenship. For many scholars the singular focus upon Muslims is both troubling and unfair. Modood (2009, p. 89) argues, 'It is quite mistaken to single out Muslims as a particularly intractable and un-cooperative group characterized by extremist politics, religious obscurantism and an unwillingness to integrate. Rather, the relation between Muslims and the wider British society and British state has to be seen in terms of the developing agendas.' For him Muslims do not raise distinctive concerns and the logic of their demands often simply mirror those of other equality-seeking groups.

The multicultural project has therefore been largely articulated around questions of identity and the forging of a national British identity.[5] Yet both the meanings and representations of these identities have been appropriated and contested by the various groups in question. In her work Avtah Brah has traced the emergence of an Asian group identity not as 'a singular but rather a multi-faceted and context-specific construct' (2005, p. 60). This identity fractures along many lines, notwithstanding religion, caste and language differences. The work of Stuart Hall in the 1990s and his focus on new ethnicities and cultural hybrid identities shifted the focus from such dominant categories of identity as 'Black' or 'Asian' to new identities and their manufacture and communication to emphasize new forms of identity and political agency (see Hall, 1992). The emergence of a Muslim discourse has undoubtedly led to accusations of cultural separatism and the revival of the debates on precisely what type of integration multiculturalism actually provides (2009, p. 166). Modood argues that one way of better understanding this renewed assertion of a religious identity, in the case of Muslims, is to understand the emergence of a Muslim political agency, which allows identity and claims-making to be reconceptualized in the same way and as part of race- and gender-equality debates.

The rights of citizens as members of a wider social and political community are realized via a relationship with the state, endowing us with a legal status. However, as individuals, as Taylor (1994, p. 25) points out, our identities and conceptions of ourselves as free and individual beings are also, and most importantly perhaps, forged as part of a dialogical process with ourselves and others, using certain given 'cultural scripts'. In this way culture becomes an important part of us all and reflects how we see the world, how we participate and evaluate it for ourselves. Ayelet Shachar (1999, p. 89) points out that this has led to extensive discussions on the type of multicultural citizenship model adopted in Western democratic societies and the ability to deal with the complexities of culturally diverse communities: 'The multicultural understanding of citizenship therefore departs from the perception of all citizens as individuals who are merely members of a larger political community, and instead views them as *simultaneously* having equal rights as individuals and differentiated rights as members of identity groups' (emphasis added).

The 'rights' debates

More recently debates on the limits of 'multicultural citizenship' have been located within the discourse of rights and in particular the conflicting relationship between individual and community rights. Under liberal political theory the principles of individual choice, personal freedom and religious toleration are grounded in the notion of individual rights. Within this tradition, group rights are viewed with suspicion and seen as inherently dangerous and oppressive if they fail to acknowledge conflict and diversity within the group. Recently, however, liberals have begun to argue that group interests may, in fact, be accommodated within the framework of individual rights (Taylor, 1994). For many the rise of a 'politics of identity' has brought such tensions to the fore with the claim for recognition of groups' rights being based upon fixed constructions of identity. For Squires, the benefits of multiculturalism are innumerable if it is grounded in a 'diversity politics framework' (2001, p. 115). This attempts to move away from the pitfalls of identity politics and focuses on the need to develop a fully inclusive political citizenship that enables all citizens to 'have equal opportunity to take part in the decision-making process whereby rules are formulated' (Squires, 2001, p. 123).

One kind of critique of liberalism comes from 'communitarians' who argue that liberalism has failed to encompass the concept of 'community' adequately within its analysis of rights. These critics claim that liberalism, by assuming that the individual exists prior to a community, fails to capture the reality of human experience. By contrast with liberals, communitarians aim to place the individual within a community, seen to play a defining role in identity formation. According to Sandel, the introduction of 'community' into the liberal conception of rights enhances self-consciousness and individual identification with a wider subjectivity of 'participants in a shared identity, be it family, community, class or nation through a sense of participation and engagement with others' (Sandel, 1982, p. 79). Belonging is central to the communitarian ideal. Human beings are defined as being socially interdependent, connected over their life course through complex social networks. People are continuously 'made' through their engagement with their society and its institutions (Bay, 1978, p. 45). 'Community' thus provides a sense of social selfhood and identity, a moral biography embedded in the 'story of those communities from which I derive my identity' (McIntyre, 1981, p. 205). What we are or are able to become depends to an important extent on the wider community in which we live. The limitations of the 'communitarian' approach are in its failure to address the issue of difference and diversity within a group. For Hirsch, the communitarians fail to acknowledge the negative dimensions of 'community': 'Both homogeneity and moral education can be politically dangerous in several ways: by encouraging the exclusion of outsiders; by encouraging indoctrination or irrationalism; by compromising privacy and autonomy' (1986, p. 14).

The notion of community constructs boundaries, which involve processes of exclusion as well as inclusion. The development of the individual thus becomes dependent upon the community yet this fails to recognize that individual and group rights may diverge. The issue is, therefore, how a theory of cultural minority group rights may include recognition of difference, including gendered difference, within groups. The principle of recognition may open a Pandora's Box, as van Dyke points out, 'from which all sorts of groupings might spring, demanding rights' (1995, p. 234). To avoid this proliferation of 'groups' claiming 'recognition', Fiss (1996) identifies two characteristics of a social group, which differentiate it from 'mere aggregates': its 'entity' and its 'interdependence'. By entity he means that the group has a distinct existence and identity apart from its members, and that individuals derive their sense of well-being, status and identity from their membership of the group (see Dunleavy and O'Leary, 1987, p. 57).

Unsurprisingly such debates on the place of Islam in Western European societies are often expressed via gender and gender relations and the 'subordinating' effect Islam is perceived to have upon Muslim women. Western women are often presented as 'enlightened' and the bearers of liberal legal ideals such as equality and non-discrimination while Muslim women are presented as the 'other', victims of cultural and religious practices in violation of their human rights. Law thus becomes the site upon which constructions of Muslims as the 'other' take shape, where internal traditions of dissent within Islam are sidelined and deemed anathema to Western intellectual thought and reason. This is why, at present, the dominant view of Islamic legal tradition and human rights is presented as incompatible, in opposition and at best producing an uneasy tension with Western liberal values of human rights. Indeed, the very idea of Islam embodying the universalism of human rights, justice and equality as discussed in mainstream multicultural and political theory seems at odds with its presentation as a culturally relativist ideology that emphasizes the impossibility of individual free will, consent and reason. The current totalizing of Islam is not only dangerous in its explicit Islamophobic tone but also in that the relationships between religious legal practice and the rights discourse surrounding faith, freedom, democracy and equality are a lot more complex than the integrated/separated trajectories currently presented. This will be discussed in later chapters of this book.

The implications of presenting Islam as a unified monolithic entity are not only intellectually problematic but raise the question of what we understand as truth and authority in law (and Islam). If there appears to be little space for genuine political and cultural contestation and exchange in the forming and reforming of a community, then we are left with the dichotomies of modern versus traditional, West versus non-West, liberal and secular versus undemocratic and religious, which do not reflect the complexity entailed in identity and religious identity within minority diasporic communities. Yet the 'problem of Islam' in Europe brings to the fore the classic liberal dilemma of individual choice versus community autonomy. Demands made by Muslim communities for the right to self-regulation in matters of family law and increased visual symbolization of Muslim dress and attire in the public space mean that such discussions often revolve around conflicts generated by liberal conceptions of community and community claims-making, with the Muslim community of believers (*umma*) in turn raising questions on the extent to which Muslims are *truly* loyal to the state.

The current discourses on the clash of secularism versus the rise of religiosity among Muslims and the perceived social conservatism among Muslims fit in neatly with a specific understanding of multiculturalism and constructions of belonging and 'otherness'. One way of better understanding the relationship between identity and group rights is to draw upon feminist scholarship, which in turn draws upon the notions of agency, *habitus* and subjectivity to better understand the relationship between identity, religious practice, authority and belonging. However, and just as importantly, this scholarship analyses how the rights discourse frames tolerance as espoused in policies of multiculturalism, in particular anti-discrimination legislation. This is addressed in Part II of the book.

A critique of liberal legal ideology

Critical legal scholars point out that at its most basic, the liberal legal framework simply operates to maintain and ensure the existence of the hegemonic social and political order, consolidating the power of the state and operating as a closed and autonomous system of rules, norms and regulation (Kelman, 1987). Over the past two decades modern and postmodern critical scholarship has critiqued the positivist postulations of law, challenging the three key modernist claims of law: individual rationality as the single source of values, the formal or abstract universalism of the law, and the centrality and meaning of state justice. This critique informs us that the law must be understood as a specific, historical and socio-political practice which operates in a social field of complexity, fragmentation and conflict and thus law can only ever be understood as a specific form of historically constituted sociality. Perhaps most importantly, at the heart of these debates lie questions of justice, citizenship and rights.

Positivism in English law can be traced back to the nineteenth century with scholars such as John Austin (1995 [1832]) and Jeremy Bentham (1996 [1789]) who focused on the questions of law and morality and jurisprudential questions on precisely what the law was for. As Norrie (2005, p. 21) points out, this period in jurisprudential thinking was based upon the need to control, maintain and stabilize bourgeois industrial society: 'Once the conditions for industrialisation had been achieved, it was more important to consolidate "what is" than to dream dangerously about what might be in an ideal world of metaphysical abstractions. What "ought to be" should be no more than a deduction based upon the facticity of what had already been achieved.' This shift from the moral standpoint of the individual to a positive theory of law led to the pursuit of a coherent, logical and rational legal system.

In his seminal work, *The Concept of Law*, Hart re-established the links between law and philosophy and developed a form of legal jurisprudence in which legal concepts such as command, rule, sovereignty and sanction are analysed to better understand the ways in which law is formed and *how* legal relations take shape (Hart, 1994). This analysis was closely followed by Dworkin's critique in *Law's Empire*, where a positivist understanding of law, one based upon rules and procedure was replaced by developing the idea that judges do not make law but simply determine the outcome of the cases by applying legal principles (Dworkin, 1986). In his work Dworkin accepts that there is substantial disagreement about what the law 'really' is, and that the production of meanings is achieved by the interaction of the interpreting subject and the object of interpretation (see Davies, 2002, p. 64).

Modern and postmodern theories of law share the perspective that law is 'embedded in its respective socio-cultural context, taking many different forms' (Menski, 2006, p. 103). Theories on legal pluralism critique the positivist interpretations of law and redefine the parameters of law as just one part of the existing social milieu within all societies (Griffiths, 1986, 2002). In particular Moore's concept of the semi-autonomous social field has been widely applied in socio-legal literature and illustrates how law is simply a part of social life and should therefore be treated as such (Moore, 1972). Menski (2006, p. 108) sums up the value of this contribution: 'Moore's seminal work shows that, in any given legal system, a variety of sub-systems exercise limited autonomy in the construction and application of socio-legal norms. An understanding of law that is narrowly focused on state-law and national legal systems is therefore too rigid.' Law therefore emerges as a social fact which operates alongside many other social facts in any particular society.

In turn the sociological approach to the study of law stresses the autonomy of the individual and how legal specificity emerges within 'certain social relations and mediating them' (Fitzpatrick, 1992a). Socio-legal scholarship in this way focuses on the social dimensions of law and this often takes place as part of law-in-action critiques with a focus on the question of justice. This approach has also been subject to criticism for its focus on the Western legal polity but it does contribute to our understanding of the emergence of different legal forms specific to particular historical periods. For example, Derrida (1990, p. 941) advocates a deconstructivist critique of law: 'a critique of juridical ideology, a sedimentation of the superstructures of law that both hide and reflect the economic and political interest of the dominant forms of society'. Western law operates on the need to maintain the 'fixed legal subject', and what becomes clear is the move towards a sociology of law coupled with a postmodern idea of law and legal relations that has increasingly focused on questions of immigration, cultural diversity, integration and the management of ethnic difference. Legal scholars such as Shah (2005, 2006), Pearl and Menski (1998) and Werner Menski (2006) draw upon the concept of legal pluralism to re-evaluate the concept of law 'in a culturally diverse, plural society' (Shah, 2005, p. 1) and explore the relation between cultural diversity, legal pluralism and the state's response to conflicts generated by the settled diasporic communities and their continued practice of cultural/religious norms and values. In particular it is the family and wider kin groups that are presented as the two key sites upon which such legal conflicts are based.

For many legal scholars the underlying questions addressed by historical and socio-legal approaches focus on questions of justice and morality. In his seminal critique of Western liberal legality, Norrie argues that liberal law is inherently contradictory and that justice is a form of ethical judgement that lies outside the boundaries of positive law. For Norrie the contradictory elements of law are partly created by, and remain linked to, attempts to guide action by reference to abstract ahistorical criteria, while the institution of law remains tied up to socio-historically defined social relations. Law has to ignore and deny the relevance of its socio-historical ties if it is to appear as an internally coherent system of rules, doctrines and decisions. That is why positivistic theories of law describe the totality of law in terms of legal rules and doctrine which are to guide the practice of law, while ignoring broader social contexts in which rules and doctrine need to be interpreted before they are transformed into legal practice. By overlooking the significance of the broader social and historical context out of which emerge not only legal practice but also institutions of law, they obscure and mystify the relationship between legal practice and the societal context of law (Norrie, 2005, pp. 28–31). To unpack this, Norrie refers to the idea of 'legal subject as a responsible agent' which is represented by such doctrines as *mens rea* and *actus reus*. He argues that liberal theory, which underpins the subjective principles of criminal law – 'affirming the need for intention, foresight, knowledge and belief concerning actions and their consequences' – is highly individualistic and atomistic (2005, p. 53). Not even the atomized liberal understanding of human action can completely ignore society, which is why the previous account of social action is restricted by recognizing the need for mutual cooperation. Liberal law abstracts the agency from 'the context of social conflict and deprivation which generates crime' and excludes 'that context from the judicial gaze' (2005, p. 30). Instead, it provides a partial and mystified image of the individual and society that allows it to justify an individualized relationship between legal and moral judgement. This critical reassessment not only challenges the ontological premises which frame the formalist definitions of law but also explores the relation between law, religious identity and the move from individual notions of identity towards a communitarian identity. For Banakar (2008) the question of liberal legality therefore raises critical questions regarding the accommodation of minority, religious and cultural demands and the law must engage with the idea of justice and ask whether positive law is capable of delivering the form of justice which is required in a plural society. From the standpoint of structure, conceptions of legal subjectivity (identity) act as modes of selection – of exclusion and inclusion – of the relations that inform entities. The seemingly universal legal subject is in fact a social and historical figure, whose abstract characteristics function to instantiate a political and moral order and to exclude alternative and competing voices and claims (Norrie, 2005, p. 151).

Liberalism and the question of justice

For many scholars Rawls' *A Theory of Justice* serves as the starting point to the liberal response(s) to cultural and religious diversity (Rawls, 1999). In his conception of the 'good life' Rawls argued pluralism was not only a positive aspect of modern-day liberal societies but also an intrinsic element to human development and activity. Moral differences, he argued, underpinned human endeavour and creativity, and were a crucial element of stable societies. Thus the question was how just, stable and equal societies could be built around differences and of the recognition of those differences. His theory of justice is underpinned by a series of universal liberal principles which lie outside the formal mechanisms of state justice: these are arrived at in a rational way and have been described as a 'shared theory of the human person or human nature' (Parekh, 2000, p. 82). In his later work, most notably *Political Liberalism*, Rawls (2005) develops his ideas of justice, truth and autonomy that make no claim to truth and questions of justice and do not form part of any particular comprehensive doctrine in a fixed way. As Parekh points out, 'For Rawls the ideas of free and equal persons and society as a system of voluntary cooperation between them are central to the political culture of democratic societies' (2000, p. 83). Ideas of justice are free standing and citizens are free and equal persons because they all possess two crucial moral powers, namely the sense of justice and the capacity to form, revise and pursue a conception of the good. In this way the liberal political conception of justice is able to deal with the question of pluralism and cultural and religious difference.

However, critics point out that Rawls' political conceptions of person-hood, autonomy, morality and justice are based upon fixed principles of political liberalism that remain intolerant to alternative conceptions of justice. As Parekh points out, 'Like many liberals he is sensitive to moral but not cultural plurality, and takes little account of the cultural aspirations of such communities as the indigenous peoples, national minorities, subnational groups, and the immigrants. Although these groups make different demands, they all seek cultural autonomy in one form or another, and hence some departure from the conventional liberal preoccupation with a homogenous legal and political structure' (2000, p. 89). The specific claims to cultural autonomy are addressed by Rawls who argues that no society is able to accommodate all different ways of life and that homogeneity is both inevitable and in some instances necessary and desirable. Parekh among many others remains critical of this inevitability arguing that the outcome of homogeneity serves the interest of the majority and in fact goes against the very principles of liberal conceptions of justice, autonomy and personhood upon which political liberalism is based.

Thus the emergence of multicultural societies in Western Europe has led many to question what should the political structure of a multicultural society precisely entail. Parekh points out that a multicultural society faces two conflicting demands: fostering a strong sense of unity and common belonging among its citizens and recognizing the value of cultural diversity. He argues that 'since human beings are attached to and shaped by their culture, and their self-respect is closely bound up with respect for it, the basic respect we owe our fellow-humans extends to their culture and cultural community as well. Respect for their culture also earns their loyalty, gives them the confidence and courage to interact with other cultures, and facilitates their integration into wider society' (Parekh, 2000, p. 196). For Parekh, therefore, the role of the state in fostering justice underpins the success of multiculturalism and the successful integration of minority ethnic groups. He argues that it is 'of the utmost importance that the institutions of the state should be, and be seen to be, impartial in their treatment of the members of different communities' (2000, p. 209). If conflicts arise, then the state is clear in its objectives that they must be resolved via dialogue with representatives of those who are subject 'to the contested norm of mutual recognition. Reconciliation should be dialogical.' But how is such a relationship expressed in practice? In multicultural Britain how have these relationships been forged? Tully (2007, p. 27) explains this process can be varied and multifaceted and often depends on the type of deliberative democracy put into practice and the nature of the conflict to be resolved.

For Habermas, direct liberal participation in civic society is the important key whereby renewed forms of civic participation allow citizens a greater say in the recognition of norms to which they are subject and in this way 'only those norms can claim to be valid that meet (or could meet) with the approval of all affected in their capacity as participants in a practical discourse (Habermas, 1996, p. 66). So how is a norm accepted by the group in question? Again Habermas argues that the group involved must come to a stage of recognition rather than the norm being imposed and then deemed unacceptable. This can only happen via a dialogical exchange of communication. As Taylor explains, 'The forms of recognition that individuals and groups struggle for are articulated, discussed, altered, reinterpreted and renegotiated in the course of the struggle. They do not pre-exist their articulation and negotiation in some unmediated prescriptive pre-dialogue realm accessible by individuals. They are worked out in dialogical relations with others' (1994, p. 34).

In this way law should institute a process of communication 'in a self-regulated democratic process of decision-making'. Law then acts as a mechanism of mutual understanding. Citizens must be in a position to participate in the decision-making processes as subjects rather than consumers. Habermas' theory on juridification underpins this idea of formalization of relationships in the private spheres which has had the effect of reducing the role of citizens to the role of consumers. This private exchange and bargaining of recognition of values is dangerous, limiting and undemocratic. In this way the point is not to start with the debate in terms of equality versus recognition but to actually listen to the groups in question and to consider carefully what their claims are actually about. Tully proposes a model of democratic dialogue as a situation of 'reasonable disagreement' and 'reasonable dissent' where procedures need to be in place for engagement and disagreement (Tully, 2007). There are different types of dialogue: deliberative democracy, communicative democracy, deliberative liberalism, agnostic democracy, perspicuous contrasts, the fusion of horizons and counter-hegemonic globalization (see Benhabib, 2002; Mouffe, 2000; Santos, 2005). Within each of these categories there are different types of interlocutors with different relations and levels of representation to the individuals and communities that they represent.

Yet the practice of law-making illustrates the complexity of the dialogical experience and the limitations of the decision-making institutions. Critical legal theorists point out that law and the process of adjudication continue to be vulnerable to partiality and normative subjective positions which may fall outside the Dworkian principle of law as defined by internal coherence, logic and structure (Dworkin, 1986). It is argued that law is political and all legal decision-making is ideological which does not mean that law cannot serve a reformist agenda but that it should not be perceived as a neutral body of norms, values and principles which can be applied to all. Thus many legal scholars readily accept that justice is always a process that is partial and selective. This process is upheld by judges and in this way 'legal reasoning is irredeemably marked by the divisions in society' (Banakar, 2008, p. 71). Foucault (1977) points to the modes of governmentality that fix the parameters of recognition and justice.

In the light of such critiques, is there a bias in law which disadvantages Muslims? In current social and political discourse, ideas of Muslims as irrational, dogmatic and threatening are endemic in Western liberal democracies. Our conceptions of justice are formed by our interaction with these ideas and by our conceptions of morality, difference and equality which are not essential and ahistorical but do play an important function in the preservation of ideas of the 'other'. These ideas permeate normative discourse on Muslims and the perceived chasm between Islam and the West. As Webber (2007, p. 73) points out, 'Conceptions of justice are always wrapped up with assumptions – about human nature, relative worth, the capacities and predispositions of the sexes, the extent and causes of evil, the pre-requisites of material production, the specific consequences of action – that depend at least in some measure on empirical judgements.'

The establishment of the multicultural citizenship model takes shape as part of legal relations where a legal rationale is worked out by state-law processes that aim to protect the rights of minority communities without violating human rights norms. As Shachar points out, 'In legal terms, the move towards a multicultural citizenship model raises potential conflicts among three components, identity groups, the state and individual rights' (1999, p. 89). Subsequently the transnational nature of migration has led to much discussion on the plurality of legal systems in Europe. There are various explanations for both the process and evidence of this change and its location within a transnational global context. As regards Western Europe the focus has been on the impact 'mass migrations from the South, particularly to Europe, but also to other parts of the global "North" have had upon the apparent uniformity of state law' (Menski, 2006, p. 15). There is now a strong body of scholarship which analyses the ways in which migration has directly led to structural adjustments in various legal systems and particularly the ways in which European legal systems have had to grapple with a renewed assertion of religious identities (see Benda-Beckmann et al., 2005). This literature is usually situated within the context of international law and pays particular attention to the 'constellations of plural legal orders' (Benda-Beckmann et al. 2005, p. 6) and local concerns where the legitimacy of domestic institutional structures is open to critique. Yet the complex and variable configurations of law operating in a multicultural setting mean that the interconnectedness of the nature of state-law and civic relations and its power brokers must not be ignored. As Rohe (2008, p. 56) points out, 'Only the state can decide whether and to what extent "foreign" law can be applied and foreign customs can be practised on its territory. Thus the legal system is not "multi-cultural" as far as it concerns the decisive exercise of legal power.' In this way the emergence of multicultural legalism merely reinstates law in very specific liberal forms which continues to be based on a formal rational sense of law which neither accepts nor permits alternative interpretations. And as discussed in the previous section, at the heart of these discussions lie the fundamental questions about the historical development of legal theory and the significance and nature of law in an increasingly complex, diverse and globalized world.

For legal anthropologists, discussion has focused on the different types of model legal systems that can be adopted in order to reflect the plural and culturally diverse nature of Western democratic societies. These legal models are often categorized according to the various state policies on how to deal with minority ethnic groups – for example, 'assimilation', 'overlap', 'segregation' and 'acculturation' – and in this way different European societies adopt different models according to their needs, demands and the political interests of the state.

Law is an important potential source of power and the pursuit of justice in response to the challenges presented by diverse cultural and religious communities reveals contradictory practices. The *effects* of a plural and multicultural society upon the development of English law have been extensively documented over the past 20 years by anthropologists, sociologists and, increasingly, legal scholars. In her work Ayelet Shachar (2005) discusses the normative arguments in support of both 'soft' and 'hard multiculturalism' while discussing the extent to which cultural and religious norms and practices should be accommodated in the public sphere(s). However, there remains a deep mistrust and suspicion as to whether the liberal–democratic constitutions 'that guarantee freedoms of political communication and anti-paternalist decision-making' (Bader, 2009, p. 115) can withstand conditions of strong or deep cultural and religious pluralism. As Bader succinctly points out, the sphere of religion and the public practice of religion seem to be more problematic:

> The fear and distrust of religious reasons is clearly very intense, since the ways that 'exclusionary secularists' seek to control, regulate and

discipline 'allowable' reasons and participants in public debate seem plainly incompatible with fairly extensive constitutional freedoms of political communication.

Bader (2009, p. 115)

What is clear, however, is that the fundamental questions about freedom of religion and the right to religious practice currently lie at the fore of contemporary debates about national and international security and human rights. As Knights (2007, p. 19) points out, 'While the freedom privately to hold particular religious or philosophical views is unlikely to give rise to practical difficulties, the extent to which manifestations of religious belief are considered acceptable in society is a vexed issue.'

Cultural pluralism in English law

As discussed earlier liberal political theory operates according to the principles of individual choice, personal freedom and religious toleration, grounded in the notion of individual rights. Within this tradition, group rights are viewed with suspicion and seen as inherently dangerous and oppressive if they fail to acknowledge conflict and diversity within the group. Recently, however, liberals have begun to argue that group interests may, in fact, be accommodated within the framework of individual rights.

This raises a number of important conceptual and theoretical questions regarding the relation between individual and group rights, how these are to be distinguished and how clashes between individual and group rights may be reconciled. Embedded in these is the key question of what makes a community a 'community of rights'. Does the state, in granting individuals the right to enjoy their culture, have an obligation to foster that culture and ensure its survival?

According to Christian Bay (1978):

> Liberals have persistently tended to cut the citizen off from the person; and they have placed on their humanistic pedestal a cripple of a man, a man without a moral or political nature, a man with plenty of contractual rights and obligations perhaps, but a man without moorings in any real community, a drifter rather than a being with roots in species solidarity.[6]

A similar definition might serve to define 'community'. Communities nest within one another: local, national and global. They also intersect: British Muslims belong to the global Muslim *umma*, for example. Britain as a national community has its own specific legal system, but Britain is also a member of the international community that recognizes transcendent human rights.

The public/private dichotomy in English law remains central to constructing the boundaries within which the free practice of cultural customs and religious beliefs is deemed acceptable. The law seeks not to intervene in matters that it defines as belonging to the private domain. As Lacey (1992, p. 106) points out, however, this avoidance is not politically innocent as the law tends to intervene selectively in the regulation of the 'private' domain. For many years, for example, the state was reluctant to intervene in cases of domestic violence, often leaving women in the dangerous situations as documented by Southall Black Sisters (1990) among Asian women.

English law is based on a liberal notion of universal neutrality. The Race Relations Act 1976 aimed to promote equal opportunities and to eliminate discrimination in employment, housing, education and the provision of goods and services. The legal system has over time recognized certain other demands of ethnic minority groups. For example the Shop Act 1950 exempted Jews from Sunday trading laws. The Slaughterhouses Act 1979 allows the slaughter of animals for the purpose of obtaining kosher and halal meat for the Jewish and Muslim communities. Since 1976, a Sikh with a turban may ride a motorcycle in Britain without wearing the otherwise compulsory crash helmet (Motorcycle Crash Helmet (Religious Exemption) Act 1976). Voluntary-aided religious and denominational schools are funded by the state, as are army chaplains and university theology faculties. Furthermore the European Convention on Human Rights upholds freedom of thought, conscience and religion and this was enshrined in the Human Rights Act 1998 but applies directly only to public bodies. The Race Directive (2000/43/EC) and EC Equal Treatment Framework Directive (2000/78/EC) which aimed to harmonize race equality legislation across the EU has also been incorporated into English law. The Race Relations Act 1976 (Amendment) Regulations 2003 which implemented provisions of the Race Directive, cover discrimination on the grounds of nationality and colour. The Employment Equality (Religion or Belief) Regulations 2003 made it illegal to discriminate against people in employment and vocational training on the basis of their religion and belief. The Equality Act 2006 widened the scope to include the provision of goods, facilities and services, education, the use and disposal of premises, and the exercise of public functions. The religious discrimination regulations give protection against discrimination on the grounds of 'any religion, religious belief or philosophical belief' in a similar way to existing sex discrimination and race discrimination laws. The Equality Act 2006 widened this to specifically protect 'lack of belief' as well. The Racial and Religious Hatred Act 2006 creates an offence of inciting (or 'stirring up') hatred against a person on the grounds of their religion.

The courts have also ruled on what is defined as an ethnic and racial group. For example, in *Mandla* v. *Dowell Lee* (1982) a Sikh boy was excluded from carrying any religious symbols to school. Lord Denning argued that Sikhs were not racially distinguishable from other Asians. The House of

Lords, however, took a wider view of 'ethnic minority' and seven criteria, including a common religion, were established. Thus the headmaster was found guilty of indirect discrimination under the Race Relations Act 1976, and Sikh children are allowed to carry religious symbols to school. Poulter argues that, given liberal principles, we must be clear about the limits of cultural pluralism 'which need to be imposed in support of the overriding public interest in promoting social cohesion' (1994, p. 156). This view is shared by Lester and Bindman (1972, p. 23) who warn that cultural tolerance must neither become a 'cloak for oppression and injustice within the immigrant communities themselves' nor must it endanger the integrity of the 'social and cultural core' of English values as a whole.

Making provisions for ethnic minority groups seeking to practise religious customs and practices has raised the question of the need for 'special treatment'. This is because, as Montgomery (1992, p. 193) argues, 'Provisions providing for formal equality may result in greater restrictions of the freedom of minority groups than is experienced by the majority.' Such restrictions must be viewed in the light of the legal commitment to protect rights of religious freedom that make it necessary to devise special rules for particular groups. But does recognizing a group right mean compelling all members of the group to partake of the right in question, even against their will?

Montgomery outlines four different types of group rights. The first is where individuals acquire rights by virtue of their membership of the group, once membership is established. This principle has been applied in English law to Quakers and Jews, for example, who are allowed by the Marriage Acts 1949–86 to solemnise marriages. Their special privileges date from 1753 and they are not subject to the Marriage Act regulations.

The second type of a 'group right' recognizes a 'private' space in which 'a self-contained parallel system of rules would operate'. The Ottoman Empire operated with a plural system, according autonomy to religious groups or *dhimmis* to manage their family law internally. Drawing on this tradition some sections of the Muslim community in the UK would like to claim legal autonomy in matters of family law, to enable Islamic law to be applied in the 'private' sphere of family relations. If this claim were accepted in Britain, a different system of personal laws would govern Muslim citizens from those applied to the community at large. But this would raise the issue of how to deal with those individuals who did not wish to conform to the traditional customs of their communities.

Clearly, such a group right is problematic if it is based on the *exclusive* recognition of a single common identity for all the members of a cultural and religious minority. As Montgomery points out, support for such a right rests on a number of assumptions. First, the group must have some discrete identity that enables its members to be distinguished from outsiders. Second, the group must be essentially homogeneous in respect of its desire for the special treatment. Third, not only must the group generally want special treatment, but also the treatment must be of a nature which creates liberties that can be exercised by all. The claim for an exclusive or territorially based separate personal law system remains problematic since the cultural boundaries of groups are rarely unambiguous. This is because, as Van Dyke (1985) points out, 'Individual people are likely to feel part of one group in some contexts and of another in relation to different issues.' Boundaries are more easily defined when minorities are concentrated territorially, as is the case with indigenous minorities. A further option, which has been adopted in India, is to create two parallel systems of personal law: customary/religious and civil, and allow all citizens the right to choose between them.

The third type of group right is a dispensation or entitlement allowing members of the group, as a collective body, to act in a way which would otherwise be unlawful. For example, section 19 of the Sex Discrimination Act 1975 allows qualifications and authorizations to be withheld from one sex 'for purposes of organized religion' in order to comply with the doctrines of that religion or avoid offending the religious susceptibilities of a significant number of its followers.

Finally, the fourth type of group right is a right permitting some individual members of a group to have special privileges deriving from that membership. For example, in both the Jewish and Muslim communities, designated members of the community have the right to slaughter animals differently from the rest of society. Muslim girls have been allowed to wear headscarves to school, contravening the school uniform, while a similar dispensation allows Jewish schoolboys to wear religious caps. Prior to changes to the law, Muslims and Jews were exempt from Sunday trading prohibitions.

Clashes between individual and group rights, then, are most likely to occur when full autonomy is granted to a 'community', as was the case in the Ottoman Empire, or under colonial indirect rule. Finnis (1986) underlines the paradox that group rights are, on the one hand, powerful in challenging state hegemony and acting to restrict state power but, at the same time, they also may restrict individual freedoms, as collective decisions and values cannot be guaranteed to coincide with the individual concerns of certain group members.

Despite his strong advocacy for an active and transformative multiculturalism, Parekh (1995) is critical of calls for autonomous group rights from different religious groups. He believes that Britain cannot allow separate legal systems for different communities without violating the fundamental principles of common citizenship and equality before the law. The law, he points out, has evolved and accepted cultural differences in case law without violating these principles (see Sandberg 2011).[7]

2
South Asian Muslims and State-Law Relations

It is the beyond the scope of this book to provide a comprehensive background, context and critique of the settlement patterns of South Asian Muslims and state-law relations in Britain. Therefore, this chapter seeks only to provide some contextual background upon which to better understand the ways in which the practice of Muslim family law may take shape in Britain). Today there is an expansion body of scholarship that traces both the historical and contemporary lives of British Muslims (see Geaves, 1996a; Abbas, 2005; Ahmad, 2006; Gilliat-Ray, 2010) that testifies not only to the interdisciplinary nature of this work (transcending the disciplines of politics, anthropology, sociology, geography, religious studies and more recently law) but also illustrates the complexity of tracing community development and settlement patterns.

South Asian Muslim settlement in Britain

The history of South Asian migration and settlement in Britain has been extensively documented (see Ballard, 1994; Abbas, 2005). Commonly referred to as 'New Commonwealth' migrants[1] and recruited in response to the chronic labour shortages that accompanied post-war economic expansion in the 1950s and 1960s, such groups initially became the subject of public debate in connection with their assimilation into British society (see Rex, 1989).

According to the 2001 census figures, Pakistanis comprise 747,285 or 1.3 per cent of the total British population.[2] Of the total 4.6 million people in the UK who belong to ethnic minority groups, half are of Indian, Pakistani and Bangladeshi backgrounds. The census data in 2001 also revealed the geographic distribution of Pakistanis in Britain and this highlights interesting settlement patterns. For example, 19 per cent of all British Pakistanis reside in London, while 21 per cent live in the West Midlands, 20 per cent in Yorkshire and Humberside, and 16 per cent in the North West.

Migration from Pakistan began in the 1950s, primarily from rural farming areas of the Mirpur district and some parts of Punjab.[3] In relation to female migration, Anthias and Yuval-Davis have challenged the commonly held view that women migrants came to Britain as mere dependants on their husbands (1992, p. 97). Instead, women remained important contributors to the family in terms of waged and unwaged work (see Ahmad, 2006). Perhaps not surprisingly, as with other migrant workers, Pakistanis were originally positioned at the lowest labour stratum, employed as unskilled or semi-skilled labourers and were disproportionately represented in textiles, clothing and footwear, metal manufacture, transport and communication, and the distributive trades.[4] South Asian Pakistani women found themselves in low-paid jobs primarily in the textile industries to support their low-paid husbands in order to contribute to the family income while continuing to maintain family responsibilities (Brah, 1993). As Gilliat (2010, p. 210) points out, 'This work was often undertaken alongside responsibility for above-average-sized or extended-family households, and limited funds to purchase labour saving devices such as the structure of the local economy. The opportunities available to women varied according to their capacity in English, their qualifications and external constraints, such as the structure of the local economy.' Recent research indicates that Pakistanis continue to be disadvantaged with respect to unemployment and occupational and educational attainment (see Brah, 1993; Ahmad, 2006).

The particular circumstances under which Pakistani communities have settled in various parts of the country have been extensively documented in anthropological and sociological research.[5] Early literature presented such communities as fixed, unchanging and inherently traditional. Cultural practices were reified to produce specific understandings of such communities based upon cultural and ethnic difference. For example, early literature on Pakistani presence in Britain questioned their 'ability to adopt western attitudes and their tenacious retention of traditional beliefs and lifestyles' (see Shaw, 1988, p. 35). Anwar (1979) point to the 'myth of return' while focus on the 'imposition' of purdah and the continued practice of Islam as examples of conservative and traditional family values and practices.

As discussed earlier, today there is growing literature which seeks to understand identities as multiple, fluid, dynamic and partial and which can only be understood in interaction with other identities, ethnicities and social structures (Anthias and Yuval-Davis, 1992). This has led scholars to focus on the 'cultural and religious identity' of the community to better understand how cultural and religious values and practices interact and conflict in the public sphere. In her study on Pakistanis in Oxford, Shaw (1994, p. 37) examines the implications of continued traditions such as *biraderi* (caste) kinship membership, kinship migration and informal networks such as the tradition of *lena-dena* (the giving and receiving of gifts) which sustain family and community relationships and provide a sense of belonging and identity. However, as Werbner points out, although one of the early aims of Pakistani communities was to sustain a cultural identity 'as a culturally enclaved minority in the west, British Pakistanis are having to come to terms with an experienced, everyday loss of autonomy and cultural control which permanent settlement in Britain entails' (1994, p. 226).

The proliferation of research on issues of identity, belonging and citizenship has also been coupled with scholarship on the formation of mosques, cultural organizations and ethnic minority business (Werbner, 2001). The political activities of Pakistanis, in particular as Muslim councillors, have been traced by Purdum (2000) and in Bradford by Samad (1997). These academic studies have been accompanied by social policy initiatives which focus on employment and educational attainment. More recently this scholarship has moved to the complex, shifting and fragmented identities within the Pakistani diaspora. For example, Alam, Kalra and Fieldhouse's anthropological study of first-generation Pakistanis in Oldham (2002) contrasts with the work of Jacobson (1998) on second-generation Pakistanis in London. This understanding of identity as fluid and changing[6] has led to conclusions that, at specific times, a particular aspect of the group identity will emerge that has more importance than at other times (Modood, 2000). In Britain empirical research suggests the emergence of a 'renewed' Muslim religious identity within South Asian Muslim communities (Afshar, 1994; Anwar, 1992; Dwyer, 2000; Burlet and Reid, 1998; Werner, 2002; Modood, 2006). In this way the Pakistani diaspora has been transformed as part of the 'Muslim diaspora' or Muslim *umma* (community) (Castells, 1997). Furthermore, it is argued that the loss of autonomy within local Muslim communities living in the West has led to a renewed assertion of an Islamic identity, one that is based on the identification of a global Muslim community (Ahmed and Donnan, 1994, p. 79). As Werbner explains:

> While South Asian culture in Britain has been relatively innovative and responsive to diasporic experiences, this has been far less the case for the transnational movement of Islam into Britain. Instead, the wide variety of different religious streams, denominations, and movements evident in South Asia has been transposed into Britain almost wholesale, along with the migration of Muslims from the subcontinent. Major religious organizations and movements such as Tablighi Jama'at, Jama'at-i Islami (in Britain known as the UK Islamic Mission), Deobandis, and Ahl-e Hadith compete with new Islamic movements such as the al Muhajirun or Khizb-ul-Takhrir, imported from the Middle East, which are attractive to some young South Asian Muslims. All these groups have their institutional embodiments in the United Kingdom.
>
> (2005, p. 482)

The impact of such religious movements have been explored in relation to the racialization of Muslims in Britain following events such as the Rushdie affair, the 1991 Gulf war, September 11, 2001 and the terrorist attacks on 7 July 2005 (7/7); and in connection with the tenuous relationship between religious pluralism and liberal democracy in Britain, and threats posed by the assertion of a renewed British Islamic identity. For many scholars this has led to a focus on the rights and obligations of Muslims as minorities in Britain in order to develop practical agendas for 'participatory citizenship' (Lewis and Schnapper, 1994; Soysal, 1994; Shadid and Koningsveld, 1996b; Werbner, 2000; Parekh, 2002; Modood, 2008).

In Britain the concept of 'active citizenship'[7] underpins what Anwar, 1992 describes as 'the status, duties and responsibilities of South Asian Muslims in Britain' (1998, p. 6). The relationship between community, state institutions and policies of integration demonstrates the ways in which ethnic minority communities and their families are situated and managed in multicultural Britain. In particular sociological literature has drawn attention to the concept of diaspora as a conceptual framework to better understand the process of migration and the dynamics of minority communities vis-à-vis new understandings of 'belonging', 'home' and 'homeland'.

Such literature better explains how a group comes to be situated, helps to understand the distinct historical experience of the group in question and analyse what impact the diasporic journey may have had upon the formation of the community (Brah, 1996; Soysal, 1994; Werbner, 2000). Anthropological accounts on South Asian communities in Britain from Ballard (1996) and Werbner (2000) consider the interplay of social and cultural practices with the significance of individuals belonging to communities and families. According to Ballard the notion of *desh pardesh* encapsulates how South Asian Muslims reconstruct a 'home away from home' to maintain cultural and religious links with original homelands and to keep 'customs' and culture 'alive' in Britain (1996, p. 4). In this way kinship and familial relations are understood as a mechanism in which marriage practices take shape and form part of an ethnic pluralism and renewal (Bhachu, 1985; Werbner, 1990). As Werbner explains, 'It is perhaps a truism that diasporas are complex and heterogeneous social formations. They differ both historically and in terms of the particular social and economic context of settlement (2004, p. 478). The anthropologist Roger Ballard[8] (2008) describes South Asian Muslim families as part of the 'corporate' family structure. According to Ballard, corporate families exist in many ethnic communities but are particularly associated in the UK with families of South Asian origin. There are differences, and distinctions can be drawn between many different family types but core characteristics are identifiable within each set. For example, he explains that in European kinship the critical relationship that forges families together is between nuclear family members whereas a wide network of inter- and intra-generational ties and obligations binds members of corporate families and women's personal conduct is connected to notions of honour and shame which then affect the whole family. He points out that these characteristics have assisted transnational families to negotiate a globalized world in which they face structural disadvantages of immigration control, discrimination and poverty.

State engagement with British Muslims

As discussed in Chapter 1, the twin goals of promoting social cohesion and political solidarity underpin the values and ideals of Western liberal–democratic states and the crucial issue of cultural pluralism underpins discussions of rights, legitimacy and justice. More recently, and in particular over the past two decades, political theorists have addressed these questions with increased urgency and renewed vigour in relation to the conflicts generated by cultural and religious differences. Moreover, the focus on Muslim communities and individual and community demands to practise the Muslim faith in the public sphere has taken centre stage. It seems that in most Western European states the emergence of 'difference-sensitive' laws and policies has accompanied increasing concerns about the impact of cultural diversity and religious pluralism upon the stability and cohesion of these societies as a whole. However, critics also point to problems of viewing communities in a fixed and deterministic way that ignores the disintegration of political stability and solidarity within and between groups and leads to inconsistent understandings of justice, equality and stability. As Shabani (2007, p. 1) points out, 'The classic challenge of how to operationalize the tension between the permanence of difference in politics and the goal of solidarity has become acute once again, but this time on a qualitatively new level; that of post-recognition.' In other words, the classic debates of recognition and difference versus equality and justice need to take into account the complexity and fractures that group membership entails. We cannot therefore simply assume that group demands promote the needs and interests of their members.

So what is the role of law in this process of change, adaptation and recognition in relation to Muslim identities? Can law recognize and accommodate diversity while preserving individual autonomy, agency and identity? What are the ideals of law and what of the conflicts on the ground? For Habermas (1996, p. 23) the modes of governmentality and state-law relations fix the parameters of all the desired forms of recognition, inclusion and redistribution, and in this way 'the plurality of ways in which specific sets of rules of interaction and of mutual recognition impose arbitrary principles of exclusion, assimilation, marginalization, subordination and so on, on individuals and groups'. This raises the question of the subtle and at times complex ways in which issues of identities and inequalities are built into the fabric of law. As critical legal theorists point out, the assumed autonomy of law as fixed and determined in reality is constituent upon factors including the legitimating powers of trust and cooperation upon which law relies to enforce its authority. The idea of the rule of law therefore must be understood as part of what constitutes as the 'social' (see Fitzpatrick, 2009).

The claims to specific forms of recognition take two distinct forms, either they manifest with the rise of specific conflict or they are advanced in a more abstract form under the context of rights, identity and culture. Tully (2007, p. 22) points out that central to this is the process and struggle for recognition – 'that is, struggles over recognition are relational and mutual rather than independent and multiple'. He goes on, 'Struggles over recognition are struggles over the intersubjective "norms" (law, rules, conventions or customs) under which the members of any system of government recognize each other as members and coordinate their interaction. Hence struggles over recognition are always struggles over the prevailing intersubjective norms of mutual recognition through which the members (individuals and groups under various descriptions) of any system of action coordination (or practice of governance) are recognized and governed.' This process of recognition is also coupled with the social, economic and political context in which claims are made. For example, the heightened tensions over terrorism and the policies of counterterrorism have also led to increased anxiety among many Muslim communities, and coupled with the fact that many Muslims remain marginalized in employment, education and housing in numerous European countries[9] has led to a strained relationship with the state (see further in the chapter).

In his early work Lewis (2002) has traced the role of religious movements in South Asia that continue to influence religious practice and thought within South Asian Muslim communities in Britain today. These movements have been broadly described by Lewis as 'the reformist Deobandis, the quietist and revivalist Tablighi Jana'at, the conservative and populist Barelwis, the Islamist Jana'at-i-Islami and the modernists' (Lewis and Schnapper, 1994, p. 36).

The complexity of mosque formation, organizational and religious rivalry and the development of religious practice and thought among Muslim communities has been traced back to the influence of these particular movements (see Ballard, 1994; Werbner, 1996). For example, Geaves (1996a, p. 149) draws attention to the fact that Deobandi religious centres emerged in Britain with the arrival of South Asian Muslim migration in the 1960s. These groups were the first to build mosques and successfully create religious networks which lay the foundations for future religious practice and thought. Geaves (1996a) also draws our attention to the fact that about half of all British Muslims identify with the Barelwi movement – a movement that emphasizes the importance of religious leaders and scholars (identified as *pirs* and *ulama*) and is divided on ethnic, class and caste differences. The expression of specific religious identities within these movements has led to the proliferation of Muslim religious organizations in Britain that seek to provide voice and representation in the interests of British Muslims.

The largest organisations include the Muslim Council of Britain (MCB), the British Muslim Forum (BMF) and the Islamic Foundation, each of which serves a particular constituency with specific needs and demands.

The organizational patterns of Muslim political leadership and the question of local and national representation illustrate the complexity and nature of Muslim state engagement. Gilliat-Ray (2010, p. 105) explains, 'Most Muslims who arrived in Britain for unskilled and semi-skilled work in the post-war years did not envisage either the eventual migration of their families, or their permanent long-term settlement in Britain. Those formal or semi-formal associations that were formed by Muslims in Britain in the 1960s and 1970s tended to revolve around the interests of particular ethnic groups, and were often internally directed initiatives which aimed to provide practical help and support in terms of housing, employment, immigration or welfare.' Two key questions therefore emerge: what are the domestic political considerations in the formation of these groups and what are the organizational structures and their linkages to the state? In their work, Fetzer and Super (2004, p. 7) draw upon resource mobilization theory to better understand this linkage and relationship between religious organizations to the state and analyse the nature of this relationship. They explain the usefulness of 'resource mobilization theory' which rejects 'the assumptions of the prevailing explanations that held that the collective action was a spontaneous and disorganized activity and that movement participants were essentially irrational. By contrast, resource mobilization theory assumed the rationality of participants in a social movement and focused on the capacity of organized groups to acquire politically significant resources for their collective purposes.'

It is generally recognized that the development of community groups and state relations is dependent upon community resources and often the lack of state resources. Political theorists have applied resource mobilization theory therefore to better understand the fractured relationship between Muslim organizations and the state. In her work on Pakistanis in Manchester, Werbner (1990) closely analyses the emergence of community leadership and the role of the 'community leader'. She explains that these individuals embody the needs and aspirations of the local community and have 'mastered some aspects of the wider culture and are concerned to bridge the gap between the community and the society as a whole. They do so by attempting to increase their influence among local politicians and other representatives of the state. In their negotiations with them the emphasis is placed upon shared symbols and values' (pp. 321–2, quoted in Gilliat-Ray, 2010, p. 107).

In their study, Shadid and van Koningsveld argue that Muslim groups remain largely ineffective as they lack the resources which would allow them to bargain effectively with the state. They point out that 'Muslims in most western European states have thus far been unsuccessful in creating representative organizations at national levels which can function as spokesmen for the Muslim communities with the respective government' (1995, p. 3). Political mobilization of Muslim groups in Britain is divided by ethnic, national, caste and linguistic divisions. These divisions are further fractured along the two branches of Islam (*Sunni* and *Shia*) and the multifaceted nature of this difference has long been discussed by numerous scholars. In their work, Vertovec and Peach (1997) argue that the state deploys such divisions to ensure key demands remain unmet. Thus the dialogical relationship between minority groups and the state is one based upon struggles over cultural, ethnic, linguistic and religious modes of recognition and which can be contrasted with struggles over the distribution of resources. For Tully it is the underlying power struggles, values and norms which determine the nature of these struggles and he points out that individuals belong to multiple groupings and associations: 'While the system of legal rules is the most obvious example, they can be cultural, religious, familial, educational, class, corporate, customary and covert. Individuals are usually subject to many overlapping norms of mutual recognition and corresponding identities' (2007, p. 5).

Following the 9/11 and 7/7 terrorist attacks in New York and London, the MCB emerged as the group with which the state chose to engage in dialogue to manage and deal with issues of security and introduce a series of policies to counter the threat of 'home-grown terrorism'. This type of dialogue was based on a fixed understanding of what was represented as the 'moderate Muslim' and endowed this group with the tacit power to represent the voices of all British Muslims. The tension between voice, representation and the labelling by government of some categories of Muslims as increased the risk of group members (mainly young Muslim men) reinforced the prevailing myth of Muslims and Muslim men in particular as the 'dangerous other' (see Bano, 2010). A number of new initiatives were introduced, in particular the PREVENT strategy which seeks to prevent people from becoming terrorists or supporting terrorism (see Sayyid and Vakil, 2010) which only further aggravated the tensions between Muslim communities and the state. Politically the very logic of this dialogical relationship with the MCB was problematic as the chosen delegation of community leaders was neither representative nor had any real power to affect policy decisions. This relationship broke down in March 2009 with the then Communities Secretary, Hazel Blears, who publicly cut off ties with the group.[10]

Critiques on community and religious leadership and their influence upon government social policy in the regulation and maintenance of minority ethnic/religious communities have focused on the 'non-representative' status of such leaders. The feminist sociologists Anthias and Yuval-Davis (1992) were one of the first sets of scholars to question the role of such groups and individuals in 'multicultural Britain'. In their pioneering work, *Racialized Boundaries*, they explored how cultural and religious differences under the context of multiculturalism become paramount rather than 'tackling the central problem of racism itself: unequal power relations which bring about "modes of exclusion", inferiorization, subordination and exploitation' (1992, p. 3). In particular they drew attention to the role of women within these communities and the problem of social and cultural control by community and religious leaders and authorities. The issue of gender control and violence against women has been further addressed by feminist activists, including the black feminist women's organizations Southall Black Sisters (SBS) and Newham Asian Women's Project (NAWP). Pragna Patel (SBS) explains, 'In Southall, as in other minority communities, the police have from time to time invoked language and cultural and religious differences as reasons for non-intervention in response to Asian women's demands for protection against domestic violence. Consultation with community leaders takes place at formal and informal levels for a number of reasons, including the need to gain "community" approval for police operations' (2003, p. 176). Such a critical view which draws attention to the dangers of affording community leaders local power has also been shared by scholars who point to the strategic use of groups and individuals by the state. For example, Kundnani (2007) provides an in-depth analysis of the ways in which these groups govern and seek representation and concludes that they do not seek to promote issues of social justice and equality but 'it is rather the state that they aim to mobilize to intervene in the community on their behalf – for example by funding educational and cultural activities that endorse their ideology. The result is, often, the closing down of spaces, particularly for the young and for women where communities can come together to tackle the injustices they face' (p. 183). Therefore the extent to which this type of political representation is both feasible democratic and practically achievable remains open to question. The use of community leaders by the state to promote a state-centred approach to resolving community tensions and wider concerns (such as 'home-grown' terrorism) has instead led to concerns of promoting tensions within communities and a fear among British Muslims deemed as the outsider-within, citizens who are effectively viewed with suspicion and disloyalty (see Abbas, 2005). Gilliat-Ray (2010), however, also questions the extent to which such groups such as MCB influence the daily lived experience of British Muslims. Instead she explains that for British Muslims 'their own self-representation and personal development within family life, within educational and employment settings or within local religious institutions is, for many, a much more immediately pressing consideration' (2010, p. 111).

Muslims in Europe

The presence of diverse Muslim communities in Europe has raised questions on the extent to which Muslims practise norms and values based on religious belief and identity that are deemed antithetical to the values and aspirations of Western European liberal democracies. Indeed the emergence of transnational and translocal communities and its consequences for liberal legality has of late received extensive and sophisticated scholarly attention. From this body of literature we are better placed to understand the underlying socio, economic and political factors that carry this process along and consider how possible conflicts and interactions take shape (see Shah and Menski, 2006). We see how identities, allegiances and relationships are built and forged, and their impact on local institutions, agencies and local populations (see Benda-Beckmann, Benda-Beckmann and Griffiths, 2005). We are able to learn the ways in which social actors, networks, communities expand and emerge and this raises fundamental questions on what we understand as the self, community, religion and the role of the law in the process of identity formation.

The legal dimension in particular plays a significant role as in its positive form it delineates the boundaries of the public/private spheres (and those deemed insiders/outsiders), and how conflicts between the legal and non-legal take shape. In their work, Benda-Beckmann, Benda-Beckmann and Griffiths describe law 'as a powerful form of cultural expression that operates as a potential source for social, economic or political power, constraining and enabling social practices, with both intended and unintended consequences' (2005, p. 2). In particular the mobility of law as a process of transnational laws and translocal relations as a series of linkages to local and national laws interacting, intermeshing and in conflict can create new visions of law and legal relations in Western societies and the rest of the world. As regards Western Europe the focus has been on the 'mass migrations from the South, particularly to Europe, but also to other parts of the global "North"' (Shah and Menski, 2006). As discussed in Chapter 1 there is now a body of scholarship which analyses the ways in which migration has resulted in structural adjustments in various legal systems and in particular the ways in which European legal systems have had to grapple with a renewed assertion of religious identities. The role of the state in both promoting and limiting the recognition of such practices has been subject to some criticism. Against this backdrop we have an emerging body of scholarship which seeks to better understand the relationship between religion and multicultural citizenship while reconceptualizing our understanding of notions of equality, religious belief and state-law relations. For example, in Britain, scholars (see Malik, 2006; Sayyid, 2000; Modood, 2007) document and explore the tensions inherent in much of Western liberal political theory on the normative values that underpin the liberal political state, with the social and legal regulation of minority communities and conflicts generated by claims for the recognition of cultural and religious practices. For many it seems blindingly obvious that Western states are simply unable to cope with the pluralism generated by diverse migration patterns and the emergence of plural and heterogeneous societies.[11]

As discussed in Chapter 1, increasingly scholars focus on the possible differences generated by majority and minority Muslim communities and raise the question of how such differences may generate different claims, rights and responsibilities. Discussion has largely focused on the different types of integration models recognized by legal systems in order to reflect the plural and culturally diverse nature of societies. European societies are grouped as being modelled on four key types – assimilation, overlap, segregation and acculturation – and each legal system reflects this difference. Yet transnational migration also illustrates recent examples where Muslims living in different European societies share common concerns and points of conflict: for example, the banning of Islamic headscarves across Europe, the role of Islamic scholars in Europe and the Muslim world and in particular the role of the Internet where Islamic scholars issue edicts and fatwas (e.g. the emergence of European initiatives such as the European Council for Fatwa and Research; see Ali, 2010). The place of Islam in Europe therefore continues to be subject to extensive social and political commentary with a more recent focus on the rising numbers of Muslims in Europe.[12] In particular the visible presence of Muslims in public is deemed so problematic that political initiatives have begun to limit this presence. The Muslim scholars Ramadan (2004) and An-Naim (2008) have explored the limits of religious practice coupled with the rise of secularism in Western European societies and each points to the areas of convergence and commonality between religious and secular practice. Both promote the idea that European Muslims are able to successfully integrate into European civic societies. Further, the idea of the emergence of a specific 'European Muslim' identity has been developed by Ramadan (2004) where he explores strategies for dual identity, dual language and the reformation and reformulation of Islam in the West in order to provide 'western Muslims' with a coherent set of tools to live as believers in non-Muslim societies (p. 23). There are a number of studies that point to the modern rise of Muslim religiosity in Western European societies which can be explained as both a product of and a reaction to Westernization.

The French sociologist Roy, for example, describes the current religiosity within Muslim populations as a new form of Islamic religiosity, which he maintains has parallels with similar quests for new forms of spirituality in the secular environments of the West. 'Islam', he writes, 'cannot escape the New Age of religion or choose the form of its own modernity' (2007, p. 3). In this way new forms of Muslim religiosity cannot be understood with reference to the traditional portrayal of Islam as bounded, fixed with immutable categories of belonging as in the distant past. Roy also insists that the continual portrayal of Islam as a single culture serves an important purpose: to preserve the mythical notion of Western civilization and progress vis-à-vis traditional Islam. If Muslim populations are expressing new forms of religiosity, then the contexts in which they are doing so need to be better understood and explained. Various judicial and legislative decrees in Western Europe, prominently among them the French law banning Islamic headscarves, are examples of this objectification. So what is the relationship between Islam and civil society? This is a complex question, but many commentators draw upon Gellner (1983), the two key proponents of the 'clash of civilizations' discourse, who argue quite simply that Islam is a dangerous political ideology that undermines both liberal democracy and civil society. Yet civil society is a much a contested terrain as is Islam. And Turam (2004, p. 260) points out that Islam's role in either propelling or undermining civil society is largely assumed to occur through the September 11 climate that has reinforced the predominant assumptions of clash, hostility and distrust as essential qualities of the Islamic revival.

This raises the question of the extent to which Islam and Islamic practice in the West can be understood as part of the social, political and civic process in Western liberal societies. In Britain, for example, the greater visibility of religious symbols in the public space has led to a sustained argument that we are witnessing a rise in religiosity. Unsurprisingly perhaps, the focus has been largely on Muslim communities and their demands to practise their faith in the public sphere, which may conflict with British norms, values and customs. Debate on Islam in the West is also closely linked to questions of immigration, loss of cultural identity for majority societies and constructions of Muslims as the 'other', and contemporary discussion focuses on the idea that Islam is incompatible with modernity. In this way, as Savage (2004) points out, the increasing Muslim presence in Europe has reopened debates on several issues: the place of religion in public life, social tolerance in Europe, secularism as the only path open to modernity and Europe's very identity. One of the ways European countries respond to this 'Muslim question' is by effectively nationalizing, if not secularizing Islam. Savage (2004, p. 57) adds: 'These governments are trying to foster nationally oriented Islam as subordinate to the state as well as to European norms stretching back to the Treaty of Westphalia, the Enlightenment, and Napoleonic rule.'

More recent conflicts in Europe have led to discussions on developing Europe-wide initiatives to both protect and promote the rights of minorities. On September 2005 what is now commonly referred to as the 'cartoon crisis' erupted in Denmark. A series of cartoons depicting the Prophet Muhammad were printed in the Danish newspaper, *Jyllands-Posten*. The newspaper argued that the cartoons were included in the newspaper as part of its campaign to explore the issue of self-censorship and ability of newspapers to criticize Islam and Islamic norms and values.

In November 2009 a new European crisis erupted when an estimated 57.5 per cent of Swiss voters voted in favour of a ban on building minarets in Switzerland. This result was all the more remarkable for the fact that Switzerland currently has only four minarets and that Swiss Muslims have been described as being extremely well integrated into Swiss society. Although this result itself produced widespread condemnation both from religious and secular authorities (including the Vatican and various human rights organizations) it also reflects the continuing and strained relationship in Western European societies over the management of ethnic diversity and the regulation of religious communities. In France the issue of veiling and, in particular, the extent to which full-face veiling transcends French values of republicanism and sexual equality currently dominates political discussion. In July 2010 the Lower House of the French Parliament approved a ban making it illegal for women to wear the full veil in public and this measure, approved by the Senate in September 2010, is now in place.[13] On 16 January 2010 *The Times* newspaper reported that the UK Independence Party is to call for a ban on the *burka* and *niqab*, claiming that they are an affront to British values.

In particular anti-discrimination law and the emerging human rights framework in the European public sphere remain crucial in protecting the rights of cultural and religious communities. For example, the Refah Partisi case[14] brought to the fore questions of European compatibility with Islamic norms and values. In this case it was decided that Shari'ah was not compatible with liberal values of European democracy. There is now a growing body of European case law which addresses the questions of Muslim integration into Europe and a growing scepticism among some scholars that Muslims are currently being represented as the 'other' in Europe, unable and incapable of integration and peaceful coexistence (see Shah and Menski, 2006).

The recognition of South Asian Muslim customary laws in English family law

In contrast to the early twentieth century, legal practitioners now readily recognize the plural systems of laws operating within different societies. Menski (2006) refers to the emergence of a 'plurality conscious jurisprudence' which draws upon concepts such as legal pluralism and hybrid legal cultures to better understand the limitations of single legal uniformity while raising questions of what we understand about the relationship between law and society. Menski (2006, p. 83) argues that Western law must take account of interlegality and pluralism to be conceived as 'a universal phenomenon covering both Western and non-Western societies, and at the same time appearing in not only the dual structure of state law and minority customary law but also the triple of customary law, national law and international law'.

Legal pluralists often turn to the work of the Austrian jurist Eugen Ehrlich to better understand the relationship between law and society. Twining (2000, p. 226) points out, 'Pioneers of the sociology of law, most notably Ehrlich, argued that a realistic depiction of the law in action had to take into account "the living law" of sub-groups, as well as "the official law" of the state. They saw that these could diverge significantly and that sometimes the other would prevail. This was an important step not only in the direction of "realism", but also away from the idea that the state has a monopoly of law-creation.' Law, he argued, derived from social facts and thus could only be better understood in relation to the historical and social context in which it was situated. Living law thus becomes an important tool in which to better understand how law evolves, takes shape and can be understood in relation to power, agency and coercion.

In contrast to positivist interpretations, this empirically enriched way of understanding how state-law relations contribute to other social factors allows us to introduce the important component of agency into the analyses. Living law is thus described as that 'which is not fixed in legal statements and yet dominates life. The sources of its knowledge are above all modern legal documents, but also the direct observation of life, of trade and other activities, of habits and customs, and of all organizations, those which are legally acknowledged as well as those which have been overlooked or marginalised, even the legally disapproved ones' (Menski, 2006, p. 95).

Ehrlich and living law are useful ways of understanding how Islamic law operates and takes shape as Muslim law in a multicultural setting. Yet what precisely constitutes Shari'ah and Shari'ah law for Muslims continues to be debated between both Muslim and non-Muslim scholars around the world. As Menski (2006, p. 20) points out, 'Muslim law, too, is in reality a family of legal systems with immense internal diversities, rather than one uniform law. All that is common to all branches of this great tree are the basic conceptual roots, evidently of a religious nature, presenting an alternative vision of a natural law system, since Muslim law is not primarily made by the state.'

As discussed earlier, it has been argued that in a multicultural and heterogeneous society a commitment to cultural diversity and pluralism in the area of family life is essential. The contention is that the law should uphold and support a diversity of family arrangements whether or not they are reflective of differences in race, culture or religion (Bainham, 1995, p. 235). Raz (1986, p. 38) argues that 'the phenomenon of a multicultural society goes beyond mere toleration and non-discrimination. It involves recognition of the equal standing of all stable and viable cultural communities existing in a society.' Raz suggests that we need a radical policy of liberal multiculturalism that would transcend an individualistic approach but would at the same time 'recognize the importance of unimpeded membership in a respected and flourishing cultural group for individual well-being' (1986, p. 44). A redefinition of society would mean there would no longer be majority and minority groups but rather a 'plurality of cultural groups each of equivalent worth'. He accepts that some cultures or some features of them may be unacceptable to the society as a whole, because of their oppressive aspects. Even Raz and Bainham, however, fail to consider the need to take into account power imbalances in the institution of the family: who determines what is considered acceptable or unacceptable behaviour within the institution of the family?

The issue of arranged marriages is a crucial case in point. A basic condition of a legally valid marriage is that it should be a voluntary union, a principle upheld in *Singh* v. *Singh* (1972). A marriage may be voidable on the grounds of lack of consent. The courts take the view that the cultural traditions of those ethnic groups in which arranged marriage is practised must be respected. A number of cases, however, have examined the issue where parents have exerted pressure to marry. In *Singh* v. *Kaur* (1981), a reluctant Sikh bridegroom's protests about his arranged marriage to a young woman in India led to a series of arguments with his parents. The court, however, rejected his petition for nullity on the grounds that the evidence of pressure fell far short of the threat to 'life, limb or liberty', then thought to be necessary to vitiate an apparent consent. Lord Justice Ormond argued that the practice of arranged marriages could not be undermined in the Asiatic and other communities. In *Hirani* v. *Hirani* (1983), however, a 19-year-old Hindu girl succeeded in her petition for nullity. In order to prevent her association with a young Muslim man, her parents had forced her into marriage and threatened her with eviction if she failed to go through with the ceremony. Lord Justice Ormond judged this to be

a classic case of a young girl, wholly dependent on her parents, being forced into marriage with a man she has never seen in order to prevent her (reasonably from her parents' point of view) continuing an association with a Muslim which they would regard with abhorrence.

The judge, applying the principle of true consent, allowed the young woman to reject a cultural practice she considered oppressive. The issue of forced marriage is addressed further in Chapter 8.

Likewise in Islamic law marriage is a contract between consenting parties in the presence of witnesses (Pearl, 1987). Unlike the civil law, however, Muslim law does not recognize a marriage between a Muslim woman and a non-Muslim man. It does, however, recognize polygamy, prohibited under English law. According to Islamic law, men can take up to four wives, even if they rarely do so, with clear repercussions for internal familial power relations.

Problems of power inequalities within the family are also evident in the case of divorce. Under Islamic law, for example, a divorce can be obtained in a number of different ways: through *talaq* (unilateral repudiation by the husband), *khul* (divorce at the instance of the wife with her husband's agreement, and on condition that she will forego her right to the *mahr*) *faskh* (husband acts unreasonably) and *mubara'ah* (the non-consumation of the marriage) *ubara'at* (divorce by mutual consent). In current English family law there is only one way to obtain a divorce, under the Matrimonial Causes Act 1973 on the grounds that the marriage has irretrievably broken down and where the decree is made absolute. The question of recognition of a unilateral divorce (*talaq*) has been the subject of considerable litigation culminating in the House of Lords judgement in *Quazi* v. *Quazi* (1979). Lord Justice Wilberforce held that

(a) No *talaq* which is pronounced in England will be valid in England regardless of the domicile of the parties and also regardless of whether the husband goes abroad to an Islamic country to appear before the Arbitration Council as laid down by the Muslim Family Ordinance 1961.[15]

(b) If both the parties are habitually resident in UK for more than one year, the English courts will not recognize a *talaq* pronounced anywhere other than the country of nationality or of domicile of the parties. If only one party, or neither party is habitually resident in the UK for this period, then a *talaq* pronounced in a third country (other than the country of the nationality) will be treated as valid in England only if it is valid by the law of the domicile of both parties.

(c) There is a residual power to refuse recognition of a *talaq* otherwise valid under the provisions of the Recognition of Foreign Divorces and Legal Separations Act 1971. The discretion operates broadly within the framework of public policy grounds (the House of Lords in *Quazi* v. *Quazi* (1979) considered this discretion would be exercised very rarely).

After a divorce, Islamic law only obliges a husband to support his wife during the three-month period of *idda* (Nasir, 1986). The husband does have to pay her any deferred *mahr*, however, and the English courts have been prepared to order these payments (see Fournier, 2010).[16]

These brief cases illustrate that under English law religious/cultural traditions can be practised within the private sphere of the family as long as they do not conflict with liberal legal principles of 'equality before the law' and 'common citizenship' (Parekh, 1990). However, 'personal religious legal systems' (e.g. Islamic legal systems) are not recognized in their totality as legitimate under English law. Indeed, they are currently critiqued by a growing number of Muslim women scholars and activists (Mernissi, 1992; Wadud, 1999; Barlas, 2006). Personal laws are defined as 'customs' which, like English common law, are allowed as long as they do not conflict with English statutory law. Thus Muslims can get married in an Islamic way as long as the marriage is registered with the state. For Muslims in Britain, then, voluntary adherence to Islamic Shari'ah law and the setting up of Muslim courts on the model of rabbinical courts is likely to be the preferred solution for those seeking to pursue a fully Islamic way of life (Shadid and Koningsveld, 1996b). This is discussed in more depth later in the book.

Muslim family law in Britain

In Britain there have been some demands for Muslim personal laws to be recognized in English law under the context of multiculturalism and the 'rights' discourse. In 1970s the Union of Muslim Organisations (UMO) was one of the first groups to demand the formal recognition of Shari'ah law into English law (see Nielsen, 1987). Today, however, these demands remain sketchy and do not necessarily reflect the viewpoints of many British

Muslims. More importantly perhaps, we have seen the emergence of a new group of specialist legal practitioners, including the solicitor Aina Khan and the barrister Ahmad Thompson who specialize in providing advice and legal representation on issues of Muslim law in Britain.[17]

In English law, religious laws and practices are defined as ethnic customs (Poulter, 1992, 1998) which are recognized, as long as they are not deemed 'unreasonable' nor clash with the principles of English law (this also includes violation of any international treaties to which Britain may be signatory). Pearl and Menski (1998, p. 68) notes that the framing of religious and community claims derive from a Western human rights framework and asks 'who determines the criteria for what is acceptable and what is not? Should the official law restrict itself to controlling the limited space that it recognizes, knowingly ignoring the rest of the social field, or should it attempt to control the entire field while being prepared to make concessions to diversity?'

More recently this point has been addressed by the Archbishop of Canterbury, Dr Rowan Williams, in his speech on cultural and religious diversity to the Royal Courts of Justice in February 2007.[18] Dr Williams argued that the minimum universal liberal values of justice, equality and fairness must – in response to moral and cultural diversity – be applied in a manner whereby all members of society are able to express their identity and loyalty to both a religious identity and the state. The case was made for the positive accommodation of some unspecified form of Islamic law in Britain under English law. He argued that the legal system in Britain needed to engage constructively with the religious concerns and motivations of members of the diverse communities which make up contemporary British society. He pointed out that a shared common culture can only grow out of complex interactions and we should both respect and nurture this diversity in order to unite around a more common way of life. More specifically still, the Archbishop considered whether Shari'ah councils should be given formal legal recognition in a similar fashion to the rabbinical courts operating in Britain, the Jewish Beth Din. Although he was careful not to restrict his general argument to Muslims per se, but more broadly to all those belonging to religious communities, the focal point was Muslim and the recognition of Shari'ah in English law. Lord Phillips, the Chief Justice at the time, added further weight to the argument when he stated that 'there is no reason why principles of Sharia law, or any other religious code, should not be the basis for mediation or other forms of alternative dispute resolution' (Phillips, 2008, p. 4). Both speakers suggested that Islamic mechanisms of family disputes could perform a function not dissimilar to that of the Jewish Beth Din courts who deal with matters relating to marriage and divorce.

Using the case of British Muslims as an example to consider the possible accommodation of religious systems of law into English law, however, proved extremely contentious (see Bano, 2008). The speech presented a rather deterministic picture of Islam and Muslims with the focus on their public visibility rather than the genuine intercultural interactions that are representative of different and heterogeneous Muslim communities in British society (see Parekh, 1997). However unintentional this may have been, this interaction between the individual, faith-based practices and the law was not given sufficient reflection and inevitably led to extensive media coverage on Muslim demands and the emergence of deep disagreements. The troubled reception of the lecture also indicates how contemporary liberal thinkers continue to be challenged with questions of how to manage cultural, religious and ethnic diversity in multicultural Britain.[19]

Legal conflicts

In Britain, the establishment of church and state has led to vociferous debates on the privileged status of the Church of England and its dominance in the law-making process. Over the past 25 years this has led to increased calls for a clear separation between religion and the state which, it is argued, would lead to more inclusive citizenship for all groups in society (Saghal and Yuval-Davis, 1992). In law, faith-based arguments for the recognition of religious practices in the civic and public spheres have received considerable attention, in particular with the implementation of the Human Rights Act 1998, the Racial and Religious Hatred Act 2006 and the Equality Act 2006. This latter piece of legislation introduces a positive duty on public sector bodies to promote equality of opportunity between women and men and eliminate sex discrimination. It also protects against discrimination on the grounds of religion or belief in terms of access to goods, facilities and services.[20] In recent years several political and legal philosophers have examined the complex relationship between law and faith and the role of faith in different legal decision-making processes. Multicultural theorists such as Taylor (2007), Modood (2008) and Kymlicka (2005) analyse the inter-relationship between differing interpretations of the 'good', 'moral and reasonable pluralism' and new forms of social organization that require new capacities and duties in response to the multicultural accommodation of cultural and religious practices. Many of these scholars draw on the work of Rawls and his ideas of justice as fairness to tackle the tension between reason and faith. In her work Malik (2000a and 2000b, p. 131) points out that there are a number of faith-based justifications (beliefs, practices and customs) that fall under the category of reasonable pluralism which must therefore be viewed as part of on a different standard. She explains: '[M]any faith-based commitments are justified by reference to facts not amenable to the standards of proof and evidence typically employed in reason-based analyses. These arguments are based on tradition, narratives, custom and culture which provide the bases for legitimation.' In particular the bonds of community and the terms of membership of that community are often determined by such criteria, and therefore differences at the level of human capacities, emotions, motivations and values must also be recognized.

As mentioned, one such focus on 'difference' has been the increasing securitization of Muslims across Europe and the introduction of initiatives where security and terrorism underlie central concerns about Muslim integration. In relation to Muslim family law practices in the West and the need to 'contain' such practices, it raises the question of what precisely is being practised by Muslims. Malik (2009) points out, quite rightly, that the terms such as 'Shari'ah' and *'fiqh'* that are commonly used to describe the practise of Islamic norms within Muslim communities need to be unpacked. She explains: '[O]ne way of capturing the nature of Muslim demands is to avoid the use of the generic term Shari'ah in favour of use of the category Muslim legal and ethical norms. The term Muslim legal and ethical norms also captures the fact that some Muslims are calling for the accommodation of norms that derive from their understanding of their religion. These include not only standards derived from the Shari'ah and *fiqh* but also general ethical principles derived from Islamic religious culture.' The practice of 'Shari'ah law' can then be better understood as the application of norms and values rather than a legal system which operates outside constitutional and state law. Furthermore questions of what constitutes Shari'ah and Shari'ah Law for Muslims continue to be debated among Muslim and non-Muslim scholars around the world.

As discussed in Chapter 1, the multicultural project has largely been articulated around questions of identity and the forging of a national British identity. In recent debates on multiculturalism in Britain the relationship between minority ethnic groups and the responsibility of the state to ensure the successful integration of all ethnic groups into mainstream society has come under sustained attack from all sides of the political spectrum (Goodhart, 2004).

As discussed in the previous chapter in his work the political theorist Tariq Modood traces the emergence of a specific Muslim identity in the UK and Europe while challenging the commonly held idea that Muslims more than other groups are demanding rights and are subsequently 'particularly intractable and uncooperative' (2009, p. 166). Modood argues that one way of better understanding this renewed assertion of a religious identity – in the case of Muslims – is to understand the emergence of a Muslim political agency – which allows it to be reconceptualized in the same way as race and gender equality debates.

The establishment of the multicultural citizenship model takes shape at the sphere of legal relations where a legal rationale is worked out by state-law processes that aims to protect the rights of minority communities without violating human rights norms. As Shachar points out, 'in legal terms, the move towards a multicultural citizenship model raises potential conflicts among three components, identity groups, the state and individual rights' (1999, p. 89). In her recent work Yuval-Davis (2011) criticizes this analysis as part of 'the politics of belonging' which, she argues, fails to sufficiently engage with questions of power, difference and identity within groups especially on issues of discrimination and gender equality. She has also warned that 'in multiculturalist types of solidarity politics there can be a risk of uncritical solidarity' (1997, p. 130).

In the UK the state accommodation of Muslim religious practices has increasingly become a source of tension and dispute. The demand that the state recognize Muslims' religious status and accommodate this justly and fairly raises the question of how the state views some practices to be reasonable and just while others are deemed unreasonable and unjust. In Britain, for example, debate and conflict has arisen over a number of different issues, including issues on civil liberty restrictions, state education and dress codes, exclusion from discrimination protections and the public funding of private Islamic schools among other issues. The issue of dress codes has focused on the right of pupils to manifest their religion in school contrasted with the rights of schools to enforce their own rules on school uniforms. As Knights explains: 'The United Kingdom has not sought to legislate directly on the issue of religious symbols including clothing in state-maintained schools. The resulting situation is one of considerable plurality – some schools have uniform policies, while others do not. Some schools have prescribed alternative uniforms to take into account the religious and cultural traditions of their pupils' (2007, p. 117).

The question of freedom of religion is currently addressed in English law with the incorporation of the Human Rights Act 1998 which came into force in October 2000. Among other rights it guarantees the right to freedom of religion:

1. Everyone has the right to freedom of thought, conscience and religion; this right includes freedom to change his religion or belief and freedom, either alone or in community with others and in public or private, to manifest his religion or belief, in worship, teaching, practice and observance.
2. Freedom to manifest one's religion or beliefs shall be subject only to such limitations as are prescribed by law and are necessary in a democratic society in the interests of public safety, for the protection of public order, health or morals, or for the protection of the rights and freedoms of others.

There is now a large body of scholarship that analyses the relationship between religious practice and belief and discrimination law (see Addison, 2007; Vickers, 2008). In Britain two high-profile cases seem best to illustrate this conflict between Islamic religious practice and public space, both involving Islamic dress code for Muslim women and the use of the Human Rights Act 1998. In *Begum* v. *Denbigh High School Governors*[21] the House of Lords ruled that the exclusion of Shabina Begum for her unwillingness to comply with school uniform requirements was not in violation of Article 9 of the Human Rights Act 1998. In this case the claimant Shabina Begum, a young Muslim woman, sought the right to wear a *jilbab* as part of her school uniform. Her insistence on wearing the *jilbab* meant that she contravened official school policy and was excluded from her local school, Denbigh High. She claimed that the school was in breach of Article 9 of the ECHR: the right to freedom of thought, conscience and religion. She challenged the decision of her school and the majority judgement found that her right had not been infringed, on the basis that in the interests of social cohesion, the school had legitimately infringed her right to wear the *jilbab*. Relying on the Grand Chamber of the Strasbourg Court's judgement in *Sahin* v. *Turkey* (2005),[22] the majority recognized:

> the need in some situations to restrict freedom to manifest religious belief; the value of religious harmony and tolerance between opposing or competing groups and of pluralism and broadmindedness; the need for compromise and balance; the role of the state in deciding what is necessary to protect the rights and freedoms of others; the variation of practice and tradition among member states; and the permissibility in some contexts of restricting the wearing of religious dress.
>
> *Begum* (paragraph 32)

The *Azmi* v. *Kirklees* (2007) case involved a Muslim woman who worked as a school teaching assistant and refused to follow an instruction not to wear a full-face veil when assisting a male teacher in class. She was suspended and brought claims for direct and indirect religious discrimination and harassment on the ground of religion or belief. Again the appeal was dismissed, as the tribunal found no indirect discrimination and that the local council's ways of achieving its aim was deemed proportionate. Such cases have led to increased discussions among scholars on questions of minority rights and Islam, identity, belonging and citizenship in multicultural societies. Western commentators and legal scholars now discuss at length the limits of religious practice and belief and many query the need to accommodate and respect cultural and religious diversity in Western societies. For some the politics of multiculturalism and the recognition of cultural difference have led to rise in a politics of cultural separatism; but for others the liberal principles of justice, equality and human rights justify the protection of all cultural and religious minority communities. As Bhandar (2009, p. 12) points out,

> The contestations over the rights of girls and women to wear (various forms of) the veil has been articulated in a discourse of rights, recognition and plurality in the UK context. While the juridification of the conflicts in the cases of Shabina Begum and Aisha Azmi necessarily meant

the framing of a range of issues in the language of rights, the broader discussions, such as those mentioned above, as well as subsequent discussions about Britishness and British values ha[ve] for the most part remained within the realm of legal rights, social policy, and the political ethos attached to a desire to establish a particular nationalist vision. In other words, the contestation over the *appropriateness* and *permissibility* of girls and women to engage with certain types of veiling has been situated in the juridical-political sphere of individual legal rights, multicultural-ism and national identity.

More recent work has considered the impact of state policies of counterterrorism and anti-terrorist legislation as directed towards Muslim communities. For example, in his work Banakar (2008) analysed case law including the ruling in *R* v. *Malik*[23] to examine how the legal and policing measures to combat the threat of terrorism interact with the ethno-cultural relationships in contemporary Britain. He found tensions between govern-ment policy and the judiciary which led to a conflict between state policy and the role of the law in upholding and promoting the rights of the individual.

From British Pakistani women to British Muslim women

For the past four decades, literature on British Pakistani Muslim women has traced the processes of social change within local Pakistani communi-ties as they relate to gender often with a focus on the dynamics of gender relations within family households and marriage practices. However, one important conceptual change has shifted the analyses from ethnicity to religion and the emergence and strong affirmation of an Islamic identity among British Pakistani women (see Jacobson, 1997; Burlet and Reid, 1998; Hennink, Diamond and Cooper, 1999). Therefore the critique of essential-izing black and minority groups as classless and ungendered groups and the theorization of the relationship between race, class and gender is now commonly accepted in social science thought. This has meant a much bet-ter understanding of the complex interrelationship between religious and ethnic identities and social change within minority diasporic communities in Britain (Anthias and Yuval-Davis, 1992).[24]

It is estimated that there are approximately 800,000 Muslim women in Britain today (see Communities and Local Government, Empowering Muslim Women, 2008, quoted in Gilliat-Ray, 2010, p. 210). We now have several studies charting the lives of women from Bangladeshi and Pakistani backgrounds, with a particular focus on education and employment pros-pects (see Dale et al., 2002; Ahmad et al., 2003). This research points to the fact that women from Pakistani and Bangladeshi backgrounds are less likely to have formal qualifications and to be in professionally paid employment.

As Gilliat-Ray points out, 'Muslim women continue to face and overcome various obstacles to their engagement in the labour market that emanate both from within and outside their own communities. It is an environment of potential prejudice and Islamophobic hostility for Muslim women, bound up with stereotypical and gendered assumptions about them and their ability to "fit in"' (2010, p. 215).

As discussed briefly earlier, Brah (1996) in her work points out that early contribution to the family income took shape in low-paid factory work or 'home working' often to supplement the income of poorly paid husbands. As Gilliat-Ray points out, 'Many women were aware that, while convenient for them, such work was often exploitative, isolating and costly in terms of their health and well-being' (2010, p. 211). Current research draws our attention to the disparities in education and employment statistics and the consequences of this. For example, Butler (1999, p. 149) explains, 'Muslim women are having to confront not only the sexist assumptions from within their own communities ... but also from British society as a whole. Thus although their parents culture may place restrictions on their lifestyles, the sexist and racist stereotypes that exist in British society restrict them even further. Standing up for their rights as women means challenging traditional gender relations within Pakistani and Bangladeshi culture, but it also means fighting against their image as exploited and oppressed victims which pervades British "common sense" notions of Muslim women in general.'

Yet the twin issues of transnational marriage and migration trends that continue to receive considerable attention by scholars (see Bhachu, 1985; Gardner and Grillo, 2002; Bhimji, 2009). Recent writing on South Asian British Muslim households reveals an interesting insight into the dynamics of gender relations and Pakistani Muslim identities (Butler, 1999; Jacobson, 1997; Burlet and Reid, 1998; Hennink, Diamond and Cooper, 1999; Bhimji, 2009). Muslim marriage, household, kinship and familial relations underpin a renewed emergence of Muslim identities in contemporary British society, and anthropological accounts trace family life and its intricate relationship between marriage, honour and kinship ties both in Britain and in relation to the transitional relationships with the countries of origin (Shaw, 1988; Ballard, 2006).

Transnational marriage within South Asian communities has traditionally been represented as the cornerstone of most marriages. Dale and Ahmed (2008) report that 43 per cent of men and 57 per cent of women aged between 19 and 50 years have a spouse who has migrated to Britain to marry. Such statistics have led to vociferous debates on the sheer number of migrants entering Britain on the basis of marriage while masking their real intent to improve their economic position. State initiatives on combating forced marriages have also led to arguments that such transnational marriages promote inter-generational and inter-cultural conflicts and that young South Asians should be encouraged to marry British-born Asians

(Wilson, 2006). The traditional representation of marriage for many South Asian women is one based upon a fixed, essential and determinate ideal, often seen at odds with 'Western' concepts of individual choice, consent and personal autonomy. Instead marriage within Pakistani Muslim communities is represented as a generational clash between parents and their offspring where the personal values of individual choice and consent clash with family expectations and community demands. Indeed much of the literature on marriage practices within South Asian communities tends to focus upon the problems associated with arranged and forced marriage with marriage ostensibly represented as static, traditional and fixed, based upon traditional Islamic principles and firmly entrenched in family relationships and community ties (Wilson, 1978, 2006; Ballard, 1996; Bhopal, 1999; Samad and Eade, 2002).

In her work on Muslim marriage, Ahmad (2006) explains that as with other evolving social and cultural practices, marriage must also be understood as a complex and contested process that encompasses a wide and multifaceted set of meanings and experiences for all its participants. Thus for many scholars a rethinking of marriage, as a lived experience, involves a move away from pathologizing it as a fixed and immutable cultural practice where individual autonomy cannot ultimately be expressed (Sharma Hutnyk et al., 1996; Ahmad, 2006). For example, Ahmad points out that many participants use marriage as a way to better understand who they are and 'what they will become' (Ahmad, 2006, p. 135). The intervention of state policies in seeking to eradicate forced marriage (see Chapter 8) has also led to important discussions on the distinctions between arranged, own-choice and forced marriages.

Therefore the portrayal of marriage within South Asian communities solely in terms of power, control and coercion is not only misleading but, as scholarship suggests, simply inaccurate. Instead, marriage must be understood as a complex and subjective experience that embodies cultural and religious values and familial expectations but also encompasses multiple 'meanings', differentiated according to age, ethnicity, class background and economic wealth as well as differences in sectarian religious practice and familial obligations. These multiple and complex variables are also relational upon the structures that make up family and kinship relations that are interwoven and can often be contradictory and at times in conflict. Yet it is within this context of 'entanglement' and contestation that the lived experiences of British Muslim women can be better understood. In her work Ryan (2011) adopts a Goffmanian framework to explore how such women may experience and resist stigma and she questions what normality means for Muslim women living in multicultural Britain and points out that meanings are complex and deeply layered according to multiple and conflicting variables and brings to the fore questions regarding how Muslim women's agency is expressed.

Muslim women's agency

Over the past three decades feminist theorists have grappled with the question of how to reconcile Western interpretations of sexual equality and the autonomy of women's agency with cultural and religious difference.[25] Debates have been largely focused on a clash-of-values scenario, where liberal notions of equality, free will and free choice have been deemed 'progressively modern' and open to all, whereas the continued adherence of women belonging to minority communities to religious and traditional ties is presented as illiberal, backward and a barrier to the enhancement of women's rights. Yet feminist writing also provides a clearer conceptual understanding of the relations of multiple identities and multiple forms of inequality (see Cooper, 2004). For Fraser (1989, p. 65) the issue raises a number of key questions: 'Which identity claims are rooted in the defense of social relations of inequality and domination? And which are rooted in a challenge to such relations? ... Which differences ... should a democratic society seek to foster, and which, on the contrary, should it aim to abolish?' Thus, for many feminist theorists claims of cultural and religious difference – part of a pluralist model of power that affords minority groups limited yet significant autonomy – can be recognized only if they do not involve the oppression and subordination of women. A particular cause for concern for liberal feminists has been whether the practice of personal laws within the family context leads to the unequal treatment of women within these communities. It has led to interesting scholarly debates about the question of female oppression and personal agency.

The influential scholar Young, in her book *Justice and the Politics of Difference* (1990), provides five criteria of oppression: exploitation, marginalization, powerlessness, cultural imperialism and violence. She draws upon the category of 'woman' as the social constituency to understand how the different dimensions of oppression may affect different groups of women and this can be better understood in relation to other groups such as elderly people or gay and lesbian groups. In contrast, Fraser (1990) approaches oppression as a process whereby social collectivities operate along a spectrum from injustices of distribution to those of recognition. In this way Fraser links particular social relations to distinct societal structures (economic and cultural) on the one hand and forms of redress (recognition and redistribution) on the other.

For many feminist legal scholars the focus has been on the question of equality and on the need to provide a critique of the ways in which legal regulations construct, and respond to, intersecting orders of inequality. This approach draws upon the work of MacKinnon (1987), namely that the law tends to reflect masculine values: many of the values around which the law is built, including its assumption of an individualistic 'reasonable' person, are those used and valued by men. Scholars such as Williams (1988) and

Crenshaw (1989) draw upon intersecting identities (in this case race, class and gender) to illustrate how the law and legal relations fail to grasp the complexities of black women's lives. For example, juridical liberalism expressed via legislation such as anti-discrimination legislation remains inadequate in understanding the position of minority ethnic women who may be situated in multiple social locations. As such these laws simply fail effectively to redress the claims of discrimination.

More recently postcolonial feminist legal scholarship has identified and critiqued the hierarchical positions of power that many Western feminists occupy in equality debates. For example, Spivak (1990) and Mohanty (1987) have challenged the representations of non-Western women made by both liberal inclusionist and structural bias approaches to women's human rights. As Merry (2006, p. 61) points out, there is an urgent need to attend to cultural and religious differences and to see similar types of oppression in both majority and minority communities. In addition to questioning First World feminist understandings of culture and religion, such critics also challenge the structural bias, with its focus on culture, as the principal site of women's oppression. As Obiora puts it, 'the truth of the matter is that, despite popular feminist discourses, culture may not be the dispositive influence on the responses of women' (quoted in Engle, 2005, p. 62).

So how does such postcolonial and feminist difference scholarship help us to better understand the question of religious difference and the expression of Muslim women's agency and choice as members of religious communities in the UK?

Feminist analysis of the public and private divisions offers important insights into the feminist goals of autonomy, equality and women's capacity for decision-making. Feminist interpretations of autonomy encourage women to make personal choices that include the autonomy of being and the right to go against what is considered as the norm. This raises a number of important questions relating to how we understand autonomy, choice and agency and whether ultimately autonomy and equality can ever be reconciled. As Charusheela (2004, p. 197) questions: 'Can we conceive of worlds in which women act differently from men, attain different outcomes based on criteria we do not ourselves agree with, and yet do so as autonomous choosing beings expressing a desired identity for themselves?' She goes on to list a number of questions that lie at the heart of current feminist debates:

> What do we do when women in a foreign culture assert as a choice actions or behaviours that do not lead to equality? What do we do when women in asserting their right to autonomy of cultural identity and national self-determination do not attack a social construction of gender we deem patriarchal, nor seek to replace it with notions of human autonomy or choice that we consider marks of female emancipation?
>
> (2004, p. 197)

Many have focused on the issue of internalized oppression – the barriers, boundaries and divisions that suggest that such women are part of a pattern of social coercion versus false consciousness, as they are unable fully to understand what is truly in their best interests. Understood in this way many women are simply unable fully to exercise their choice and autonomy. For example, women's apparent consent to marriage in the face of coercive social, cultural and structural forces has often been broadly interpreted as acquiescence to patriarchal authority, whereas agency is equated with women's declared resistance, often through the strategy of exit (Goddard, 2000, p. 3).

Others have argued that the very idea of choice in the context of more overarching systems and networks of power and domination is problematic (Wilson, 2006). Inter-generational changes among British Asian communities in the UK have also been interpreted as evidence of the rational exercise of agency by young British Asian women through strategic manoeuvres, and through compromise and negotiation within structural constraints (Samad and Eade, 2002). Feminist engagements with issues of choice and definitions of agency can be underpinned by broad and sometimes false distinctions. The scepticism of either/or choices of belonging to families and communities is now well documented and for the past two decades feminist theorists have been grappling with the criticism that their analyses of women's oppression are ethnocentrically universalist. As Anne Phillips (2007) points out, while there is broad agreement in principle that ethnocentric universalism is to be avoided, there is also much disagreement about how this can be achieved without falling into debates on cultural relativism.

Contemporary discussions on the right to veil go to the heart of current feminist concerns on whether veiling acts as a *constraint* that limits the choice of Muslim women. The discussions on the veil and veiling in the UK do focus on the autonomy of Muslim girls and women *freely* to veil themselves, and thus such discussions embrace ideas that Muslim women have little choice but to veil and therefore displace any notions of autonomy and decision-making in the process of choosing to veil (Bhandar, 2009). For Barlas, the veil 'has become so overinvested with meaning that one can no longer speak of it in any simple way'; in Western societies it has become a 'Muslim cultural icon' (2006, p. 57). As Motha (2007, p. 140) points out, 'The veiled woman troubles feminism and secularism in much the same way. Both feminism and secularism face a problem of finding a consistent position that respects individual autonomy, and simultaneously sustains a conception of politics freed from heteronomous determination.'

In 2006 Jack Straw MP, the then Foreign Secretary, expressed his discomfort at meeting with Muslim female constituents who wore the veil (with their face covered), and stated that he was in the habit of asking women to remove their veil in his office. He further stated that women should not wear veils that cover their face. Characterizing the veil as 'a visible statement of separation and of difference', he said that, above all, his discomfort lay in the fact that the veil, in his view, prevented him from having a truly 'face-to-face' encounter with his constituent (see Bhandar, 2009). Drawing upon this example and the Government Green Paper titled *The Governance of Britain*, published in July 2007, Bhandar points out that Jack Straw's comments reflect anxiety about the issue of social cohesion and the perceived need for common British values. So on what basis has this specific form of clothing become a symbol for constraint and disempowerment of Muslim women? As Charusheela quite rightly points out, 'Unless one decides that all social markers of gender-difference are always and everywhere constraints, there is no intrinsic aspect of the veil that can make us decide to locate it as constraint while we leave out stockings and skirts and all other markers of female–male difference in apparel norms in other societies' (2004, p. 196).

Thus not all Muslim women seek to exercise their agency as understood by Western feminists in order to enhance Western feminist interpretations of their autonomy. Within the context of a patriarchal system, women will often act to uphold gendered norms, such as beauty culture, or adopt disciplinary bodily technologies like elective cosmetic surgery (Frank, 2006). Most feminist celebrations of women's agency are in service of the politics of emancipation, and such accounts interpret women's lack of autonomous impulses as acquiescence to patriarchal power structures, and see women's desires as informed by 'oppressive norms of femininity' (Morgan, 1991; Wolf, 1991). Waggoner (2005, p. 24) discusses the question of ethics in discussions of agency and draws upon the notion of 'ethical embodiment'. He explains: 'The idea it preserves is that a strong model of agency (as radically autonomous) is a fiction, since subjects are always formed and shaped by conditions not of their making, but there is nonetheless more to subjectivity than those conditions and their effects alone. Causal conditions are capable of giving rise to undetermined moments of self-reflection, self-interrogation, openness to the unforeseeable.'

One argument that does not conceptualize agency as oppositional has been discussed extensively in Mahmood's account of the women's piety movement in the mosques of Cairo, which uncouples agency from liberatory politics (2006a). Thus the complexity of women's actions in different contexts can be understood in multiple ways. Wendell (1990) points to the role of structural inequalities while retaining a strong sense of respect for women's agency and responsibility to act within the constraints and possibilities presented by their context. That this agency, which has been defined as 'the socioculturally mediated capacity to act', can emerge in particular situations and places and at particular times has been noted in research examining the impact of education, employment, class and the perception and reality of racism on women's marriage choices. However, there has been far less exploration of how personal histories, emotions, motivations and institutional arrangements – as well as practical concerns such as access to information and perceived access to services – have a bearing on women's agency and the language they use to talk about it.

3
Background to the Study

In Britain today we have seen the emergence of community and family reconciliation/mediation mechanisms that seek to resolve matrimonial disputes outside both the traditional framework of state law and in conjunction with state-law mechanisms. For example, the work of Shah-Kazemi (2001) and Bano (2007) illustrates the emergence of Shari'ah councils operating within diasporic Muslim communities that act as ADR mechanisms to resolve matrimonial disputes within the family, home and local communities. This development has been followed by the emergence of the Muslim Arbitration Tribunal (hereinafter referred to as MAT) which operates as a civil law mechanism under the auspices of the Arbitration Act 1996 to produce decisions that may be enforced and relied upon in the civil courts. Therefore in Britain today, we currently have a three-tier approach to resolving matrimonial disputes: state civil law procedure, unofficial community mechanisms (Shari'ah councils) and the new Muslim Arbitration Tribunal.

In the 1990s the legal anthropologist Werner Menski (1997, 2001) first published a series of articles based on his research which documented the ways in which South Asian Muslims practised, utilized and perceived 'law' in Britain. Drawing upon the work of Masaji Chiba (1986), he described this new understanding of law as a complex process of legal and cultural practice that drew upon Islamic and English legal precepts of law (mixed in with cultural norms and values) to form a new hybrid understanding of legal practices in Britain which he broadly described as *Angrezi Sharia*. He went on to develop his work to illustrate both the dangers and problems associated with what was then largely described as 'ethnic minority laws' practised under the rubric of state law. In particular he argued that state ignorance of such practices left vulnerable parties with little if any legal protection and allowed some individuals within groups to circumvent the law in order to promote personal interests at the expense of more vulnerable members. More importantly perhaps, he argued that the consequences of this had led to privatized unofficial and de-regularized systems of religious laws operating in private which undermined both the authority and recognition of state law. And while promoting the principle of diversity in law and the diverse ways in which individuals seek to resolve matrimonial disputes, he argued that the law must evolve to recognize multiple systems of dispute resolution that more specifically include rather than exclude personal systems of family law that are based upon the lived social experience of individuals. In this way the universal principles of liberal legality, justice, equality before the law and common citizenship then have real meaning to all in society, applicable to all irrespective of differences in ethnic, cultural and religious backgrounds (see Pearl and Menski, 1998).

This work provided the impetus for a whole new body of scholarship in Britain (see Shah-Kazemi, 2001; Yilmaz, 2005; Bano, 2007). This book contributes to this new scholarship and is based upon two empirical research projects. The first, is based upon my doctoral research completed in 2004 which analysed the experiences of a group of British Pakistani Muslim women using Shari'ah councils to obtain a Muslim divorce certificate in England. This study produced insights into the workings of a small number of Shari'ah councils in England and the experiences of British Muslim women using these bodies to obtain a Muslim divorce certificate. The second, a project funded by the Ministry of Justice titled *An Exploratory Study of Shariah Councils in England with Respect to Family Law* (Bano, 2012) 'maps' the number of Shari'ah councils operating in England and provides some overview of the type of dispute resolution process within Shari'ah councils.

My interest in this area is both personal and professional. On a personal note as a British Muslim Pakistani woman I was intrigued to discover why my peers may choose to use a Shari'ah council to resolve matrimonial disputes upon family and relationship breakdown. More importantly, what are the personal consequences, if any, for these women in their use of these bodies? Were the rights of Muslim women in effect being eroded in the private sphere outside the protection of state law? Was the emergence of Shari'ah councils the impetus to introduce a parallel legal system in Britain whereby Muslims would be encouraged to use religious bodies to resolve family law disputes simply on the basis of their religious identity and belonging to a particular Muslim religious community? Why do some British Muslim women choose to use the services of religious bodies which may appear (at least to some both within and outside the community) as patriarchal in nature and unequal in their protection of the rights and interests of Muslim women? Was this a clear-cut example of social coercion, and the exertion of family and community pressure compelling Muslim women to use these services? Prior to this new scholarship that explicitly draws upon empirical research to better understand the practice of Muslim family law in Britain, existing explanations were largely based upon theoretical understandings frequently discussed under the rubric of multiculturalism across disciplines (in particular politics, philosophy and history). For example, the rise in theoretical debates in liberal political theory, as discussed in Chapters 1 and 2 and often summed up today as the Okin (1999)-inspired debate of 'Is multiculturalism bad for women?' that focussed on liberal conflicts between the rights of the individual versus the rights of the community (see Taylor, 2007). This scholarship questions the increasingly perceived tenuous and fractured relationship between the rights of the individual and moves to accommodate group rights in the name of culture and religion, with little analyses on protecting vulnerable members of the group, most often women.

These debates also mirrored a theoretical re-examination by legal scholars drawing upon a postmodern analysis of law which sought to better understand the practice of cultural and religious systems of law at times in opposition to state law. Some of this analysis drew upon the practice of multiculturalism in Britain and the idea of cultural rights that were based upon fixed notions of religious and cultural norms, values and practices and understood as essential and homogeneous in nature: in other words such scholarship seemed to make clear that you either belonged to your community or you did not, the traditional insider versus outsider debate. Yet I began to wonder whether individuals actually experience identity and law in such a fixed and structured way. More importantly, I was aware that decades of sociological research had given us plenty of data to reveal that identity can never be understood in such a fixed or essential way. Of course, this is not to deny that individuals, communities, groups and networks may not operate along fixed structures and boundaries based upon fixed notions of belonging and identity in order to maintain group loyalty, cohesion and commitment (in what they may perceive as a challenge to their survival). But in reality sociologists have also drawn our attention to the fact that for many individuals living within cultural and religious communities, identity is far more fragmented, messy, complex and contested. And furthermore Islamic scholars too point to the complexity of Muslim identity that is also based upon personal and group contestation when questioning Islamic norms, values and ethics – a process which underpins Islam and Islamic thought in which choice and belonging to a Muslim community then becomes more autonomous and consensual rather than being predicated exclusively upon group membership and belonging: the Muslim *umma*. So how can Muslim dispute resolution in matters of family law be understood in Britain today? And why do existing debates continue to be framed in the context of those who belong to the community and seek the formal recognition of religious councils in Britain and those who perceive this as a challenge to liberal legality and liberal values of fairness, justice and equality?

Doctoral research 2000–4

Selecting the methodology

The central methodological questions for my doctoral research related to formulating ways to observe how Shari'ah councils operate in practice, and to encourage British Pakistani Muslim women to speak about their experiences of using them to obtain a Muslim divorce. The first method, observation of four Shari'ah council 'proceedings', was chosen for a number of reasons. As discussed earlier, existing research documents the development of Shari'ah councils in Britain as evidence of an emerging parallel legal system. Thus the socio-legal reality of Muslims in Britain is presented as a complex scenario whereby official and customary laws interact to produce a new set of hybrid laws. The present study attempts to problematize this approach by examining the gendered nature of the informal legal sphere(s). In doing so it deconstructs the binary oppositions of 'state law' and 'customary law' and seeks instead to explore the contested 'space/s' that Shari'ah councils occupy as an empirical reality rather than a theoretical construct. Research included observing counselling and mediation sessions, interviews with Shari'ah councils' scholars and observation of 'council' proceedings when a religious divorce certificate was issued.

The observation research aimed to explore the extent to which marital disputes are settled within the context of family, home and community by the intervention of non-state agencies such as Shari'ah councils. The issue of mediation in English family law has been presented as a dilemma for the liberal state that grapples with regulating family life while also preserving it. The relationship between 'family' and liberal political theory has focused on the family threatening 'citizenship' and loyalty to the state for it is deemed to undermine democracy through its emphasis on loyalty to family networks rather than the state (Maclean and Kurczewski 2011).

In addition to observation, analysis of Shari'ah council case files allowed me to explore the nature of the correspondence between Muslim women and the councils. This is important as some women do not attend the Shari'ah council and all contact is made via correspondence. The files can therefore provide an insight into the administrative procedures applied by the councils when issuing divorce certificates.

The third method comprised in-depth qualitative interviews with 25 Pakistani Muslim women to elicit their experiences of using Shari'ah councils to obtain a Muslim divorce. It is the 'voice' of the women that the research seeks to bring out. A feminist approach to interviewing was adopted, as explained later (see Stanley and Wise, 1988). In particular, the study explores the women's motivations for using Shari'ah councils, drawing upon their experiences of marriage and analysing strategies to obtain a religious divorce. In doing so it considers how women balance social expectation based on cultural duties with religious obligations and how gender frames the relations of power on which negotiations may be based within the family and unofficial decision-making bodies (Griffiths, 1997). In particular it considers how socially sanctioned parameters that embody notions of honour and shame interact and affect their decisions and autonomy. The differential position of women within the family, home and community is well documented and 'gives rise to the exercise of different forms of power, which impact upon individuals' abilities to negotiate with one another. These forms of power not only differ on the basis of gender, but also vary between members of the same sex and across generations' (Griffiths, 2005, p. 68).

The challenge of researching 'sensitive' issues

Conducting research on 'sensitive' issues raises a specific set of ethical and methodological challenges. Sieber and Stanley (1988) define sensitive topics as those studies in which there are 'potential consequences or implications either directly for the participants in the research or for the class of individuals represented by the research'. This can include topics that involve taboos for the local community, for example sex or death, or topics which may be sensitive in relation to the socio-political context in which the research is undertaken (Lee, 1999).

Research on Shari'ah councils can be deemed 'sensitive' for a number of reasons. First, issues of marriage and divorce embody notions of familial honour and shame and consequently remain confined to the private spheres of family and home. The implications of discussing private matters through what is ultimately viewed as a public forum can have detrimental effects for the women and their families. During observation of Shari'ah councils, a number of scholars voiced concern about the implications of discussing personal matters of marriage and divorce 'in public' with a complete stranger. It became apparent that my presence was deemed an 'intrusive threat' by some councils since I was attempting to gain entry into areas deemed 'private' by respondents, their families and the communities to which they belonged. One religious scholar explained:

> You must understand confidentiality is of utmost importance in our work. It is very difficult for our people to discuss these issues and we spend a lot of time and effort convincing them to seek our help. Divorce is shunned in our communities and rightly so. It should not be given the air of respectability but that doesn't mean we condemn those who want to divorce. Divorce is permitted in Islam and we work with Muslims to achieve the best possible situation … to allow someone they don't know to sit through our sessions would mean they would lose our trust and confidentiality.

A further issue concerned the rise of Islamophobia and the perception of 'risk' associated with collaborating with the research project. Again discussions with religious scholars revealed concern about the possibility of such research contributing to the demonization of Muslims and what one scholar described as 'the growing climate of fear and discrimination against Muslims'. One Muslim female worker at a Shari'ah council voiced concern about the possibility of the research contributing to existing stereotypes of Muslim women as passive victims of archaic religious traditions:

> It is quite understandable why Muslim women don't want to contribute to research projects because mostly we're presented as some kind of alien species, especially if we choose to practice our faith. For example, discussion normally is confined to why we would choose to wear the hijab ... well if we're Muslims why shouldn't we? And also you have to remember that it's not that many of us are reluctant to discuss issues such as marriage and divorce in the public space but it's the lack of tolerance and understanding in this space that makes us reluctant to engage.

There were also concerns from religious scholars on the presentation of data. One scholar informed me, 'We discussed your request at our weekly meeting and a number of us are concerned about what will happen to the material once you've completed your project.' When access to the council's proceedings was permitted it was made clear that, as a Muslim researcher, I was expected to present the data in a fair and accurate way.

Gaining access to some Shari'ah councils for observation research proved challenging, lengthy and problematic. It is well documented that the aim of observation fieldwork is to provide a rich insight into the organization under study, yet this process can be limited when access to private organizations is controlled and in some cases blocked by its 'gatekeepers' (see Punch, 1986). Some writers point out that the 'access processes' need to be more fully explored. For example, Lee (1999, p. 67) complains that 'neither has much attention been paid to patterns of access and non-access across studies, [n]or to the potential consequences of differential accessibility to some settings rather than others'. In this study the absence of direct measures, a result of restricted access to Shari'ah councils, meant that comparisons between the bodies could not be sufficiently drawn.

The gendered experiences and realities of Muslim women's lives mean that a multifaceted approach to conducting feminist social research must be adopted. Further, the influence of the religious and gender identity of the researcher on the research process is subtle and complex. McCarthy, Holland and Gillies (2003, p. 23) question, 'how do we place ourselves as researchers, with our own sympathies and particular perspectives, within such multiplicities?' The dichotomies of 'insider/outsider' are too limiting and fail to capture issues of difference and commonality when the researcher shares similar ethnic/cultural and religious identity.

Do we need a radically different approach to conducting socio-legal research on 'sensitive' issues within minority diasporic communities? Research findings suggest we need to incorporate notions of difference and diversity into the feminist analytical approach. As Hall (2000, p. 209) points out:

> The temptation to essentialize 'community' has to be resisted – The fantasy of plenitude in circumstances of imagined loss. Migrant communities bear the imprint of diaspora, 'hybridization' and difference in their very constitution. Their vertical integration into their traditions of origin exists side by side with their lateral linkages to other 'communities' of interest, practice and aspiration, real and symbolic.

The concept of 'standpoint differences' allows us to draw upon different theoretical approaches while recognizing the complexity of 'individual histories, shared family lives and standpoints of gender, generation, class and ethnicity ... all interwoven in these related but individual accounts' (McCarthy, Holland and Gillies, 2003, p. 19). This approach allows us to interrogate what we understand as culture, community and identity as fluid, changing and contested entities, which are open to social and cultural contestation within diasporic communities. As a researcher, I was able to draw upon these multiplicities and move away from the traditional dichotomy of Muslim women as subordinated and oppressed within local Muslim communities.

Interviewing Pakistani Muslim women

Feminist ethnographic research emphasizes notions of 'reflexivity' and 'situated knowledge' where the relationship between the respondent and the interviewer is acknowledged and recognized and thus becomes part of the data and not external to it.[1] It contests the traditional constructions of 'knowledge' and 'society' defined within a structuralist paradigm and underlined by patriarchal norms and values. The feminist approach emphasizes the personal and subjective experiences of the researched subject that can produce invaluable data. Here the researchers are encouraged to place themselves in the position of the researched in order to understand the dynamics of the relationship between the two and locate all research within a historical and contextual setting.

In this study, the British Pakistani Muslim women who were interviewed came from Birmingham, Bradford and London, were aged between 25 and 40 and were from a variety of socio-economic backgrounds. I developed an interview method which allowed women to raise and discuss issues that were important to them, and not only those in which I was interested. All the women were offered anonymity for their accounts and have been given pseudonyms.

The logic for selecting this sample of British Pakistani Muslim women for interview as opposed to 'Muslim women' as a general category is twofold. First, as a result of the complex and changing nature of identity, this approach provides the opportunity to explore the subtleties of cultural difference between Muslim women. In this way, we are also able to provide an insight into the dynamics, representation and practice of power within Pakistani Muslim communities. Second, to categorize all British Pakistani Muslim women as belonging to a homogenous Muslim community presumes the primacy of a universal religious Muslim identity. It prevents one from exploring ambivalence and antagonism outside the binaries of insider/ outsider, Muslim/non-Muslim and subordinate/dominant. This does not mean, however, that some British Pakistani Muslim women do not embrace this unifying identity that homogenizes cultural and religious difference. Evidence also suggests, however, that there are also unique differences between and within the category of 'Muslim women', and by focusing upon one group of women we are able to explore the conditions under which they develop strategies to obtain a Muslim divorce and participate in family and community mediation. Hence, we can explore how identities may be ambivalent, situational and strategic.

Negotiations with female respondents were long and challenging. Matters concerning marriage and divorce are largely confined to the private sphere of the family and home, and women are often involved in lengthy and complex negotiations. They may therefore be reluctant to discuss such personal issues in a 'public forum' as epitomized by a research project. It is also important to remember that women are seen as carriers of 'collective honour' in the family and community and they play a central role in the symbolic reproduction of 'community' and its survival (Anthias and Yuval-Davis, 1992). The implications of private details becoming public may be too great for the women. Existing research literature fails to address adequately this issue of the specific methodological obstacles faced when conducting research with diasporic communities in Britain. For example, it is commonly believed that respondents agree to take part in a study once they meet the researcher, yet this is not always the case. In this study, consent still depended upon lengthy discussions and assurances on the specific ways in which the research would be used and the importance of confidentiality and anonymity. Only 25 of the 45 women who were approached and who fitted the criteria for the in-depth study agreed to take part. The other women failed to return phone calls or said that they were not ready to share their personal experiences. I spent a lot of time thinking of how I could contact the women and once contact had been made how I could stay in touch with them. A number of women expressed their concern about participating in research that might contribute to the stereotype of Muslim women as victims of a patriarchal cultural/religious system. Some women, therefore, refused to take part in the research as they felt that it might be more damaging than beneficial to them. Out of 25 women, 13 informed me that the implications of divulging private details would affect not only themselves but also their immediate families. Rubina explained, 'I have to be careful about what I say ... It's not that I don't trust you but

I have to think about what will happen if what I say gets back to my family.'
Assurances of complete confidentiality and anonymity were not enough to
convince some of the women.

This raises the question as to *why* respondents may choose to take part in
a research project. Phoenix (1994, p. 35) points out that respondents have
their own varied reasons that 'include simple curiosity; desire to talk and to
be listened to; to help with the researcher's training or the aims of the study;
[and] to complain about the aims of the study or about the specific kinds
of research'. In this sample the women were asked why they had chosen to
contribute to this study and their responses were both diverse and conflicting. For some women the study provided an opportunity to put across their
version of events. Others were keen to challenge stereotypes of Muslim
women as passive, and finally a small number of women hoped the research
would hasten the introduction of Muslim family law into English law.

The period of negotiation between the researcher and respondent to participate in the study is a formidable time for the researcher. It is during this
time that the respondents are in the powerful position of refusing to take
part and possibly curtailing the objectives of the project. Even when consent is given, however, negotiations continue. In fact, discussions with the
women over how the research would proceed and develop continued once
the interviews had been completed. Out of 25 women, eight expressed concern over what would happen to the interview tapes once the research had
been completed. Brannen (1988, p. 324) suggests that participants respond
favourably to some methods and not to others when there is an overlap
between the concerns of researchers and those of participants, and 'where
both parties are in search of similar explanations'. Perhaps somewhat unsurprisingly, the shared experiences of other women were important.

I pay tribute to all those women who contributed to this study and who
chose to share their experiences, often in difficult circumstances. As one
interviewee reported:

> I was the shameless one who wanted a divorce ... My mum would meet
> someone in the shop who would say your daughter's a whore because she
> did this, this and this and people would invite themselves to my family
> home, uncles of mine, and say you know you should now disown her
> and have nothing to do with her and all this kind of stuff. So my family
> had that for many, many years.

Pursuing this type of research depends on women placing sufficient trust
in a researcher to share these experiences with wider audiences, both within
their own ethnic and religious community, and with society more generally. The political and ethical challenges are many, but it is important that
socio-legal researches engage with the issues raised by feminist standpoint
research.

The Ministry of Justice Project: *An Exploratory Study of Shariah Councils in England with Respect to Family Law*

This project represented early work into mapping Shari'ah councils in England and Wales with three key objectives:

1. To identify as accurately as possible the number and location of Shari'ah councils in England.
2. To describe the administrative structure, funding and membership of Shari'ah councils in England.
3. To describe the range and quantity of family-related work carried out by Shari'ah councils.

It also aimed to make some preliminary recommendations regarding future research and the scope of the study was limited to providing preliminary insight into the workings of Shari'ah councils and did not focus on the experience of Shari'ah council users. Limitations in method, time frame and resources meant that the study was not able to identify all the number and location of Shari'ah councils in England and it could not therefore produce a definitive list of all the Shari'ah councils in England.

In this preliminary project the organizations that appeared to undertake Shari'ah council work were identified using Muslim directories, online searches and researcher contacts. The different sources were used to identify organizations where some kind of Shari'ah-related advice on family law matters was available to local Muslim communities. Organizations were included if they dealt specifically with issues concerning marriage breakdown, and had the capacity to issue Muslim divorce certificates. It was found that many organizations did not undertake Shari'ah council work themselves, but instead offered general advice or signposting for women and couples looking for support. A process of 'snowball' sampling, in which respondents were asked to nominate additional contacts, was also used. These methods identified 30 groups involved in this type of activity. A telephone survey of the 30 councils was undertaken and respondents included religious scholars and other key individuals within the organizations. Respondents from 22 of the 30 councils took part. No contact was achieved with five councils and three refused to take part. There were no major differences between participating and non-participating councils in terms of size of council, affiliation to a mosque or public profile. Contact was attempted with all of these. Councils where a respondent took part were located as follows:

London: Six councils
Midlands: Ten councils
The North: Six councils.

Participating and non-participating councils were compared, using information obtained from the mapping exercise to examine contrasts between size of council, affiliation to a local mosque and whether the council had a public profile. Interviews were based on a semi-structured questionnaire exploring the structure, administration and funding of councils, council membership, and processes employed.

Research challenges

The councils were generally run on a volunteer basis, were short staffed and very busy. This led to practical difficulties in speaking with respondents. There was also reluctance to discuss the private work of the councils and concerns that the research might contribute to surveillance of Muslim communities. Respondents were also wary of the stereotypical ways in which their organizations were represented in the media. A further major challenge for the research was the difficulty building up trust with respondents using the telephone survey approach. This has implications for future research.

A final list of 30 councils was identified. The researchers were confident the final sample included the major Shari'ah councils operating in England. However, during fieldwork, through discussions with contacts and respondents, it became apparent that certain small Shari'ah councils based in local community mosques or local organizations had not been included. Due to the scope of the study only those councils that were publicly well known, or well known in the local community, and those councils that dealt with family law-related matters were included in the sample. The list should not be seen as definitive. However, the findings do shed light upon a number of the major councils in Britain and are likely to highlight issues common to many councils.

Data collection

Once the 30 groups which would be included in the study had been identified, telephone interviews took place with key contacts identified within the organization. The contacts included religious scholars and key individuals who had in-depth knowledge of the organization and its services. In each case the researchers spoke to individuals who were directly involved in the organization(s).

Ethical considerations

The research raised a number of ethical considerations. All organizations that agreed to take part in the study were afforded complete anonymity. This was to ensure that any confidential issues being discussed in the interviews would not jeopardize the work of the councils and their clients. Understandably there was also a high expectation of confidentiality, which was granted. All participants were cautious about their involvement with the project due to the adverse publicity generated by media representations of 'Shari'ah courts' and 'Shari'ah law'.

Data security was a high priority. Telephone interviews were recorded by hand. Once this data was collected and anonymized it was transferred with due care to the project manager. At no point was data held on laptops. All data, both electronic and paper copies, were destroyed at the end of the project. This included the deletion of electronic 'temporary files'.

Research Limitations

As noted previously, within practical time and resource constraints it was not possible to provide a definitive list of *all* of the organizations undertaking Shari'ah council work in England. Nevertheless, the final list can be said to have included all of the major councils, as well as at least a reasonable number of the smaller ones, to provide useful information about the operation of Shari'ah councils in general.

There were a number of practical difficulties in contacting organizations by using the telephone method. These led to some limitations in the data, but at the same time consideration of these problems provides useful information for planning future research and also tells us something about the nature of these organizations. Problems of making contact included difficulties in obtaining accurate contact details of organizations, inaccurate information over which *individuals* to contact within an organization, lack of staff within councils to deal with telephone enquires and prearranged telephone interview calls being unanswered or interrupted. It was found that organizations were run on a volunteer basis, and tended to be very busy and short staffed. In addition to these practical difficulties, there was a general reluctance to engage with the research for the reasons outlined earlier.

Matters concerning marriage and divorce within Muslim communities are largely confined to the private sphere of family and home, and sometimes the local community. The work of Shari'ah councils is often understood as an extension of such familial relations. There was a general reluctance on the part of respondents to discuss such private or personal issues in the public forum represented by this government-funded research. It was argued that such matters should remain private in order to protect client confidentiality and anonymity.

A number of council respondents were suspicious that the data collected would be used by the government to undermine the work of local community organizations and mosques. They therefore refused to take part or limited their responses to 'yes' and 'no'. Some were concerned that participation might contribute to the stereotype that Shari'ah councils seek to replace civil law mechanisms for resolving matrimonial disputes and/or seek the wholesale introduction of Shari'ah law into English law. As previously mentioned another reason for shari not taking part was the concern that this project would contribute to surveillance on Muslim communities in order to 'manage' their presence in British society.

A small number of respondents specifically pointed to the report by Civitas[2] published in June 2009. This report claimed that 'Sharia law has already become quite entrenched in Britain' (p. 2) and suggested that its implementation could contravene English legal principles of equality, non-discrimination and justice. The timing of the report, just prior to the start of fieldwork for this project, influenced a small number of respondents who subsequently refused to take part, citing concern about media projection of Shari'ah councils. Some councils also reported an increase in the volume of enquiries received from the media after the publication of the Civitas report and were again more reluctant to take part.

Some difficulties in persuading respondents to take part had been expected. The use of a telephone survey adopted made it difficult to develop relationships between interviewers and respondents and therefore limited the data collected. However, this was an early exploratory study across a wide geographical area using simple and non-contentious questions and therefore the views of council users was outside the remit of this study and not sought. Obtaining more in-depth data would require researchers and respondents to build up relationships and trust over a longer time period (see the next section on the need for further research).

The need for further research

While both projects in this book have contributed to a better understanding of the range and scope of Shari'ah councils, much remains unknown. There is a need to develop our understanding of this area and therefore an urgent need for fuller, more in-depth studies of Shari'ah council activity and the experience of council users. This should be based on a more comprehensive mapping exercise, taking into account the wide range of organizations that may be involved in providing assistance to Muslim women seeking a religious divorce and possibly providing other dispute resolution services. It should also analyse how such bodies reach their decisions and the nature of the 'legal reasoning' that such decisions are based upon. A closer analysis of the 'process' of issuing Muslim divorce certificates should include some evaluation of how such bodies self-assess and are portrayed within local Muslim communities in which they operate.

Conducting research within community type organizations such as these is recognized as difficult as discussed earlier. Many potential respondents wish their work to remain private, without any form of public, media or state intervention. There are specific difficulties for the researcher, particularly in terms of accessing and negotiating participation. Both projects in this book have highlighted some of the challenges involved and the following recommendations suggest ways these obstacles may be overcome.

First, qualitative semi-structured interviews conducted on a face-to-face basis with key respondents would provide more detailed knowledge of the workings of Shari'ah councils. This method would allow the interviewer to adapt the research questions depending upon the responses obtained. By allowing the in-depth exploration of specific topics, the interviews could obtain more detailed data, and chart key similarities and differences between different types of Shari'ah councils. This approach would allow a rapport to be built up between the interviewer and respondent. It might also allow a more protected space for discussion; in the MOJ study reported here, even successful telephone calls were often interrupted.

Second, ethnographic observation research, with researchers spending time within councils, could provide further insight into how the councils actually work in practice. This has the potential to allow for better understanding of any potential conflicts or overlap with civil law mechanisms. Contacts and trust would need to develop over time. The data produced could then enable a detailed analysis of the administration and dispute resolution processes used by the councils.

Third, further research must include in-depth qualitative face-to-face interviews with Muslim women belonging to heterogeneous Muslim communities, as the primary users of Shari'ah councils, and with men also. Such an approach would be critical to understanding why some Muslim women choose to use Shari'ah council services and others do not. It could also explore the rise perceived by some in the use of Shari'ah councils.

Finally, research on Shari'ah councils requires an adequately resourced team of experienced researchers. Issues around whether or not to match researchers and respondents in terms of background and gender would need to be considered which raise questions on nature of data collated and the role of the research as an insider/outsider as previously discussed.

Organization of the book

This book is divided into two parts with nine chapters. Part I, composed of Chapters 1, 2 and 3, traces the key debates underpinning questions of Muslim family law in Britain and nature of the empirical data. The second part, Chapters 5 to 9 focuses on the emergence of Shari'ah councils and experiences of a group of Muslim women using Shari'ah councils to obtain a Muslim divorce certificate. It is recognized that the terms 'Muslim' and 'Islamic' are often used interchangeably in literature and this can lead to some confusion. The vast diversity in Islamic legal principles and jurisprudence and their interpretations means it is simply impossible to speak of Islamic law in a generic way. Therefore in this book the terms 'Muslim law' and 'Muslim family law' are used to illustrate the laws and practices of Muslims. Islamic law is used when discussing specifically Islamic legal principles and jurisprudence.

Chapter 1 reviews some of the wider debates on multiculturalism, secularism and community rights in Britain and outlines some of the key implications of formalizing privatized mechanisms of religious dispute resolution in Britain. It looks at the public discourse of rights and the manifestation of rights from the standpoint of law and religious practice: how do the current debates on multiculturalism, public religious practice and citizenship rights manifest in relation to the emergence of separate systems of personal law and practice within diasporic Muslim communities? Chapter 2 examines the relationship between Muslim communities and state-law relations and considers the conflicts generated by cultural and religious difference in Western societies. It explores the nature of marriage practices for Pakistani Muslim women in Britain, which is analysed in the context of debates on Muslim women's agency and autonomy. Chapter 3 then provides background to the study and outlines some of the key methodological questions underpinning the study while raising some of the methodological challenges faced while undertaking the research.

The second part of the book begins with Chapter 4. This chapter considers the development and emergence of Shari'ah councils in Britain. It draws on the concepts of privatized legal pluralism and multicultural interlegality to better understand how Muslim disputants handle their matrimonial disputes and settle their private affairs according to Islamic personal systems of law. The chapter includes an analysis of how such religious bodies may constitute as unofficial dispute resolution mechanisms within the local communities in which they are situated, in particular the ways in which the practice of Muslim family laws interact with the socio-political locations of diasporic communities and conceptions of 'home' and' homeland'. Chapter 5 then draws upon empirical data to provide a more detailed account of the ways in which four Shari'ah councils in Britain operate as unofficial ADR mechanisms within Muslim communities. In particular it considers how Islamic norms, ethics and values underpin and influence this process in the resolution of matrimonial disputes. It also draws upon empirical research to analyse the administrative structures and the *process and procedure* adopted by Shari'ah councils to resolve matrimonial disputes and analyses *how* the process of reconciliation and mediation takes place in this privatized space of local community and whether it disadvantages Muslim women. More specifically the chapter draws upon the ways in which mediation is reconstructed in this space as a specific form of Muslim legal pluralism shaped by common goals and strategies.

Chapter 6 draws upon empirical data to better understand the personal experiences of marriage with a group of British Pakistani Muslim women. Chapter 7 then draws upon interview data to better understand the motivations and experiences of British Pakistani Muslim women using a Shari'ah council to obtain a Muslim divorce certificate. In particular the chapter considers whether this unofficial process to resolve matrimonial disputes generates greater levels of disadvantage and inequality for Muslim women or whether their use provides an insight into one of the ways in which Muslim women's subjectivity and agency is expressed. These chapters draw upon the concepts of 'translocational positionality' and feminist debates on intersectionality to illustrate the complexities, difficulties and dilemmas involved in the decision-making process. Having suggested that the women's decision to resolve matrimonial disputes in these spaces cannot be understood via the dichotomous framework of insider/outsider or Muslim/non-Muslim, the chapter challenges the perceived rise of a specific religious identity and social conservatism among British Pakistani Muslim women. It does so by analysing differing identifications and drawing upon the complex realities of their lives to understand the specific contexts in which they may choose to utilize religious fora to resolve matrimonial disputes. This intersectional analysis adopts a constitutive rather than an additive approach, in which the different social divisions are not just accumulative but actually construct each other. An additive model of intersectional analysis tends to essentialize and fixate social identities, assuming that there is a certain way in which one is being 'black', 'Muslim', 'woman' and so on. The concept of 'translocational positionality' reconceptualizes the relationship between the categories of 'women', 'family' and 'community' and allows a more nuanced approach to the interplay of power, complexity and difference in the lived realities of women's lives (Anthias, 1998, 2002). In this way the empirical data challenge the presentation of Muslim legal family practice in Britain as bounded and fixed, and instead grounds these emerging social and legal formations in the lived realities and experiences of Muslim women's lives.

Chapter 8 considers the relationship between Shari'ah councils and English law in England. Drawing once again on empirical data, it considers the extent to which these competing sites of mediation overlap, conflict or complement each other and discusses any possible conflicts of law scenarios. The chapter questions whether these bodies are creating new forms of governance such as the Muslim Arbitration Tribunal and the use of the Muslim marriage contract in English family law prior to outlining some conclusions in Chapter 9.

Part II
Shari'ah Councils and Women's Experiences of Muslim Divorce

4
Shari'ah Councils in Britain

This chapter considers the emergence of Shari'ah councils that act as family dispute resolution mechanisms within Muslim communities in Britain. Theories of legal pluralism traditionally posit a non-state law that arises from the community that is opposed to the systems of the state and its law. In this chapter the concepts of 'interlegality 'and 'multicultural interlegality' are used to reveal that the legal field in Britain is composed of not a single state law versus non-state law but a plurality of laws that combine to structure the legality of the field. For example, writing on Muslim family law points to the emergence of parallel legal systems operating in Britain where state law may assume its singular dominance in the lives of Muslim disputants but the actual lived reality of law places greater primacy on the authority of religious legal principles. If this lived socio-legal reality is recognized then the ways in which these non-state processes affect social and legal change in matters of family law raise crucial questions about equality, rights and citizenship and in doing so also reveals competing claims and contestations over the meaning, practice and recognition of religious personal law systems within minority Muslim communities. This chapter therefore examines discussions on the role of community-based adjudicatory systems of dispute resolution in the light of contemporary discussions about individual and community rights, justice and common citizenship. The chapter also includes analysis of how such religious bodies may constitute unofficial dispute resolution mechanisms within the local communities in which they are situated, in particular the ways in which the practice of Muslim family laws may interact with the socio-political locations of 'home', 'homeland' and 'belonging'.

From legal pluralism to interlegality

Legal pluralism moves away from the study of law that is based upon abstract legal rules to understanding its meaning, practice and development in the context in which it operates. A simple but clear definition by Merry (1988, p. 875) serves as a useful starting point to understanding its conceptual framework as 'a situation in which two or more legal systems co-exist in the same social field'. This definition recognizes a plurality of legal orders as social facts and therefore challenges what we understand as 'law' in its traditional sense. To put it simply, legal pluralism recognizes multiple forms of ordering and bodies of rules which may be central to the lives of individuals but which are not dependent upon the state or state law for recognition or legitimacy. For many scholars the concept of legal pluralism therefore provides a space for critical thought, analysis and reflection where the relationship between law, culture and social change in society can be documented and better understood. As Griffiths (2005, p. 115) notes, 'it raises important questions about power – where it is located, how it is constituted, what forms it takes – in ways that promote a more finely tuned and sophisticated analysis of continuity, transformation and change in society.'

Historically legal anthropologists have analysed conflicts between differing social and legal orders in the colonial and postcolonial contexts to better understand systems of dispute resolution. The first phase of legal pluralism documented the nature of pluralism inherent in legal systems in matters of personal and family laws in former European colonies in Asia, Africa and the Middle East. Here the focus was the conflicts generated by state law mechanisms and the customary practices of indigenous communities. Drawing upon social and legal theories of the nineteenth and early twentieth centuries, legal pluralists then challenged the centrality of state law as the single source of overarching power and authority. Moving away from understanding law as fixed, quantifiable and scientific to an empirically based analysis based upon anthropological research, such scholars argued that understanding law as a social fact meant that state law could only be understood as one form of legal regulation that operates in any given social field. In reality there are therefore multiple and alternative forms of legal regulation that state law simply has little or no knowledge of.

The second phase of legal pluralism emerged with legal scholarship critiquing the role of law in Western liberal democracies with a focus on the conflicts generated between secular laws and personal systems of religious law. In particular it focused on the claims made by minority groups to practice personal systems of religious law and drew upon tensions and the conflicts of law scenarios generated by such demands. In other words it considered the extent to which the dominant legal order was willing to accommodate religious practice in matters of family law as part of state law processes. Scholars such as Sally Falk Moore produced insights into how customary systems of law interact with state law and the conflicts generated by the differing sources of law and the subsequent interpretive meanings attached to our understanding of 'law'. Moore (1972, p. 720) developed the concept of a 'semi-autonomous social field' that 'can generate rules and customs and symbols internally, but that ... is also vulnerable to rules and decisions and other forces emanating from the larger world by which it is surrounded. The semi-autonomous social field has rule-making capacities, and the means to induce or coerce compliance; but it is simultaneously set in a larger social matrix which can, and does, affect and invade it, sometimes at the invitation of persons inside it, sometimes at its own instance.' As legal pluralist scholarship moved on from the seminal question of 'what is law?' to how law operates in any particular social field, scholars such as Marc Galanter, Upendra Baxi and De Sousa Santos, among others widened their conceptual analyses to include critiques of state power, community and state-law relations. Such critiques of 'legal centralism' successfully dismantled the ideas of early legal anthropologists and law was now viewed as a part of other multiple non-state normative orders of rules and legal orders such as the family, community, school and trade unions.

The third phase of legal pluralist scholarship has focused on the *regulated interaction* between religious and secular sources of law and uncouples the strict separation of law/non-law and private versus public spheres to reveal new forms of legal contestations and multiple overlapping by different systems of power. Santos (1987) describes this as 'interlegality' while Hoekema (2005) develops the idea of 'multicultural interlegality' to describe the practice of minority religious laws in Western liberal democracies. This conceptual understanding of normative legal orders provides a better understanding of the ways in which personal systems of religious law take shape and the complexity of state legal pluralism in matters of family law. As Santos (2002, p. 5) explains:

> We live in a time of porous legality or of legal porosity, multiple networks of legal orders forcing us to constant transitions and tresspassings. Our legal life is constituted by the intersection of different legal orders, that is, by interlegality. Interlegality is the phenomenological counterpart of legal pluralism, and a key concept in the postmodern conception of law and recognizes that in the postcolonial context it becomes difficult to distinguish between different types of legal pluralism(s).

To capture the complexity of the relationships among and between legal orders, social life and semi-autonomous legal fields, Santos (2002, p. 6) introduces the concept of 'interlegality' as 'not the legal pluralism of traditional legal anthropology, in which the different legal orders are conceived as separate entities coexisting in the same political space, but rather, the conception of different legal spaces superimposed, interpenetrated, and mixed in our minds, as much as in our actions, either on occasions of qualitative leaps or sweeping crises in our life trajectories, or in the dull routine of eventless everyday life'. Santos suggests that complementarity, co-optation, convergence, assimilation, suppressions, junctions in social life and their interactions with law are just some of the possibilities under which interlegal interactions take place. His empirical work on disputes in squatter settlements in Brazil illustrates excellently this complexity of law and dispute resolution. Indeed this work reveals new forms of legal multiplicities where different aspects of legal pluralism are played out with the involvement of different parties utilizing different social, political and legal resources (see Twining, 2000). It therefore becomes evident that such analyses of the ways in which law actually operates on the ground can raise important questions on the relationship between normative pluralism, 'law' and person-orientated actions. Such scholarship also demonstrates that different legal/normative orders are neither fixed nor unchanging and the focus instead must be a shift to person-orientated interactions within the wider structures of dispute resolution inhabited by institutions such as the family, community and state law. Emphasis is therefore placed on personal behaviour, adaptation and community response.

Such analyses can be usefully applied to understanding how the multiple ways in which Muslim family law in Britain are practiced which can be viewed both as a part of and critical of state legal pluralism in matters of family law. In this way the dominant legal order adapts to the emergence of new frameworks of dispute resolution, becoming embedded with new meanings as a result of the interaction with the local legal order and/or vice versa. Hoekema (2005) describes this as a process whereby 'local law usually yields to the superior force of a dominant national system and adopts many features of the majority law; but there is also a "reverse interlegality" when the local legal sensibilities and practices in some respects affect the dominant ones'. A central theme of interlegality is that conceptions of home and belonging are challenged by migration and crossing borders, raising various conflicts of law scenarios. Hoekema (2005) develops this idea, applying it to migration in Europe and explains:

> Crossing borders is normal behaviour for many persons, certainly in the past but ever more so in the present time, people now move in and out of the legal practice of European states, and at the same time back and forth in the legal practices of their country of origin. Borders are fluid and porous regarding social phenomena as well. 'Community', 'culture', 'legal order' are terms often used in the present debates about plural societies, social cohesion and law, but these terms produce a false idea of coherence and stability of the phenomena they point at. They suggest a wrong idea about the relation of individuals to the social structure and how these presumably stable elements are reproduced.

Most importantly this scholarship introduces the role of social, economic and political processes into the equation of law and the relationship between legal relations and individual actions in Europe.

However the concept of legal pluralism itself has been subject to extensive critique with scholars pointing to its preponderance to State-law relations.

For example, Kleinhams and MacDonald (1997, p. 89), under the rubric of 'critical legal pluralism', argue that for many legal pluralists the cultural underpinnings of law are described in structured and fixed ways. Instead they view law as 'no more than a social structural network of social fields that fills the normative vacuum between legislator and subject. Social scientific conceptions of legal pluralism disempower the subject and its construction of law; they view the legal subject only as an abstract "individual" thereby eliminating creativity and effectively erasing any notion of legal subjectivity with a specific content.' Law, in this view, is an anthropomorphic creation that regulates itself in the guise of a plurality of social fields; the legal orders of these social fields themselves become the legal subject and their interaction is posited as responding to a logic of 'rational choice'. For many legal pluralists the problem can therefore lie with the mixing up of social and legal norms, namely where does the 'social' and 'legal' begin and end? Legal pluralism in this way continues to be hindered by conceptual difficulties and little attention is also paid to power relations within families and communities – often the basis of legal anthropological accounts. Consequently the strong legal pluralist approach that supports an anti-state ideology then presupposes that 'non-state or indigenous law is good' (Tamahana, 2001, p. 199). In his seminal work, 'Justice in many rooms: Courts, private ordering, and indigenous law', Marc Galanter (1981, p. 75) explores the relationship between legal pluralism and access to justice and warns against glorifying non-state law arguing that 'Indigenous law ... is not always the expression of harmonious egalitarianism. [Indigenous law] often reflects narrow and parochial concerns; it is often based on relations of domination; protections that are available in public forums may be absent.' However, legal pluralism, rather than solely being an object of analysis, can be used as a means of developing a better understanding of the particular ways in which power operates between and within law, unofficial law and social life. In this way, 'social investigators can ask who [which group in society, which social practices] identifies what as "customary law", why and under what circumstances? What is its interaction with state law, and what relationship does it have, if any, with actual customs circulating within society?' (Tamahana, 2001, p. 19).

Western legal scholars have therefore long recognized the existence of different and varied social and legal orders, operating within any given 'social field'. A postmodern theoretical challenge to the concept of law comes from re-evaluating the concept of law in a culturally diverse, plural society and exploring the relationship between cultural diversity, legal pluralism and the state response to conflicts generated by settled diasporic communities who wish to maintain their cultural/religious norms and values, a wish that can produce conflicts with official state law rules and norms. This approach, summarized by Shah (2005), conceptualizes contemporary legal conflict as a clash between diverse systems of law, both formal and informal, and it draws upon the origins and migration patterns of specific ethnic minority communities in Britain in order to demonstrate how such conflicts arise. In particular, the family and wider kin group are presented as the two key sites upon which such legal conflicts are based. As Shah (2005, p. 19) argues, 'family and wider kin groups are the primary location of self-regulation, which also gives rise to conflict and negotiation in the wider British social order. Since Asian and African laws emphasize self-regulated societies rather than positivist top-down regulation, as the British state law does, there is a fundamental clash of basic values.' Shah's critical reassessment not only challenges the ontological premises upon which formalist definitions of law are based, but also reframes discourse on the settlement patterns of dispersed communities living in the West. More recently still discussion has centred on the relationship between law and religious identity and the move from individual notions of identity towards a communitarian notion of identity along with its potential for undermining the legal principles of 'equality before the law' and 'common citizenship' (Phillips, 2007).

In her groundbreaking work on the relationship between law and the social and political context under which it operates, Moore (1978) drew heavily on the work of the anthropologist Malinowski (1948) and argued that state law rules do not pertain to the control and authority that under-pin the lives of many individuals. She explained:

> A central concern of any rule-maker should be the identification of those social processes which operate outside the rules, or which cause people to use rules, or abandon them, bend them, reinterpret them, sidestep them or replace them. To recognize that such processes are inescapable aspects of the use of rule-systems and to try to understand as much as possible about the conditions of their operation would probably be far more effective than taking the view that such activities might be fully controlled simply by tighter drafting of 'loophole' – less legislation. Social transactions usually take place in the service of objectives to which legal rules are merely ancillary shapers, enablers or impediments. Conformity to the rules is seldom in itself the central objective.
>
> Moore (1978, p. 4)

This produces a complex interplay of rules, norms and values as part of wider social and cultural processes that enable individuals to forge and develop strategies that are best suited to them. As Ehrlich (1936) argued, law derives from social facts and can only be better understood in relation to its historical and social context. His concept of 'living law' thus becomes an important tool in which to better understand how law evolves, takes shape and can be understood in relation to power and compulsion. Menski explains, 'Ehrlich's analysis highlights an inevitable gap between the official law and actual practices, so that "living law" is not simply the law as practised, but an amalgam of the official law and of people's values, perceptions and strategies, constituting a new hybrid entity' (2006, p. 93). In this way state law is never the only source of law – people look to other forms of rules and sources of authority as part of their understanding of law and legal relations. Such analyses emphasize the gap between theory and practice. The introduction of the individual and communities into our understanding of law and legal relations contributes to the analytical debate of what we understand as law. Most importantly critiques of state-law relations and the significance individuals attach to state law in their own perceptions and understandings of law introduce the concept of agency in law.

In contrast to the early twentieth century, legal practitioners now readily recognize the plural systems of laws operating within different societies. One of the first scholars to document and analyse this was the legal anthropologist Werner Menski. In his most recent work, Menski (2006) refers to the emergence of a 'plurality conscious jurisprudence' that draws upon concepts such as legal pluralism, diaspora(s) and hybrid legal cultures to better understand the limitations of single legal uniformity while raising questions of what we understand as the relationship between law and society in Western liberal societies. He explains, 'To take account of interlegality pluralism needs to be conceived as "a universal phenomenon" covering both western and non-western societies, and at the same time appearing in not only the dual structure of state law and minor customary law but also the triple of customary law, national law and international law' (2006, p. 83).

More recently research has explored the comparative nature of religious councils and tribunals operating in Britain. A recent study, titled *Social Cohesion and Civil Law: Marriage, Divorce and Religious Courts* (Douglas et al., 2011), led by Professor Gillian Douglas looked specifically at the relationship between religion, divorce and access of law. The study focused on the work of three tribunals, the Birmingham Shariah Council, the London Beth Din of the United Synagogue and the National Tribunal for Wales of the Roman Catholic Church. It found both diversity and commonalities between these three mechanisms of dispute resolution but each sought to avoid conflict with state law in matters of family law. The authors found the process of resolving disputes to be more open and flexible rather than based upon rigid religious laws. For example: 'Each religious tribunal in our study sees itself as applying a body of religious "law" in the sense of a code regarded by adherents as binding on them. However either the autonomous position of the particular tribunal, or the breadth of the rules which might be applied to the case before it, provides a degree of flexibility to the decision-maker. None of the three tribunals we studied is constrained by a system of binding precedent.' On the question of recognition, the report concludes: 'our findings show that, at present, religious annulments and divorces remain completely outside the civil legal system, and none, including Jewish divorces where the Matrimonial Causes Acts is invoked to delay the civil decree absolute, is "recognized" by the law.' This study was therefore able to provide insights into the areas of commonality and difference between these models of religious dispute resolution and the extent to which they seek to complement and/or conflict with English civil law mechanisms.

What is Muslim family law?

The term Shari'ah in classical Muslim law refers to 'definition of practice'. In day-to-day usage it refers to the body of rules and principles that make up Islamic religious law. Wheeler (1996, p. 34) points out that Shari'ah 'determines how certain aspects of everyday life are to be practised according to the model provided by the canon'.

Its application is wider, however, than the word 'law' implies, as these precepts do not distinguish between public and private activities. Rather, Shari'ah covers a broad range of actions and obligations for Muslims. Washing, cleaning, eating, marriage, divorce, bank loans, business transactions and property purchases are all examples of areas of day-to-day life that Shari'ah provides guidance or direction upon. Both civil and criminal codes are incorporated within the Shari'ah system of jurisprudence.

There is no single document or source giving a definitive listing of every Shari'ah precept. To describe Shari'ah as a framework can be misleading, since there is no ideal or typical model of Shari'ah in the world today: Shari'ah law is subject to interpretation by different religious leaders and communities. There is no one comprehensive Islamic legal system but varieties exist according to ethnic or religious backgrounds. Shari'ah is perhaps better characterized as an evolving legal philosophy (jurisprudence) with its roots in two key religious scriptures: the *Qur'an* and the *Sunna*.

The Qur'an contains the religious scriptures of Islam, while the Sunna contains the actions and words of the Prophet Muhammad (Nasir, 1990, pp. 2–3). In this way modern Islamic legal ideas have developed over time, contextual upon both time and place and more importantly the nature and type of the applications and precedents set through the practice of Shari'ah. Since the Qur'an is concerned predominantly with religious precepts, there are relatively few identifiable legal injunctions. Badr (1978, p. 188) estimates that '[o]ut of a total of 6237 verses only 190 verses or three per cent of the total can be said to contain legal provisions. Most of these deal with family law and inheritance.' Where issues or disagreements cannot be settled through religious texts, jurists look towards the *Ijma*, which refers to the body of principles arrived at through the consensus of Islamic scholars:

[T]he whole process of Muslim jurisprudence, from the definition of sources of law to the derivation of substantive rules, was an exploratory effort of the human intellect. When an individual jurist reached a judicial conclusion, it was considered more of a conjecture; however, when the ruling was the outcome of a more or less unanimous consensus, it became an incontrovertible statement of the divine body.

Masood (2003, p. 2)

Where neither the Qur'an nor Sunna is able to provide the necessary authority, a jurist may apply *qiyas*. This refers to reasoning through analogy to provide the applicable Islamic principle to decide the issue at law (Hallaq, 1999). Broadly, Islam can be divided into Sunni and Shia followers. The Sunni schools of Islam include *Hanafi*, *Hanbali*, *Shafi'i* and *Maliki*. The dominant Shia school is *Twelvers* (sometimes also called *Jafari*, which excludes the *Ismaili* and *Zaydi* sects). The way in which Shari'ah is considered, interpreted and enacted differs between these schools and, moreover, will vary according to local customs, cultural practices and traditions. As such, there is no cohesive body of Shari'ah, rather there are differing strands based upon common texts. Yet, because the schools derive their ideas from common texts, common themes emerge. Recent efforts have been made by Islamic scholars to establish a cohesive body of Islamic jurisprudence, *Fiqh al-Aqalliyyat* (or, more simply, the *fiqh* of Muslim minority communities living in non-Muslim jurisdictions) (see Fishman, 2006, p. 1).

In practice, then, despite different methodologies, the Sunni schools regard one another's decisions as valid by consensus. As the process of Shari'ah is itself an exercise in interpretation, individuals are unable to set incontrovertible legal precepts. Islamic history points to the development of Muslim jurisprudence that has led to different interpretations of Islamic law. The principles of jurisprudence are referred to as *usul al-fiqh* and the methodologies for understanding and applying Shari'ah are consensus (*Ijma*), critical reasoning (*Ijtihad*) and analogical reasoning (*qiyas*). Muslim scholars point to the tensions between the Sunna and Qur'an as the primary source of authority for Shari'ah. In Sunni Islam as mentioned earlier there are four schools of legal thought and jurisprudence, as mentioned earlier and in Shia Islam there are three schools. While each recognizes the other's parameters, orthodoxy tensions between them persist. Abdullahi An-Naim (1999, p. 33) points out that far from being 'a single logical, whole, the Shari'ah reveals a diversity of opinions not only across schools but within them as well'.

Despite these differences An-Naim (1999, p. 31) also points out that each of the schools of thought concur that men and women are not to be treated equally and that even though 'Islam is probably the most uncompromising of the world's religions in its insistence on the equality of all believers before God ... to the jurists it did not follow from the equality of "all believers" before God that men and women should be equal before the law'. Indeed there is enormous literature on the nature of the conflicts generated between the different schools of Islamic jurisprudence. In this regard the growth of divergent opinion on what was understood as Islamic law was deemed as a dangerous situation to the power and authority of Allah and which led to consensus and the closing of the 'gates of ijihad' (see Nasir, 1986). Uniformity across the four Sunni law schools was deemed necessary to safeguard the development of Islamic thought and practice. However, Esposito (1982, p. 9) points out that other extratextual sources[1] also played a key role in the implementation of Shari'ah law. Asma Barlas (2006) and Abdullahi An-Naim argue that the development of Muslim legal norms must be understood in the historical context in which they evolved and that in spite of its 'assumed religious authority and inviolability' Shari'ah is 'not the whole of Islam' but an 'interpretation of its fundamental sources as understood in a particular historical context' (An-Naim, 1990, p. 31). Not only was the method for deriving it a product of the intellectual, social and political processes of Muslim history but Shari'ah was constructed by its founding jurists. In the process some jurists tried to reconcile it with what they perceived to be the community's best interest at that time; others simply disregarded reality and addressed themselves to an ideal situation in theorizing on what *ought* to be the case.[2]

In Britain existing literature presents the socio-legal reality of Muslims in Britain as a complex scenario whereby official and customary laws interact to produce a new set of hybrid laws (Yilmaz, 2002). In attempting to develop a conceptual framework which both adopts a 'postmodern approach' to the study of law and recognizes pluralism and diversity in social life, Menski (1993) adopts the analytical framework of the jurist Masaji Chiba (1986) and constructs a legal model he defines as *Angrezi Shari'ah*. According to Menski, Asian Muslims in Britain have not simply given up Islamic law but combine Islamic law and English law to form *Angrezi Shari'ah*. He describes a threefold process generated by internal conflicts within Asian communities, leading to the creation of 'British Asian Laws' in Britain. The first stage occurred at the time of migration when ignorance of the British legal system meant that customary practices continued to be observed. For example, until 1970 many Asians did not register marriages and this later resulted in huge matrimonial disputes. Subsequently, however, Asians learnt to adapt to English law but rather than abandon their customary traditions, they built the requirements of English law into them. The result has been the second stage that new British Muslim, Hindu and Sikh law, unique to Britain, has emerged, differing in some important aspects from Indian, Pakistani or Bangladeshi laws and customs. This was the second phase, which created the corpus of precedent law Menski labels *Angrezi* law. The third stage in this process might involve abandoning ethnic customs and religious personal laws altogether and practising only state law, but as Menski argues this has not happened and is unlikely to do so. Thus English law remains the official law while *Angrezi Shari'ah* is the unofficial law. As part of this complex process, redefined Muslim laws in Britain have become 'hybrid' and thus 'all ethnic minorities in Britain marry twice, divorce twice and do many other things several times in order to satisfy the demands of concurrent legal systems' (Pearl and Menski, 1998, p. 46). This analysis contributes to a better understanding of the development of a British legal discourse which comprises a complex interplay of cultural and social values, Islamic legal practices and state law norms and values. In doing so it demonstrates how law evolves and develops over time emphasizing both the commonalities and differences between and within the different legal orders.

Shari'ah and family-related disputes

Shari'ah 'family law' is part of the branch of Shari'ah (*al-mu'amalat*) that concerns the interactions, transactions and relationships between individuals and families. Within this branch, various precepts have been established to govern and/or regulate everyday activities such as: inheritance, marriage, divorce and child welfare, (penal) punishment, food and drink, endowments, business administration and transactions. Other branches govern other aspects of Islamic life such as morals and conduct (*adaab*), religious belief (*i'tiqadat*), worship (*'ibadah*) and punishment (*'uqubat*).

Shari'ah councils in Britain

In Britain the emergence of Shari'ah councils can be traced to a diverse set of social, political and religious developments in civil society. The formation of Islamic religious organizations and their engagement with the state has been characterized by multiculturalism and the development of multicultural state policies to accommodate cultural and religious difference. And, in the past three decades, a growing number of scholars have explored the changing and contested nature of this relationship, revealing a new discursive space of engagement, contestation and negotiation between minority ethnic communities and the state. One way of viewing this new relationship is based on the claim that cultural and religious communities actively seek to avoid interaction and any possible conflict with the secular state. In the case of Muslims this retreat to the privatized sphere of local Muslim community provides the space where matrimonial disputes are resolved according to principles of Muslim family law.

Shari'ah councils have been described as 'internal regulatory frameworks' (Pearl and Menski, 1998, p. 396), 'complex informal networks' (Poulter, 1998, p.61) and sites where 'new ijtihads'[3] are taking place (Yilmaz, 2001a, p. 1). This form of Muslim self-organization is more generally described as 'Muslim legal pluralism' and has led to extensive discussion on a possible conflict of laws with English law (Hamilton, 1995; Carroll, 1997; Poulter, 1998). Indeed, existing literature presents these bodies as evidence of an emerging parallel legal system whereby Muslim family laws are reconstructed to accommodate the needs of diasporic Muslim communities in Britain (Bunt, 1998; Pearl and Menski, 1998; Poulter, 1998; Yilmaz, 2001b).

Shari'ah councils operate as unofficial legal bodies specializing in providing advice and assistance to Muslim communities on Muslim family law matters. They are neither unified nor represent a single school of thought but instead are made up of various different bodies representing the different schools of thought in Islam. In essence, a Shari'ah council has three key functions, issuing Muslim divorce certificates, reconciling and mediating between parties and producing expert opinion reports on matters of Muslim family law and custom to the Muslim community, solicitors and the courts. It is also significant that in addition to providing advice and assistance on matters of Muslim family law, Shari'ah councils have also been set up to promote and preserve Islam within British society (see Bunt, 1998). Subsequently the socio-legal reality of Muslim communities in Britain can be presented as a complex scenario of multiple state laws and personal laws. This challenges the assumed uniformity of state law (as superior, monolithic and homogeneous) and instead points to postmodern analyses of law and legal relations which highlight 'a diversity of laws' and 'interlegality' (Santos, 2002).

Yilmaz (2002) identifies four key conditions that have led to the emergence of Shari'ah councils in Britain. First, according to Muslim tradition, family issues are purposively left to 'extra judicial' regulation and this continues within Muslim diasporic communities today who choose to resolve disputes in the private sphere. Second, Muslims do not recognize the authority and legitimacy of Western secular law on a par with Muslim law. Third, the familial notions of honour and shame prevent family disputes from being discussed in the 'public sphere' and subsequently religious laws are given greater legitimacy within religious communities. And finally, the failure of the state to recognize plural legal orders has led to the development of 'alternative' dispute resolution processes in the private sphere (see Yilmaz, 2002).

This body of work challenges both the essentialism and uniformity assumed in state-law relations and celebrates cultural and religious difference in relation to the emerging parallel systems of law operating within British society. More specifically it contributes to our understanding of how contemporary societies are 'increasingly confronted within minority groups demanding recognition of their ethnicity and accommodation of their cultural and religious differences' (Hussain and Bagguley, 2005, p. 31). However, this literature also adopts a somewhat legal prescriptive analysis to understanding the emergence of Shari'ah councils and their relationship with and in opposition to state law. In short, there is little substantive and empirical analysis on the internal dynamics of power within these mechanisms of dispute resolution. Conceptualizing unofficial dispute resolution in this way is premised on the idea of homogeneity within 'Muslim communities' with little explanation on how these bodies are constituted within local communities. Furthermore, the primacy of a Muslim identity means that little is learnt about cultural and religious practices that may affect the autonomy of women using these bodies and how such processes are contested, redefined and used strategically to serve particular ends. Existing literature does not, for example, give due salience to the interconnection between the Shari'ah councils, forms of power and gender inequality.

There is no single and authoritative definition of the term 'Shari'ah council'. The criteria used to identify Shari'ah councils in this study led to the inclusion of four councils which identified themselves as Shari'ah councils and each organization specifically dealt with issues concerning matrimonial breakdown. Each organization also had the capacity to issue Muslim divorce certificates to Muslim women and all explicitly expressed their objective to support Muslims experiencing family problems who were seeking to resolve conflicts within an Islamic framework of dispute resolution. As Badawi (1995, p. 78) explains, 'Muslim law is not adversarial in nature but rather conciliatory. We seek to bring people together, to reconcile them rather than to create dissension between them.'

The history of Shari'ah councils in Britain can be traced to the development of Muslim organizations during the 1970s and 1980s with the emergence of religious and ethnic diversity and the introduction of multicultural policies to accommodate such 'difference' (Brah, 1996; Modood, 2007; Werbner, 2000). While some studies attribute such developments to state initiatives under the context of multiculturalism, others argue that communities instigated such change to forge closer ties with family and local Muslim communities. For example, in his analysis of the relationship between the emergence of cultural and religious organizations and 'ethnic governance', Vertovec (1996) concludes that minorities have their own reasons for choosing their 'idioms of mobilization' as well as 'their own orientations, strategies and levels of experience that affect the kind of state liaisons which they foster and maintain' (p. 66). The development of Shari'ah councils can therefore be understood in relation to the conditions in which they are situated. At present the nature and scope of Shari'ah council activity in England and Wales remains unknown and undocumented. However, a recent report by the Ministry of Justice titled *An Exploratory Study of Shari'ah Councils in England with respect to Family Law* (Bano, 2012) identified 30 councils that worked on issues of Muslim family law and issued Muslim divorce certificates. Although this project did not look at smaller Shari'ah councils, it suggests a relatively small number of key councils operating in England. The project found much diversity in the size of the councils, the number of religious scholars providing advice and assistance, and in the composition of council members. Most councils were embedded within Muslim communities, forming part of mosques and community centres and appear to have evolved according to the needs of the communities in which they are located.

The development of Shari'ah councils also mirrored the emergence of Muslim communities in Britain. In his study of Muslims in Bradford, Lewis points out that the socio-political establishment of Muslims in Britain via mosques and community organizations indicates a shift 'within the migrants' self-perception from being sojourners to settlers' (2002, p. 56). In particular, it is the close relationship to mosques that has shaped the type of Shari'ah councils that we see emerging in Britain.

The councils are setup by a diverse group of individuals many of whom belong to local mosques and have therefore previously been involved in supporting Muslim families with issues of family and marital breakdown. The data in both studies found that the advisors (scholars) had received formal Islamic jurisprudential training in India, Pakistan, Egypt, Saudi Arabia or Yemen while imams from Pakistan had also been involved in setting up each of these councils. There were no data regarding the type of religious training the scholars had received prior to taking up their roles as advisors in the councils as the nature of this training was not explored and beyond the remit of the study. Although belonging to different schools of thought, the scholars emphasized that the advice and guidance provided to all Muslim disputants was based on each of the schools of Islamic jurisprudence.[4]

The data revealed that Shari'ah councils formulate their services to cater to the local and specific needs of British Muslim communities and to fit in with the wider framework of dispute resolution in Islam. However, with this seemingly visible emergence of Shari'ah councils in Britain their role as dispute resolution mechanisms has also come under some scrutiny. In his study, Warraich (2001, p. 11) criticizes the conflation between South Asian Muslim family laws, localized cultural practices found in British Muslim communities and the rigid application of English family law, each a contributory factor in the emergence of Shari'ah councils. He argues that such bodies 'have appropriated for themselves the role and position of parallel quasi-judicial institutions' and directs blame at 'the lack of space in the English system for appropriate solutions to dilemmas facing people' leading to 'this confusing situation'. Instead state law, which offers adequate protection for all its citizens, must remain open, plural and flexible to the needs of ethnic minority disputants, create the spaces within the existing legal framework and adapt to the complexities that pluralism inevitably entails. However, one of the difficulties with a focus solely upon the rights afforded by state law is that very little is then understood about how individuals engage these official and unofficial laws and what the outcomes are for individuals, and in particular women, within Muslim communities. And second, little is understood about the ways in which the boundaries of state law, personal law and privatized dispute resolution are contested, challenged and appropriated in specific contexts.

Shari'ah councils are therefore a product of transnational networks, operate within a national and global landscape and mirror the local ethnic profile of Muslim communities in which they are situated. Dr Suhaib Hasan (Islamic Shariah Council) explained, 'In Pakistan I have many friends who are learned scholars in Islamic matters concerning marriage and divorce. I often consult them for advice and this helps our work immensely.' Dr Saeeda, a marriage counsellor at Birmingham Shariah Council, acknowledged that dispute resolution catered to the specific needs of the Pakistani Azad Kashmiri community in Birmingham; this meant that the Council was aware of localized cultural practices and the process of dispute resolution was therefore expressed via an ethnicized idiom. However, Dr Badawi, a scholar at Muslim Law Shariah Council, was keen to distinguish the diversity of Shari'ah councils: 'We work on the basis of Islamic principles and we draw upon a wide range of schools of thought in Islam. We are not made up of just Pakistanis and we do not adhere to Pakistani law. We are here for all Muslims.' The emergence of Shari'ah councils in Britain must therefore be understood in relation to the ways in which Muslim communities came to be situated 'in and through a wide variety of discourses, economic processes, state policies and institutional practices' (Brah, 1996, p. 182).

The relationship to mosques

The establishment, regulation and legitimacy of Shari'ah councils can be better understood in relation to their close relationship to mosques,[5] which reflects developments in Islamic religious practice. Shari'ah councils are part of the community mosque structures that facilitate Muslim settlement in Britain (see Anwar, 2008). A mosque can be described as a sacred place of worship for Muslims (the Arabic translation reads as *masjid*) which often provides educational and social facilities too, and in some cases medical care. In 2006 the Muslim Council of Britain produced a report titled *Voices from the Minarets: A Study of UK Imams and Mosques*. It defines the role of a mosque in two parts, 'firstly to meet the spiritual needs of the community signified by its role as a place of worship; and secondly to meet the practical educational and social needs of the community' (2006, p. 4). Joly (1995) points to the fact that for many Muslims mosques act as important symbols of religion and presence.

Mosques are spread out geographically and ethnically, as well as according to the different Islamic schools of thought. Mosques are classified as charitable religious organizations and are essentially free to develop their own policies within the framework of existing legislation. They operate both at a local and national level to meet the spiritual, practical, educational and social needs of the community. In this way they seek to encourage the positive integration of Muslims into British society and to foster close links among local Muslim communities. In 2009, the Charity Commission produced an independent survey of mosques in England and Wales which identified 1102 organizations of which 716 took part in the survey. It found that on average each mosque devotes 20 per cent of its work to providing the local Muslim communities with legal advice services.

Mosques are normally managed by a board of trustees, responsible for finances and overall management, and a local independent mosque committee that takes responsibility for the appointment of the imam and other paid and volunteer staff. Mosque committees donate their time out of a sense of civic responsibility (BMG, 2009). The title 'imam' is applied to, to scholars of Muslim jurisprudence and to appointed prayer leaders in mosques (Muslim Council of Britain, 2006). The imam's primary role is 'to lead ritual prayers for the congregation five times a day, perform marriages, funerals and other rites of passage, give religious advice and guidance to the community on their daily lives and religious rituals such as fasting during the holy month of Ramadan and pilgrimage during *Hajj*, collect and distribute charity, provide counselling and teaching for both adults and children' (FAIR, 2002, p. 12). An imam has been described as a 'community leader, teacher, advisor to people of all ages, spiritual guide, counsellor, social worker, mediator in disputes – there is no end to the definition of tasks that fall under the role of the imam. In addition to this they deal with the social consequences of the economic conditions of their communities' (FAIR, 2002). A number of umbrella organizations such as the Muslim Council of Britain and the Muslim Association of Britain seek to represent British Muslims in national and international fora.

Literature on planning permission for the development of mosques in Britain points to the important social and religious functions they serve (Gale, 2004). In his work on mosque development in Birmingham, Gale argues that planning permission is difficult to achieve and highly contentious. Following the enactment of Human Rights Act 1998 the issue of religious freedom and Article 9 has received considerable attention in the courts. Knights (2007) reports that in the case of the *Islamic Education Society* v. *Blackburn and Darwin Borough Council* (Application 10/04/0629, PAD 31, August 2005) the broadcast of the call to prayer (*adhan*) from a mosque was considered. She explains, 'There was evidence from a number of people in the local community who supported the amplification of the *adhan* five times a day during prescribed hours. However, the inspector rejected those views on a number of grounds. The decision reveals a highly subjective approach taken to the religious issue' (2007, p. 197).

The establishment of mosques in Britain has been extensively documented with mosque formation being closely tied to community development (see Ballard, 1994; Lewis, 1994; Eade, 1996; Werbner, 2001). As Lewis points out, 'The creation of mosques reflects the growth, location and differential settlement patterns of distinct regional and linguistic communities' (1994, p. 58). Consequently, we see the proliferation of different mosques each fragmented according to village kinship, sectarian affiliation and intra-ethnic differences. Hence in Britain, mosques cater to the needs of Muslims of various ethnic backgrounds, including Punjabis, Mirpuris, Pathans, Bangladeshis, Yemenis, Somalians and Gujaratis. In larger communities, mosques are not only based on ethnic differences but also split along the differential doctrinal teachings. In Britain the different Islamic schools of thought have been identified as *Barelwi, Deobandi, Jama'at-I-Islami, Ahl-I-Hadith, Shia* and *Ahamadiyya* (see Lewis, 1994, p. 57). Most Pakistanis in Britain belong to the *Barelwi* tradition. Mosques are thus closely aligned to the sectarian affiliation of the local community (see Shaw, 1988; Werbner, 1988; Geaves, 1996b; Lewis, 2002).

Mosques also seek to 'institutionalize' Islam within local communities and therefore provide a 'Muslim space' where Muslims can discuss a wide range of issues from an Islamic perspective. Shadid and Koningsveld point out, 'Quite logically, the establishment of these places of worship implied the creation of social spaces where new contacts could be made on the basis of a common religious identity' (1996a, p. 111). In this way, mosques act as a focal point for the Muslim community, identified as the 'Islamization of local urban space' (Eade, 1996, p. 231) and as such mosques are markers of 'shifts in ... sacred geographies [and in] the maps of meaning and profiles of power in the west' (Pieterse, 1997, p. 187).

Ahmad argues, 'The mosque is by definition the heart of the community. It has to be multi-dimensional if it is to adequately succeed in harmonizing all the varied elements within the community ... I have always felt that mosques should be venues for issues of national importance such as racism, unemployment, the environmental crisis, education, business, the arts and sport. We are being restrictive if we keep them as prayer places alone. The strength of our mosques can only materialize with their ability to attract a larger audience. They have to utilize all the skills, abilities and talents of the community' (quoted in Raza, 1991, pp. 40–1).

Growing concern about the emergence of the 'home-grown Muslim terrorist' following the attacks of September 2001 has led to a renewed interest by the state in mosques and in particular the role of imams. The reason for this intervention is not merely to prevent acts of terrorism (more recently pursued under what is known as the PREVENT strategy) but in doing so to ensure that Muslims are fully integrated into the British way of life (see Birt, 2010). Understandably this has generated concern within communities and generated enormous discussion in Muslim newspapers and magazines where such intervention is viewed with suspicion and hostility (see Vakil, 2010). A number of government initiatives such as the Home Office initiative, 'Working Together to Prevent Extremism' (2005), produced a report that focused on the need to tackle extremism within mosques. The report found that a proportion of imams are recruited from overseas with religious qualifications from their country of origin and in response there has been a growing political urgency in several Western European countries to institutionalize and create facilities for imam training Islam et al. (2005).

More recently, the recruitment of imams from abroad has led to conflict within mosques and continuing concern from the government. There are a number of institutions in Britain which undertake the training of imams[6] but there is no central body which oversees the training. This has led to concerns that imams who have little understanding of the lives of British Muslims may be contributing to disaffection and alienation within local communities. Furthermore imams are often employed from a particular area in Pakistan to ensure they reinforce these religious values imbued with localized cultural traditions, within British Pakistani communities (Bunt, 1998). Understandably this has led to criticism from British Muslims, who may speak English only, of the language barriers and generational conflict. Geaves points out, 'The imam may well not speak English but his presence becomes the focal point for legitimizing and reinforcing those customs from a particular rural locale in the subcontinent that have been transported to a few terraced streets in a British industrial city. Here the mosque functions more strongly as a means of reinforcing kinship and ethnic ties than as a means of intensifying the sense of belonging to the wider ummah whether in Britain or the Islamic world' (1996b, p. 171). Interestingly, however, in his study he found that most Muslims were not aware of the different ethnic or doctrinal biases within mosques and prayed there because of convenience.

New state initiatives to provide imams with employment rights have stipulated that imams must be British Muslims so that they are aware of British social, cultural and political life and thus are able to relate more to their younger congregations. This of course raises concerns outlined in Chapter 3, where the use of select Muslim organizations in dialogue with the state ignores the diverse manifestations of Islam within communities. Furthermore the state seeks the control and preservation of communal harmony against a background of high unemployment, low educational attainment, social deprivation and social exclusion for many Muslims in Britain (Modood et al., 1997). Not only does this approach fail to explore the underlying reasons why young Muslims may be disaffected, but it also ignores the dynamics of power within communities.

Hence we can see that the task of the imam is both challenging and complex. Apart from this national interest there has been discussion over the internal conflicts of power between different sectional interests within mosques. Raza describes this as 'mosque politics' and states:

> Mosques in Britain have become a battle ground for power politics ... It is pointless to conceal that within the last few years most of the trouble and discord have stemmed from the attitudes of some of the Ulema and Imams and these have been the reason for many of the most unpleasant scenes witnessed in the brief history of the Muslims in the United Kingdom. In some cases, the troubles have escalated to such an extent that the police have had to enforce the closure of the mosques.
>
> (1991, p. 37)

In this way we understand how mosques compete and vie for power among themselves, reflecting their importance for local Muslims. All of these problems also reflect how the mosque acts as a resource for Muslims to access, and objections on the way mosques are run are commonly discussed and debated in Muslim newspapers such as *Q-News* and *The Muslim News*.[7]

A second concern relates to the presence of women in mosques. This presence is marginal and defined according to the dictates of *purdah* which gives rise to the creation of separate space for men and women. Mirza (2000, p. 13) explains, 'The installation of separate entrances, separate seating arrangements and the bifurcation of rooms by screens or awnings to create sharp, well-defined boundaries between sections of the mosque are the means by which the contours of gendered space and the pattern of restricted interaction between the sexes are produced.' Women are not actively involved in mosque committees, they have little input in the administrative tasks of running a mosque and when they are involved, they are designated to the realm of 'women's issues'. Yet imams at mosques can play a central role in matters of marriage and divorce including introducing 'suitable' marriage partners and advising women on matters of marriage breakdown.[8] This has led to concern from Muslim women's organizations such as the Muslim Women's Helpline and the An-Nisa Society about how such advice may be steeped in local customs and practices that may sanction intra-family inequalities such as forced marriage.

In Britain the formation of mosques is closely tied to the development of Shari'ah councils. In this study, three Shari'ah councils had evolved under the guidance of an imam from a respected mosque. Prior to the establishment of Shari'ah councils, imams provided all spiritual and religious guidance to Muslims based in their local mosques and this included settling marital disputes and issuing divorce certificates. In his study, Bunt (1998) found that imams found this work to be time consuming and taking them away from their traditional duties of providing spiritual guidance and sermons for Friday prayers. This was confirmed by findings in this study. Dr Nasim at the Birmingham Shari'ah Council explained, 'We realized that some form of body was needed which could resolve family disputes. Before the Shari'ah council it was the imam who used to deal with these issues and this caused problems not only because he was not versed in dealing with all the issues that confronted him, but he didn't have the time on top of his other duties. So in that respect the Shari'ah council was formed. This body is led by religious scholars including imams.' Thus an important feature of the relationship between Shari'ah councils and mosques is that they continue to be based in mosques and imams serve as religious scholars on the council's body while operating from a separate room. Although Shari'ah councils are based within mosques, they have their own distinctive approach to dispute resolution. Mosques are classified as charitable organizations and are essentially free to develop their own policies within the framework of existing legislation. In particular mosques play a significant role in Shari'ah councils by reinforcing the significance of Islamic religious practice, a significance often underpinned by the role of imams who act as a linkage between mosques and Shari'ah councils. For example, imams often lead religious prayer at mosques and also act as mediators in resolving marital disputes within Shari'ah councils. This relationship is clearly important in its emphasis upon Islamic beliefs and morality and identification to a wider global Islamic culture (see Ahmed and Donnan, 1994).

In this study only one Shari'ah council, the Shariah Council of United Kingdom (SCUK) had little contact with a mosque; all the others were closely aligned to one particular mosque. There are two important differences between mosques and Shari'ah councils. First, unlike mosques, Shari'ah councils are not charities and therefore are not obliged to reveal details of their organizational structure nor their financial status. Second, many mosques in Britain are organized on an ethnic basis reflecting the specific needs of different groups of Muslims while Shari'ah councils aim to cater for the needs of all Muslims irrespective of ethnic, racial or national background.

Thus while some studies attribute decision-making power within the community to imams, the emergence of Shari'ah councils has led to an interesting 'separation' in the roles of an imam and religious scholar. In his study of informal decision-making in the Pakistani Muslim community in Birmingham, Bunt (1998) found imams to be in a position of power, providing advice and assistance in matters of marital and intra-family conflict. Conservative in attitude, they sought to control female sexuality and thus prevent 'outsiders' threatening the stability of the Muslim family. In comparison, the religious scholars in this study who were based at Shari'ah councils were keen to distinguish themselves from performing the traditional duties of imams (though some were also imams) but they did point to 'the mutual relationship between the imam and the Muslim scholar in resolving marital disputes' (Dr Suhaib Hasan, Islamic Shariah Council or ISC).

Divorce and Shari'ah councils

In Islamic literature, discussion on divorce often begins with the *Hadith* literature, in which the Prophet explains that divorce is permissible in Islam but only as a last resort (Engineer, 1992). In this study, each Shari'ah council reported marriage breakdown and divorce as the two key issues that they dealt with. As discussed more fully in the next chapter, under Muslim law marriage is based on a contract, the *nikah*, which can be likened in some ways to a pre-nuptial agreement. The *nikah* outlines the rights, duties and responsibilities of the parties (Pearl and Menski, 1998). It includes a sum of money called the *mahr* agreed between the parties and given to the bride by the groom. The essential elements of the formal marriage ceremony are an offer of marriage by the husband and its acceptance by the wife, in the presence of two witnesses.

There are several types of Muslim divorce and a great diversity of approaches to these among the different schools of Islamic thought. Muslim men have the right to unilaterally terminate their marriage. Such a divorce is known as *talaq*. Divorce may also be granted by mutual consent, where parties have included a term in their *nikah* (marriage contract) that permits the wife to divorce if she wishes. A further type of divorce, the *khul* divorce, can be instigated by a wife with her husband's agreement, on the condition that she forgoes her right to the *mahr* (excluding instances of neglect and abuse). *Faskh* permits the marriage to be annulled if the wife can prove her husband has acted unreasonably. Female applicants may contact a Shari'ah council when husbands refuse to grant them a unilateral divorce (*talaq*). Where a husband refuses a divorce, there are other types of divorce that require the intervention of a religious scholar and these must fulfil certain criteria (e.g. the husband deserting the wife). The next chapter analyses how Shari'ah councils justify their issuing of divorces under these various categories. Thus under Muslim law women are permitted a divorce without the consent of their husbands but this must involve the intervention of religious scholars who determine the kind of divorce to be issued.

Under Muslim law marriage is a contract and thus the different types of divorce available are based on ways in which to dissolve this contract. The different schools of tradition will therefore allow termination of this contract by 'either of the parties, by mutual agreement or by the courts' (Carroll, 1997). Yet the different approaches in classical literature on Muslim law of divorce coupled with state law interpretations of Muslim divorce in Muslim countries has led to some confusion among scholars and lawyers on the rights and limitations afforded in divorce law.[9]

Notwithstanding the diversity of literature on divorce in Muslim law, two key issues can be identified for Muslim women in Britain. The first relates to the extent to which Muslims are being divorced outside the official system and whether this creates a conflict of law scenario with English law.[10] And the second is identified as the problem of 'limping divorces' whereby a civil divorce has been obtained by the woman but her husband is refusing to grant her a Muslim divorce (Menski, 2006).[11] As Yilmaz explains, 'If the woman is not religiously divorced from her husband, it does not matter that she is divorced under the civil law, in the eyes of the community her remarriage will be regarded as adulterous and any possible offspring will be illegitimate since it is not allowed under the religious law. So, in reality, until the religious divorce is obtained, the civil divorce remains ineffective because one party is unable to remarry' (2001b, p. 16).

The type of Muslim divorce granted to women by the Shari'ah council raises an important set of questions. For example, if a *khul* is granted, it means that the female applicant must give up her right to dower or *mahr* in return for a divorce and this seems unfair. Pearl and Menski describes this process as 'Usually the wife will offer to pay a certain sum, normally the amount of the dower either given to her or promised to her, in return for the agreement of the husband to release her from the marriage tie' (1998, p. 284). Again this is a complex area and one that ensures some confusion as to the precise amount of dower the husband should receive for the *khul* (see Carroll, 1997). Aside from this issue Shari'ah councils also deal with how the female applicant is able to retrieve her dower after her husband has willingly divorced her. Nasir points out that in theory Muslim women entitled to the dower have exclusive right to it under the terms of the contract, though in practice this may vary 'according to the circumstances. She may be entitled to the whole dower, half of it or may have no dower at all' (1990, p. 103). Furthermore Afshar points out, 'What women are entitled to and what they get are very different. Married women are not expected to assert their proprietorial rights. They are not to bring conflict, but peace' (1994, p. 29). Therefore in Muslim divorce we are dealing with a complex formulation whereby 'legal discourse' in matters of religious marriage and divorce are reconfigured in the private sphere.

Islam and the custody of children

The issue of custody in Islam is contentious precisely because it is not addressed in the Qur'an and is based upon two sayings of the Prophet found in Hadith literature. The first relates to a woman complaining to the Prophet that after divorce her ex-husband wished to remove her child; upon hearing this the Prophet commented: 'You have the first right of the child as long as you do not marry.' The second saying again relates to a woman complaining that her ex-husband wishes to take her only child away from her. On this occasion the Prophet is reported to have said: 'Child, here is your father and here is your mother; make a choice between the two as to whom you prefer' (quoted in Goolam, 2001, p. 186). Yet all four Sunni schools of thought – Hanafi, Maliki, Shafi'i and Hanbali – rule that where possible the mother has prior claim to the custody of the child (see Engineer, 1995).

Interviews with the religious scholars in Shari'ah councils found that scholars avoid contested issues of access to and custody of children. However, observation research did point to informal negotiations taking place at this space and this raises wider concerns about the enforcement of Muslim legal norms that may be antithetical to the rights of women enshrined in English family law.

This process can be characterized as seeking to avoid conflict with English law. For example, the councils in this study apply the *Maliki* school of thought which does not involve the automatic transfer of the child at any age to their father and thus complies with s11 of the Family Law Act 1996 with its emphasis on the best interests of the child. Mufti Kadir, a panel member at the at Islamic Sharia Council, states:

> Family courts in the UK and the west in general are broadly in conformation with Islamic Law of custody, especially the Maliki school of thought.

The current priorities of English law centre on the needs of children and so does Islamic Shari'ah. Other perspectives reported earlier, reflect the social trend of the time. For Islamic Shari'ah courts choosing from the Maliki perspective is not strange especially if it reflects current social policy trends. Islamic Shari'ah councils have little control over custodial orders. But they have a balancing act to perform when matters are in Shari'ah Courts.

Legitimacy of Shari'ah councils under Islamic law

The emergence of Shari'ah councils in non-Muslim countries raises the question of their legitimacy under Islam and Islamic law. Upon what basis do such bodies operate as ADR mechanisms for minority Muslim communities living in the West? This question is complex and unfortunately cannot be adequately addressed within the limits of this book. Indeed this question itself has not been directly addressed in Islamic scholarship instead literature focuses upon the issues and complexities generated by migration and issues of asylum which in turn addresses questions of the rights, duties and responsibilities to and upon all Muslims living in non-Muslim countries. What can, however, be discerned from this literature is that in Islamic law there is no such thing as a 'Shari'ah council' as an institutional framework with clear historical linkages to the governance by Islamic principles of Muslims living in non-Muslim states. As discussed earlier they have evolved to cater to the needs of diasporic Muslim communities seeking to resolve matrimonial disputes. Nevertheless the practice of minority legal orders operating within majority societies as been addressed by scholars.

The early jurists demarcated boundary lines between *dar al-Islam* (the land of Islam) and *dar al-kufr* (the land of war) (see Shadid and Koningsveld, 1996a) and most jurists largely accept that Muslims are able to remain on non-Muslim lands as long as they are allowed to continue the practice of Islam. The point of contention concerns the jurisdiction of Muslim judges and the extent to which they are permitted to intervene and regulate the lives of Muslims. For many scholars, therefore, the most important issue facing Muslims in Britain is the absence of a 'communal jural autonomy in matters of personal law', something that is allowed to religious minorities or *dhimmis* residing in Muslim states (Lewis, 1994, p. 67). For example, this concept of *dhimmi* allowed non-Muslim minorities to live and practice their faith in return of a payment of tax to the Muslim ruler (see Braude and Lewis, 1982). In return they were granted state protection and the legal orders based on personal systems of law and these were found in North Africa, Eastern and Central Europe and the Caucasus (see Balchin, 2009). Furthermore the personal systems of law in Asia and Africa have been addressed and questions have been raised on their relationship to the establishment of Shari'ah in Britain (see Ahmed, 2010).

There is also much debate and discussion within Islamic texts as to the role and duties of Muslims living as minorities in non-Muslim states. This area of law is both ambivalent and open to dispute (see Fadl, 1994). Historically, migration for Muslims has been linked to forced migration and persecution during the time of the Prophet, with two Qur'anic verses (4.97–100 and verse 5.44) addressing these issues. Fadl points out, 'It seems that different jurists were addressing different scenarios in their expositions without specifically indicating the issue they had in mind' (1994, p. 150). The degree of conflict between the schools of thought has also exacerbated this confusion. For example, Maliki Muslims who find themselves as minorities must migrate to Muslim countries. Hanbali and Shia hold the view that migration is permitted as long as it does not conflict with the practice of Islam but living in a Muslim state is the ideal situation even if that state is despotic (see Esposito, 1988). Pearl and Menski sums up this confusing situation when he points outs that 'Muslims as members of minority communities in the west today, then, have no clear authoritative, uniform juristic guidance available to them' (1998, p. 64).

The polarization of this debate has, however, led to new approaches that attempt to reformulate the dichotomy of *dar al-Islam* (the land of Islam) and *dar al-harb* (the house of war). For example, Shadid and Koningsveld develop the concept of *dar al-dawah* (the country of mission) and *dar al-ahd* (the country of treaty) where Muslims can live in non-Muslim lands and organize their lives in accordance with Shari'ah. What becomes evident in the discussions is that the emergence and development of Shari'ah councils must therefore be understood in the context in which they emerge and in relation to the dynamics of power within communities that result in conflicting cultural and religious norms.

The degree to which Shari'ah councils have been transformed via the process of migration in Western liberal societies also raises interesting questions on the reasons for their emergence in different European societies. As Madeira (2010, p. 1) questions, 'why do formal Islamic law tribunals exist in some Western democracies but not in others?' The history of Muslim migration to Europe has been extensively discussed in relation to settlement patterns and differing multicultural policies (Levey and Modood, 2009). Rohe explains:

> Many Muslims in Europe still tend to seek practical solutions for organizing their lives in accordance with the demands of European legal orders and Islamic religious commands. It is only within the last few years that Muslims have also tried to formulate theoretical statements to clarify their position and possible conflicts between legal and religious rules, and to find adequate solutions for such conflicts.
>
> (2006, p. 58)

Muslim settlement in Europe is typically construed as a clash between Muslim sensibilities on the one hand, and liberal–democratic values on the other (Levey and Modood, 2009, p. 242). Differing church–state relations and conceptions of the public and private have led to varied approaches the extent to which religion can be regulated in liberal societies. For example, the separation of law and religion as epitomized by *laïcité* in France contrasts with the symbolic relationship between church and state in Britain.

Furthermore the emergence of European Muslim organizations points to a new type of European identity, based on the primacy of a Muslim identity which can also involve making political and social demands. There is an emerging body of scholarship which documents the practice of European Muslim family law. For example the European Council for Fatwa and Research operates as a privately funded, European-wide umbrella organization, comprising Islamic scholars vested with the authority to issue fatwas and guidance to European Muslims.[12] Dien explains, 'The main objectives of the council, according to its constitution, are to bring together European scholars and to aim to unite legal injunctions on various issues, thus providing both legal injunctions suitable for Muslims in Europe and research for general, public fatwa' (2004, p. 146).

In Germany, in the field of matrimonial law the introduction of Islamic norms can be found in matrimonial contracts. Rohe (2006, p. 65) points out that contractual conditions regulating the payment of the Islamic *mahr* are possible and generally accepted by the courts (although he acknowledges there is no case law on this issue) while other contractual regulations, especially those discriminating against women, could be void. In France there is no legal or any recognition of religious laws in the French judicial system (Basdevant-Gaudemet, 2000, p. 115, quoted in Madeira, 2010, p. 5). There is also evidence that Muslims living in France do not use informal, mosque-based Shari'ah tribunals. Madeira explains such differences to be based upon

> different immigrant integration policies in France and the UK, informed by different conceptions of citizenship and nationhood, [which] explain not only the different institutional choices but also the different demand for Islamic law institutions among Muslim communities in the two countries. British multicultural policies encourage the creation and maintenance of religious and cultural institutions among immigrant groups, ethnic groups and religious groups. In France, by contrast, republican policies and institutions reduce demand for Islamic legal institutions by socializing French Muslims to reject authority that is not state-based. Thus, French Muslims are more likely to develop Islam *á la française* that has little use for either formal or informal Islamic legal institutions. In the UK, by contrast, religious preferences and choices remain more autonomous because of more accommodating social and political institutions.
>
> (2010, p. 9)

The process of dispute resolution in Western Europe therefore is produced through various discursive social and political practices. That is, such adjudicatory systems must be understood in relation to the locus of multiple communities and loci of power in which they are embedded in different liberal societies. In her work Ali (2010) draws attention to the rise in Internet *fatwa* and argues that such discourses challenge historical conceptions of legitimacy of family law norms as enacted by Muslim states.

These issues have more recently been addressed in Canada. In 2003 in the Canadian State of Ontario the issue of Islamic arbitration in matters of family law took the media and policymakers by surprise. A group called the Islamic Institute of Civil Justice (IICJ) announced that they would offer arbitration in family law matters based on Islamic law. Vociferous opposition from a wide variety of groups, including the Canadian Council of Muslim Women, led to the setting up of the Boyd Review to consider the policy implications of various options (Boyd, 2004). Natasha Bakht points out, 'the idea of private parties voluntarily agreeing to arbitration using religious principles or a foreign legal system is not new. Ontario's Arbitration Act has allowed parties to resolve disputes outside the traditional court system for some time. This issue has been complicated by the fact that Canada has a commitment to upholding both a policy of multiculturalism and an international obligation towards women's rights' (2004, p. 1). The Boyd report was released in December 2004. The recommendations attempted to strike a balance by allowing religion-based arbitration to continue but only if the process and decisions were compatible with the Ontario Family Law Act. In November 2005 the government introduced the Family Statute Law Amendment Act, designed to ensure that all family law arbitrations could only be conducted under Canadian law. As Boyd explained in her report, the legislation 'provides that family law resolutions based on any other law or principles, including religious principles will have no legal status and amount to advice only. People will still have the right to seek advice from any source in matters of family law, including religious leaders. However, such advice will not be enforced by the courts' (2004, p. 472). The report found that religious arbitration in family law matters should be allowed to continue as long as safeguards were put into place which emphasized procedural safeguards to protect vulnerable parties who may be compelled to use these services. But the largest Muslim women's organization in Canada (The Canadian Council of Muslim Women) was critical of such recommendations and argued that they undermined the Canadian constitution which promotes 'equality before the law' for all its citizens. Following this response and a media backlash, it was decided in 2005 that it would no longer enforce the decisions of such arbitrations. As Eekelaar (2012) explains, 'The result was that, while religious bodies may still carry out arbitration in family matters under the Arbitration Act they must do so according to the law of Ontario or of another Canadian jurisdiction. Furthermore, regulations require family law arbitrators to undergo training in the law of Canada, that cases are screened for "power imbalances and domestic violence, by someone other than the arbitrator" and that a written record be kept of the proceedings'. And recent work has focused on this question of equality: 'if religious arbitration does have the potential to harm autonomy, what kind of legal safeguards can counteract or mitigate this potential?' and how the autonomy of vulnerable persons might be affected by religious arbitration (Ahmed and Luk, 2011)? These questions are further addressed in the final chapter of this book.

5
Shari'ah Councils and the Practice of Law-Making

For many liberal scholars the practice of religious personal systems of law raises the paradox of what Shachar refers to as 'multicultural vulnerability' (2001, p. 45), namely the dilemma of protecting individual choice and personal autonomy with group and community rights. The arena of family law succinctly illustrates this conflict, as Shachar explains: 'Clearly, when the state awards jurisdictional powers to the group in the family law arena, it enhances the group's autonomy. At the same time, this re-allocation of legal authority from the state to the group may also expose certain individuals within the group to systemic and sanctioned in-group rights violations' (2001, p. 45). Such concerns also mirror current debates over the establishment of 'Shari'ah courts' in Britain. At present the literature is scant on the ways in which Shari'ah councils govern, co-ordinate and operate privately in matters of family law within Muslim communities. And very little in actual fact is known about *how* Shari'ah councils operate as ADR mechanisms in Britain and the ways in which these bodies facilitate state law mechanisms in relation to resolving matrimonial disputes (Shah-Kazemi, 2001).

This chapter draws upon empirical data to provide a more detailed account of the ways in which four Shari'ah councils in Britain operate as unofficial ADR mechanisms within Muslim communities (see Chapter 3 for details of how the study was conducted). In particular it considers how Islamic norms, ethics and values underpin and influence this process in the resolution of matrimonial disputes. Scholarship on Shari'ah councils itself is at a preliminary stage and tends to draws upon individual council case studies. This study instead analyses the practice of council 'law-making' across four councils: the Muslim Family Support service and Shariah Council, Birmingham (hereafter referred to as BSC); the Muslim Law (Shariah) Council, West London (hereafter referred to as MLSC); the Islamic Shariah Council, East London (hereafter referred to as ISC) and Shariah Council of United Kingdom, North London (hereafter referred to as SCUK). And it seeks to illustrate how the doctrinal centrality of religious belief interacts with the 'inherent plurality of socio-cultural manifestations' (Menski, 2006, p. 279) to produce a specific form of Muslim legal pluralism. In doing so it analyses the ways in which reconciliation and mediation take shape at this privatized space within local communities and considers whether this process of dispute resolution disadvantages Muslim women.

Concept of dispute resolution in Islam

The primary sources of Shari'ah, the Qur'an and Sunna, illustrate that the concept of dispute resolution is inherent to Islam and Islamic practice. Shari'ah has developed various mechanisms of dispute resolution in matters of family law. One of the major distinctions between Islamic court-based and reconciliation-based dispute resolution mechanisms relates to their methodology and process of reasoning. In the adjudication system, the court refers to Islamic sources of law including the Qur'an and Sunna, as primary sources of Shari'ah, and uses reasoning by analogy (*qiyas* in Sunni tradition or reason, *aqhl*, in Shiite theology) and consensus (*ijma*), as secondary sources of Shari'ah. The reasoning methodology is called *usul al-fiqh* which determines the substantive regulations or practical jurisprudence (*fiqh*). In contrast, in reconciliation-based dispute resolution, the mediator/arbitrator might refer to Islamic law, in particular the Qur'an and Sunna, to encourage parties to reconcile but the primary source for settlement is the application of reason (*aqhl*) to the dispute. The judge (*qadi*) within the Islamic legal system balances the 'rights' owed to God with the rights of individuals based on Islamic law but the mediator/arbitrator balances the rights of individuals based on their own interests and consent (see University of Warwick *Manual on Islamic Family Law*, 2009).

In Islam the concepts of mediation and reconciliation are grounded in both the Qur'an and the Hadith literature. Both of these sources remain instrumental in shaping the model of dispute resolution both in Muslim majority and minority societies.

In verse 4:39 the Qur'an states:

> If you fear a breach
> Between them twain (husband and wife)
> Appoint arbiters
> One from his family
> And the other from hers
> If they wish for peace,
> Allah will bring about
> Their reconciliation:
> For Allah hath full knowledge
> And is acquainted
> With all things.

And verse 4:31 states:

> Allah doth command you
> To render back your trusts
> To those to whom they are due;
> And when ye judge
> Between man and man,
> That ye judge with justice:
> Verily how excellent
> Is the teaching which He giveth you!
> For Allah is He who heareth
> And see all things.

Other verses that promote reconciliation include verse 5:8: 'You who believe! Be decent for Allah, bearers of witness with justice, and let not hatred of a people provoke you not to act equitably; act equitably, that is nearer to faithfulness, and be careful of (your obligation to) Allah; without doubt Allah is aware of what you do.'

Such verses are underpinned by the principle of *tahkim*, meaning arbitration, found in the Qur'an and Hadith literature which seeks to maintain 'social order' in Muslim societies and acts as the key element in the resolution of matrimonial disputes. As the Qur'an states, 'Allah commands you to render back your trusts to those to whom they are due; and when ye judge between man and man, that ye judge with justice: verily how excellent is the teaching which he gives you' (4:31). Although the principle of *tahkìm* is not clearly defined in the sources of Islam, the arbitration of disputes (see Ibrahim, 1991) and the concept of reconciliation can be found in the early traditions of the Prophet Muhammad (Sunna).[1]

In this legal pluralist tradition as Rosen puts it, 'in the Qur'an the image is constantly invoked of mediation and interstitial relationships as most appropriate to handling disputes' (2000, p. 183). Nevertheless confusion regarding the parameters of mediation and reconciliation in Islamic practice can cause some difficulties though scholars point to the dynamic interaction between the Qur'anic verses and the practice of Islamic principles. For example, the Prophet as the first mediator in Islam is understood to uniquely govern and regulate different types of familial relationships. In this way the Prophet is said to have set the precedent in resolving disputes via dialogue and communication in relation to various issues. By following the example set by the Prophet, the process of resolving disputes has over time evolved into a somewhat hybrid process in relation to individual control and societal changes. It is also taken for granted that the nature of resolving disputes serves importantly to maintain and enhance social order and control in all Muslim societies – the preservation of society against chaos (*fitna*) (Rosen, 2000).

Islamic principles make clear the religious obligation upon all parties to seek some form of arbitration should the need arise. More importantly it is considered a duty upon Muslims both in an individual capacity and collectively to help resolve disputes. By following the practice of the Prophet it is important to note that this process cannot therefore be understood merely as an alternative to the adversarial approach of dispute resolution. Most scholars agree that according to Shari'ah, every Muslim community, however small its size, must be regulated as far as possible by Islamic legal norms, appropriately interpreted and applied by the most knowledgeable scholars residing in the community. Perhaps more importantly is the way in which such religious norms are interpreted in Shari'ah councils in order to create the conditions for resolving matrimonial disputes.

Muslim scholars point out that a faith-based approach to dispute resolution is rooted in Qur'anic verses that promote compromised resolution and reconciliation. One of primary Qur'anic values regarding dispute resolution is forgiveness (*afv*) which encourages Muslims to take to forgiveness (7:199; see Gopin, 2002). Other Qur'anic core principles, including *adl* (justice), *solh* (negotiated settlement), *musalaha* (reconciliation), *hakam* (arbitration), *hikmah* (wisdom), *ihsan* (beneficence) and *salam* (peace), are used to construct an Islamic framework for dispute resolution.[2]

In addition, Islamic human rights values can be considered as related source for reconciliation-based dispute resolution. Islamic scholar Majid Khadduri (1984, pp. 236–7) has illustrated the five most important principles of human rights in Islam:

(1) Dignity and brotherhood;
(2) Equality among members of the community, without distinction on the basis of race, colour, or class;
(3) Respect for the honour, reputation, and family of each individual;
(4) The right of each individual to be presumed innocent until proven guilty; and
(5) Individual freedom.[3]

cited in the University of Warwick Manual on
Islamic Family Law (2009)

As discussed, there is general agreement among scholars that Islamic doctrines emphasize the importance of resolving disputes, to all parties. The locally infused forms of dispute resolution within Muslim communities – reformulated according to local community terms – raises the question of the precise differences between Western and Islamic systems of resolving disputes in relation to family law matters. Mohammed Abu-Nimer (2001, p. 171) draws a distinction between the adversarial case-law system in the West and Islamic jurisprudential theory and practice:

The western style contains underlying assumptions that: conflict can be positive and lead to growth and creativity; facing conflict is necessary; conflicts can be managed through rational steps; the individual's needs, interests, positions and desires should be satisfied; it is often efficient to negotiate with the alternative of a likely court outcome in mind; collaborative and cooperative frameworks are essential to conflict resolution; the parties and the mediator are task oriented and an agreement should usually be written and signed.

The institutional framework(s) upon which Shari'ah councils operate are based upon specific procedural rules and principles which underpin the process of resolving matrimonial disputes. Understanding the frameworks will indicate how such bodies operate as ADR mechanisms. An overview of these frameworks reveals a somewhat generic approach adopted by the councils that comprises five key stages.

The first involves contact made by the applicant to a specific council. The second involves the council establishing the grounds upon which divorce might be permitted as stipulated in the certificate application form. The third stage forms the basis of the problem-solving process – the investigation stage – where the grounds for divorce cited in the application form are investigated by council members. The fourth stage involves reconciliation and mediation between the parties, reconciliation often being the outcome sought by council members. The final stage involves the issuing of the divorce certificate for Muslim women by the council panel. I found that the complexity of the dispute, and the time needed to reach a settlement differed due to the facts of an individual case but all largely evolved around a common framework of dispute resolution.

Two key questions emerge: what are the internal rules/processes embedded within Shari'ah councils? And what are the norms the parties themselves create during this process of obtaining a divorce certificate? Thus the inter-relationship between the institutional framework and the personalized negotiations taking place create new forms of decision-making processes. As Roberts points out, 'This process is not in itself either haphazard or chaotic. If it were, negotiations would be doomed to failure. Whatever the differences in the society, the kind or complexity of the dispute, the length of time needed to reach a settlement, or the framework, the process itself generates an internal structure of its own' (2008, p. 123). Dr Nasim, Director of BSC, explains, 'We must abide by the Shari'ah and we must ensure that all clients understand what divorce means. There may be difficulties in the marriage but divorce is not an easy option. We work within the guidelines of Islam ... We're a religious body and clients are aware of this when they come to us.' He goes onto explain that 'a large number of clients want to resolve their differences ... coming from an Islamic perspective'. This view was shared by scholars at the other Shari'ah councils. Moreover, this commitment to a specific form of dispute resolution gives shape and form to the framework upon which the dispute resolution is based. The question this raises is the extent to which Muslim women are able to negotiate their use or may be 'compelled' or 'coerced' to use these bodies to resolve matrimonial disputes as opposed to utilizing state law mechanisms.

The debate on Muslim family law and 'alternative dispute resolution' has not yet developed satisfactory explanations of gender relations and power on the one hand and the fact that the reality of women's connections to these bodies may be very complex, contested and subject to the contingent local variations of the councils on the other. This is addressed later in the book, from the perspective of female users of Shari'ah councils. While the potential for mediation and reconciliation practices emerging within local and national communities has been extensively explored, there is very little analysis on the growth of religious bodies, operating in privatized spaces and developing such services in Britain. The exercise of different forms of power and power relations within these frameworks of unofficial dispute resolution may affect the decision-making abilities of some female users. Clearly in this situation, the unofficial mediator is in an all-too-powerful position to possibly encourage or coerce the applicant into reconciling, making the potential consequences for women particularly disastrous. This argument appears to make a great deal of sense, particularly if there is little or no screening process at these bodies to determine which cases are suitable for mediation and which are not. The Family Law Act 1996 contains provisions to ensure mediation only takes place in the interests of both parties with no risk of violence or threats of violence to either of the parties involved. Section 1(d) states that 'any risk to one of the parties to a marriage, and to any children, of violence from the other party should, so far as reasonably practicable, be removed or diminished'. This view is further given expression in the Code of Practice of the UK College of Family Mediators 1998 (see Diduck and Kaganas, 1999, pp. 351–2). This section therefore analyses how gender relations are constituted in this process of ADR.

In general, this process of dispute resolution itself generates an internal structure within each council but some differences emerge in relation to reconciling and/or mediating between the parties. Notwithstanding the methodological constraints of limited access granted by the Shari'ah councils, the empirical data provide an interesting insight into the strategies, procedures and practices adopted by the councils. This insight allows a better understanding of how these bodies constitute as dispute resolution mechanisms within the local communities in which they emerge. And rather than embodying a set of shared cultural and religious norms and values the councils are imbued with and draw upon different and at times conflicting interpretations of Islamic legal principles. This is accompanied by differing relations of power between the councils that can reveal internal contestations, conflict and change between them and in their relationship with state law.

Council size and administration

The four councils studied vary in size, structure and the type of advice given. Their size depend on a number of factors such as the number of religious scholars available, the council's affiliation, the size of the related mosque, the availability of space to set up the service and the number of divorce applicants. All councils reported 'user demand' as key and the primary reason for their existence. However, services were limited due to the availability and expertise of religious scholars, donations and volunteers.

Types of advice given

Each council reported marriage breakdown and divorce as the two key issues which they dealt with. As discussed in Chapter 2, in relation to divorce, female applicants can contact a Shari'ah council to obtain a Muslim divorce certificate when husbands refuse to grant them a unilateral divorce (*talaq*). Under Muslim law women are permitted a divorce without the consent of their husbands but the intervention of a religious scholar is essential to determine the type of divorce to be issued.

The councils in this study generally formed part of a wider range of community services, rather than being distinct and separate bodies. All councils offered reconciliation and mediation services, discussed further. The advice given to applicants was reported to be based upon 'Islamic interpretations' of family and marriage rules and guidance based on the two key sources in Islam, the Qur'an and the Sunna. Issues such as ancillary relief, contact with and custody of children, sale of homes and domestic violence were outside the scope of this research. Although some anecdotal evidence was found it is *not* possible to report on whether or not these are discussed by the councils. More general matrimonial advice can also be given at local mosques by an imam (religious scholar). Advice can also be given by Muslim counsellors based in local cultural or religious organizations although they do not issue Muslim divorce certificates.

Each council relies on community and family networks to advertise services, often by word of mouth. Respondents reported that all services were funded by charitable donations, often via local mosque donations or funding appeals to the local Muslim communities. The councils were described as 'community organizations' that 'act in good faith' and provide a much needed service for Muslim women that involves 'minimal charge and no financial gain' (Sheikh Abdullah, SCUK). Mohammed Raza, at the MLSC explained, 'We act in the best interests of Muslim women ... they come to us for advice and with guidance from Allah we help them as best we can.'[4] Most strikingly, this space of dispute resolution is conceptualized by the scholars where Muslim applicants can resolve their disputes within a Islamic context and Muslim approach thereby fulfilling their religious obligations.

Council panel members

The administration of councils is generally overseen by a panel comprising religious scholars and volunteers. In this study each council reported the use of a panel, which was closely affiliated to the mosque committee and which facilitated the process of resolving disputes. Each council panel was headed by a 'chairman' who, after discussions with other panel members, had the final say as to whether a divorce certificate would be issued to the applicant or not. As discussed later in this chapter, although divorce under the Shari'ah is available to Muslim women, this is neither the guaranteed nor the inexorable outcome.

The respondents in this study identified themselves using terms such as imam, Qadi, Mufti, Sheikh and Maulvi (these titles are explained on page 119). All the scholars were male and aged between 35 and 80. The study found no evidence of Muslim women acting as religious scholars or forming part of the council panels.[5] However, Muslim women did form part of the counselling and mediation services offered by some Shari'ah councils (see further). Council panels could also include individuals from within Muslim communities, including professionals such as GPs and Islamic schoolteachers. Panel members were closely involved in the local mosque and chosen to represent the diversity of experiences within Muslim communities. Only one council reported the involvement of women on the council panel and this was to facilitate and manage the dispute resolution process but did not involve giving advice.

Little variation was found in the types of religious training the religious scholars had received prior to taking on their roles as advisors in the councils. The councils reported that all the scholars also acted as fully trained imams. They had received formal Islamic jurisprudential training in India, Pakistan, Egypt, Saudi Arabia or Yemen. The nature of this training was not explored. Although belonging to different schools of thought, the scholars emphasized that advice and guidance based on all schools of Islamic jurisprudence was available.

The councils were largely set up within mosque premises, occupying a room in the mosque or based in a local community centre with weekly drop-in sessions for clients and panel meetings taking place on average once a month. All the respondents considered Shari'ah council work as a part of the more general services offered by mosques. Each council permitted scholars to take home files but all final decisions as to whether a divorce certificate could be issued were taken by the council panel rather than an individual scholar. It was reported that religious scholars spent an average of 10–15 hours per week in dealing with divorce applications. There was general agreement that offering such services generated a considerable workload for all those involved. However, the work was described as part of an Islamic 'duty' to help all Muslims resolve disputes with an Islamic spirit of community and in an environment based on Islamic rather than secular values.

Process of resolving the dispute

In his pioneering work on negotiation, mediation and dispute resolution, Gulliver (1979) explores the relations between parties in order to better understand the decision-making processes which underpin reconciliation and mediation practices. He argues that the two parties are themselves key to the decision-making process and upon entry to the negotiation process they each reach a joint decision in order to resolve the dispute. He explains, 'In negotiation there are two distinct though interconnected processes going on simultaneously: a repetitive, cyclical one and a developmental one. A simple analogy is a moving automobile. There is the cyclical turning of the wheels … that enables the vehicle to move and there is the actual movement of the vehicle from one place to another' (1979, p. 82). Gulliver outlines six key stages in the dispute process and points to the complex interaction of norms, values and ethics that underpins the decision-making process:

1. Searching for an agenda
2. Defining the agenda
3. Exploring the field
4. Narrowing differences
5. Bargaining
6. Ritualizing the outcome

This type of negotiation process is shaped by what Gulliver calls the 'search process' (Gulliver, 1979, p. 192) and the involvement of all the parties. In this case the applicants for a divorce certificate learn about what the Shari'ah council has to offer and the religious scholars consider their ability to resolve the dispute. This conceptual framework as developed by Gulliver (1979) is useful as it allows a closer analyses of the ways in which dispute resolution processes can take shape.

The study found that all the councils adopted some kind of a formal process prior to a divorce certificate being issued. In each of these councils there were two or three primary advisors and a council panel of five to 12 religious scholars who met on a monthly basis to discuss cases and issue divorce certificates. The two religious scholars (the primary advisors) dealt with each applicant on a personal basis, meeting regularly with the applicant, her husband and usually both sides of the family. This was done in order to ensure that the facts of the case were collated from the applicants and their families. All the councils required the parties who had an English civil law marriage to have completed a civil divorce prior to obtaining a Muslim divorce. Three meetings typically took place before the Muslim divorce certificate was issued or withheld.

The process began with a set of documents sent to the applicant outlining the procedures involved in obtaining a divorce certificate. This may include information on a registration fee, a form requesting the agreement of the applicant to abide by any decision, a letter of acknowledgement of the application and finally a request for certain basic information about the dispute.[6] The BSC and ISC adopt a similar set of procedures with variations on the fee charged to cover the administration costs.

Once contact had been made with the Shari'ah council, the next stage involved the client completing an application form which detailed the grounds for divorce. In fact, the 'grounds for divorce' cited in the application form often provided the basis for the type of divorce certificate to be issued to the applicant. According to Dr Saeeda at BSC, it allows the parties an opportunity to consider why the marriage has broken down and more importantly raise the possibility of reconciliation. She explained, 'Applying for a divorce with us is not as straightforward as it may seem. We meet with the applicant and their families, sometimes with the husband too ... Myself and Saba take down the details and we ask them to fill out forms and provide concrete evidence to back up their claims.'

The data revealed that there was very little variation in the administrative process between the councils. This process was described as follows:

- Applicant makes contact with the Shari'ah council to obtain a Muslim divorce certificate.
- A meeting takes place between the applicant and the religious scholar.
- The applicant is asked to fill in an application form citing the grounds for divorce and pays an administrative fee.
- A divorce notice is sent to the husband asking for his version of events.
- If there is no response from the husband, a further notice is sent out.
- Once contact has been made with all parties, a meeting is arranged to consider reconciliation.
- If contact is not made with the husband and his family, then the religious scholar continues with the process to issue the divorce certificate.
- If reconciliation fails, then a process of mediation begins.
- The religious scholar considers what type of divorce certificate can be issued.
- Once all meetings are completed and evidence has been collected, a copy of the file is passed to all members of the council panel.
- A date is set for a meeting of the panel to discuss all cases, where all panel members make a collective decision as to whether a divorce certificate can be issued.
- A divorce certificate is sent to the applicant *or* she is asked to collect it.

With each Shari'ah council the religious scholar(s) attempt to include all the parties involved in the matrimonial dispute in order to verify the basis upon which the divorce certificate can be issued.

There are in essence two key aspects to this process of dispute resolution, the emphasis placed upon reconciling parties and, should this fail, the type of Muslim divorce certificate issued to female applicants. Distancing themselves from the dangers of forced reconciliation, each religious scholar was, however, keen to promote the willing participation of female applicants. The rise in applications for a divorce certificate in some areas was in part explained by what was perceived as the increasing confidence of Muslim women to challenge unacceptable behaviour in marital relationships and their confidence to instigate religious divorce proceedings. A number of scholars made reference to the uncertainty generated by modern Western societies that were deemed to be based upon secular and consumerist values and contributed to the breakdown of the Muslim family. Sheikh Abdullah (SCUK) explained, 'In Islam we have very clear principles on how Muslim women must be respected and protected as wives, sisters and mothers. Women nurture the Muslim family and today we see these roles being undermined and destroyed with an emphasis on material wealth. Twenty years ago we would not have had so many young women walk away from their marriages as we see today.' By contrast, scholars such as Dr Nasim at BSC welcomed the presence of Muslim women at Shari'ah councils and the renewed visibility of Muslim women in 'British life'. For him, Shari'ah councils enabled Muslim women to 'challenge oppressive cultural traditions and free themselves from unwanted marriages'. Likewise, Sheikh Abu Hassan blamed parental pressures that forced young women into unwanted marriages and Muslim men for 'failing to recognize change and moving with the times', all of which ultimately contributed to the rise in divorce applications.

The onus, therefore, is upon the female applicant to contact a Shari'ah council to obtain a religious divorce certificate. However, each scholar was keen to emphasize that Muslim women are neither coerced nor obliged to contact a council to reconcile with their husbands or, failing this, to obtain a Muslim divorce certificate. Nevertheless, as discussed previously, there is an obligation upon Muslims to resolve disputes within an Islamic framework of Muslim values and principles and this can be accentuated for those Muslims who choose to live in non-Muslim countries. As Sheikh Abdullah explained, 'As Muslims, we have a duty to live according to the Qur'an and Sunna even though we may have chosen to live in non-Muslim countries. I think it is incumbent upon us to live up to this responsibility because of the effect of Western influences upon our children and ourselves. It is easy to neglect our duties in this secular environment.' While emphasizing the importance of 'embedding' Islamic values into British Muslim communities while countering what was perceived as the constant and real threat of secularism in British society, the scholars were keen to describe Shari'ah councils as community organizations that were unique in their position to share and promote common Islamic values within Muslim communities and to encourage tolerant and acceptable behaviour in British society. For these scholars, therefore, Shari'ah councils can play a pivotal role in strengthening both a sense of belonging for British Muslims as individuals and as part of a wider Muslim *umma* while in part promoting the core values of citizenship, equality and justice.

Yet as discussed later in this book, the power relations aligned within Shari'ah councils may in effect regulate, supervise, observe and define the behaviour of women, dictating acceptable patterns of behaviour and promoting particular outcomes (Foucault, 1977). Given the 'observed' general similarities in this approach to resolving disputes, the differences relate primarily to the subtleties in the practice of mediation and reconciliation. Here, the powerful role of the mediator in constructing ideologies of Muslim family and marriage plays a pivotal role in the ways in which the dispute is framed and its outcome.

Cases

The research found that Shari'ah councils appear to deal primarily with Muslim divorce, each reporting between 80 and 200 cases each year. These figures vary according to the size of the council, its location, expertise and the number of volunteers. However, the precise nature of these cases was not fully explored with each council due to restrictions of access to council case files. For example, we do not know whether the figures included general enquiries, or only cases of Muslim women seeking to obtain a Muslim divorce certificate as this data was simply unavailable.

Case files were kept on the premises (most often the local mosque or the centre in which the council was based) and filed according to the applicants name and/or a file reference number. All materials are deemed confidential but the interviews did not reveal the process as to how materials were gathered and filed. When asked if there had been a growth in demand for their work, approximately half the councils reported a rise. The other councils reported little if any rise and explained variations in the number of divorce applications as the result of increased knowledge within Muslim communities of the existence of Shari'ah councils. The next sections analyses this process of issuing divorce certificates in more depth.

Stage one: Searching for an arena

The first stage in the process is finding an arena acceptable to both parties where the dispute will be resolved. As Roberts points out, 'The arena covers not only the geographical or social location but also who is involved – for example, parties with decision-making authority, and other participants such as partisan representatives or support persons' (2008, p. 126). Shah-Kazemi (2000, p. 306) points out that the type of arena can vary according to the needs of the parties and often can be determined by ethnic, cultural and religious values the parties identify with. She explains, 'Each venue indicates a particular set of ground rules for the disputants, and within the context of minority ethnic communities the difference between social mores at home, at venues amongst the member community, and in the wider social domain is exaggerated. The dynamics of migration, the concomitant insecurities and need for self-preservation and simply the fact of being in a minority has implications for the way in which the family dispute is tolerated and the importance the dispute acquires in the life of the family' (2000, p. 306).

Analysis of a small number of case files reveals that the applicant makes contact with a council via telephone or letter and through scheduled and unscheduled appointments.[7] All councils reported that in the majority of cases the applicants first telephone to enquire about the possibility of obtaining a Muslim divorce certificate and the financial costs involved. Should the applicant wish to proceed with the divorce then a set of documents is sent to the applicant outlining the procedures involved. This may include information on a registration fee, a form requesting the agreement of the applicant to abide by any decision, a letter of acknowledgement of the application and finally a request for certain basic information about the dispute (see Shah-Kazemi, 2001, p. 11). At this stage there is little discernible difference between the councils with variations only in the level of fees they charge to cover administration costs.[8] As Dr Saeeda at the Birmingham Shari'ah Council explained, 'We have no choice but to make a small charge. We work as volunteers and in order for the service to operate effectively we must ensure that our administrative costs are covered.'

A key difference between the councils, however, is whether a divorce certificate can be issued by post and without any face-to face contact with the applicant. Mohammed Raza at MLSC explained that at times it became necessary to issue certificates in this way: 'We get cases from all over the country and we cannot realistically expect all our clients to visit us in London. This doesn't mean that we hand out divorces to anyone who requests one. We make thorough checks and act in good faith.' However, other scholars voiced criticism of such an approach pointing to the difficulties in attempting to reconcile the parties. Maulana Abu Saeed at ISC explained, 'For us it's important to meet with our clients, to reason with them and make sure they understand the consequences of their decisions.'

Criticism of issuing divorce certificates by post led some scholars to be concerned about the problem of applicants simply 'forum shopping' between councils if they were dissatisfied with one council's decision. As Sheikh Abdullah explained, 'I do recognise that some councils make thorough checks as best they can but what we see happening is that if an applicant does not like our decision then they will go off and find a different Shari'ah council and if, for example, the applicant never has to visit the council then it only makes it easier for them to go off to other councils whenever they choose to.' Conceding that choice for applicants was also necessary to accommodate the needs of all Muslims, he argued that self regulation between the councils was crucial in order that council verdicts held moral authority and were not unwittingly undermined by conflicting council decisions.

Stage two: Defining the agenda

The second stage in the dispute process defines the agenda upon which the dispute can be resolved and for the scholars to clarify the basis of the dispute between the parties. The disputants must therefore come together to decide the parameters of the dispute, and the normative framework of the dispute resolution process is determined by the disputants and the religious scholars. In this case the common starting point for Muslim disputants is their religious identity as Muslims. In other words this religious identity can contribute to the willingness of the applicants to participate in the process and the rights afforded to them under Islamic law. As Shah-Kazemi points out, the view that Muslims hold about divorce is 'influenced by the fact that divorce has been a right available to both men and women since the inception of the religion, contrary to the view held by Hindus that marriage is an unbreakable lifelong union, which until recently, could only end upon the funeral pyre' (2000, p. 312).

This stage begins with the applicant completing the application form in some detail and outlining the grounds for divorce. It is clear that the application form also acts as a tool to encourage possible reconciliation and if not then determine the type of divorce certificate to be issued. According to Dr Saeeda at BSC, it allows the parties a crucial opportunity to consider the reasons why the marriage has broken down. As for the application form itself, it is interesting to note that each council has devised a form that to some extent mirrors legal practitioner documentation. For example, three councils (MLSC, ISC and BSC)[9] refer to the applicant as the 'Petitioner' and the application form is titled 'The Petitioner's Submission'. The language in these documents therefore works rhetorically to ensure the applicant takes seriously the nature of Muslim divorce proceedings. Sheikh Abdullah at SCUK explained, 'We've attempted to develop a process whereby the clients understand that you don't just get a Muslim divorce if you want one. They have to understand the seriousness of divorce and this process helps us as the clients have to provide evidence, that they need documentation and ... well just the process the way it works.' In this way the application form therefore is deliberately formulated to convey the seriousness of the dispute resolution process and to prevent 'forum shopping' to become the norm.

For example, a typical application form requests general details of age, address and the grounds for divorce. It states: 'Please outline a maximum of five grievances against your husband to be considered as the main areas for your separation and request for an Islamic divorce. You are requested to be precise and concise. Please bear in mind that the Shari'ah council may ask you to provide evidence to support your submissions.' The factors cited include bigamy, domestic violence, adultery, forced marriage and wider familial conflict. It is noteworthy that the applicants take this opportunity to provide detailed accounts describing the events leading up to the marriage, reasons for the breakdown of the marriage and the current situation the applicant finds herself in and provide an insight into the experiences of the women.

Extracts from two cases illustrate some of the reasons given for the breakdown of the marriage.

Case A

1. My husband had previously had an Islamic marriage to somebody else but only in an Islamic way. He never told me. When I found out I asked him whether it was true and he lied and denied it but after getting proof he finally admitted it which completely shook me altogether.
2. I later realized that he had married me because he was trying to get to stay in this country.
3. After the birth of our child he began to act very strange and refused to register the birth and state that the child was his. Which I have always taken as doubting the child is his.
4. He is unreliable, a liar and a crook. He has hidden many things, which I have later found out about. After separation a few friends have questioned him about his behaviour but he has always denied it.
5. I do not want him to have any contact with the child as I am in fear of him and fear that if contact were given he may try to harm the child in some way.

Case B

1. He is impotent.
2. He has been verbally and physically abusive towards me since the day we were living together.
3. He has subjected me to mental torture and made me cry every single day.
4. He intends to go to Pakistan and remarry without my consent.
5. He has threatened to kill me on several occasions.

The application form is frequently supported by additional information, often up to an additional three to five pages detailing personal experiences and the breakdown of the marriage. Clearly, then, the applicant uses this opportunity to put forward her reasons for seeking a Muslim divorce. For the councils the application form acts as a first indicator of the possibility of issuing a divorce certificate and 'to disentangle fact from fiction'

(Dr Nasim, BSC) but also to seriously consider the possibility of reconciling the parties.

Stage three: Exploring the field

Once the application for divorce is completed an investigation begins to verify the applicant's version of events and for the parties to come together and possibly resolve the dispute, without divorce. Although there seems to be no foolproof means of verifying the claims made in the application form, it is generally assumed that the burden of proof falls upon the applicant who is expected to act according to Muslim values of truthfulness, honesty and sincerity and this is explicitly stated in the application forms.

Interview data also revealed that scholars are keen to challenge the applicants' submissions in the application form and once the application is submitted, the applicants' husband is given the opportunity must challenge and/or disprove the allegations put forward. Mohammed Raza at MLSC explained, 'First ... we will send a copy of the woman's allegations to the husband. If he challenges those allegations, then definitely we will demand the applicant produce evidence to prove those allegations. But if he accepts those allegations or he doesn't reply to our notices or he ignores those allegations, then perhaps we will take the initial submissions of the applicant as sufficient for our purpose.'

Where access to case files was permitted, I gained an insight into this process. At MLSC, the process of gathering evidence centres on a number of notices being sent to the husband. The first notice includes three requests for the husband to

1. Make every possible effort towards reconciliation urgently through your own resources;
2. To grant your wife a proper Islamic divorce;
3. Contact us immediately, through written correspondence only, to present your own side of the case showing reasons why you should not divorce your wife.

If the husband fails to respond to this notice a second notice is sent which states:

Please note that if these circumstances remain unchanged and you do not respond to the laws of the Shari'ah, the members of the Council comprising eminent scholars, imams and Muslim barristers representing various Schools of Muslim law (Fiqh) in Britain may consider issuing a document with the effect of pronouncing your Nikah dissolved (Tanseakh) on the basis of grounds valid in the divorce laws of Ilsma. We trust as a Muslim brother you will co-operate with us in resolving this dispute.

Failure to respond to this notice results in a final divorce notice being sent. The registrar, Maulana Mohammed Raza explains, 'What happens after issuing that notice is almost different in every case. There are cases where after receiving this notice husbands act realistically, they agree to a divorce or they issue a divorce. Or they can just ignore our letters; they don't think that we are an adequately constituted authority so they just throw our letters into the bin. Or they can put their defence to us and challenge all the allegations submitted by the wife in her application. So it's a lengthy, a very sophisticated and complicated process where each case is different from the other.'

The BSC and ISC follow a strikingly similar procedure but the SCUK deals with the issue somewhat differently. Here, a joint meeting is arranged between the applicant and her husband to compare and discuss the evidence presented by both parties. The evidence can, however, only be accepted as valid once it can be verified by three male witnesses.

Analysis of 25 MLSC case files revealed that in 17 cases, two notices were sent out to the husband and in eight cases a total of three notices had been sent. There were a total of 19 responses from the applicants' husbands and most of these challenged the grounds for divorce. It is interesting to note, however, that in 20 cases, rather than produce any 'evidence' with which to challenge the grounds for divorce cited by the applicant, the husband requests some form of mediation in the hope reconciling. Yet the basis for reconciliation is often tempered with uncompromising sentiments. For example, in one case the husband states, 'I am prepared to reconcile with my wife and forgive her for what she has put me and my family through. But she must change her behaviour; she is selfish and unreasonable and puts her needs first without any regard for the rest of us.'

The issue of what constitutes 'evidence' as stipulated in the application form is crucial in determining the type of divorce certificate issued. Thus an important part of the investigation process involves clarifying the reasons for the breakdown of the marriage and establishing the grounds for divorce. Not only does this determine whether a divorce certificate can be issued but it also acts as a pretext to the possibility of reconciling the parties.

As discussed earlier, there are different ways in which a *nikah* contract can be dissolved without the intervention of the husband. The one most commonly used by the councils in this study is known as the *khul*. As discussed earlier, here the wife is able to instigate divorce in return for a payment to her husband, which usually involves the return of the *mahr*. In doing so she forfeits her right to any form of maintenance. The other types of divorce that are instigated by women are *mubara't*, where the marriage has not been consummated due to the fault of the husband and both parties agree to dissolve the marriage; and finally the *faskh* or *tanseekh* where the *nikah* contract may stipulate the right of the woman to divorce her husband, but this must involve the intervention of the religious scholar. Inevitably the different interpretations of divorce within these broad categories can lead to confusion for the female applicants. This is addressed in the following two chapters.

The issue of what constitutes as grounds for divorce and 'evidence' underpins the decision-making process. Case-file analysis reveals that the grounds for divorce at the ISC are

1. If the husband suffers certain physical defects, which are well known in Shari'ah and are considered to be legal grounds for nullification of the marriage.
2. When the husband accuses the wife of unchastity. In such a case, the process of *li'aan* is to be applied.
3. When the husband is missing.
4. When the wife embraces Islam but the husband refuses to do so.
5. When the husband ill-treats the wife or fails to perform his marital obligations or does not maintain her in spite of having the means to do so.
6. When the husband does not or refuses to comply with the judge's order to divorce his wife for one of the reasons mentioned.

With the SCUK, the following grounds form the basis for divorce:

1. If the husband causes direct harm to her: for example, bodily damage, leaving wounds and bruises or physical humiliation.
2. If the husband causes indirect harm to her such as not providing food, shelter and clothing or oppressing/harming her children or he becomes a *faajir* – for example, homosexual, alcoholic and so on.
3. If she hates him and cannot tolerate him any more even if he is good towards her. This will cause harm to her, as she will become sinful by not fulfilling her duties towards her husband.

These grounds include the caveat, 'NB: As for the first and second grounds, the husband is not entitled to the jewellery or any dowry that has been paid and he is liable to pay the dowry or remainder of it if it has not been paid in full. As for the third ground, the husband is entitled to the jewellery and mahr that has been paid.'

Despite the subtle differences found between the councils in the grounds for divorce, it becomes clear that four key factors determine the outcome of which kind of divorce certificate can be issued: the validity of marriage, physical and/or emotional abuse, wider familial conflict, the possibility of reconciliation and *other* factors (e.g. desertion/impotence). In relation to each of these five grounds, material evidence is required by the scholars in order to verify the claims made by the applicant.

Is the marriage valid?

The rise of forced marriages was seen by all the scholars as one of the primary reasons for women seeking a divorce. Hence one of the most important grounds for divorce centres on the validity of the marriage itself. Aside from understanding *why* the applicant had chosen to marry, the scholars were keen to explore whether the marriage was valid according to Islamic law. Dr Nasim at BSC explained, 'In Islam we have very clear guidelines of when a marriage is a valid marriage. Unfortunately we see all too many cases of young women and men being forced into marriage in the name of Islam. This is not only morally wrong but also un-Islamic. Parents would do well to remember that there is no compulsion in Islam.' While these sentiments were shared by other scholars, case-file analysis also revealed that the issue of forced marriage was addressed by the religious scholars during the process of collecting evidence. It is interesting to note, for example, that references to forced marriage in case-file notes are often referred to as 'alleged' cases of forced marriages. During interview Sheikh Abdullah at SCUK explains, 'We have no way of verifying that the marriage was forced. We accept that some marriages are forced ... but remember some women agree to the marriage but then change their minds and then claim they had been forced into marriage. Our duty is [to] deal with the issue as we see it.' The councils have attempted to deal with this problem by issuing *fatwas* regarding what constitutes a forced marriage in Muslim Islam and the importance of consent in marriage.

There is also a focus on the process of marriage itself and the formalities of marriage in order to determine its validity. For example, each applicant is asked to produce documentary evidence such as a *nikah* certificate and/or civil registration certificate, and if for some reason the applicant is unable to provide this evidence, then an affidavit is required to authenticate the fact that the marriage had indeed taken place. If the marriage has not been registered according to civil law, then the applicant is required to produce a copy of the *nikah* certificate and documentary evidence of the wedding, including visual recordings of the wedding and/or photographs, to prove that the marriage did indeed take place.

Physical and/or emotional abuse

Physical and emotional abuse is cited as a key ground in the divorce application form. Again the councils require documented evidence to verify the allegations put forward by the applicant: for example, in cases of domestic violence this can include police reports, court injunctions and family court orders restricting access to children to prove that emotional and physical abuse has taken place in the marriage.

Wider family conflict

A common complaint cited by the applicants in the application form is 'family interference' in the marriage, summed up by one applicant who stated that '[h]is family made everything much worse, they always interfered telling him what to do and how to do things ... is this allowed in Islam?' Another stated that the reason for pursuing a divorce was the 'constant taunting for not being a proper Muslim wife'. The applicants are not expected to produce evidence to verify these allegations but these claims are rigorously discussed and challenged during the reconciliation and mediation sessions and the religious scholars explained that they often request the presence of family members to 'explain their (the parties) behaviour'.

The possibility of reconciliation

Reconciliation and mediation shape the process of dispute resolution which means that at any time during this process the divorce application is halted if either party is willing to reconcile.

Overall the process of collecting evidence to determine whether a divorce certificate can be issued can be eclectic as well as complex. It encapsulates the power of religious scholars to determine what constitutes evidence while simultaneously placing the onus on the applicant to produce verifiable documentation. The process can therefore result in lengthy delays.

Stage four: Bargaining

The mediators

The religious scholars described themselves in different ways using titles such as 'Registrar', 'imam', 'Mufti', 'Sheikh', 'Maulana' (or 'Maulvi') and/ or 'Qadi'.[10] The use of each title is based upon the varied and traditional *Darul Ulama* systems of Islamic education and scholarship. Each title refers to a specific and well-defined level and type of education attained by each of the scholars in question. For example, the title imam implies the non-completion of an *Alim* course. Maulana is a title conferred upon the completion of a basic Alim course. Mufti and Qadi are titles conferred upon an individual who has completed a basic Alim course which has been supplemented with a two-year course in Islamic law. This study did not yield any information on the nature and type of training undertaken by each scholar.

There is some dispute regarding the appointment of mediators and the legitimacy of their verdicts within Muslim communities. For some scholars only a religious scholar who is trained to provide Muslims with religious and spiritual guidance can be appointed as a mediator while others argue that any member of the local Muslim community with varying expertise and qualifications in Islamic law and jurisprudence has the right to intervene and attempt to resolve matrimonial disputes (see Rosen, 1989). This reflects the disagreement among Muslim jurists about the extent of the mediator's authority. For example, Hanafi and Shafi'i schools are of the opinion that mediators have no authority to issue a binding verdict and their role is merely to recommend a solution which the spouses have the right to either accept or reject but other jurists argue that a Qadi has the full authority to attempt to reconcile parties or annul the marriage (see Esposito, 1988).

It is interesting to note, however, that the scholars in this study were keen to avoid using the term 'religious judge' as a deliberate attempt to avoid any confusion with judges presiding over English law and to avoid any confusion over the legality of Shari'ah council divorce certificates in English law. As Dr Nasim at the BSC explained, the verdicts and divorce certificates issued by the councils are not legally binding under English law and council verdicts serve to uphold 'the moral authority of the Muslim community'.

The process of unofficial mediation

This study did not specifically focus upon the ways in which official and unofficial processes of reconciliation and mediation may meet, interact or be in conflict, but some general points can be drawn from the data collected (as discussed in Chapter 6).

In marital disputes, the complex relationship between individual party responsibility and the nature and extent of state intervention raises questions regarding the extent to which unofficial dispute mechanisms (in this case Shari'ah councils) assume an important and pivotal space in the dispute resolution process. So, for example, to what extent do such unofficial mediation bodies provide advice and assistance in matters of family law specifically catering to the needs of the minority groups in question? Several scholars have identified the spheres of official and unofficial mediation as fixed, distinct and separate, which provide different types of services (Shah-Kazemi, 2001; Yilmaz, 2001a). For example, drawing upon her findings, Shah-Kazemi observes that '[w]hile the MLSC performs a mediation function through the manner in which they intervene in marital and intra-family disputes, they do not often mediate in matters that are now becoming more formally associated with mediation in England, as the organization has a deliberate policy of not conflicting with civil law mechanisms' (2001, p. 55).

While this study found a similar or generic approach adopted by each of the councils in relation to reconciliation and mediation practices, it is also fair to note that such a dichotomous approach, as official and unofficial/private mediation as two separate spheres of dispute resolution, in fact obscures not only the social relations upon which the two approaches are based but we also learn very little of the dialectical relationship between the official and unofficial law. As Santos points out, at some level this dichotomy between state and non-state dispute resolution is inevitably blurred and ultimately misleading (1987, p. 35). Instead, the 'emerging' relationship between official mediation practices and a state-sponsored move towards privatized bodies increasingly mediating in marital disputes reveals a more complex relationship. Furthermore this inter-relationship where official and unofficial mediation can come together cannot be perceived as partial and incidental but also one of complementarity. This does not, of course, point to a definitive and unproblematic link between the two approaches but instead points to situations where the two approaches may come together and find common ground.

This move towards private ordering and community mediation has particular implications for women users of Shari'ah councils. According to Poulter
(1995) Muslim women may feel compelled to participate in such processes
due to family and community pressures (and concerns about damage or the
loss of 'family honour'). A move towards such forms of private ordering can
therefore have a negative and detrimental effect on the rights of women
afforded under state law. Viewing Shari'ah councils as patriarchal and 'conservative' in nature, which serve to maintain the existing unequal power
relations in the family and community, Poulter (1998) remains sceptical of
the ability of such ADR mechanisms to deliberate fairly and equally on family law matters. Paradoxically, however, he argues that if such bodies were
given formal recognition and state funding, that would allow state accountability and provide Muslim women with protection if they were compelled
to participate in such processes. Under this proposal the 'full panoply of
the remedies of the English legal system would still be available to Muslim
women' (1995, p. 86). In this context, English law could then remain as the
preferred method of dispute resolution and Shari'ah councils would also be
able to operate as a 'facility for those who feel that the English courts are
not responsive enough to their religious or cultural needs' (1995, p. 86). This
point is discussed more fully in the following chapter but some scholars
remain critical of such initiatives arguing that state law cannot define the
parameters of Islamic ADR as the former is essentially based upon Western
concepts, norms and values which can conflict with Islamic systems of
dispute resolution (Pearl and Menski, 1998; Yilmaz, 2001b).

How does the mediation process take shape?

This study found that for many councils the process of mediation is principally an opportunity to attempt to reconcile the parties. It is by no means
an uncomplicated process and gives rise to an interesting set of social and
cultural practices, based upon religious principles and cultural norms,
overlapping and, at times, in conflict. What becomes clear, however, is the
centrality of gender relations that frame the terms of the negotiations upon
which reconciliation and mediation are based. In this way the role, position
and representation of Muslim women remain critical to the outcome of this
process.

Interview data with religious scholars revealed the primary importance
attached to resolving the dispute and reconciling the parties. Reconciliation
is understood both as a moral duty upon all Muslims (to preserve the sanc-
tity of the Muslim family) and a religious obligation (a divorce cannot be
pronounced without the parties first agreeing to attempt reconciliation).
Mohammed Raza, at MLSC, explained: 'We do not just distribute divorces
on a footpath ... we are not encouraging divorce, that's not our role. When
a woman rings here to find out about divorce or to request an application
form, we are initially reluctant to issue a divorce application. We ask her

that you should try to rethink your position because divorce is something that is considered a stigma in society and divorce is nothing good for you and if they have children that will be another problem after divorce, so we discourage it.' The data also revealed that despite the reluctance of religious scholars, the most likely outcome was the eventual issuing of divorce certificates. In this study the religious scholars explained that their intention was not to control the outcome, but instead to provide a 'space' at the councils where the couple could be reminded of their 'Islamic duties as husband and wife' (Dr Hasan). It was also described as an opportunity 'to discuss personal matters from an Islamic perspective with the guidance of learned Muslim scholars' (Maulana Abu Saeed).

Therefore this framework of dispute resolution encourages Muslim women to engage and participate in reconciling with partners and to resolve the dispute amicably from an Islamic perspective. Of course, this process is not a simple one and the religious framework upon which it is based is neither fixed nor homogenous across the councils. Instead it can be better understood as one based on the involvement of multiple parties with multiple meanings of Muslim marriage and family relationships and it is between these multiplicities that a more insightful picture is emerging of this process of resolving disputes.

Central to this process is the religious scholar who seems to occupy a somewhat ambiguous position between reconciling the parties and facilitating the successful outcome of the divorce application. In English law, mediation is predicated on the decision-making capacity of the individual (see Chapter 6). The crucial point here is that the parties themselves retain authority and responsibility for reaching and making their own decisions (Roberts, 1997, p. 2). In this context, mediation is clearly differentiated from reconciliation services as it provides the conditions upon which negotiations are based in the context of family breakdown. It embodies third-party intervention but the authority of all the decisions remains with the parties themselves. McCrory (1981, p. 56) outlines four key characteristics of mediation:

- The impartiality of the mediator
- The voluntariness of the process (because the mediator has no power to impose a settlement)
- The confidentiality of the relationship between the mediator and the parties
- The procedural flexibility available to the mediator

Unofficial mediators, in this case religious scholars based at Shari'ah councils, can be distinguished from official mediators in three key ways. The most obvious distinction is the standpoint of the mediator him/herself. In the case of Shari'ah councils, the approach to mediation is conceptualized and understood as being part of an Islamic framework whereby all negotiations derive from sources based upon divine revelation. Secondly, these mediators are often senior members of the local Muslim community and therefore can claim an insight into local familial conflicts based upon personal knowledge and experience.[11] And finally unofficial mediators work on a voluntary basis to ensure their autonomy and independence from community and state intervention. Of course, this also has the consequence that such bodies avoid state accountability (see Poulter, 1998).

The following section draws upon observation data to consider the ways in which reconciliation and mediation take shape at Shari'ah councils. In particular it analyses two identifiable features of this process – the role of the religious scholar as the unofficial mediator and the extent to which wider family intervention shapes the nature of this process. The experiences of Muslim women are then discussed in the subsequent chapters.

Shari'ah councils observed

The Muslim Family Support Service and Shari'ah Council, Birmingham (BSC)

The Muslim Family Support Service and Shari'ah Council (BSC) based at Birmingham Central Mosque was set up in 1996 to deal with matrimonial disputes within the local Muslim community. The council offers both a reconciliation and mediation service under the authority of five appointed religious scholars who meet three times a year to discuss cases, meet with applicants and clients, and issue council divorce certificates. The council works in tandem with the marriage counselling service, run by female counsellors, which was set up within the mosque in 2001 in response to the growing number of queries regarding Muslim divorce.

The task of dealing with inquiries, preparing case files and providing counselling to applicants is led by Dr Saeeda who at the time of the fieldwork headed the counselling service at the council and her assistant. Applicants must first attend on average three counselling sessions with Dr Saeeda prior to their case file being sent to the council panel for consideration of whether a divorce certificate can be issued. Therefore this council places a particular emphasis on using a female counsellor to consider the reasons for the breakdown of the marriage and the possibility of reconciling the parties. During interview Dr Saeeda explained: 'As a Muslim woman I am aware of the need to approach reconciliation with caution. In fact the only time we don't consider reconciliation is when the woman is facing violence and we get a lot of cases where women tell me their husbands physically abuse them. It's not tolerated under English law and it's certainly not tolerated under Islam.' On occasions when women do wish to reconcile with violent husbands, she explained that she intuitively uses her position to dissuade any such attempts.

She therefore seeks to disentangle oppressive cultural values that she argues are based upon social and familial pressure from Islamic marriage principles which encourage individual choice and personal fulfilment. For example, she explains that forced marriage, emotional and physical abuse and the family dominance of women are synonymous with cultural practices that confer male authority in the family household and marriage practices. Instead during the counselling sessions women applicants are told that violent husbands 'are unlikely to change their ways' and they are encouraged to report all incidences of violence and abuse to the police. At the same time she presents Islam as an empowering tool for women with its emphasis on autonomy, choice and consent that is based on divine will and a supreme being who has created a complex but totally logical world for all believers:

> You must not submit to your parents' wishes. It is your life and not theirs. Islam does not compel you to marry someone against your wishes. If he wants to remarry let him take responsibility for the divorce. Allah knows he is the one who is sinning so let him be punished for this. Women should remember there is no compulsion in Islam. Allah knows best.

By making gender visible and central to the dispute process, she provides new insights into the dynamics of these sessions. She is clearly able to communicate with the women by occupying a position of trust and understanding. She later explained, 'a lot of women tell me of the pain and suffering they go through and they're genuinely distressed. You don't contact me at the counselling service on a whim, wanting a Muslim divorce.' Instead she blames family pressure as the main reason as to why some women, victims of domestic violence, may be keen to reconcile with violent husbands. She does, however, acknowledge that all women must consider reconciliation prior to obtaining a Muslim divorce certificate.

Observation of six counselling sessions enabled me to study a total of 26 cases. A key finding is the role, nature and involvement of wider family members in the dispute process. This is best illustrated by the fact that in 24 cases, a family member accompanied the applicant to the counselling session(s), including a mother, father, sister(s), brother(s), uncle(s) and cousin(s). During the session itself, each applicant was questioned about the marriage, the reasons for its breakdown and nature of family intervention in the marital dispute. Discussion often focused on family honour and attempts made to salvage the marriage in order to avoid shaming the family and possible ostracism for parents by wider family members. For example, 19 women described divorce as shameful for their families and in one case, a client explained, 'Divorce is something that families keep hidden; it's not something they celebrate.' Observation also revealed the extent to which the family mediated in the dispute prior to contacting a Shari'ah council where often all options had been exhausted.

It is notable that the female applicant was often accompanied by a male member of her family and Dr Saeeda expressed concern that this may result in her failing to disclose the reasons for the breakdown in her marriage. For example, in one case the brother of the applicant began to explain why she sought a Muslim divorce but Dr Saeeda intervened mid-sentence, looked at the female applicant and stated, 'if you want an Islamic divorce why don't you speak and tell me; you don't need a man to speak on your behalf.' On another occasion the father of a female applicant began to explain his daughter's situation and again Dr Saeeda immediately intervened, 'if there's anything to tell me, she'll do it. If I need any information from you, I'll ask you.' These examples illustrate how Dr Saeeda is aware of familial pressure on the women who may be encouraged to reconcile and she clearly seeks to use these sessions to clarify the women's desired and preferred outcomes. It also became clear that some female users of the counselling service brought along family members in order to counteract any pressure from the mediator to reconcile and thus friends and/or family members can therefore act as a support mechanism.

In the sessions observed, only three women sought reconciliation with their husbands whereas most women revealed that they had been involved in lengthy discussions with their families in the hope of reconciling prior to contacting the council. One applicant explained to the counsellor, 'We tried for months and months. When we couldn't sort things out, my parents got involved but things just didn't work out.' When further probed about the nature of this family intervention she replied, 'Well, some members of my family got together, had a meeting and tried to sort things out. But they just didn't want to know. It never worked out because they weren't interested in sorting things out.'

The extent to which notions of honour and shame compel some of these female applicants to seek family mediation must be seriously addressed. As Dr Saeeda, explained, 'These women have been through mediation [within the family], they have tried to reconcile with their husbands and I believe them, that's the threshold for me.'

Of particular concern can be the role and presence of the applicant's husband in the reconciliation process and this also raises a set of dilemmas for Dr Saeeda. First, she must track the husband down for 'his version of events'; she explains, 'It's not that we don't believe what the women are saying, but in Islam, it's our duty to see what he has to say, to give him an opportunity and so then we can make an informed decision as to whether we should continue with the reconciliation.' This again leads to concerns about the possibility of violent partners being involved in this process which state law mediation prohibits. Even though, as indicated earlier, Dr Saeeda does not proceed with reconciliation where violence has previously occurred in the relationship or is a continued threat; nevertheless it also became clear that once contact was made with the husband, some women were at risk of renewed threats of violence and abuse. For example, in one session, the applicant informed Dr Saeeda that her attempts to trace her husband had led to threatening phone calls from him. She explained, 'I don't want a reconciliation so I don't want you to contact him. If you do, things will get worse; he's violent and I'm scared of what he might do.' More worrying still was the fact that in this case the applicant's husband had been issued with an injunction order prohibiting any contact with the applicant. Yet Dr Saeeda feels she has little choice but to seriously consider reconciliation if the applicant is to proceed with the Muslim divorce. The study revealed a further eight women complaining to Dr Saeeda about the subsequent threats they received from husbands once contact had been made. The women challenged the claim that their husbands must participate in this process of reconciliation. As one client explained, 'If you continue to write to him or speak to him, he will harass me even more. He doesn't want me to get this divorce, so he will use every opportunity to make my life even more difficult.' The idea that husbands must participate in this process therefore raises serious concerns about the safety of female applicants.

The reasons given by husbands for refusing to pronounce the *talaq* ranged from the applicant's unacceptable behaviour, to a failure of their wife to respect their in-laws and newfound family. Many wives were accused of a reluctance to embrace traditional interpretations of Islam that conceptualizes the role of a 'wife' in a traditional, passive and subordinate way, with the insistence that women ascribe to a particular set of norms and values defining their measure of social worth according to male interests in the family, home and community. This taken-for-granted assumption on the supposed role of Muslim women is challenged by Dr Saeeda who explained that 'the project for all Muslim women is to challenge the presentation of women's lives as *nashuz* [female disobedience]'. For this reason, she attempts to challenge ideas about the duties of a Muslim wife by referring to the responsibilities of a Muslim husband. Although the sincerity of Dr Saeeda's approach to resolving dispute is not in doubt, in practice it had little effect as many husbands who attended the reconciliation meetings insisted that reconciliation could only be achieved on their terms and therefore the parties were rarely reconciled.

Clearly some women found such counselling distressing but others were actively engaged in this process as discussed in the following chapters. Given these contradictions and tensions, three aspects of this process emerge that give rise to serious concerns: first, as discussed previously, the nature of family intervention in the reconciliation process; second, the role of the husband in the counselling sessions; and finally, the extent to which family law matters are being negotiated in this 'unofficial space' with little if any state law protection. Each of these is discussed in more depth in the following chapters.

The council meeting

Once the reconciliation meetings have taken place and there is no prospect of reconciling the parties, the next stage involves the case file being sent to the council panel to determine whether a divorce certificate can be issued. Prior to this council meeting, Dr Saeeda sends the applicants a letter explaining that the council will meet to consider the divorce application. All applicants are expected to attend this meeting and if they are unable to attend their case is then reassigned to the next council meeting. During interview Dr Saeeda revealed that the council panel expects her to prepare a case file outlining the facts of the case, reasons for the failure of the marriage, details of the counselling sessions and reasons for the failure of the parties to reconcile. Dr Saeeda is able to accompany the female applicant to the council meeting but only under the proviso that she cannot contribute to the proceedings unless she is asked to do so by the council panel. Hence her presence at the council meeting is to support the women during the meeting rather than contribute to any scholarly discussions or as to whether a divorce certificate can be issued or not. She accepts this position and explains to the female applicant that 'you will have to push for your case and tell them you do not want any reconciliation' and 'be prepared to answer all the questions' and that 'it's best to be honest'.

I observed two council meetings where a total of 24 cases were discussed by the council panel. Panel members were expected to read the case files prior to the meeting itself. During the first part of the meeting the panel members discussed and agreed the number of cases they were to review and flagged up any potentially difficult cases. It is interesting to note that issues of access and custody of children were also discussed. The female applicants were questioned on the type of access their husbands were given to the children and the reasons why reconciliation had failed. Questions regarding access to and custody of children created some dissension between the council panel members as it presented a conflict of laws scenario with state law principles. Part of the confusion might pertain to the assumptions held by some council panel members that fathers should be granted access to children in all circumstances or that the threshold for deciding such cases differs in Islamic legal thought. The following observation highlights some of the dangers that can arise when such issues are discussed in such a privatized space without the protection of state law.

Parveen was 26 years old and had two young children, aged two and four years respectively. Born in Birmingham, she described herself as a 'British Pakistani'. In 1998, she married a British Pakistani, which she described as a 'love marriage'. Both the requirements of civil and religious marriage were fulfilled and she cited violence and 'emotional abuse' as the grounds for which she was seeking a Muslim divorce.

The council panel members requested that she attend the council meeting in order to clarify a number of 'unresolved' issues. It quickly became apparent that two scholars remained unconvinced that the applicant had seriously considered the option of reconciling with her husband which they argued would serve the interests of the couple's two children. The following extract reveals the exchange between the applicant and one council member.

Council member: Did you consider getting back together with your husband for the sake of the children?

Applicant: Yes, I did but we've been separated before and we tried to work things out then but it didn't happen. I just know this time it's the end; it's not going to work.

Council member: Why?

Applicant: Because he'll never change. I don't want to get back together with him. This time I want a clean break and that's why I'm here. I want a divorce, I want out.

Council member: Have you thought what effects your decision will have on your children?

Applicant: Yes, I have but it's better they don't see the violence, don't see what he does to me. I want them to grow up in a safe environment.

Council member: But ...

Applicant: (Interrupts him) Look I understand what you're getting at. You want us to get back together and Dr Saeeda has explained to me that in Islam you have to try and make things work before you ask for a divorce. But I'm telling you I've tried everything, I was a good wife and I am a good mother but I can't live like this. I want a divorce.

The client was visibly upset and though Dr Saeeda acts only in a supportive role she asked to intervene. After being given permission to do so, she explained to the council panel: 'Myself and Parveen have discussed these issues for weeks and weeks. There is no possibility of her reconciling with her husband and I support her one hundred per cent. If you look in the case file, you'll see my recommendation.' Clearly angry with the stance of this particular council member, she later explained: 'These men have no understanding of what women go through. It makes me so angry! I spend so much time and effort making my recommendations to the council but some of them don't even bother to read them.' It seems that some council members are frustrated by the low number of couples who are successfully reconciled and are therefore ready to embrace a less objective stance with little consideration for the possible consequences for the women involved. Further by exemplifying the possibility of reconciliation as uncontentious and easily achieved, they fail to acknowledge the unequal power relations within the marriage (this point is addressed in the following chapters).

Observation of a second council meeting also revealed long discussions about disputes regarding access to children. In one case a scholar reported that the applicant's husband had been in touch with the council demanding that the council intervene and negotiate some form of access to his children. This particular council member was keen to implement a possible solution and the next extract illustrates the potential dangers.

Religious scholar: In respect of the children what arrangements have you both come to?

Applicant: I don't want him to have any contact with my child and the courts agree with me. I have a court order ...

Religious scholar: But what does your husband want?

Applicant: I have a court order [shows him the order] which says that he's not allowed any direct contact with my child, only indirect contact, he can send cards and letters but that's all.

Religious scholar: Why did the courts come to this conclusion?

Applicant: Because he lied. He told them that he paid maintenance when he didn't and that he had done all these other things when he hadn't. They could see what kind of a person he is; he doesn't really want any contact, he's just doing this to get back at me.

Religious scholar: Well, I spoke to him this morning and he told me that he does want to see his daughter and that if he doesn't get to see her he will take other steps. He may become violent towards you and to prevent this from happening I think we should arrange for him to see his daughter at the mosque.

In this case this council member was very persistent and the female applicant continually challenged him to explain that she had with her a copy of a court order which prohibited her husband from contacting her or having any access to her daughter. However, the council member simply ignored this and suggested that the mosque could be used as a neutral place where the husband could be allowed some access to his daughter. At this point the applicant became, very visibly upset and angry said, 'Look I haven't come here to discuss my daughter, I came here to get a divorce.' Dr Saeeda then intervened, 'This is wrong. There is no question of negotiation.' At this point the chairman asked the applicant to wait outside and explained to all the panel members, 'We cannot issue a directive which is against the courts. Our discussion is merely academic. We have no power of enforcement.' After a few more minutes of general discussion the panel agreed that a divorce certificate should be issued and Dr Saeeda was asked to inform the applicant of their decision.

As discussed later in this book the most striking finding of the council meetings therefore is the concomitant discussion on reconciliation and access to children. Practical and pragmatic decisions in resolving marital disputes cannot be achieved without understanding the standpoint of the women applicants themselves. Without its flexibility and openness this process loses its ability to serve as a locus for Muslim women to resolve the marital disputes from an Islamic perspective.

The Muslim Law (Shariah) Council (MLSC), West London

The Muslim Law (Shariah) Council was established in Ealing, West London in 1985. One of the first Shari'ah councils to be established in Britain, it provides 'legal' opinion on various issues and comprises 21 *ulama* reflecting the four schools of *fiqh* present in Britain. The late Dr Zaki Badawi, one of the founding members of the council, described the objectives of the Shari'ah council, 'to resolve problems confronting Muslims in the light of the Qur'an and Sunna and according to the agreed principles of the Islamic jurists' (1996, p. 106). The Shari'ah council operates from the premises of the Muslim College in Ealing and is affiliated to the Muslim Council of Great Britain. The Muslim College has charitable status and pays its shared secretary through voluntary donations.

Permission to observe council proceedings was declined on the grounds of protecting client confidentiality but two key religious scholars, Maulana Mohammed Raza and Dr Zaki Badawi, agreed to be interviewed. Together with analysis of a small number of council case files, this provides an interesting insight into how the process of dispute resolution at this council takes place.

A key difference between this council and the BSC is that potential applicants are not required to participate in reconciliation sessions, but should the applicants wish to consider reconciliation then the council provides a separate counselling service where applicants are able to meet with a trained Muslim counsellor. Key to the success of reconciliation is the role of the husband. As Maulana Mohammed Raza explained:

> We ask the husband that he should try for reconciliation and if he agrees to it then we offer a full reconciliation service at the Shari'ah Council ... we have a trained counsellor for that purpose. Our first priority remains reconciliation. In our notice that is sent to the husband or to the respondent we ask several things and first of those is that you as a husband must try for reconciliation. If he agrees and says 'fine I want to reconcile, could you arrange something' then we try that.

This approach is based on the understanding that most female applicants are reluctant to pursue reconciliation, as they have exhausted this option prior to any contact made with a Shari'ah council. Mohammed Raza concedes, 'I think the husbands they try or they raise this question in more cases than the wives that contact us. In 95 per cent of the applicants [who are women], they tell us right in the beginning that reconciliation is not an option for them now ... when they come to us.'

Analysis of ten case files revealed that all female applicants were asked to consider reconciling with their husbands, but this option was taken up by only two applicants.[12] Instead evidence from the case files suggests that the failure of family intervention and what is loosely termed as 'unofficial family mediation' simply convinced many applicants there was little point in trying to reconcile.

Extracts from case files next illustrates the extent to which this process of obtaining a divorce certificate can be challenged, contested and negotiated by the involvement of different parties.

In Case A, after a four-month period during which the reconciliation and investigation aspects of the process were completed, a note in the file by the religious scholar concluded that the husband should be given further time to try and resolve the marital problems and seek some form of mediation through his family or the local community. The female applicant was clearly angry with this decision and wrote to the council to protest at their decision:

> Dear Mr ...
> Further to our conversation of today I confirm that I am unhappy with the three month extension that you have granted to my husband in respect of my divorce case. As explained to you, from having been told the response of his letter he has approached neither my brother [n]or father in order to resolve the matter. No extended family or local community are involved, or have subsequently been involved. On the basis of his evidence in the letter I fail to understand why you have granted him thee months extension for resolving the matter since I do not wish for a reconciliation and neither is my husband pursuing for one.

The applicant was clearly frustrated by the religious scholar's repeated attempts to reconcile the parties.

In Case B the applicant agreed to a reconciliation meeting at the Shari'ah council on the understanding that her husband agreed to grant her a Muslim divorce. She wrote to the council:

> As confirmed by yourself I would like to exercise my option of a meeting being arranged with the appropriate parties concerned, and a resolution being reached with my husband signing the divorce.

She stated quite clearly that her husband should be made aware of her intentions. In this case the woman was very reluctant to enter into any form of mediation but felt she had little option but to do so. Her letter stated, 'if we are to proceed with a meeting, then for it to be mutually beneficial my husband should be made aware of the reasons for meeting in this way.'

Therefore the emphasis upon reconciliation can lead to the women developing strategies to participate in this process while keeping in mind their own objectives in obtaining a divorce certificate (see Chapter 6).

In Case C, a 27-year-old British Pakistani woman stated in her application that she had been forced into marriage with a distant relative. Both parties were British citizens and had been residing in Manchester. The marriage was not registered according to civil law but a religious ceremony had taken place (the reasons for this were not given) and the marriage was subsequently consummated. The marriage had lasted two and a half years and the couple had been 'separated' for four months prior to the application for a Muslim divorce. The reasons for the breakdown of marriage were given as

1. Deception – he lied about his qualifications and age
2. Consumption of alcohol
3. Gambling that led to debts
4. Cannot financially support his wife

On receipt of the application, a letter was sent to the applicant. It stated:

Dear Sister
Assalamu Alaykum
We acknowledge the receipt of your application form for an Islamic divorce. However we note that despite our clear guidelines that were sent to you with the application form, you have not sent a copy of your Islamic marriage certificate.

We request that you send this document to us immediately otherwise your case will be delayed. If you are not in possession of your Islamic marriage certificate, then please complete the enclosed declaration form and go to the solicitor or oath commissioner where you can countersign the declaration. Once this completed declaration has been received by us, we will initiate the proceedings for an Islamic divorce.

A week later the applicant sent a copy of the marriage certificate to the council. A note stated, 'divorce notice to be sent to C'. Each time a divorce notice was sent to the applicant's husband a short note was made in the case file. Over a period of eight weeks three divorce notices were sent.

No further action was taken on the case and in the next piece of correspondence the applicant queried the delay:

Dear Mr ...
I had lodged an application to your organisation since 22/05/01 for an Islamic divorce. I was advised it takes about six months. Unfortunately

I have so far not heard from your Council. Can you please update me on the proceedings?

Yours sincerely

There was no response to this letter; however, a few days later, a note in the case file stated that the applicant had again contacted the council by telephone. There were no notes regarding the nature of this telephone conversation but a note stated 'have informed client and Mr ... will call'. A further note dated a few days later stated that the council member had telephoned 'the petitioner' to explain that the delay had been caused by the husband failing to contact the council to put forward his version of events. During interview, Mohammed Raza elaborates on this point further, 'You see delays do occur and clients do get upset or think that we're not doing enough ... but we must try and get the husband's version of events. In Islam evidence is only accepted if it is thoroughly checked and verified. We're not in the business of handing out divorces to anyone who wants one.'

There was no further contact with the applicant until the council was satisfied that enough time had been given for the husband's response. Approximately two months later, the applicant was sent a letter informing her that the council had come to a decision:

Dear Sister
Assalamu Alaykum,
Your case has now been discussed by the members of the Shari'ah Council and in the light of the fact that your husband has refused to contact us we have decided to issue you with a divorce certificate.

A copy of this letter was sent to the applicant's husband and this impelled him to contact the council, indicating that he would be in touch shortly with 'details presenting my side of the case'. He was clearly upset that the council had issued the divorce certificate and claimed 'this is an injustice and against Islamic law'. The council responded with a letter to the applicant informing her that the divorce certificate had been suspended and that 'the council will reconsider and investigate some of the matters raised by Mr ... in this respect and then to deliberate over this case'. The scholars made clear that they were obliged to take this 'evidence' into account. The applicant then wrote to the council to express her shock and dismay at the suspension of the certificate explaining that

My husband has no intention of reconciling and no intention of putting forward his version of events. He is merely making my life more difficult. I want a divorce and he's trying to stop it from happening for no reason but to make things even worse.

The case file contains a letter dated two weeks later from the applicant's husband in which he refuted all the grounds for divorce but did not provide any 'evidence' to verify his claims. Instead he wrote, 'C is the one acting unreasonably, she has refused all offers of family mediation and has kept all the money given by my family'.

There are no other documents in the case file apart from a brief note, dated two months later which stated that a divorce certificate had eventually been granted but only once the applicant had agreed to return the dower.

Analysis of this one case file at the MLSC provides an interesting insight into the process of obtaining a divorce certificate for the female applicant. Despite the difficulties and delays, we can see ways in which the applicant engages with this process. Moreover, this analysis suggests that husbands may wish to delay the process and prevent divorce certificates from being issued. Consequently the councils issue a *khul* certificate which means that the applicant must give up her right of *mahr*, a problem identified by Pearl and Menski (1998).

The Islamic Shari'a Council (ISC), East London

From its offices in Leyton, East London, The Islamic Shari'a Council (ISC) is one of the most renowned Shari'ah councils in Britain. It was established in 1982 and draws its religious scholars from ten different religious organizations in Britain.[13] This council deals with over 350 cases a year and describes itself as a 'quasi-Islamic' court applying Islamic rules and principles in order to resolve matrimonial issues. It also encourages the active engagement of all Muslims within the local Muslim community by 'fostering and encouraging the practice of the Muslim faith according to the Qur'an and the Sunna' (1995, p. 3). The council is closely affiliated to the Islamic Cultural Centre based in Regent's Park Mosque in London.

As with the previous councils ISC adopts two key stages in the process of issuing a Muslim divorce certificate. First, it provides reconciliation and mediation sessions in the hope of reconciling the parties and should this fail then the council panel convenes to decide if a divorce certificate is to be issued.

With this council a religious scholar acts as the mediator and this can inevitably lead to some difficulties. The following excerpt is taken from observation notes of a mediation session involving a young woman and her estranged husband. While the facts of this case are applicable only to the parties involved, this particular case raises a number of tensions pertinent to many other cases.

In this case, Z was 30 years old and has been previously married. She described her marriage as 'forced' and had two young children aged six and four respectively. In 2002 she married W, a 35-year-old British Pakistani with the consent of her parents. Both parties were practising Muslims of British Pakistani descent and met via the 'Muslim Marriage Bureau', a service that brings together potential marriage partners.

This extract provides an example of an exchange between the religious scholar and the applicant.

Religious scholar:	In your application you said you had asked his family to intervene and help sort out the problems.
Applicant:	Yes, yes I did but they weren't interested ... not interested in sorting things out. They made things worse blaming me for everything. Everyone blames me.
Religious scholar:	Why is that?
Applicant:	It's him; he's so clever, so manipulative, he can make anyone believe anything. Really he can, even my parents are on his side. But they don't know what it's like to live with him; it's awful. I can't move out of the room without him asking where I'm going.
Religious scholar:	He doesn't trust you?
Applicant:	No.
Religious scholar:	Why not? Have you given him any cause not to trust you?
Applicant:	No, no ... I don't know why he's like that but he has so much *shak* [suspicion].
Religious scholar:	Did you fulfil your duty as a Muslim wife?
Applicant:	Yes, yes I did. Everything I did, I did for the family and him but still I'm not allowed to go out; if I work he tells me I'm flirting with the men; it's so difficult. I feel as though I can't breathe. I've tried, I really have.
Religious scholar:	Are there any specific reasons you want a divorce?
Applicant:	Yes, I can't stand it anymore. I can't stand him, he disgusts me and he hit me.

The applicant was informed that her husband was waiting outside and was keen to participate in the meeting with the hope of reconciling. The applicant became very upset repeating that she did not wish to meet with her husband nor seek any form of reconciliation. She explained this to the religious scholar, 'I don't want to meet with him, please don't make me. He frightens me.' Yet having been assured that she did not have to meet with her husband is she refused, she was also informed that under Muslim law the scholar had to consider the issue of reconciliation and mediation seriously. He explained, 'Look you don't have to sit next to him, you don't have to look at him but you have made a number of allegations and I need to confront him with these allegations and get his version of events.'

The religious scholar was therefore insistent that some of the allegations put forward would need to be further clarified in the presence of her husband to ensure all parties are treated fairly. She was very reluctant to do so but eventually agreed under the proviso that she did not have to be seated next to him and did not have to agree to his demands. The religious scholar accepted these conditions and argued that 'if he was to try and make up then we must ... it is our duty to try'. Once the husband joined the meeting, he refuted all the 'allegations' made by his wife and sought to reconcile. When asked whether he was violent towards his wife he replied, 'yes I admit it; once, just once. I didn't mean to hit her but she made me so angry.' The session ended with the applicant and her husband seeking to divorce.

What this session revealed is the dangers of imposing reconciliation upon vulnerable parties. In most cases the scholars seem aware that reconciliation is unlikely for the couple but it is pursued as an 'Islamic' duty which they must fulfil and in such circumstances female applicants can find themselves constrained by such conditions. This is discussed in more depth in the following chapters.

The council meeting

Once the scholars conclude that there is little hope of reconciliation the case file is sent to the council panel meeting for the scholars to consider whether a divorce certificate is to be issued, and if so which type of certificate.

The council panel, made up of six members and one 'administrator', meets each month in a seminar room at the Islamic Cultural Centre, Regent's Park Mosque. Each scholar is given a summary of the details of the cases to be discussed at the meeting. Observation of one Shari'ah council session revealed that up to 24 cases could be discussed in a single council meeting. The main issues for discussion were concerns over *mahr*, validity of an affidavit, evidence, access to children, forced marriage, domestic violence and mediation and reconciliation.

The most important factor in such council meetings was the presence of the parties and questioning why the husband had placed obstacles to the divorce. For example, in one case a husband stated that his wife has been influenced by 'women's organization, who are non-Muslim and who favour women to live by Western influences and standards'. The husband claimed that his wife's Western way of life was having a detrimental effect on their children's lives and he asked the council to intervene to convince her to adopt a more 'Islamic way of life' to enable them to reconcile. If they were to separate, he sought the intervention of the council to ensure that he was given access to his two children. The council members discussed at some length their concerns over whether they should intervene on matters concerning access to children. They were aware that the courts had issued an order stating that the husband must be allowed limited access (not specified) and that the wife must comply with this. The council scholars agreed they could not intervene and the husband should instead approach his solicitor to resolve the matter of access to his children. They did, however, agree to arrange a meeting with his wife to draw 'her attention to the fact that as a Muslim mother she has a duty to bring up her children as Muslims'.

On occasions when clients were requested to attend these meetings, the discussion focused on the possibility of reconciliation. The extract next illustrates this process. Both the applicant and her husband were required to attend the session. The applicant arrived with her father and sat facing the scholars facing her husband.

Religious scholar:	Why are you refusing to reconcile with your husband?
Applicant:	We've tried to make things work but it's not going to work. Things have gone too far and he hit's me; that's why he's not allowed to see the children.
Religious scholar:	Who advised you to restrict access to the children?
Applicant:	Social Services ... the children are scared of their father because of the violence. I have a duty to protect my children, that is my priority.
Religious scholar:	Is there anything else?
Applicant:	Yes, I also want you to know that he has never provided for his family. I have to work and pay all the bills and the mortgage; as a Muslim man he has a duty to provide for us but he never has.

The scholars then turned to her husband. He spoke in Urdu and argued that he did not want a divorce and claimed that his wife was simply too domineering and taunted him constantly, and must change her behaviour. He stated, 'She is a disgrace to what it means to be a Muslim woman and she has "shamed" not only herself but the whole family.'

When asked to respond to the allegations put by her husband the applicant argued that she had never committed adultery and he was lying and deceitful. She then produced bank statements which she argued proved that she paid the mortgage and she also produced 'police reports' which stated that the police had been called to their house during a domestic disturbance.

Another religious scholar then addressed them both and explained that though he was aware that there were many problems between them, as Muslims they both had a duty to try and reconcile for the sake of their children. Both the applicant and her husband remained silent. A third scholar then suggested that the three of them go into a separate room to discuss ways in which reconciliation could be achieved. The female applicant began to protest but the scholar intervened, saying, 'Just come and talk, it won't take long and if you've really made up your mind it won't affect it.' Unfortunately permission to observe this meeting was declined but in the meantime the other scholars discussed the issue with the applicant's father and asked him, 'why have you not attempted reconciliation?' He argued that he had done so several times over the past nine years but had now come to the conclusion that they must separate permanently in order for them both to be happy.

The religious scholar, the applicant and her husband re-emerged 45 minutes later. Nothing was said and both parties took their belongings and left. The scholar who was party to this meeting reported back to the council panel that they were unlikely to reconcile because it seemed 'the wife has made her mind up that she no longer wants to remain in the marriage'. The council decided to issue a religious divorce certificate but only when the civil procedure for divorce was finalized. A scholar stated, 'We're not in a rush, let them get on with it' and they agreed to write to the wife informing her of their decision.

Interestingly the scholars were very reluctant even at this stage to issue a divorce certificate in the hope that reconciliation could be achieved. In terms of mediation this space can also be used to negotiate *mahr* settlements for husbands. One of the scholars explained:

> There are cases where we have refused applications of divorce, where we have discovered the man is not to be blamed and he is offering everything to the woman so without any reason why is she asking for a divorce and there is principle in the Shari'ah for that as well and that is in that case you have to buy your divorce from your husband. The husband has got the right to put a price on it. We will negotiate the price where the woman is unable to prove anything against the husband. We would say to her, 'well look your case is a *khul'* then what are you doing, are you in a job, what is your bank balances, things like that. We will collect all the information and then we will call the husband and say, 'Look she doesn't like to live with you; you cannot force a woman against her wishes so you have to divorce her. This is the price in the opinion of the Shari'ah council; seems to be reasonable so accept it and divorce. You will get all the jewellery back, all the expensive items back; the money you have paid as *mahr*, it will be returned to you, plus £500, £1000 whatever is within the means.' We will offer that to the husband and if he is adamant, 'no, no even then I won't divorce', then he will lose everything and the Shari'ah Council will dissolve the marriage.

The Shari'ah Court of the UK (SCUK), North London

The Shari'ah Court of the UK is based in Tottenham, North London and was set up in 1992. It is headed by a group of local imams to advise Muslims on marital disputes from an Islamic perspective. The council panel comprises one imam, a Muslim solicitor and three male witnesses from the local mosque who meet with new and existing clients every week. All meetings with clients are run on an appointments system and an average of four cases are discussed at any one session. The council is open three days a week, from Tuesday until Thursday between 11 a.m. and 2 p.m., and the staff work on a voluntary basis.

The process of mediation and reconciliation at the SCUK rests primarily upon the participation of family members, including those who may have arranged the marriage. In these terms, the particular contribution of the 'family' underlies the paradigm upon which reconciliation and mediation is sought. During interview Sheikh Abdullah explained, 'In Islam, marriage is the foundation of the Muslim family and we recognize that for the marriage to succeed the family plays a vital role. To that end yes, we actively seek the involvement of family members.'

Observation identified two key features to this process. First, there was a pervasive view that marital disputes could not be resolved without the intervention of parents and possibly other family members. Parental consent was considered vital to the happiness of the married couple and consequently, parents were invited to participate in the process of dispute resolution. Second, all reconciliation sessions were conducted in the open involving all the parties with little, if any, opportunity for the female applicants to discuss any issues in private.

The religious scholar's position was observed to be one of central control in the process. As an individual, he 'presided' over all sessions and all applicants were expected to attend a minimum of three sessions before a decision on whether to issue a divorce certificate was made. In doing so, this discourse engaged implicitly in a nostalgic appeal to the past, to a situation where Islam, community and Islamic values provided the solution to the perceived increase in marital disputes. The scholar used this space to develop a critique of Western mass culture and the modern forms of consumerism to challenge the perceived fragmentation of Muslim belief and practice in the West. More precisely the views of the scholar are based upon a strict distinction between the sacred and profane that reflects the specific patterns of dispute resolution. Muslim women are associated with being mothers, wives and daughters, to be protected and cherished, so an applicant's desire to divorce is conceptualized as threatening the stability and continuity of the traditional Muslim family.

During each session, a 'Muslim solicitor' and three male witnesses accompanied the scholar. Though rarely at the forefront of the discussions, they seemed to occupy a strategic, symbolic importance in fulfilling the requirements of Islamic law whereby it is deemed that the evidence of Muslim women must be verified in the presence of three male witnesses. This approach, which hinges upon a contested understanding of the rules of evidence in Islamic law, embodies both a nostalgic return to traditional Islam and illustrates the tension between an essentialized, fixed representation of Muslim women and the complex realities of their lives.

These tensions were captured during observation of six sessions. The sessions were all conducted in English and lasted approximately 35 minutes. Twelve cases were described by scholars as 'ongoing' and five new cases were opened and discussed. Upon arrival each applicant was asked a series of questions to determine why a divorce certificate was being sought. Some women obviously welcomed the opportunity to explain their situation.

For example, 26-year-old Rizwana was seeking a divorce after just ten months of marriage. She was accompanied by her father and brother and explained she had been forced into marriage against her will. She was articulate and passionate when detailing the reasons for the breakdown in her marriage. She explained, 'I was against getting married from the beginning but I didn't want to go against my parents' wishes so I did what I thought was right. I married him. But he couldn't cope with the responsibility of being married and my parents agree we should get divorced.'

Interestingly the most important dynamic in this process was the relationship between the scholar and male members of the applicant's family. The scholar did not address female applicants directly and instead used the medium of male family members to communicate with them. This drew attention to the fact that women occupied a very marginalized role in the whole process and by contrast, questions were directed at men, all of whom were expected to contribute to the process.

Of the new applicants, four women had not registered their marriages according to civil law and this produced discussion on the legitimacy of a Muslim marriage in Britain. A large number of women complained they had been forced into marriage and the marriages had not been registered by their husbands to ensure that they had no legal protection should the marriage end. In all cases the scholar engaged in lengthy discussions over what he described as the 'Muslim principle' to reconcile and explained that with enough influence from male members of the applicant's family the parties could be successfully reconciled. At the end of first session, an order was issued in all the cases for the applicants' husbands to attend the next session so that the process of reconciliation could begin. This 'order' was sent to the husband. In cases where his whereabouts were not known the sessions were postponed indefinitely so that there was an opportunity to locate him.

As a strategy to encourage the individuals to reconcile, family members were also encouraged to attend the sessions. If the husband refused to attend or was unavailable, he was asked to provide a male witness who could bear witness to the fairness of the proceedings. Often the sessions were delayed if one male witness was unable to attend. All the female applicants were asked to produce a written submission of their claims prior to the second session and this provided the basis for the reconciliation. Interestingly, in the second and third sessions a large number of the husbands did attend the reconciliation sessions. Out of a total of 12 cases, seven husbands attended the sessions.

The concept of reconciliation sat uncomfortably with this process of resolving disputes. This space was male dominated with the presence of male family members, male witnesses and the male 'judge'. It is within this context that negotiations took place and were based on gendered constructions of Muslim identity and female responsibility. Reconciliation was defined primarily as the acceptance of 'Islamic moral values' by the female applicants and was based on the preservation of the Muslim family whereas the failure to reconcile was equated with female disobedience. For example, in a number of cases where the applicants were accompanied by parents, the judge laid the blame for the breakdown of marriage on the women, even in cases where they had been forced into marriage. He went on to explain, 'Most women need guidance when marrying, even if they are over the age of consent; so it's the duty of parents to make that decision for them.'

This study reveals the inherent contradictions and tensions in this process of dispute resolution. The process is embedded in 'absolute relativism' (Frow, 1995, p. 57) and based upon an essentialist model of Muslim community as an insider/outsider. In the identity of Muslim women is ascribed to share cultural understandings and there is little room for challenging this cultural and religious order.

During the observed sessions, Sheikh Abdullah also revealed that on a number of occasions social workers had requested to attend the Shari'ah council sessions to 'understand Islam particularly when there are conflicts over access to children'. This issue was not addressed in this study, but if this is the case then it certainly points to the dangers of practitioners using this space to gain an understanding of Islam that may influence or determine issues of access to children. What could be at stake is both the welfare of the children and the women applicants as discussed in later chapters of this book.

Enforceability of divorce certificates?

The issue of enforceability of Muslim divorce certificates in English law was not addressed in this study. However, as discussed in this chapter, the councils actively sought to avoid any conflict with civil law or procedure in matters of family law and the respondents stated that certificates were issued for the personal use of applicants and not viewed as legal documents to be recognized under English law. The scholars did report that there were no community mechanisms or sanctions in place to enforce the terms of the divorce and this was left to the goodwill of the parties concerned.

6
Personal Experiences of Marriage

Marriage, in this study, is categorized in the traditional three-tier approach; 'arranged', 'own-choice' and 'forced' marriage.[1] The data revealed that 13 interviewees defined their marriages as 'arranged' marriages, eight had chosen their own spouses (but with the approval of their families) and four had been 'forced' into marriage.[2] However, given the problematic nature of what is understood as consent in marriage and the subtle and complex interconnections between these categories, such classifications of marriage must be used with caution.

It is interesting to note that while the analysis between the types of marriage and the heterogeneous nature of this group of women revealed a number of commonalities regarding attitudes and expectations of marriage, differences also emerged in relation to the age, generation, education and class background of the interviewees. Most women in this study considered marriage and having children as a natural course of events but this was neither universally nor uncritically accepted. In fact, interview data revealed that discussion about the reasons to marry centred upon personal choice, religious considerations and family expectations with strong affirmations of the importance of their consent to the marriage.

Reasons for marriage

The reasons given by the women for their decision to marry ranged from age, family expectations, 'family pressure', gaining independence to a reluctance to conduct sexual relationships outside of marriage. Perhaps unsurprisingly, parents and the wider family played an important role in the process of decision-making and to this end family concerns concentrated on what was considered the appropriate age for the women to marry to the family acceptance of a personal choice of spouse. Traditionally, a woman is considered of marriageable age from her late teens until her mid-20s (Anwar, 1998; Bhopal, 1998) but, of course, this range varied considerably within the sample and interestingly reflected generation, age and class differences.

For example, the younger women reported they had been expected to marry between the ages of 24 to 28 years whereas older women had married between the ages of 18 to 22 years. There was no discernible difference between the two groups of women from Punjabi and Azad Kashmiri backgrounds as they reported similar reasons for marriage.

> I was brought up knowing that I would have to be married by the time I was 18. That's just the way it went back then. Marriage is important to Muslim families and young girls are taught this at a young age but I think most wait until they're a little older these days.
>
> Anisa (Bradford)

> I don't believe it's just an Asian thing because women from all backgrounds face the pressure to get married or have to consider getting married. But in our communities, marriage carries the added burden of *izzat* and so there's always some pressure.
>
> Hina (London)

> You can talk to lots of Asian girls at college and they'll all tell you the same, going to college is really important because it gives us a few more years of not having to get married; that's what I did.
>
> Shabana (London)

> Well the thing about marriages and particularly perhaps Pakistani marriages is that there is something that is set in motion that happens when you are fairly young, perhaps 12, 13 and this process starts to happen and you're an incidental part of it.
>
> Yasmin (London)

The data also revealed the personal expectations the women attached to marriage and the bargaining strategies that some women adopted in their attempt to delay the marriage. Other factors such as age and their position in the family (e.g. being the eldest or the youngest sibling) revealed different expectations of marriage.

> I was the eldest and I was expected to get married. It sounds strange but I knew I had to because of the *izzat* thing and that it probably wouldn't be as bad for my sisters.
>
> Noreen (Birmingham)

> I was 29 and was getting a lot of pressure from my parents to get married. I was promised that I would be made the 'senior sister-in-law' and we thought of this as a big honour.
>
> Farah (London)

For parents in particular age signified the best chances of their daughters' prospects to marry. Marriage can therefore be seen as part of a longer-term strategy by family members to fulfil familial obligations while upholding wider kinship group expectations and seeking to satisfy the needs of their daughters. As Berger points out,

> Individuals do not create or contest meaning as unified, autonomous subjects from an essential human core, but always from already being positioned in several discourses. This does not mean that discourses are constructed outside of actual relations and then placed upon passive individuals. The meanings constructed by discourses are in fact created, used and contested by all participants who are in different ways in them. Even members of strongly marginalized groups are not simply passive recipients of a dominant discursive meaning about them.
>
> (2002, p. 181)

In this way the meanings attributed to marriage can be understood as part of complex social and cultural formations that cut across many different social, cultural, religious and personal identities.

Arranged marriage

The arranged marriage process can be measured against a set of variables such as individual agency, the process of negotiation, dialogue and type of family intervention which for many can produce a positive outcome. In the most 'straightforward' arranged marriages, the question of power, authority, coercion and, most importantly, consent remain paramount as a basis for negotiations. In this way, the arranged marriage process often occupies a difficult space between the consensual participation of both parties and family members and the subtle forms of coercion and pressure applied by family members in order for the individual to comply with expectations of marriage. In their research, Stopes-Roe and Cochrane (1999, p. 95) construct a typology of arranged marriages that illustrate the subtle differences inherent within the arranged marriage process and the conceptual problems in clearly demarcating the forced marriage process from the arranged marriage process. They categorize the types of arranged marriage in three ways: the 'traditional pattern', the 'modified traditional pattern' and the 'co-operative traditional pattern' and point to the underlying tensions of power, dialogue, consent and coercion between all three categories. Furthermore the values of kinship, matrilineal networks and *biraderi* which often underpin family and community structures can result in conflicts between Western ideas of marriage based on individual choice of marriage parties and South Asian customs of marriage based upon family involvement and parental consent.

Bhopal argues that there are profound differences between arranged marriages and Western-inspired notions of marriage, 'the most significant being, in the West individuals retain the right to autonomy and personal responsibility for their lives. For South Asians, a lower age of marriage is desirable and customary since individuals have no need for courtship patterns' (Bhopal, 1999, p. 59).[3] This way of understanding the arranged marriage process can be useful as it provides an insight in the different normative criteria attached to the arranged marriage process. Such a view lies at the paradox of the arranged marriage process whereby an individual's decision to participate in this process may be influenced by the notions of duty, family honour, respect and family expectations. However, it is also important to note that such a paradigmatic approach is unlikely to tease out the tensions and contradictions inherent in the arranged marriage process. Because of issues of honour, conflict, loyalty and belonging in families, marriage cannot be simply understood in an either/or deterministic way.

Feminist scholars have long pointed to the regulatory powers of family and the inequities found in the family structure which privilege male interests and power (O'Donovan, 1985, p. 57). In this study, a number of women reported that due to the unequal power relations in the family, male members of the family were not only given greater choice of marriage partner but also given greater flexibility over when to marry. As Sameena (London) explained,

> It's different for men; they don't have to start thinking about marriage until a lot later. But for us it's different. Once you're at college, that's it; the family starts talking about when you should get married. It doesn't mean you have to get married straight away but it's just that they start talking about it.

Therefore unequal social relations and power, within the family and household, hierarchically distributed according to age, position and sex permeate the traditional Asian family structure. For Anwar (1998, p. 32) such social relations remain embedded within notions of 'family respect', 'prestige' and 'honour' that together act as mechanisms to keep the family structure intact. Yet the multifaceted, heterogeneous nature of families also reveals that these understandings of respect and honour are likely to throw up a wide range of meanings based upon personalized and subjective experiences of marriage. As Rose points out, 'Characterization of the family as a site of family subordination, however accurate, fails to capture the complexity of familial powers, of the duties, obligations, pains and pleasures which have been constituted through the familialization of the subjectivities of both women and men' (1987, p. 74).

In this study the term 'family expectations' cropped up in 22 interviews and was used to describe family relationships with parents and elder members of the wider family. It was also used to discuss restrictions imposed upon the women and their choice of marriage partner and notions of honour – *izzat*. Anthias and Yuval-Davis point out that the concept of family honour relates to rules regulating sexuality, marriage and the family, and 'communal boundaries often use differences in the way women are socially constructed as markers' (1992, p. 114). Such markers include women as the natural preservers of 'family honour'.

Wilson (1978, p. 5) describes *izzat* as 'essentially male but it is women's lives and actions which affect it most. A woman can have izzat but it is not her own, it is her husband's or father's. Her izzat is a reflection of the male pride of the family as a whole. [What is more] saving her izzat [and through that their own izzat] is perhaps the greatest responsibility for her parents or guardian.' In this way the role of women as preservers of family honour means that only they can increase the honour of the family through obedience and only they can 'lose it' and thus shame the family. This notion of 'family honour' within South Asian communities has therefore been described as a process used to control female sexuality through restriction of movement (Anthias, 1992; Afshar, 1994; Bhopal, 1999). In her study of the structure of female authority within Pakistani households in West Yorkshire, Afshar points out that the significance of *izzat* is the way in which women are expected to conduct themselves both in the private and public spheres. As Anthias points out, 'A significant element is to be able to control the behaviour of the women in the family, both wives and daughters, for any transgression by them is an imputation of a failure to exercise proper patriarchal control' (1992, p. 78). Yet the way in which 'family honour' operates within the family, home and community context(s) must also be understood in relation to the specific family and community context(s) to which the women belong. Nevertheless, as existing literature suggests, the significance of family honour to the marriage process raises fundamental questions of human rights and the right to choose a marriage partner based on personal choice, consent and autonomy. It also raises conceptual problems of what we understand as an arranged, forced and own-choice marriage with the issues of consent and coercion being at the forefront of different interpretations.

In this study the women recognized that their marriages served an important function to preserve familial and kinship ties vis-à-vis relationships with their spouse and newfound families. But perhaps the most salient finding was not only that the women were critically aware of the ways 'family honour' affected their choice of marriage partner but the shifting and entangled definitions of 'family honour' and its centrality to the marriage process.

> Women of our mothers' background were not in a position to challenge what was going on in terms of *izzat*, shutting up and staying quiet. I think one of the things we're doing is redefining what *izzat* means. We're

claiming it back; *izzat* is our own. I don't agree that *izzat* is keeping male honour in the family. I think that's total rubbish. We all have *izzat*. Men have *izzat* and they're responsible for it; it doesn't mean they can go out and have girlfriends and drink and gamble and do what they want. I think it's blown out of proportion by Western writers.

Yasmin (London)

I suppose me getting married was important for my parents, because of the honour thing ... but don't we all have this honour? I just sometimes worry that it's all exaggerated – you know the way *izzat* controls every-thing. Well it doesn't, not in my experience anyway.

Shaheen (London)

The meaning of honour within the family context illustrates the extent to which tensions persist. As Welchman and Hossain (2005) point out the effects of family honour that can at times often only be understood in rela-tion to the highly specific and individualized contexts to which women belong.

In this study the significance of family honour to the marriage process raises the question of the extent to which the women's decision to marry was contingent upon family honour, parental consent and belonging. The data that follows produces some interesting narratives on the experiences of the women while simultaneously drawing our attention to the fragmented, shifting and highly individualized meanings the women attached to the notion of 'honour'.

For example, a number of women expressed complete satisfaction with the arranged marriage process, describing it as an 'equal' process for all participants, including family members. For Fauzia (Birmingham), despite considerable uncertainty about her prospective husband, the shared values of family, cultural norms and religious values together enabled her to par-ticipate in a process that had been largely organized by her family. A friend of the family had suggested a possible suitor to her parents, who had given their permission for the couple to be introduced and then meet separately, but with the consent of both families. Fauzia had not considered herself to be peripheral to the process of arranging her marriage.

He was from a middle-class family. He was presented as a 'suitable match' and it was agreed we would have chaperoned meetings with a view to marriage. They were very well educated and I thought this was an envi-ronment that I would feel comfortable [in]. I wanted to keep my parents involved as much as possible so that we could make the decision together as a family so that they know what's going on and I feel open enough to tell them what's going on with me. And also at the back of my mind if anything goes wrong, you know, no one can point the finger at me and say, 'Well, you went out with him alone, why didn't you find out?' At least this way I felt I was being protected should anything ever happen in the future and that my parents would always be there. So I was very careful about that.

Such strategies therefore had meant a shift in the responsibility of finding a suitable marriage partner to her parents which in turn had helped to strengthen her position in the arranged marriage process. She was aware, however, that the process was accompanied by some contradictions.

The only problem I felt a little uncomfortable about was the fact that they weren't very religious, but I thought that's OK because well I don't see myself as too religious. I mean I don't pray five times a day and I don't wear the *hijab*. I'll do other things but not those things, so I thought there really won't be a problem.

Some women therefore participated willingly in the arranged marriage process and described being empowered by this process which also afforded protection against any unwanted interest and personal intrusion. In this way, such women described that they were able to successfully navigate the competing demands that had been placed upon them.

The important thing for me was that my parents listened to me. If I didn't like him, you know, if we didn't have anything in common, they did understand and we moved on. For me that's what an arranged marriage is – making sure your parents understand what their role is in the whole thing, though sometimes we all get it wrong (laughs).

Anisa (London)

Yet the nature of family involvement in the arranged marriage process varied in the sample, with issues of consent to marry and choice of marriage partner at the forefront of discussions. The ambivalence described by some women regarding their decision to marry also reflects the contradictions in categories such as arranged, own choice and forced marriages. For example, some women found it difficult to delineate any differences between the categories whereas other women were keen to stress the differences and point to their participation in the process.

Having an arranged marriage was the only option for me and I never thought about challenging my parents. Getting married the way I got married was like for ... well for keeping the family together, you're meant to be keeping the ties together. It's meant to be like this, you know some sort of guarantee that if anything goes wrong, then you've got the family there to help sort things out. Yeah, I'd have another arranged marriage.

Shazia (London)

The family is my bedrock; without them you don't amount to much. I mean it, I really do ... it's the people in the world that care for you, that you know will always be there for you.

Nasima (London)

Such congruent findings are likely, therefore, to throw up a wide range of questions relating to issues of personal decision-making and individual autonomy in the arranged marriage process. For Sameena (London), marriage was based upon the values of family loyalty and respect.

My sisters all had arranged marriages ... we all did, our parents used to say that we had to marry someone in the family, because an outsider couldn't fit in and they would cause trouble...It wasn't like people sat me down and said you should get married. I think what happened is that my family didn't think I was going to have a career, so therefore what else is there to do and as long as I'm at home, the family home, I'm their responsibility, you know, in terms honour and *izzat*.

Such a view lies at the paradox in the arranged marriage process whereby an individual's decision to participate in the process maybe heavily influenced by notions of duty, family honour, respect and family expectations while choosing to participate in the arranged marriage process. In this way loyalty to parents and the wider family appears to lead some women to ignore what may seem like obvious difficulties inherent in this process of marriage.

I'm sure there was times [*sic*] when I thought, 'Do I really want this?' But what stopped me was thinking, 'Well, I'm sure it's going to work out because we're both getting married for the same reasons, we both know what it's all about.' Well, that's what I thought.

Naheed (London)

In her research, Bhopal (1999) found little evidence that challenged the traditional practice of arranged marriages[4] in South Asian households and suggests that due to the fact that women are accorded less power within the family and household, the arranged marriage process further disadvantages them and creates what she describes as a 'private patriarchy' (p. 67). This explanation points to the endemic barriers experienced by women that can restrict their participation and their ability to negotiate favourable outcomes in the arranged marriage process. Many women therefore are simply unable to develop strategies to challenge parental authority and are given little space in which to instigate any real change in the marriage process. As Raheela (London) explained:

> It was more my uncles and aunts and the elders of my family that got together and they chose a good family in Pakistan, and they approached my parents, not me, and there was a family conference, and at some point I was told about this process happening and I was allowed to say yes or no.

At the same time other women were able to negotiate and then renegotiate over a period of time the terms of their participation in the arranged marriage process. Therefore a dialectical process that involves parents and family members on the one hand and prospective marriage partners on the other in practice defines the boundaries of the marriage process. As Salma (Bradford) explained:

> My parents did the hunting down if I can call it that. I mean they looked out for people they thought were suitable, people that they thought I would get on with and I was OK with that. It was always understood that they would do that. I was told of certain people and I was allowed to meet with them if I wanted to. So you see it wasn't forced or anything ... I did my bit too.

Some women, therefore, clearly felt that parental support and involvement could act as a mechanism upon which potential partners were viewed and this relationship was based upon evolving and dynamic reciprocal values of family and religious commitments.

Bradby (1999, p. 157) found that young Pakistani women developed tactical strategies to delay marriage and were able to negotiate the age they should marry if they entered into higher and further education. According to Butler, by preventing their behaviour from coming to the attention of their parents, it was possible for young women to delay marriage and engage in activities deemed questionable by families (1999, p. 134).

This data therefore reveals the diversity of women's experiences in the arranged marriage process and the multiple meanings the women attached to their personal understandings of the arranged marriage process. Interestingly, the women shifted the emphasis away from understanding the arranged marriage process as part of simple notions of paternal control and coercion to ideas of family commitment, mutual inter-dependence, compromise and negotiation. In doing so, they were able to reconceptualize the arranged marriages process to one based upon personal experience and individual choice. Keeping our minds open to these more complex understandings, therefore, allows a more nuanced understanding of the arranged marriage process but recognizes that for some women it quite obviously remains a very difficult and protracted process.

Forced marriage

In this study four women reported they had been forced into marriage. In each case the women were painfully aware of family demands to marry imposed upon then and for a multitude of reasons were less able to resist the pressures. For example, Zareena (Bradford) expressed regret that she had eventually agreed to her parents 'wishes' to marry a distant cousin in Pakistan, despite her vociferous opposition to their choice of marriage partner. She conceded that these protests had not been enough to challenge parental authority and in particular her father's authority in the household which had left her with little option but to accept the marriage.

Given the complexities of how notions of family honour, duty and respect underpin the marriage process, it is not surprising that some women regard this as the only option in order to fulfil family demands.

Most recently, in Britain we have seen a shift in focus in challenging the practice of forced marriages under the rubric of combating 'honour crimes'. Hossain and Welchman describe an honour crime as 'patterns of conduct cutting across communities, cultures, religions and nations manifested in a range of forms of violence directed, in the majority of cases, against women, including murder ("honour killings") and forced marriage' (2005, p. 2).[5]

The issue of forced marriage is being addressed at a national and increasingly international level.[6] In Britain the murders of young women who had been killed for refusing to marry[7] has mobilized a 'multi-agency' approach in tackling the problem. A forced marriage has been described as 'a marriage without the full and free consent of both parties' and 'where people are coerced into a marriage against their will and under duress' (Welchman and Hossain 2005, p.5). Existing provisions in civil and criminal legislation prohibit the practice of forced marriage. For example, the Marriage Act 1949 and the Matrimonial Causes Act 1973 govern the law on the validity of marriages in England and Wales. A forced marriage can be made null and be deemed voidable (civil proceedings for nullity) according to section 12c of the Matrimonial Causes Act 1973 which states that a marriage shall be voidable if 'either party to the marriage did not validly consent to it, whether in consequence of duress, in marriage mistake, unsoundness of mind or otherwise'. The issue of duress has also been extensively addressed by the courts. In *Hirani* v. *Hirani* (1982) (4 FLR 232) the test of duress for these purposes was whether the mind of the applicant (the victim) had been overborne howsoever that was caused.[8] Under criminal law, although there is no specific offence of forced marriage, perpetrators can however be prosecuted for a range of offences, including kidnapping, child abduction, false imprisonment, assault and battery, blackmail and threats to kill.[9] In June 2012 after a six month consultation process the Home Office announced that new legislation is to be put forward to Parliament in 2013 making forced marriage a criminal offence as discussed later.[10]

Interestingly, however, there remains little clarity over the meaning of a forced marriage, which has led to criticisms that existing approaches are ineffective. For example, a study on forced marriage by the Council of Europe (2005, p. 5) described it as 'an umbrella term covering marriage as slavery, arranged marriage, traditional marriage, marriage for reasons of custom, expediency or perceived respectability, child marriage, early marriage, fictitious, bogus or sham marriage, marriage of convenience, unconsummated marriage, putative marriage, marriage to acquire nationality and undesirable marriage – in all of which the concept of consent to marriage is at issue'. This definition categorizes a wide range of practices as amounting to forced marriage. In Britain, however, there has been a deliberate initiative to draw a clear distinction between an arranged and a forced marriage in order to avoid labelling all arranged marriages as forced marriages. For example, the Home office report, *Forced Marriage: A Wrong not a Right* (1999, p. 3) states, 'Forced marriages are not arranged marriages. In an arranged marriage the family will take the lead in arranging the match but the couples have a choice as to whether to proceed. In a forced marriage there is no choice.' Yet most commentators also readily accept that there is a narrow distinction between a forced and an arranged marriage based on difficult issues concerning consent.

There have been a number of UK initiatives on forced marriages. In 1999 a working group on forced marriage was set up by the Home Secretary to investigate the extent to which forced marriage was practiced in England and Wales. In the same year the Community Liaison Unit was set up by the Foreign and Commonwealth Office (FCO) which was given the responsibility of dealing with the international dimension of forced marriages (see further). In 2000 the report *A Choice by Right* was published by the working group and this report focused on clarifying the arranged/forced marriage distinction and providing clear guidelines to public bodies such as the police, schools and social services as to what can be deemed a forced marriage. In 2002, police guidelines were issued by the Association of Chief Police Officers to better equip members of the police force in dealing with forced marriages (see Phillips and Dustin, 2004, p. 535). Each of these initiatives has focused on the option of exit for vulnerable women forced into marriage. Community attempts to persuade the state to adopt a dialogue-centred approach via the use of mediation services have met with resistance from women's organizations.[11] It is argued that in practice, women's attempts to reconcile with families can lead to undue levels of social pressure to reconcile with families in the face of a continued threat of being forced into marriage.

In September 1999 the FCO and the Home Office published a consultation document titled *Forced Marriage: A Wrong not a Right*, the aim of which was to consider whether a specific offence on forced marriage would help the state combat its practice. This consultation invited responses from various community and women's groups as well as faith organizations and victims of forced marriage in an attempt to provide a comprehensive analysis of the practice of forced marriage and to consider whether the law provides adequate protection or whether there was a need to introduce a specific criminal offence on forced marriage. This culminated in the introduction of the Forced Marriage (Civil Remedies) Protection Act 2007 which came into force in autumn 2008. The Act inserts a new part 4A into the Family Law Act 1996, creating a new Forced Marriage Protection Order or FMPO (part 4A is found in ss63a-s63). The High Court or a County Court can make an FMPO to protect a woman from being forced into a marriage, from any attempt to be forced into a marriage or to protect a person who has already been forced into a marriage. The courts are given wide discretion and the orders can contain any prohibitions, restrictions or requirements that the courts deem appropriate. An application can be made by a woman, a third party or another person who is given leave by the court to make an application. In this respect, the order differs substantially from other orders such as occupation orders or non-molestation orders as only the party wishing protection can make these orders and the orders are not restricted to associated persons. Therefore, from the outset, the government had aimed not to offend communities who partake in the cultural practice of arranged marriage. However, more recently this approach has been challenged. First, in June 2011 Prime Minister David Cameron announced a consultation on making forced marriage a criminal offence. Second, the issue of transnational marriage and prohibition of forced marriages have been challenged by the Supreme Court. In the Quila and Bibi cases (2010 EWCA Civ 1482; 2009 EWHC Admin 3189) the court ruled that the government's ban on non-EU spouses under the age of 21 from entering the country was an unlawful interference into the couples right to family life under Article 8 of the Human Rights Act 1998. As mentioned earlier the government is due to criminalise forced marriage with a draft bill due to be put to Parliament in 2013. There remains however much contention over the criminalisation of forced marriage with critics pointing out that it may not only drive the practice underground and also have the unintended consequence of criminalising whole communities (See Gill 2012).

In their study of UK initiatives to combat forced marriage, Phillips and Dustin (2004) point to three broad solutions: regulation, dialogue and exit, of which the British state has favoured the option of exit. This approach seeks to provide vulnerable young women with the support, protection and resources to exit families and local communities who may be instigating and colluding in a forced marriage. Such an approach is based upon the principle of protecting the rights of vulnerable women, rather than challenging internal cultural values. Phillips and Dustin point out, however, that given the complexities of family honour, duty and respect coupled with notions of belonging in the family home and local community, women forced into marriage are unlikely to exercise the 'exit option' due to the psychological effects of being ostracized and alienated from family and local communities. This finding was confirmed in the study particularly among younger women anxious about the consequences their exit from the family may have upon their younger siblings.

> The only girls that I knew who had left the community were brought back the next day and married off. That was my only experience of women leaving the community ... they probably went to Birmingham town centre or something and they were brought back ... so I didn't particularly want any of that.
>
> Sadia (Birmingham)

Even when some women did consider the option of exit and leaving the family home, concerns of being marginalized from their local community and their families prevented them from doing so.

> I couldn't just leave; I know everyone would turn their backs on me and anyway where would I have to go? I do feel constrained at home but I know being on the outside isn't all it's made up to be. I know some girls who've run away and they're really alone and with no support. I couldn't do that because ... well I just couldn't live that way.
>
> Nighat (London)

Attitudes to leaving were therefore circumscribed by belonging to close-knit communities where conformity and pressure to comply remain commonplace. Furthermore the personal and emotional costs of leaving the family household and community were calculated as simply being too high. The potential loss of family honour had compelled these women to comply with the marriage.

In this study the women forced into marriage described threats by family members to disown them to accusations by family members of disloyalty and a perception by family members that their actions represented a challenge to parental authority and control. None of the women reported incidences of physical abuse but it is quite possible that they were simply unwilling to divulge such personal details. Simultaneously, a number of women reported that they had in fact little choice but to agree to the marriage:

> I didn't care what they [extended family and community] thought of me, I really didn't, but it's my parents ... my parents will suffer so I had to think of what the community thinks for their sake.
>
> Shazia (London)

Of the women forced into marriage in Pakistan, little description was given of the marriage ceremonies and instead discussion focused on their confusion about the validity of the marriages and questions surrounding whether they could use immigration rules to prevent unwanted spouses from entering into Britain.

> I was taken to Pakistan, without knowing I'd be forced into marriage. I honestly thought we were going on holiday. Anyway I really don't want to go into it but just to say that I've written to immigration to tell them not to let him in.
>
> Zareena (Bradford)

Paradoxically, for some of the women who had been forced into marriage, the continued intervention of family and, in particular, parents remained vital to them in their future plans to remarry.

'Own choice'/love marriages

Of the sample, eight women had chosen their own spouses but even in these cases the women had only gone ahead with the marriage once the consent with family members had been obtained. As already noted, due to the difficulties in conceptualizing issues of choice and individual decision-making in the arranged/forced marriage spectrum, the interviews with this category of women yielded considerable discussion on parental consent, family involvement and community reaction to the choice of marriage partner. Unsurprisingly perhaps, parental consent remained a crucial factor in the women's decision in whether or not to proceed with the marriage.

Typically the women who chose their own husbands adopted strategies in order to gain parental approval. As Farhana (London) explained:

> I first told him [her father] about Naveed and he just mumbled something about 'keeping my honour' and that was it. He just expected me to be discreet; he just didn't want to think about what I might be doing.

Aside from parental consent, these women had also been concerned about the possible detrimental effects of their decision to marry upon their younger siblings:

> I did understand where my parents were coming from because in Asian communities it's the norm to marry in your own *biraderi* and I knew my parents were going to get a lot of stick from the community.
>
> Hina (Birmingham)

The capacity of the family therefore to encourage and consent to 'own choice'/love marriages remained an important factor and to a large extent dominated the decision-making process. This may mean that the outcome for the women and their decision to marry are somewhat conditioned by relations of parent and family involvement. However, by increasing the participation of the family in the marriage process, the women were also able to stimulate conversation, dialogue and discussion with family members and have a real influence on parental consent to go ahead with the marriage and prove their choice of marriage partner. However, invariably for those women who were now in the midst of divorce proceedings, their choice of marriage partner and decision to marry had since become a source of regret.

> I should have listened to them; I know that I made a mistake. I mean it's not as if they were forcing me to get married. I just thought he was the right person.
>
> Sadia (Birmingham)

The experience of Muslim marriage, the *nikah*

Interview data revealed that issues of family honour, parental authority and consent in marriage were discussed within an Islamic context to encourage solutions. For example, all the women described Islam as empowering and some of the younger women interviewed felt that codes of behaviour explicit within the Qur'an had been distorted by male figures of authority in order to impose greater restrictions upon their freedom and autonomy. In her research with Pakistani Muslim women in West Yorkshire, found that many young Muslim women are choosing to adopt the Islamic identity, for example, by donning the headscarf as part of a universalist Islamic identity in order to assert their rights afforded to them in Islam. She points out, 'Amongst Muslims, women have traditionally been the appointed site of familial honour and shame and the representatives of the public face of the society's apparent commitment to its faith. Thus Muslim women are both the guardians and the guarded'.

Consequently Islam and personal faith played a key role in the decision-making process 'insofar as faith is in accordance with right reason'. A number of women, for example, explained that they acted in accordance with their faith when opposing forced marriages as their faith encouraged and expected their full participation in the marriage process. Allying themselves to Islamic principles pertaining to marriage allowed these women a greater role in the decision-making process. Muslim feminist scholars point out that although women are deemed the custodians of the religion it has been men who have interpreted the norms and values of Islam. As Afshar explains, 'Women, whether they have wished it or not, have been required to reflect the religious commitment of the group in their attire and behaviour as well as in most aspects of their lives' (1989, p. 129). This has been a problematic relationship where over time women have had to negotiate their position in relation to the patriarchal environment that they find themselves in (Kandiyoti, 2007). The following extracts illustrate some of these dilemmas.

It took me a long time to realize that in Islam marriage is based on mutual consent, love and trust and when I'd decided that I wasn't going to take the abuse any more I took this to my parents. Of course they refused to speak to me but in my heart I know that I'm doing nothing wrong because it was wrong in the first place ... it should never have happened.

Yasmin (London)

As a Muslim I understand the importance of honour ... I don't accept that this honour means we don't have the choice to marry the person we choose or whether we can go to college or not. That's not about honour, it's about control. In Islam we have these rights and I try to explain this to my parents.

Noreen (Birmingham)

Concerns were also expressed about community expectations that made it harder for some Muslim families to accept their choice of husband.

Even if my parents had given me more freedom it just would have caused them more problems. People talk about you: 'Oh she's doing this and that.' But what can you do?

Rabia (Birmingham)

In Islam marriage is a civil contract between an adult woman and an adult man who have the legal capacity to enter into such an agreement.[12] In Arabic a Muslim marriage is described as a *nikah* (meaning to perforate) or *aqd* (meaning to tie a knot). The marriage contract is not sacrosanct but is revocable. The requisites of a valid *nikah* contract include 'legal capacity' (individual to be of sound mind and has reached puberty), consent, acceptance and the dower or *mahr*.[13] In her work Ali (2000) draws attention to the fact that the *nikah* is neither unified in theory nor in practice but its significance to the institution of the 'Muslim family' cannot be underestimated. She explains, 'the central idea in Muslim family law is the institution of *nikah* or marriage. Almost every legal concept revolves around the central focal point of the status of the marriage. It is through marriage that the paternity of children is established and relationship and affinity are traced' (2002, p. 157).

The significance of marriage to Islam and the Muslim family has been extensively discussed in Muslim literature and mirrors Western feminist scholarship that documents the social and historical relationship of marriage on the basis of sexual rights and financial obligations. In her work Mona Siddiqui traces the historical origins of the *nikah* contract as a verbal contract and explains this as 'where the words spoken are in the nature of a "perfomative utterance", i.e., by virtue of the words being spoken, the status of the man and woman changes to that of husband and wife. That the offer may be made explicitly by the woman implies a certain autonomy which she can exercise' (1996, p. 51).

Under Hanafi law any free and sane adult can enter into marriage. As discussed before, one of the essential elements in the *nikah* contract is the free consent of the individual contracting into marriage. Ali explains the significance of consent as 'the focal point on which this entire debate rests appears to be the legal competence of the adult female, a capacity which is considered suspect' (2000). Even bearing in mind that of the four Sunni schools of thought in Islam, the Hanafis advocate that an adult woman should marry in her own right, this creates a sense of ambiguity and confusion in relation to issues of personal consent. As discussed in Chapter 1, in Britain most Pakistani Muslims are of Sunni origin and belong to the Hanafi school of thought.

In Islamic law, the issue of consent in marriage has been discussed in the context of marriage 'of a minor and the role of the guardian and the way in which consent may be assured is problematic' (Siddiqui, 1996, p. 52).[14] It is accepted that a lack of consent from the woman invalidates the marriage and the principle of *kafa'a*[15] which is the principle of compatibility and/or equality, and may give the power to the guardian to apply to a Qadi to set aside the marriage. This is generally referred to the '*wali* of the bride', in essence the guardian of the bride who must be an adult, sane Muslim man, usually the father or other close relation. Siddiqui points out, 'There is a tension running through the Hanafi arguments; family involvement in the arrangement of marriages is part of the social fabric and yet men and women, having reached legal majority, have the right to choose their own partners' (1996, p. 53). Hence under the laws of marriage a woman may be given the right to choose the marriage partner and demand consent in marriage but her position is ultimately subordinate to that of her father or male guardian and in this way 'the ties that bind a woman to her male relatives ensure both her protection and subjugation' (Siddiqui, 1996, p. 53). This seems to suggest that the principle of consent in Islamic legal principles can be counterposed against the lived realities of British Muslim women's lives. For example, personal definitions of consent may clash with the principles of Muslim family law, an example being that of a *wali* (male guardian) who can represent the bride and conclude the marriage on her behalf. Some scholars have interpreted this to mean that a Muslim woman does not have to be physically present at the ceremony for the marriage contract to take place – she can be in a different room, house and even different country, while her *wali* makes the contract of marriage on her behalf, although he must seek permission from the bride prior to acting on her behalf.

This issue has been addressed in *KC* v. *City of Westminster Social and Community Services Department* (2008).[16] In this case the appellants (K and N) appealed against a declaration that the marriage of their son (C) was not valid under English law. K and N were British nationals of Bangladeshi origin who were domiciled and habitually resident in England and Wales. C, who suffered from autism and severe impairment of his intellectual functioning, lacked the fundamental capacity to marry under English law. Marriage was not, however, precluded in Bangladesh and C was married in a Muslim ceremony conducted over the telephone, he being in England and his bride being in Bangladesh. The parties accepted that, as a matter of law, the marriage had been celebrated in Bangladesh. In declaring the marriage to be invalid under English law, the judge applied the dual domicile rule, refused recognition of the marriage on the grounds of public policy and rejected submissions made by K and N that, pursuant to the Matrimonial Causes Act 1973 s.12(c), the marriage was merely voidable rather than void and the court therefore had no power to deny it recognition.

The extent to which the *nikah* ceremony is performed as part of the Muslim marriage process in Britain remains largely under-researched (Shaw, 1988). In her study, Mirza describes the marriage process for Muslims in Britain as 'a series of discrete events each with a particular function, with its own customs and traditions, all contained within a firm but not unvariable order. Many of these events have a well-established lineage and, crossing geographical and cultural boundaries, have retained similarities across very different contemporary Muslim societies' (2000, p. 4). From this perspective the marriage process can be described as more than merely ceremonial but also embodies socially transformative norms – in flux and constantly evolving. The 'sites' of religious and civil marriage are therefore transformed by the emergence of hybrid cultural and religious practices and the marriage processes are open to change, contestation and interpretation.

Moreover, the *nikah* ceremony itself only constitutes one aspect of the Pakistani marriage process. Werbner, drawing on her extensive work with British Pakistanis in Manchester, describes the marriage process as fourfold: the *Mehdi*, the *nikah*, the *Rukhsati* and finally the *Valima* with each step constituting a move away from sexual chastity and moving towards sexuality (1990, p. 46). And Mirza explains, 'Each step marks a further stage in the alteration of the condition of the bride and groom, as those forbidden from expressions of their sexuality, and prohibited to one another, to their recognition as sexually active individuals in the conjugal unit. The sequence of marriage events is therefore an explicitly transformative process with each stage utilizing colour, space and the gaze in a specific manner, each defining and signifying the sexual state of the couple – with particular focus upon the bride – at each point in this process' (2000, p. 9). From this perspective the marriage process embodies a confluence of the past and the present, whereby notions of 'homeland' and 'belonging' are reconstructed to produce new cultural idioms in which new forms of hybrid marriage practices emerge.[17]

These processes create new understandings of marriage and the ways in which social, cultural and religious norms underpin the Muslim marriage process. Thus while the process seeks to balance family expectations and traditions on the one hand with individual choice and consent on the other, in practice the process inhabits a gendered social space that is based on social norms and values that constitutes gendered Muslim space (Mirza, 2000, p. 19). And it is within this gendered space that the experiences of the women can be better understood to consider how this process can both include and sideline Muslim women.

Civil registration of marriage

The Muslim marriage contract, the *nikah*, contracted in England is not recognized as a valid marriage[18] (Ahsan, 1995, p. 22; Pearl and Menski, 1998, p. 167) even if the parties believe the marriage to be valid (Yilmaz, 2001b, p. 4). The data in this study showed that less than half the sample who had married with a partner domiciled in England had registered their marriages according to civil law, meaning that the largest group of women in this sample were in effect unmarried according to English family law. The types of marriage ceremonies are depicted in the next figure.

This raises the obvious question of why the majority of women in this study had not registered their marriages according to the formalities of civil law which affords women greater legal protection should the marriage end in divorce. It may also reinforce the argument pursued by some legal scholars who argue that, in order to accommodate the needs of British Muslims who intentionally choose to avoid using state law, some kind of parallel legal system needs to be introduced in matters of family law (see further). At first glance, this absence of formal registration of marriage seems to legitimize

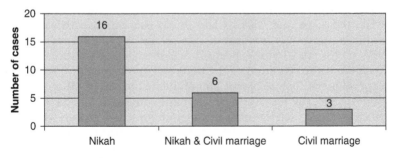

Figure 6.1   Types of marriage ceremonies

this argument but as data in this study illustrate we see on closer inspection that the picture may be a little more complex. What becomes clear is that in the majority of cases in this study, the women had in fact expected their religious marriages to be registered in accordance with the Marriage Acts but upon completion of the religious ceremony and once consummation of the marriage had taken place, some husbands had simply refused to register the marriage according to civil law.

At present all marriages which take place in Britain must be conducted within the framework of the Marriage Acts 1949–94. Under this framework, Jews and Quakers are afforded special treatment whereby they retain the right to determine who should marry couples, when and where, leading to concern that other minority groups are denied equal recognition (Poulter, 1998). In response, the government published a White Paper (1987) with proposals to put all non-Anglican marriages on an equal footing (for discussion on the elements within a Muslim marriage contract, see Doi, 1984, p. 56).

As discussed in earlier chapters, there are long-standing debates on the extent to which religious personal laws should be accommodated within the framework of existing English law. The essence of these arguments is that Muslim women are deliberately failing to register their religious marriages according to the formalities of civil law, therefore raising the need to introduce a formal process that is able to accommodate the needs of all Muslims in Britain. What becomes clear is that non-registration must be understood in relation to power relations and the positioning of women in family and marriage relationships (Anthias, 2002). For example, it is difficult to ignore the relations of power and the gendered cultural norms and values that underpin the decisions made by husbands and male members of the newfound family, many of whom choose not to formalize the marriage according to civil law. These women had experienced a loss of decision-making and autonomy in the marriage process; they had relied upon a level of trust and reciprocity from their husbands that the marriage would be registered and this trust had been violated. One interviewee explained:

> I think a lot of people are naïve; they just trust their husbands that they will get a registered marriage. It's not that they don't know about registry or that they don't want it; they are just naïve in believing their husbands. I tell all my friends now that you must have a legal marriage first because if you have an Islamic marriage first then they will not agree to do a civil marriage. I mean you can do it on the same day there's nothing stopping you doing that. Because I really think that guys would begin to take marriages more seriously.
>
> Salma (London)

All these outcomes led some women to call for the introduction of a parallel legal system as a means of redressing their situations. The next extracts from interview data reveal some of the underlying reasons why marriages were not registered according to civil law.

Well to tell you the truth I honestly thought that the Muslim marriage certificate would be recognized and I was quite shocked when I found out that it wasn't. I thought, 'Hold on a minute we got married, didn't we? I had a massive wedding; I've got the wedding photos to prove it, the wedding cassette to prove it. I have all this to prove it so how can they turn round and say to me that sorry, no it's not recognized.' The only difference is ... the only thing that we didn't do is swap some vows in the registry office, I mean that's the only difference.

Mina (London)

Well I understand that Islamically it says that you have to have a *nikah* in order for your marriage to be recognized, but I would have been happy if it had been registered straight away, then I would have felt that I am on the safe side at the end of the day. I'm not happy with what happened to my marriage at all, my marriage was planned and the breakdown of my marriage was planned.

Shazia (London)

I said to him we need to get registered and he said, 'Oh no we don't because the Muslim certificate is recognized now.' And I was so naïve, I believed him, so I thought, 'Oh well, it must be.' He said, 'Yeah well I thought it wasn't as well and last time I got registered it was just a big hassle to divorce' and I believed him.

Sadia (Birmingham)

What happened was when I got engaged he promised me we'd get registered, we'll get a house of our own, we'll do everything when I got into our marriage because they had a bad family name, in that they treat the daughters-in-laws [*sic*] so badly that's the reason why they refused to let us get registered. I said to my husband, no we have to get registered because it's the law in this country that we get registered but he kept saying, 'Yeah, yeah, we'll do it', but he never would. Anyway a year later I started getting worried because I thought if something happens then I would have nothing. I said to him, 'You know I'm worried – what if your mother says, "Oh, you know, kick her out." I just don't feel safe.' And he said, 'Oh no, nothing's gonna happen like that. Islamically we're married, we don't believe in getting registered, that's just this country's law.' He turned around and said that our family only believe in the *nikah* and that's it. So he just refused and they were just playing it cleverly.

Parveen (Birmingham)

Before I married him I did say I'd like to get registered and he said, 'We'll do it after we get the *nikah* done, that's what more important' and personally that is how I saw it then too, but I see it differently now obviously. At the time for me Islam was number one; I was more bothered about Islam rather than anything else really but that doesn't mean I didn't want to get the marriage registered. I did and I knew that I may not be protected with just having a *nikah*. It was exactly a week after we got married I got a little concerned and I asked him when are we going to get registered and he said, 'Well no, we're not', and I said, well, 'Why?' and he said, 'Well because if we split up you'll want half of everything that's mine and I went, 'Oh is that what you think' and I was absolutely gutted because that wasn't my reason. I did not marry him with the intention of splitting whereas he had looked far ahead.

Sabia (London)

It is noteworthy that these extracts reveal the precarious situation in which many of the women found themselves. For example, of the sample, only two women had been unaware of the validity of the *nikah* according to English law and believed they were legally married. A further two women had agreed with their husbands to forego civil registration for financial reasons. But the largest group of women who had not registered their marriages were those who were aware of the need to comply with civil law and had fully expected their marriages to be formalized. The consequences for the women being intentionally misled led to their facing a multitude of social and legal problems.

Those women who had believed that their *nikah* had been a legally recognized form of marriage also speculated on the lack of available information for their misunderstanding. Blame was directed towards imams and community leaders.

I think the imam who married us should take the blame because surely it's his duty to explain everything to us before we go through with it. Surely imams should know that the *nikah* isn't recognized in this country.

Mina (London)

I find it shocking that Pakistanis have been in this country for decades and decades and still no one seems to know if the *nikah* in England is recognized or not. Solicitors and the community need to be trained, especially the imams. We go to them for advice, so it's really important they know at least what's going on.

Shazia (London)

Hence these women clearly lacked power and position within their new-found family to successfully negotiate the formal registration of marriage and they remained dependent on the willingness of their husbands to comply. Many disempowered women described their bitterness on having relied upon their husbands' trust only to be let down.

Case law and the validity of religious marriages

As discussed previously, a religious marriage that is not conducted in compliance with the formalities and procedures of marriage as enshrined in English family law can produce a legally invalid marriage. In English law, the legal formalities include age, sex, consent, sound mind and fulfilling legal procedures as to what constitutes as marriage. Therefore all religious marriages taking place at unlicensed buildings must have their marriage registered in a licensed building to give it legal validity. One requirement here is that in order for the building to be licensed for marriages it is must be a 'separate building' and 'a place of meeting for religious worship'.[19] Consequently the majority of mosques have been excluded from this process, as many mosques are part of larger buildings that include community centres. Thus in 1998 there were only 109 mosques in which a marriage could take place out of 561 that were certified as public places of worship. Thus, only 189 Muslim marriages were recorded as taking place in 1998 (see Probert, 2002, p. 408).[20] Yet as Probert (2004)[21] demonstrates, recent developments in case law have brought to the fore the contentious issue of when a religious marriage is deemed valid, void, non-existent or presumed to be valid in English law, and questions, 'How strong is the presumption in favour of marriage at the start of the twenty-first century? Is it possible to presume that a valid marriage has taken place where there is evidence that the only known ceremony was invalid?' (2002, p. 399). In other words, what status should be given to marriages that are celebrated outside the provisions of the Marriage Act 1949 but where the parties believe the marriages to be valid?

We have some case law that raises some of the conflicting issues arising over the validity of a religious marriage. In *Chief Adjudication Officer* v. *Bath* (2000),[22] the courts addressed the issue of the validity of a religious marriage in an unlicensed building. In *A-M* v. *A-M* (2001)[23] and *Gandhi* v. *Patel* (2001),[24] the courts discussed the validity of polygamous ceremonies in the private sphere, challenging the basis upon what constitutes as a valid marriage. Probert points out that both rulings have only further increased the confusion as to what is deemed a valid religious marriage. For example, in the Bath case the courts ruled the marriage was valid on the basis that there were no 'provisions invalidating it' (Probert, 2002, p. 401). Hence due to the fact that the marriage could not be deemed void it was concluded to be a valid marriage. This contrasts with the ruling in *Gandhi* v. *Patel* and *A-M* v. *A-M*, where it was held the applicant had 'failed in multiple respects to comply with the formal requirements of the Marriage Acts, and therefore ... was incapable of creating a marriage recognized as such under English law' (Probert, 2002, p. 403).

In *G* v. *M* (2011)[25] the applicant was part of an Islamic marriage performed in her flat in London. She argued that all the parties had believed this marriage to be valid under English law and the question once again was whether this marriage was a valid marriage, a non-marriage or a non-existent marriage? In this case a petition for nullity was issued but the judge also made it clear that this ruling was based only on the facts of this case and should not be taken as precedent for other cases. This case law demonstrates that this area of law remains both ambiguous and unclarified.

One further requirement is that the marriage is conducted either by a person authorized to conduct a civil ceremony or by a member of the community authorized to do so, and that the marriage does not conflict with the conditions for a valid marriage under English law. The Act also requires that certain declarations are made for the marriage to be valid, which are taken from the procedure for a valid civil marriage (Ali, 2010, p. 2).

So what are the primary differences between what constitutes a valid marriage under English law and Islamic law? Ali explains, 'It is not a requirement under Islamic law that the parties to a marriage must be over the age of 16, and a man in Islam can take up to four wives. Both these examples would invalidate a marriage under English law.[26] In order to solemnize a *nikah*, and have it recognized as a civil marriage, the imam conducting the *nikah* would have to ensure that it does not contradict what is considered valid under English law' (2010, p. 2).

Another interesting development regarding the validity of the *nikah* under English law relates to those marriages that are conducted abroad. For application of law in relation to religious personal matters, it is the law of the domicile which is taken into account under the English legal system (see Hamilton, 1995). In this study, five marriages had been conducted in Pakistan and upon return to Britain three women chose to register their marriages according to civil law with the remaining two choosing not to do so. This situation has led to a conflict of laws scenario whereby both applicants and practitioners are confused regarding the validity of a religious marriage that has been conducted abroad. In his study Warraich (2001) points out that for British Pakistanis a *nikah* that has been contracted in Pakistan is a valid form of marriage due to the fact that under Pakistani law second-generation British Pakistanis are considered as dual nationals. He argues that the failure of English family law to recognize the pace of social change in South Asia (in its understanding of Muslim family law principles) has contributed to this confusing situation of precisely when a religious marriage constitutes as a valid marriage (2001, p. 13).[27] In an attempt to clarify the issue he points out that if a woman has not registered her marriage in the UK she 'can seek to have her marriage validated in Pakistan because mere registration of marriage can be done at any time' (2001, p. 46). In other words a religious marriage can easily be registered in Pakistan and avoid questions of the legal validity.

Empirically there is evidence to suggest that some women as dual nationals are willing to access remedies in other jurisdictions such as Pakistan (as women are actively involved in developing strategies to remedy their situations), but equally others are simply unwilling to utilize remedies available outside Britain. Therefore it would be wrong to conclude that by simply reconceptualizing such conflicts from English jurisdictions to that of Pakistan necessarily provides a solution to these problems. Instead such conflicts must be understood as part of the entanglement of law, identity and belonging and must take into account the complex social dynamics and identifications that are associated with the marriage process. For example, in this study of those women who had married in Pakistan, categorically stated that they did not wish to use remedies available to them as dual nationals in Pakistan. As one interviewee, Sameena (London) put it:

> This is my home, I'm British and this is where I want the law to help me. I don't want to go back to Pakistan, certainly not after what I've been through.[28]

Thus religious marriage inhabits an interesting 'space' where religious values, identity and where law interact and the experiences of Muslim marriage for British Pakistani Muslim women are contested, challenged, adapted and accepted.

Locating the 'self' in the *nikah* process

Muslim marriage, as with all experiences of cultural and religious practice, is mediated by complex relations of power. This space is experienced differentially by its participants and its boundaries shift and adapt over time. In this section the women's personal experiences of *nikah* are analysed. Of particular interest are the ways in which the women challenged, resisted, accepted, redefined or displaced the 'boundaries' of the *nikah* process and the meanings and negotiations they attached to it. For example, how did they perceive the religious, symbolic and functional aspects of such a process? What procedures did they rely upon and what were the outcomes of their participation?

Of the sample, 22 women described in personal terms the 'importance' they attached to the *nikah*. Being married 'under the eyes of God' was a commonly used phrase and the experience of Muslim marriage represented not only an important symbolic marker as part of their personal religious identity but the practice legitimized their marriage in the form of a public ceremony which allowed them to publicly display their membership to the Muslim *umma*:

> I've never questioned it; it's all part of being a Muslim. If you're a Muslim you would have one ... it doesn't even have to be that you're really

religious. Getting married in God's eyes is more important than getting married for English law.

Raheela (London)

I very much saw the civil side of it as something that we just had to do. Had I never had that I would have still felt very married because I had the *nikah* because that's a very sombre, a very real experience.

Anisa (Bradford)

The registry marriage was a formality; it was the *nikah* that was important. It's the *nikah* that's binding in the Islamic setting and it's at that point whether you have the registry marriage or not that you're considered to be married by people in the family, the community, you know, people who know you, know your family. We're all Muslims and we know what's important to us.

Sameena (Birmingham)

Well the Islamic marriage is very important for me. I could get married in a civil registry office and not regard myself as married, I might be legally married but I wouldn't be married in my heart and in my mind.

Fauzia (London)

The *nikah* was very important to me and it was at that point I felt married. But we did both feel it was important for us to also register the marriage. I'm a British Muslim so in a way both ceremonies kind of represent who I am. For me it completed my marriage ... and of course the law gave me protection, I understood that.

Noreen (Birmingham)

It's difficult to explain what it means. It's not the most crucial thing for Muslims but I guess we all do it because that's just the way it works. I mean it doesn't make me feel any more Muslim than I already feel ... if that's what you mean?

Farhana (Birmingham)

The data reveal that for many interviewees performing the *nikah* forms an integral part of their future lives as married women. Indeed it can be viewed as part of their complex religious identities and an integral part of their Muslim identities. For others, however, it simply fulfilled a functional role in a social context where their participation was simply part of the overall marriage process.

The ceremony has been described as follows: 'One matrimonial party expresses "ijab", willing consent to enter into marriage, and the other party expresses "qubul", acceptance of the responsibility in the assembly of marriage ceremony. The contract is written and signed by the bride and groom and their two respective witnesses. This written marriage (*Aqd-Nikah*) is then announced publicly' (Hussani, 2010).

The *nikah* is addressed with a marriage sermon (*khutba-tun-nikah*) by the Muslim officiating the marriage. The sermon invites the bride and the groom, as well as the participating guests to a life of piety, mutual love, kindness and social responsibility. In marriage ceremonies, customarily a state-appointed Muslim judge (*Qadi*) officiates and keeps the record of the marriage contract. However, any 'trustworthy practicing Muslim' can conduct the *nikah* ceremony, as Islam does not advocate priesthood (Hallaq, 2001).

The marriage contract/certificate is filed with the mosque (masjid) and a copy is given to the parties. Marriage is considered as an act of worship (*ibadah*). It is virtuous to conduct it in a mosque, keeping the ceremony simple. The marriage ceremony is a social as well as a religious activity. There are three primary requirements: (1) mutual agreement (*Ijab-O-Qubul*) by the bride and groom, (2) two adult and sane witnesses and (3) *mahr* (marriage gift) to be paid by the groom to the bride either immediately (*muajjal*) or deferred (*muakhkhar*), or a combination of both.

The process of the *nikah* therefore embodies a wide range of experiences for Pakistani Muslim women that include social strategies, practical compromises and, for some, dealing with issues of coercion and parental pressure to marry. Most interestingly this dynamic lived experience of the *nikah* process also brings to the fore issues of consent in Muslim marriage. The findings on the experience of religious marriage in real-life situations lead to interesting insights on how the women understood the meaning and limits of consent in Muslim marriage. As Hunter and Cowan (2007, p. 12) point out, 'Put simply, consent and female subjectivity are bound together by issues of power: the power men exercise over women, women's power over themselves and their own lives, and the belief in the need to further empower women.'

This idea of consent as one of empowerment was discussed among the women with terms such as 'being empowered', 'permitted' and 'my rights' being frequently used. The idea that Islam promotes equality between the sexes emerged significantly as some women spoke with enthusiasm of Islam as a spiritual journey, drawing upon Islamic thought to better understand their duties, rights and autonomy as Muslim women. No discernable differences emerged between those women of a Punjabi or Azad Kashmiri background and the discussions primarily focused on the need to develop fuller understandings of what marriage in Islam actually means for all parties involved.

> When my parents starting talking about getting married, I started reading around what marriage in Islam actually means. What I read made sense to me. As a Muslim woman I have the choice to marry whoever I want as long as he's a Muslim. My parents wanted me to have an arranged

marriage because that's what Pakistanis do and I did understand that was important to them. I'm not saying that culture isn't important to me, because I love speaking Punjabi and everything else but I wanted to choose who I could marry and Islam gave me that.

Sadia (Birmingham)

I've read quite a bit around Islam and Muslim women and rights in marriage and all that ... I understand it's very important to make sure a woman gives her consent. But I think most parents still want to give their consent to who you marry; even if they're a Muslim, they still think that's the most important thing. So I had to sit my parents down and talk to them, you know, explain that it's my consent that matters!

Shabana (London)

An understanding of the rights afforded to Muslim women in marriage enabled many of these women to interrogate and challenge the power relations in the family regarding matters of choice of marriage partner and issues of consent. Using Islamic rules as a base upon which to interrogate cultural practices that may have denied them the space to voice their opposition to the marriage, these women were able, therefore, to negotiate and in some cases to see through a solution.

It was interesting to note how discussions of consent in marriage within the Islamic framework were brought to the fore. As Drakaopoulou (2007) explains, 'Endorsement or rejection of consent is therefore predicated not only upon how effectively it communicates women as autonomous, rational and responsible political, social and economic actors, but also the anticipation of what will affirm real women's agency and mastery over themselves and strengthen their equal standing in private and public life.'

Ali points out that under Muslim law a Muslim woman has the capacity to enter into a marriage contract without the consent of her parents; however, she accepts that 'the notion of a woman being able to exercise her choice by entering into a contract of marriage is seen as an affront to the male honour as she is considered the izzat of the family and negotiating a marriage contract with a male without an intermediary poses a threat to existing social structures' (2002, p. 167). This viewpoint was confirmed by findings of this study.

For example, some women explained that the cultural framework of marriage within British Pakistani communities is based upon gendered roles and responsibilities that prohibit individual decision-making. Islam, however, based on values of equality and justice, provided clearer guidance on issues of consent and choice of marriage partner. With some interviewees this also led to discussions on how religious observance, including donning the Islamic headscarf and the *hijab*, had enabled the women to create spaces within the family context upon which they were able to challenge marriages arranged by parents (see Afshar, 1994).

More importantly, for women who had been forced into marriage, the strength of redefining marriage according to the tenets of Islam also lay in the struggle between a search for transforming oppressive cultural practices and a search to express themselves as British Muslims. As one interviewee explained:

> I wasn't allowed to say no; so no, my permission wasn't even a factor. For me, Islam was a way of telling my parents that I did have rights as a woman, a Muslim woman, I have the right to choose.
>
> Zareena (Bradford)

In Islamic literature the principle of the 'option of puberty' (*khiyar-al-bulugh*) addresses the issue of forced marriage and acts as a measure that is designed to free those women who have been forced into marriage. There is no divine revelation on this issue but it has been discussed among the various Islamic schools of thought (see Engineer, 1992). For example, in Hanafi law, if a young woman is forcibly married prior to puberty she can repudiate this contract once she reaches puberty. Other Sunni law schools recognize this option in the case of jest or duress (see Nasir, 1990). Such debates point to issues of the control of female sexuality and the idea that Muslim women who remain virgins are essentially under the control of their fathers or other male members of the family who act as their guardians. As Pearl and Menski point out, 'The woman only becomes capable of contracting herself in marriage when she ceases to be a virgin by reason of a consummated marriage or an illicit sexual relationship' (1998, p. 142). Therefore marriage in Islam is based on a contractual relationship where the consent of interested parties underpins the validity and enforcement of the contract.

In this study, the women's *nikah* ceremony was performed in various locations – the family home, the wedding premises (often described as the 'wedding hall') and the local mosque. It is useful to note that Islamic literature imposes few restrictions on where the marriage can take place. Interestingly no marriages were performed in a licensed mosque according to the Places of Worship Registration Act (1855) and only one interviewee had checked prior to the religious marriage ceremony as to whether or not the mosque had been registered as a licensed building. Unable to clarify this issue, she had nevertheless gone ahead with the *nikah* on the understanding that her religious marriage was shortly to be registered under civil law.

Eade (1996) points out that the location for the *nikah* ceremony largely depends upon family expectations and cultural traditions and is created 'purely by ritual and sanctioned practice and is not dependent upon the creation of any juridically claimed territory or formally consecrated space, or indeed, the production of architecturally specific place' (p. 231). At one level, this was confirmed by findings in this study. For example, a number of the women reported that their decision as to where the *nikah* ceremony should take place was taken after lengthy discussions with immediate and extended members of their family and often rested upon family expectations and cultural traditions, sometimes both in Britain and Pakistan. Such women described in great length the involvement of family members and friends in arranging the *nikah* ceremony which included the length of the ceremony itself, the role of family members in organizing the imam to perform the ceremony and the terms of the marriage contract. Agreement to how this process took shape therefore could be complex and involve lengthy negotiations. Other women, however, had had minimal participation and little family involvement in the negotiations.

> My mum made it pretty clear that the *nikah* was going to happen in our house. Apparently that's the way it's always been done in our family and yes, I was ok with that. She discussed it with me and I was ok with it.
>
> Nighat (London)

> We had the *nikah* first. My parents did that. We had it in the wedding hall and the imam came from his aunt. I think traditionally the imam who conducts the ceremony is meant to come from the groom's side; they're meant to provide you with the imam. So the imam came from the aunt and he was known to the family for about 30–40 years. He had done their aunt's marriage and all her brothers and sisters marriages in Pakistan.
>
> Fauzia (London)

In terms of the length of the ceremony and the participation of the women, it was described as 'short' and involving their minimal participation.

> It was really quick, over in like two minutes. He [the imam] asked me whether I gave my consent and I said yes; I mean he only asked me once, which I don't think is right. Then he said something in Arabic and that was it really. All over in two minutes in my parent's front room.
>
> Sameena (Birmingham)

> I don't remember much about it because it happened so quickly but then I think it's meant to be like that in Islam, you know, marriage is just a contract, somebody asks you, you say yes and then that's it.
>
> Zareena (Bradford)

> Maybe I would have liked more involvement but I don't think it's meant to be a long and drawn out … practical thing, its more symbolic and that's what it was, symbolic.
>
> Naheed (London)

The presence of witnesses at the *nikah* ceremony generated interesting discussion. Under Hanafi law, a contract can only be fulfilled in the presence of witnesses, which can be either two males or one male and two females (see Nasir, 1990). The presence of witnesses also acts as a symbolic public representation that the marriage is taking place. As Mirza points out, 'The presence of the witnesses is essential for the valid solemnization of a marriage as their attendance ensures publicity, this being the decisive symbol that demarcates the line between lawful wedlock and fornication or *zina*' (2000, p. 14). In this study, the witnesses to the *nikah* ceremony comprised primarily the male members of the family, including fathers, uncles and brothers. By contrast, female witnesses were involved in only two cases and in each case involved family friends. The presence of witnesses acquired specific meanings and significance for the women as described next.

The husband and wife are not supposed to be in the same room. Basically they pray and everything and make *dawah*. There must be three witnesses present and when he is ready they ask him, 'Do you want to marry this woman', three times and he says, 'Yes', and then he signs the certificate to make sure he agrees and he's happy with the marriage. After that they come to me and I was at my mum's house: three men come, three witnesses and they ask me, 'D'you want to marry this man', and I said, 'Yes, I do', three times and then you sign the book.

Fareeda (Birmingham)

There's two witnesses from his side, one witness from my side. My witness was my uncle and his witnesses were his two uncles. My part of it was that before they come and do the *nikah* bit in the mosque they come and ask me whether I agree to the marriage. I was at home and they came over, they asked me, well, they basically said, 'You are getting married to such and such person and do you agree to it', and you have to say *geehaa* [yes] three times and that was that, done. Then they go to him. I'm not sure what happens in the mosque but basically they ask him the same question. I think they do a lot of prayers.

Salma (London)

Women aren't allowed in the mosque so it was upstairs in my mum's house and it was just us ladies in the room. Then they went to the mosque where he was and they said to the maulvi, the girl has said yes three times and she signed this paper and that was the marriage certificate. Then he went through more or less the procedure but it's just a bit longer because what they do before is give a bit of a lecture before the *nikah* itself, you know, they just tell him about how they should look after a wife etc. After they ask[ed] him what they asked me and I think the men have to say yes twice, I think so I'm not quite sure, and then basically then everyone congratulated him and then he came to the hall where the reception took place. And that is it ... basically everyone eats.

Shabana (London)

I can't say it's religious really because he didn't actually read anything from the Qur'an or give a sermon. Like my brother got married recently, it was quite different and the chap who married them was from the London mosque and he prepared a special sermon and made it quite a special occasion and he's known for this. That's why it's so very different, each sermon or each marriage contract is so different according to what mullah is doing it.

Rabia (Birmingham)

Initially the imam didn't ask me three times, so my mum had to ask him to do what he hadn't. He asked me just once and my mum had to go and get him to do it properly and then he came and asked me three times.

Fauzia (London)

These experiences illustrate some of the ambivalences the women experienced with the *nikah* as the process is neither straightforward nor uncontested. In fact, the *nikah* marks the physical presence of the different parties involved, including the marriage partners, male witnesses, the imam, parents and wider family members. For some women, therefore, this process was difficult, protracted and complex. Some women complained that they had been sidelined in the process as a whole, as their participation was minimal in what was in actual fact supposed to be a shared ceremony. For others, both the meaning of the *nikah* and their presence as participants was symbolic on a deeply personal level and understood as part of what it meant to them to be a Muslim woman, transcending any obligatory requirements. Yet all the women in this study interacted, engaged and closely identified with the *nikah* ceremony. Significantly, for those women who had been forced into marriage, the *nikah* ceremony certainly did not mark the end of their attempt to challenge the issue of consent in marriage and ultimately the validity of the marriage itself, but for these women it was also closely associated as a marker of discipline and control and understandably these women disengaged with the process to a large degree. However, for many women the *nikah* represented the most distinctive part of the Muslim marriage process which fulfilled specific duties and provided social and moral legitimacy to their marriages within the Muslim community and under the 'eyes of God'.

It sort of marked a different status in the eyes of people. It was from then on that I had the status of coming into the family. I mean lots of doors opened then, I mean socially and community wise that I wouldn't have had otherwise.

Anisa (Bradford)

The discursive framework of the *nikah*, therefore, is undoubtedly based upon specific gender relations that underpin the marriage process. The formal aspect of this process, the *nikah* contract, creates an interesting space for many women who are able to challenge the unequal cultural norms embedded in marriage practices for women belonging to Pakistani Muslim communities.

Negotiating *mahr* in the *nikah* contract

A final element of the *nikah* contract involves the *mahr* or dower, described as 'a sum of money or other property which the wife is entitled to receive from the husband in consideration of the marriage' (Mehmood, 1995, p. 87, quoted in Ali, 2000). The Qur'anic verse 4:4 states, 'And give the women (on marriage) their *mahr* as a (*nikha*) free gift.'

Precisely what the *mahr* constitutes is open to some dispute in Islamic literature. Ali points out that rather than being perceived as a form of consideration in the contract it is largely understood as a debt to be repaid to the wife by the husband in event of death (2000). In this way the *mahr* is an effect of the marriage contract and not an exchange for the marriage. The amount of *mahr* is expressly stipulated in the *nikah* contract.[29] It is therefore a mandatory requirement that can either be paid immediately or be partly deferred. As Ali explains, 'If there is a written record of the marriage contract then details of the *mahr* would normally be included within it as it is an essential element of the marriage contract; although an Islamic marriage is still valid without a *mahr* being declared, when the wife is then entitled to call for a *mahr*, the value of which is to be determined by an Islamic judge based upon certain conditions. If a dispute then arises as to the *mahr* it may be possible to apply contractual principles under English law to enforce the agreement in the civil courts'[30] (2010, p. 3). Hussaini (2010) describes *mahr* as 'a token commitment of the husband's responsibility and may be paid in cash, property or movable objects to the bride herself. The amount of *mahr* is not legally specified; however, moderation according to existing social norm is recommended. The *mahr* may be paid immediately to the bride at the time of marriage, or deferred to a later date, or a combination of both. The deferred *mahr*, however, falls due in case of death or divorce'.

The contractual nature of Muslim marriage has led to interesting discussions on the extent to which the *nikah* allows women 'some legal autonomy in order to bargain over her own destiny' (Haeri, 1990, p. 57). Muslim feminist literature points to the underlying assumptions of ownership and purchase within the marriage contract and its legitimacy as a patriarchal understanding of the male–female relationship. For Muslim feminist scholars, concerns are raised over how female bodies become obvious sites for sacrifice, discipline and control (see Abu-Odeh, 1996; El-Nimr, 1996). Coulson maintains that the *nikah* contract constitutes a sale due to the 'transfer of an absolute propriety' (1964, p. 111). This is accepted by Haeri (1990) who argues that the *nikah* embodies an inherent determinism of male–female relations that act as a justification for the existing sexual inequalities and explains, 'Because marriage is a contract from an Islamic point of view, the phenomenon of intercourse, *vatye*, is inevitably intertwined with monetary exchanges. The underlying assumption here is two-fold. First, as "purchasers" in a contract of marriage, men are "in charge" of their wives because they pay for them and, naturally, they ought to be able to control their wives' activities. Secondly, women are required submit to that for which they have been paid for, or promised to be paid. It follows therefore that women ought to be obedient to their husbands' (Haeri, 1990, p. 58). The ideological representation of women as wives, daughters and mothers therefore remain central to the role of *mahr* in the *nikah* contract.

Three key issues emerge from the data in this study: first, the confusion between the *mahr* and dowry; second, the failure by the women to negotiate a 'reasonable' amount of *mahr* as part of the *nikah* contract; and, finally, the limited use of the *nikah* contract to retrieve the *mahr* upon breakdown of marriage and divorce.

In this study only 13 of the 25 women obtained a copy of the *nikah* contract upon completion of the marriage ceremony. The contract included personal details such as name, age, address, date of birth, the date and place of marriage, and the signature of witnesses. As for the *mahr*, the women reported each receiving a nominal sum, ranging from £100 to £200. For most women, therefore, the *nikah* contract simply became synonymous with the *nikah* ceremony rather than seen as a key document that could be invoked to claim *mahr* upon the breakdown of marriage.

For women whose marriages had not been formalized and registered according to civil law, however, the *nikah* contract was considered of significant value and importance. In cases where the religious marriage is not formally registered, the *nikah* contract then is firmly rooted in understandings of 'justice' where women are actively engaged in strategies to claim the *mahr* and/or challenge the amount of *mahr* stipulated in the *nikah* contract. It seems that shifting the understanding of the significance of the *nikah* contract as a general document to one which is used to enforce the rights of Muslim women can also depend upon whether the marriage has been formally registered or not. In this way the *nikah* contract serves as a useful mechanism allowing the marriage breakdown and the divorce to be in some ways managed, negotiated and settled.

Interestingly the data revealed a conflation of the terms used by the women to refer to *mahr* as '*mahr*', '*haq mehr*', '*jahez*', 'dower' and 'dowry', and to some extent this complicates the ways in which the *mahr* was understood as being a central part of the *nikah* contract. The following extracts highlight some of the narrative found in these discussions.

Haq mehr is the property or the sum of money or whatever you want it to be which the woman can ask for from her husband at any time during the marriage but at the divorce it has to be passed over. I know from other people's weddings that you know things can stop there for hours and hours, you know, because there's a problem with the *haq mehr*, you know, like the guy's side is saying, you know, 'We thought we'd get something else', and the girl's side think something else has been arranged. Or sometimes it's so enormous the sum the girl couldn't get out of the marriage because the guy's side wouldn't be able to pay that. There's a lot of politics around the amount that you put forward. But Islamic law says it should be something like for three months or something like that.

Shabana (London)

The whole idea of the *mahr* is that you show the value of that particular individual. It has to be a reasonable amount of money as well, that's the other thing that I was aware of as well; it can't just be something that's a throwaway sum of money that's not going to cause any hardship to the man if there is a divorce. It's got to be something that means something to him, not that's something that's just done for the sake of doing it. For me it's a form of protection and I was quite definite on that.

Fauzia (London)

The imam was in the room with my father and some men and he talked to my father about whether he was happy giving me away and what the *haq mehr* should be. You know we hadn't even discussed it before. I didn't know what it meant and I don't know what they decided.

Rubina (Birmingham)

The problem arose at the time of the *nikah*, like when we were talking about what was going to happen and all the procedures. But they hadn't mentioned anything about the *mahr* or clothes, you know, exchanging of gifts and we were beginning to think this was a bit strange. My mum was getting a little worried because it had come up to two weeks before the wedding and still nothing had been mentioned. In our family it's important for the girl to be given clothes before she gets married. My mother told my future mother-in-law and the response was, 'Well as far as the *mahr* is concerned we're going to set it at the same amount as we set our other son's and I can't allow her to have a higher *mahr* than my other daughter-in-law. As far as I'm concerned they're equal.'

Sameena (London)

Nothing, I have nothing to show that it's an Islamic marriage. I don't even have a certificate. I think he did make a certificate and he said come next week but I never went back. At that point I didn't think it was important so I don't know what the dower was for my marriage but I think they gave us some clothes.

Nasima (London)

Of course, this confusion between *mahr* and dowry does not in itself deny the value the women placed upon the *nikah* contract and the centrality of the *mahr* to the *nikah* contract. Instead what becomes evident is the complex interwoven religious marriage process to cultural expectations and practice all interacting within a cultural setting that then shapes the temporal and spatial boundaries of the *nikah* ceremony itself (Bhabha, 1994). In this way some women sought to distinguish between religious and cultural practices to draw attention to centrality of the *nikah* ceremony and the importance of *mahr* to the *nikah* contract. Therefore most women were also placed at the margins of decision-making and negotiating the terms of the *mahr* as a stipulation of the *nikah* contract. Interestingly these women also called into question their personal lack of knowledge and their general ignorance of Islamic principles that they believed had eventually led to their troubled circumstances and the breakdown of marriage.

For me to get the *nikah* right was really important. But I didn't know. I was really stupid at the time. I really didn't know everything. I knew some of what I was entitled to but I really didn't know the level of my rights. For instance, I didn't know I could stipulate terms of divorce at the time of the *nikah*. I didn't know I could ask for the rights to divorce at that time or I didn't know I could stipulate various other things at the time of the contract. I just went as far as saying that 'Look, if you're going to give a *mahr* it has to be a reasonable amount and it has to be an agreement between me and him not your parents or not your aunts or anyone else'.

Fareeda (London)

I did not know much about it actually. I think I learnt more about the *nikah* after I got divorced. Like, for example, that in Islam you can have prenuptial arrangements, you don't have to change your name when you get married, in fact it's better to keep your own name, you don't have to agree to live with the guy's parents. It's up to him to look after his family but he's got no right to impose it on you, things like that. So I found out things like that and I was surprised really. I could have said that before I married him but I didn't because I don't think it's the right way of starting a relationship by splitting him from his family if he doesn't want to do that. I didn't want to come between them but I didn't make that as a condition. I now know a lot of girls do that these days.

Salma (London)

When the imam was conducting the ceremony, although he had written the correct amount of the *mahr* on the certificate that he had, after I said yes three times and I was seated officially next to my husband and when they got me to sign the thing, I noticed on the certificate next to the *mahr* amount they had written 'deferred' and I didn't know what that meant. And I saw it and I thought well I didn't agree to this but there was about 100 people there and I couldn't say anything. I just noted it and I thought, 'Well, it shouldn't really mean anything', so I just signed my name to it but no one had consulted me as to whether this *mahr* was deferred or not because the understanding behind the *haq mehr* is that it's supposed to be paid to the wife preferably before the marriage is consummated. There wasn't any mention of it being paid. I mean it doesn't have to be paid but at least I could have been spoken to about why a deferred term was included in the contract.

Naheed (London)

What becomes clear is that for this group of women the gendered nature of Muslim marriage can sideline the role, position and participation of the women, meaning that some were simply unable to engage with the process and actively negotiate the terms of the *nikah* contract and the amount of *mahr*. This is not to lose sight of the fact that the women described the *nikah* ceremony and contract as an important and significant part of the marriage process. Furthermore, there was by no means a taken-for-granted consensus on the significance of the *mahr* in promoting the rights of Muslim women upon breakdown of marriage. Certainly the interview data reveal the significance placed on the *nikah* contract in cases of non-formalized and legally registered marriages. This has led to attempts by some religious scholars to strengthen the *nikah* contract by producing and introducing a standard *nikah* contract for all Muslims in Britain, a development discussed in Chapter 8.

Conclusion

It is unsurprising that the most salient finding with the women in this sample was the extent to which they challenged the norms of the cultural group to which they belonged. Many of the women in the sample were actively engaged in the process of redefining the notion of 'family honour' and negotiations. As Bhachu points out, 'ethnic cultural values are represented as repressive traits that they must accept rather than as values they continuously adapt, choose to accept, reproduce, modify, recreate and elaborate, according to the circumstances in which they are situated' (1999, p. 24).

The interviews revealed the complex relationship between the women and their families. As Brah points out, the family 'remains an area of acute ambivalence for women' as it provides them 'with a sense of belonging and family support in the struggles against the onslaughts of racism' (1996, p. 98). The multifaceted context of families means that the women occupy different social positions and access different sources of power within the family. Thus, for example, some women reported that as the eldest of siblings they were better able to negotiate terms of marriage, as parents were more likely to listen to their concerns by virtue of their age and position in the family. Similarly a large sample of the women reported it was female members of the immediate and extended family who took the decision on who should marry and then went on to broker the terms of dowry and dower. We are thus given the impression that the different sources of power to which women have access can result in them actively colluding in cases of forced marriage and such a view challenges the presupposition of an underlying family truth based solely upon patriarchal power. Herein lies the paradox whereby the understandings and interpretations of marriage can often appear as contradictory and complex. Furthermore, existing literature pays little attention to how the arranged marriage process can itself be reformed. Nor has there been much discussion on the use of modern mechanisms – for example, Muslim marriage websites and agencies – in arranging marriages. In this study very few women used such services but this is most probably reflective of the limitations in the sample rather than indicative of the use of such methods.

In this study the women were keen to discuss the ways in which the arranged marriage process could be reformed. And recognizing this method of marriage as a tradition based on cultural values allowed them the possibility of it being modified. In some cases the women explored the possibility of disposing of the term 'arranged marriage' and renaming it as an 'assisted marriage'.

> The term 'arranged marriage' has got such a bad press now with all the focus in the media. I think we need to start again, where we have 'assisted marriage', you know, where parents help us … assist us in marriage.
>
> Fauzia (London)

> I think it's time the arranged marriage thing changed because I think a lot of the time the individual gets forgotten in the process. Like, for example, my cousin – the arranged marriage things worked out really well. I mean they're a really successful couple, fantastic in fact and are a really good role models. But for me it just didn't work out. I think this needs to be challenged, that to understand that what may be good for

one individual may not be good for someone else. It's this blanket that we have to change.

                                                            Anisa (Bradford)

For other women, entering into the marriage process itself limits the choice for women.

I personally don't think either systems work and for me I would just go with the system that causes the least amount of heartache to my parents and family.

                                                            Raheela (London)

Yet for many women combining traditional and contemporary values to create new ideas of identity which facilitate individual growth and aspirations within the basic family structure are crucial. Nevertheless pressure to get married remains strong and the institution of arranged marriage is often perceived as the only acceptable form of marriage, which can lead to inter-generational conflict. Thus for the majority of women, marriage remains a process of negotiation, compromise and struggle. This may suggest that parental involvement in the marriage process is far greater than studies suggest and the nature of this involvement is complex, entailing material, emotional and psychological factors. Afshar points out, 'Women are the perceived transmitters of cultural values and identities and are the standard-bearers of the group's public and private dignity. Yet women themselves are burdened with a diversity of values and identities which may not always converge to produce a rich entirety' (1989, p. 129).

There are many social, cultural and religious reasons why British Muslim women choose to participate in traditional religious marriage ceremonies. In the popular imagination Muslim marriages are often seen as being *arranged* or *forced* which in turn subscribes to the idea that the experience of marriage for all Muslim women is based upon oppressive and archaic religious traditions. From the standpoint of the women in this study, marriage was described as a complex and complicated affair and the significance of family honour to the marriage process also raised the question as to whether the commitment to marry was contingent upon wider social influences experienced by all women in minority and majority communities. What becomes clear in this study is that the family can both provide a space for negotiating which differences are important but also produce a story of struggle and oppression itself. Because the issues of honour, choice, conflict, loyalty and belonging exist in all family relationships, it is important to capture divergent experiences effectively that cannot simply present marriage in a fixed and deterministic way.

7
Muslim Women, Divorce and Shari'ah Councils

Alternative dispute resolution (ADR) mechanisms as epitomized by Shari'ah councils have become important arenas in which to promote civic and social integration while acknowledging that their existence and use can be a threat to this very process. For Muslim women the use of these privatized spaces within which to resolve family law disputes raises fundamental questions of agency, autonomy and choice. This chapter draws upon interview data with a group of British Muslim women to better understand their motivations and experiences in using a Shari'ah council to obtain a Muslim divorce certificate. In particular the chapter considers whether this unofficial process to resolve matrimonial disputes generates greater levels of disadvantage and inequality for Muslim women or whether their use provides an insight into one of the ways in which Muslim women's subjectivity and agency is expressed.

Representations of the 'Muslim woman'

Razack (2008, p. 125) argues that Europe has long had a legal fascination with the Muslim woman's body as a *culturally different body*. Such critiques are useful to better understand how specific ideas of Muslim women are mediated through the law to produce the dialectical representation of Muslim women both as agents and victims of their communities. Contemporary liberal thinkers, shaping the terms of liberal values in Western societies and the postcolonial world, have been able to advance a rather conservative agenda in and through liberal rights discourse not in opposition to it (Kapur, 2005, p. 19). For many of these thinkers the focus on Muslim women serves as a yardstick to consider the conflict between community rights and the rights afforded by the liberal state. As Razack (2008, p. 86) points out, 'Women's bodies have long been the ground on which national difference is constructed. When the Muslim woman's body is constituted as simply a marker of a community's place in modernity and an indicator of who belongs to national community and who does not, the pervasiveness of violence against women in the west is eclipsed. Saving Muslim women from the excesses of their society marks western women as emancipated.' The current presentation of a cultural clash in the West is organized around the idea of the Muslim 'other' – essentially in conflict and disloyal to the values of liberalism and the liberal state and, in Razack's words, producing a form of cultural 'European superiority' (2008, p. 124).

Muslim women belong to many diverse communities and their lived experiences must therefore be understood as complex, strategic and at times contradictory (Afshar, 2005). Over the past three decades feminist theorists have grappled with the question of how to reconcile Western interpretations of sexual equality and the autonomy of women's agency with cultural and religious difference. As discussed in Chapter 2, debates have largely focused on a clash-of-values scenario where liberal notions of equality, free will and personal choice have been deemed 'progressively modern' and open to all, whereas the continued adherence of women belonging to minority communities to religious and traditional ties is presented as illiberal, backward and a barrier to the enhancement of women's rights. In these debates the law and juridical liberalism (e.g. anti-discrimination legislation) serve as the starting point to enhance the rights of all women. Admittedly this dichotomous approach of Western liberalism versus traditional practice and the universal applicability of 'Western modernity' with the ideas of enlightenment to non-Western traditions and in non-Western contexts has been the subject of intense critique. For example, theorists such as Spivak (1988) and Mohanty (1991) were among the first to challenge the ahistorical overgeneralized constructions of Muslim women as members of minority religious communities. Rooting themselves in both a postcolonial and feminist critique, they challenged the epistemological roots of Western scholarship that focused on the subordinated position of women belonging to minority, ethnic and religious communities. Going against the grain of traditional Western feminism, Spivak (1988, p. 25) highlights the hierarchical positions of power that Western feminists occupy and the need to critique feminist 'subject positions', the failure of which renders many feminist arguments of personal choice and equality simply inadequate and limited.

Perspectives like these also emerge in the scholarship on agency. By framing the question of individual agency within those in non-Western societies (and the idea of human rights interconnected to Western liberal democracy) and in terms of the extent to which Western democratic principles can be applied to raises the rhetoric of a 'clash of civilizations'. A key debate in human rights literature is the conceptualization of cultural human rights. Purkayastha (2009a, p. 290) points out that

> The notion of cultural human rights has gotten mired, almost exclusively, on debates about the hijab, honour killings, stoning rape victims (along with genital mutilation, forced marriages, and polygamy). Cultural human

rights were developed to protect minority cultures from extinction in the midst of a powerful majority culture. The world's indigenous people, for instance, have sought cultural human rights protection to revive and sustain their identities. Yet, most of the discussions of cultural human rights do not focus on organized attempts to promote cultural extinction. Nor do many 'transnational' feminist activists who claim to speak for 'global women's rights' systematically consult with local groups that actually work on these issues.

However, providing cultural rights is not simply a matter of making provision for multiple sets of 'personal and family' civil laws based on the idea that religions and cultures are unchanging and non-diverse. These same laws have also been used by men to subordinate women in their communities (see Purkayastha, 2009a, p. 292).

In the UK a number of legal issues have been addressed and policy measures introduced which have a particular relevance for Muslim women. Most prominent among these have been the right to veil at school, to wear the *jilbab* at the workplace, policies against forced marriage and debates on the introduction of Islamic law in the UK. Underpinning each of these debates is the question of consent versus social coercion and the extent to which Muslim women are able to express their autonomy and agency living within Muslim communities. For example, women's apparent consent to marriage in the face of coercive social, cultural and structural forces has often been broadly interpreted as acquiescence to patriarchal authority, whereas agency is equated with women's declared resistance (Goddard, 2000, p. 3), often through the strategy of exit. Others have argued that the very idea of choice in the context of more overarching systems and networks of power and domination is problematic (Wilson, 2006). Inter-generational changes among British Asian communities in the UK have also been interpreted as evidence of the rational exercise of agency by young British Asian women through strategic manoeuvres, and through compromise and negotiation within structural constraints (Samad and Eade, 2002).

The complexity of women's actions in different contexts can be understood in multiple ways. Wendell points to the role of structural inequalities while retaining a strong sense of respect for women's agency and responsibility to act within the constraints and possibilities presented by their context (Wendell, 1990; Chetkovich, 2004). That this agency, which has been defined as 'the socio culturally mediated capacity to act' (Ahearn, 2001, p. 112), can emerge in particular situations and places and at particular times has been noted in research that has examined the impact of education, employment, class, and the perception and reality of racism on women's marriage choices (e.g. Bredal, 2005). However, there has been far less exploration of how personal histories, emotions, motivations and institutional arrangements, as well as practical concerns such as access to information and perceived access to services, have a bearing on women's agency and the language they use to talk about it. How women perceive their situation (and their choices) and thereby exercise their agency may indeed change over time, as the configurations of the various forces that affect their decision-making change.

Furthermore, not all Muslim women seek to exercise their agency as understood by Western feminists in order to enhance Western feminist interpretations of their autonomy. And within the context of a patriarchal system, women will often act to uphold gendered norms, such as beauty culture, or adopt disciplinary bodily technologies like elective cosmetic surgery (Frank, 2006). Most feminist celebrations of women's agency are in service of the politics of emancipation and such accounts interpret women's lack of autonomous impulses as acquiescence to patriarchal power structures, seeing women's desires as informed by 'oppressive norms of femininity' (Morgan, 1991; Wolf, 1991). Waggoner (2005) examines the question of ethics in discussions of agency and draws upon the notion of 'ethical embodiment'. As he puts it: 'The idea it preserves is that a strong model of agency (as radically autonomous) is a fiction, since subjects are always formed and shaped by conditions not of their making, but there is nonetheless more to subjectivity than those conditions and their effects alone. Causal conditions are capable of giving rise to undetermined moments of self-reflection, self-interrogation, openness to the unforeseeable' (2005, p. 239).

One argument that does not conceptualize agency as oppositional has been voiced in Mahmood's (2006a) account of the women's piety movement in the mosques of Cairo, which uncouples agency from liberatory politics. In this important study we learn how Muslim women not only engage with mosque movements but also actively create new spaces and hence create new meanings of faith, freedom and belonging. For Saba Mahmood the imperative for all feminists is to consider the terms of these women themselves, both their understanding and relationship to God and how they are able to negotiate this. In this way she challenges traditional liberal philosophy which emphasizes individual choice as of primary value. She describes these Egyptian Muslim women's strong desires to follow socially prescribed religious conventions 'as the potentialities, the "scaffolding" ... through which the self is realized', not the signs of their subordination as individuals. She argues that their desire to take the ideals and tools of self-reference from outside the self (in Islamic religious practice, texts and law) challenges the usual separation of individual and society upon which liberal political thinking rests. She tells us we need to question the (modern American) distinction that underlies most liberal theory between 'the subject's real desires and obligatory social conventions' (see Abu-Lughod, 2002).

Research on the marriage practices of South Asian Muslim women in Britain has also uncovered instances where young women have spoken about their need to uphold certain traditional norms out of a positive need to assert their belonging to a community under siege (Bredal, 2005). In her study Bhimji (2009) examines the ways in which British-born South Asian Muslim women engage with Islam through study circles. She argues that the religious spaces within which the women participate allow them to assert various identities, as well as agency, as they collectively search to comprehend Islam. In traversing these religious spheres, women transform them from male-dominated sites to spaces wherein feminine, political and cosmopolitan identities are expressed. Anitha and Gill (2009) also express caution in conceptualizing Asian women's choices around the binary framework of coercion versus consent arguing that by 'examining the socio-cultural construction of personhood, especially womanhood and the intersecting structural inequalities that constrain particular groups of South Asian women in the UK ... consent and coercion in relation to marriage can be better understood as two ends of a continuum, between which lie degrees of socio-cultural expectation, control, persuasion, pressure, threat and force. Women who face these constraints exercise their agency in complex and contradictory ways that are not always recognized by the existing exit-centred state initiatives designed to tackle this problem' (p. 165).

Women, therefore exercise their agency in complex and often contradictory ways as they assess the options that are open to them, weigh the costs and benefits of their actions, and seek to balance their often competing needs with their expectations and desires. While there remains a need to recognize gendered power imbalances at the same time, there also remains a need to respect women's exercise of agency.

Using Shari'ah councils

Freely exercising one's choice to use a Shari'ah council to obtain a Muslim divorce remains a underlying concern for many feminists and all those wary of recognizing religious bodies as ADR mechanisms in family law disputes. Consigned to the 'private sphere', Shari'ah councils are largely unregulated by state rules in family law matters and this can therefore have far-reaching consequences for Muslim women and their capacity for decision-making in the face of family and community pressures.

As discussed earlier, the view of women's successful attainment of subjectivity and their exercise of personal choice raises fundamental questions in relation to their experiences of using institutional community frameworks underpinned by patriarchal values. A key condition prior to issuing a divorce certificate is the requirement set by the councils for Muslim women to consider reconciling. Feminists draw attention to the fact that many community and religious organizations are institutionally patriarchal (Patel, 2008) and therefore using such fora can lead to greater levels of intercultural gender inequality for women. But what are their reasons and motivations for obtaining a Muslim divorce certificate? Are they avoiding the use of civil law mechanisms in favour of privatized dispute resolution to settle matrimonial disputes? Is justice therefore being administered in the 'privatized space' of Shari'ah councils, effectively under the 'shadow of law'? (see Griffiths, 2003). More specifically are women being encouraged to reconcile with violent or dangerous partners? Are they compromising their rights in relation to custody and access of children? Does this form of Muslim family justice curtail the women's citizenship rights and undermine the notion of 'equality before the law'?

As discussed in Chapter 4, female applicants contact a Shari'ah council on occasions when husbands may refuse to grant them a unilateral divorce known as a *talaq*. In her groundbreaking study titled *Untying the Knot: Muslim Women, Divorce and the Shariah*, Shah-Kazemi (2001) explored the reasons why women chose to use a Shari'ah council. The single-most important reason to emerge in this study was the women's need to obtain a religious divorce certificate rather than a desire to save their marriages. Shah-Kazemi points out that the women who chose to use Shari'ah councils saw this use as part of their religious identity, a finding confirmed in this study. Furthermore this interaction with the councils was negotiated in different ways and their different cultural, ethnic and traditional backgrounds as well as their personal experiences, affected the way in which they used the councils. The subjective experiences of Muslim women may not therefore easily rest within the dichotomy of free will versus social coercion and the idea of a free and autonomous person as found in Western philosophical literature as discussed in Chapter 1. Instead the social and lived experiences of Muslim women using these bodies may point to more sophisticated analyses of their motivations for using these bodies and raises wider questions relating to their agency, autonomy and the exercise of free choice. As Mahmood (2006a, p. 167) points out, 'different modalities of agency' come into play when Muslim women exercise their agency in relation to patriarchal institutions.

Islamic divorce and the rights of Muslim women

The *legitimacy* of divorce in Islam has been discussed extensively in Islamic literature with scholars drawing upon the Qur'an and the Hadith literature to reveal that divorce is permissible in Islam but only as a final resort (Engineer, 1992; Esposito, 1988). While numerous scholars have analysed the ethical and spiritual dimensions of Islamic divorce (in the context of preserving the institution of Islamic marriage), it is the contractual nature of Muslim marriage that permits the different types of divorce available to Muslim women. Carroll points out that the different schools of Islamic legal tradition allow termination by 'either of the parties, by mutual agreement or by the courts' (Carroll, 1997).

Notwithstanding the diversity of literature on divorce in Muslim law there are two key issues that pose possible tensions for British Muslim women. The first relates to the extent to which Muslims are being divorced outside the official legal system and whether this creates a conflict with official law.[1] Menski identifies this problem as 'limping divorces' where a civil divorce has been obtained by the woman but her husband is refusing to grant her a Muslim divorce (Menski, 2001).[2] This has meant that women who may have been divorced through civil procedure continue to be married under Muslim religious law and those who may have been divorced abroad may not be legally recognized in this country as divorced and thus continue to be legally married. This leads to a conflict-of-laws scenario and Yilmaz describes its implications: 'if the woman is not religiously divorced from her husband, it does not matter that she is divorced under the civil law, in the eyes of the community her remarriage will be regarded as adulterous and any possible offspring will be illegitimate since it is not allowed under the religious law. So, in reality, until the religious divorce is obtained, the civil divorce remains ineffective because one party is unable to remarry' (2001b, p. 16). To address such a legal quagmire, scholars of law have suggested that legal practitioners and the judiciary must be equipped with a better understanding of Islamic norms, values and principles in order to avoid any confusion and/or conflict between state law and religious socio-legal principles. Consequently there have been various attempts and initiatives developed by several state-based legal bodies to better understand ethnic minority customs and practices.[3]

The second issue relates to the type of Muslim divorce granted to the women by the Shari'ah councils. If a *khul* is granted, it means that the female applicant must give up her right to dower or *mahr* in return for a divorce. Menski describes this process as follows: 'Usually the wife will offer to pay a certain sum, normally the amount of the mahr either given to her or promised to her, in return for the agreement of the husband to release her from the marriage tie' (Pearl and Menski, 1998, p. 284). Again this is a complex area and there is some confusion as to the precise amount of *mahr* the husband should receive for the *khul* (see Carroll, 1997). Aside from this issue, Shari'ah councils also deal with how the female applicant is able to retrieve her *mahr* after her husband has willingly divorced her. Nasir points out that in theory Muslim women who are entitled to the *mahr* have exclusive right to it under the terms of the marriage contract, though in practice this may vary 'according to the circumstances. She may be entitled to the whole dower, half of it or may have no dower at all' (1990, p. 103). Furthermore Afshar points out that 'what women are entitled to and what they get are very different. Married women are not expected to assert their proprietorial rights. They are not to bring conflict, but peace' (1994 , p. 129).

In his study of Muslim legal pluralism, Pearl and Menski points to what he describes as 'the legal de-recognition of Muslim divorces ... in the United Kingdom' (1998, p. 382). By this he means the lack of provision in English law to recognize religious law as an official form of divorce. In the present, revised English family law there is only one way to obtain a divorce – on the grounds that the marriage has irretrievably broken down, after a two-year separation where the decree is made absolute. Muslim divorces granted through a 'non-judicial process' known as the *talaq* (Poulter, 1986, p. 98) are generally not recognized as valid in Britain, a situation which has led to the creation of 'limping marriages' as described before (Pearl and Menski, 1998, p. 383).

In this study obtaining a Muslim divorce was important to all the women and given as the primary reason given for contacting a Shari'ah council. Given the fact that the issue of divorce is fraught with difficulties and tension for women within South Asian Muslim communities, the focus of this research was to better understand the strategies adopted by the women in their quest to obtain a Muslim divorce certificate. In the course of the fieldwork it became apparent that the women had little alternative than to approach a Shari'ah council to obtain a religious divorce when their husbands refused to grant them a unilateral divorce. It also became clear that they often had to struggle against the prevalence of patriarchal attitudes endemic within Shari'ah councils and the confusion, at times, as regards the advice given by religious scholars based upon different and at times conflicting interpretations of Islamic divorce generated for the women. Hence questions arise regarding the processes and procedures that are involved in obtaining a Muslim divorce and the experiences of female users of Shari'ah councils. These relate to issues concerning negotiations, conflict and decision-making both within the family, community and via such unofficial dispute resolution bodies. So how did this sample of women negotiate issues of marriage breakdown and divorce within the family, home and community? And at what point was contact made with a Shari'ah council?

The breakdown of marriage

This study showed that, as well as playing a central and vital role in the organization of the marriage, the family played a vital role in both organizing and facilitating attempts to reconcile the parties when marriages broke down. Within the family context attempts at reconciliation could take shape in various ways and the women each reported that they had been involved in lengthy discussions with their families, and in some cases imams, to explore the different ways in which they could possibly save their marriage.

In a majority of cases the women reported that they had been blamed for the breakdown of the marriage and were being typically characterized as the primary 'marriage wreckers' for instigating divorce. Therefore despite being subjected to intense levels of pressure to reconcile with husbands, it is interesting to note that the women also reported being able to express themselves and challenge social and cultural norms such as family honour. These challenges were commonly perceived within their communities as dishonourable and socially unacceptable during these attempts to reconcile. In her work on mediation within ethnic minority families, Shah-Kazemi (2000, p. 312) points out that family mediation takes on a particular significance for minority ethnic communities where both spouses and wider family members perform specific roles and each have the capacity to act to resolve the dispute. In this way all parties involved in this process bear both rights and responsibilities, and the concept of a free, autonomous and rational individual as understood in Western literature on individual capacity and decision-making cannot apply so easily.

The data in this study revealed the emphasis the women placed on family intervention to resolve the marital dispute because the family was perceived and understood as being inextricably linked to the marriage. As one interviewee explained:

> The thing with arranged marriages is that when it breaks down you're not really left alone. It's the family that arranges it so when it breaks down they go into this motion of trying to sort things out.
>
> Shazia (London)

> Yes I did expect my family to help me and yeah I do think it was because I had an arranged marriage. I suppose the way I got married was different to how my English friends get married and they probably don't expect the kind of help that I got.
>
> Humeira (London)

The reasons for the breakdown of marriage in this sample were cited as forced marriage, family interference, 'clash of upbringing', adultery and domestic violence. Eighteen women reported that they had experienced some form of emotional, sexual and/or physical abuse during their marriages and a small percentage of women continued to face this threat (see also Thiara and Gill, 2010). In this sense it would be a mistake to ignore the detrimental impact traditional norms that are based upon family and moral ideas of responsibility may have upon some of the lives of these women. The reasons for breakdown of marriage were premised upon inter-family inequalities with discussion focusing on issues of power, negotiation and struggle. In relation to 'family pressure' many of the women described relationships with in-laws as being particularly difficult and fraught. Those who opposed or challenged their in-laws' authority were ostracized and alienated from other members of the family. For other women the control of their physical movements meant they were given very little space to assert their independence within the family context. In three cases this had led to increased levels of domestic violence.

The extracts that follow provide a brief snapshot of the effects on the lives of these women.

> It wasn't that bad in the beginning but over time he became very violent and by the end I wasn't allowed to go out by myself.
>
> Mina (London)

> I tried to commit suicide. I used to go to my doctor and I used to complain to him all the time. He told me to leave. At one time I never used to eat.
>
> Sadia (Birmingham)

> My dad was never on my side. When he found out about the problems, he always used to shout at me saying that I must do everything they tell me to do. He only said that because he was scared that I was going to end up divorced and he kept saying, 'Don't get divorced, don't get divorced.'
>
> Zareena (Bradford)

Patel (2008) identifies the control of women within minority communities and families as an issue that needs greater attention. She also argues that the state affords black and minority women little protection. Organizations such as Southall Black Sisters[4] and Newham Asian Women's Project[5] have over the past three decades developed critiques on state accountability and the limitations of strategies to support vulnerable women. For many of the women in this study, leaving the marriage could prove a difficult and traumatic experience. One interviewee, Sameena (Birmingham), explained the lengths that she had undergone prior to leaving the marriage:

> I knew I had to be really careful because they wouldn't have let me go. But one day when they were all out I just left and took my children without any belongings. I went to the health officer and they put me into a bed and breakfast.

While many of the problems the women faced were premised upon inter-family inequalities, the women were also vocal in arguing that they were not accountable for the actions of their husbands and all recognized that Islam permits a Muslim woman the right to divorce – a mechanism that was used to protect themselves against abusive marriages.

This study showed that divorce is not an easy option for British Muslim women and the majority of women only considered this option after years of verbal, emotional and physical abuse. Family intervention in attempting to resolve the dispute was taken as a sign that their parents and wider family cared enough about them to attempt to save their marriages but that did not mean that the women did not come into conflict with notions of obedience, the language of duty, respect for authority and a sense of piety culminating in forms of moral pressure and social conditioning to maintain the honour of the family.

Transnational marriages

The high levels of transnational marriages that take place between British-born Pakistanis and Pakistani nationals raise a number of questions regarding their legal validity and immigration barriers. In English law transnational marriages are deemed valid as long as they comply with the Marriage Acts 1949 and 1994. Charsley and Shaw (2006) point to the popularity of transnational marriages between British Pakistanis and Pakistani nationals, which distinguishes this group from other South Asian groups in Britain. The authors report that such marriages are based upon kinship obligations, emotional ties and a socio-economic strategy. Their empirical research with British Pakistanis in Bristol draws on the concept of *rishta* (a good match) and illustrates how this concept acts as an emotional tie among siblings, parents and the prospective spouses in order to forge the marriage relationship and which then ensures its continuing practice and importance. Charsley (2005a) reports that the majority of such marriages take place in Pakistan after which an application is made by either the husband or wife to enter into Britain. Under the current UK immigration rules the applicant, for admission as the spouse or fiancé of a person settled in the UK, is required to demonstrate that 'each of the parties intends to live permanently with the other as his or her spouse and the marriage is subsisting'.[6] This rule is aimed at the prevention of marriages of convenience (Wray, 2006, p. 163). Scholars point out that the abolition of the Primary Purpose rule (see Shah, 2005) in 1997 has led to an increase in Pakistani transnational marriages. Under this rule applicants could be refused if the clearance officer was satisfied that the marriage was undertaken primarily in order to gain entry into Britain. As Wray (2006, p. 163) points out, 'the difficulties in proving that the purpose of the marriage was not primarily immigration were multiple and fell almost solely, as they were designed to do, upon arranged marriages from the Indian sub-continent'.

In her work Charsley (2005b) has explored the gendered dimension of transnational marriages, explaining that 'the marriage of a child presents an opportunity to strengthen connections between much-missed kin separated by migration decades earlier. Parental exegeses also stress the need to protect daughters, conceptualized as vulnerable to mistreatment by in-laws. For some, the marriage of a daughter in Britain to a trusted relative who has been raised in an Islamic society is one response to this risk.' Her focus on migrant husbands also reveals an interesting insight into the asymmetry in expectations of marital 'adjustment' and compromise, masculinity and the position of the uxorilocally resident son-in-law (*ghar damad*) (2005b, p. 386).

In this study the reasons for the breakdown of transnational marriages were cited as domestic violence, forced marriage and 'a conflict of upbringing' between British Muslim women and their Pakistani spouses. As one interviewee explained:

> I think there's a conflict with women who are brought up here and men who come from Pakistan to get married. We just saw things differently. For him it was a problem that I wanted to work, that I was pretty independent and this was important to me. It didn't mean I couldn't be a good wife, but he just couldn't see things from my point of view.
>
> Zareena (Bradford)

In her report Shah-Kazemi (2000) found immigration regulations to be a significant 'equation' in the breakdown of marriage arguing that had these regulations not been in place the outcome of the marriage may have been very different. She points out, 'If immigration regulations were not in existence, and unrelated to marriage, men would not be interested in exploiting women solely for the purpose of immigration, women would not be vulnerable to the pressure to allow the marriages to continue, nor indeed would the women go through the hardship of having to wait for their husbands' (2001, pp. 33–4). In this study those women who had been forced into marriage while in Pakistan held the view that immigration legislation in the UK could be utilized to prevent their husbands from gaining entry into the country (see also Bhabba and Shutter, 1994). It was also clear that in two cases where entry had been allowed the interviewees had sought the advice of police and the Home Office in their attempts to deport their husbands. As one interviewee explained:

> For the past three years he's made our lives hell. He constantly harasses us and his family used us so he could come into this country. I want him out and I'll do everything in my power to make sure it happens.
>
> Nasima (Birmingham)

However, in both cases the women reported little success. While it is easy to condemn these strategies, which effectively give the state a further excuse to introduce even tighter controls and restrict immigration (see Patel, 2003), it is also important to understand the underlying issues which may compel such women to resort to such drastic tactics.

The decision to leave

The data revealed a close correlation between the women's decision to leave a marriage and the level of financial independence they enjoyed. For example, those women who were financially dependent upon their husbands were more likely to have remained in the marriage when compared to those who were not.

Fauzia (Birmingham) confirmed that her decision to leave the marriage had been made easier with the knowledge that her family could provide her with financial support. In turn, Salma (Bradford) drew attention to the 'assumed link between tradition and being backward'.

> I am traditional and that's important to me. I like to wear Asian clothes and, you know, do Asian things but people make assumptions. Like my in-laws, they thought that my parents would never want me back if they treated me badly and if I wanted to leave, just because of my religion and the way I was. I felt as though I was tricked into the marriage and when I told his family they said, 'Well, so what?' As if I would just stay in the marriage.

She had left to return to her parents' home. It is also useful to point out that those women educated up to university level also mentioned their educational attainment as a contributory factor in the breakdown of marriage. For example, Parveen (Birmingham) described how the difficulties in the marriage were compounded by the fact that she was perceived as being 'too educated' and hence 'too independent'.

> I did everything they wanted me to do. I cooked, I cleaned, I looked after them as well as my husband but still it was never enough. Just the fact that I'd been to college, that I had an education, was a problem for them.

At the same time, the interviews revealed that some women had experienced specific problems because of being labelled as 'too Westernized'. Interestingly these views transcended class and educational differences. A number of the interviewees were keen to emphasize the weight of family expectations.

> I could never win in the eyes of my in-laws, never. I could never do right, that's how it always felt ... I wasn't traditional enough, I just didn't fit the mould of a traditional girl and that's what my mother-in-law really wanted.
>
> Shabana (London)

> He started imposing things on me, like you have to wear a scarf, and I'm not really comfortable with it, you know, and I told him, 'Well, I'm not really comfortable with it and I don't believe I should do something that someone is making me do it.' Islam is within myself. I do it because I want to do it. I'm not saying I don't have any intention of it, I will do

it but not just yet and he was more worried about his Dad than himself. The impression I got was that he wasn't really that bothered himself; he was more bothered about his family.

Nighat (London)

But in my in-laws' family it was like, you can't go out, you can't do this, you have to wear a scarf all the time, you have to wear shalwar kameez all the time, you can't wear anything else. 'So OK', I thought, 'Oh my God, I can't live like this!' Eventually I spoke to a friend of mine; she's quite religious and she told me that women couldn't be compelled to do things in Islam – it's wrong and it's un-Islamic.

Humeira (London)

In Islam we need women's voices to be heard. Not just talk about the need for change but actual change and the acceptance of recognizing women as equals.

Anisa (Bradford)

I always did what they told me because my parents taught me that when you get married you should never speak in front of your mother-in-law. But in this family they really used Islam against us. If we argued and said something was wrong they would just bring Islam into it, saying Islam says this and Islam says that but whenever they did anything bad to me they brushed Islam under the carpet and do what they want because Islam never said you can treat your wife like that. Islam says that a wife is equal to your Mum but I was never treated like that.

Sadia (Birmingham)

Such descriptions of 'being controlled' and the lack of empowerment within the newfound family household eventually proved a catalyst for many of these women to seek change in their lives and to exit the marriage. It also demonstrates how the women were able to draw upon Islam to demand equality and respect in the family household (see also Barlas, 2006).

Unofficial family mediation

Historically the legal provisions supporting couples in matters of family breakdown are premised upon philosophical and political bases on the extent to which the state *should* intervene in matters of marriage breakdown, separation and divorce (Eeklaar and Maclean 2004). However, few studies explore the nature of 'unofficial family mediation' (which takes place in 'private' with no official intervention) or analyse the normative frameworks of family- and community-type intervention.[7] For example, the ways in which cross-cultural mediation takes shape is of particular significance for understanding the ways in which disputes are resolved within minority ethnic and religious communities. Shah-Kazemi (2000, p. 304) points out that 'negotiations within the domain of marital disputes assume a very particular complexity as the dynamics of both gender and identity-defining normative ethics shape the setting in which the negotiations take place'. Therefore the extent to which the religious and cultural identity of the participants and the mediators may influence the ways in which the disputes are resolved raises the question of what is the decision-making capacity of the individuals involved. Shah-Kazemi (2000, p. 307) points to a number of key factors which influence this process: 'The dynamics of migration, the concomitant insecurities and need for self-preservation and simply the fact of being in a minority has implications for the way in which any family dispute is tolerated.'

The family and the family network may play a central role in the resolution process. In this study the family provided the normative framework upon which all negotiations were based. As well as arranging the marriage, the family played a vital role in facilitating attempts to reconcile the parties upon the breakdown of marriage. The interview data revealed the inevitable conflicts and disputes that had been generated by the breakdown of the marriage and of the sample 20 women explained that they had been involved in lengthy discussions with their families prior to making any contact with a Shari'ah council. Shah-Kazemi (2000, p. 312) points out that family mediation takes on particular significance for individuals who belong to minority ethnic communities. This was confirmed by findings in this study where intervention of family members is closely associated to their role in arranging the marriage. As Shah-Kazemi (2000, p. 316) explains, 'the knowledge of normative family structures such as the dynamics of the extended family, or the prevailing attitude towards elders is axiomatic in achieving dispute resolution. The complexity and importance of these wider family relationships can have a greater impact on the dispute than any problems in the marriage of the couple.' So what are the cultural prescriptions that govern the way in which disputes are resolved? And what are the specific cultural and religious norms that enter into this process of negotiation?

Interview data reveal that this process of dispute resolution gives rise to a set of obligations and responsibilities for all parties involved:

Well, there is a system to prevent breakdown and it's a very invisible one, a very subtle one and it starts with your own family. The community at large are prepared to play a reinforcing part and what your family is doing is they say, 'Are you alright?' and you're expected to say 'Yes, how are you?' You're expected to say, 'I'm fine', and what you do is you make sure that everything that happens in your household remains there; nothing goes outside of that.

Nasima (Birmingham)

When I eventually decided to leave home, I called my family together. My family had no idea what had been going on and how abusive he had been and all the neglect and all the treatment that myself and my daughter had had, because why should they? Because he never made it public and also I think people let things go because they don't want to know. But they were very upset that I hadn't told them and once I had done.

Rubina (Birmingham)

The data revealed three types of unofficial family mediation that can be broadly categorized as the intervention of the immediate and extended members of the family; the involvement of local community members and/ or family friends; and finally advice from an imam, often based at the local mosque. In the management of the marital dispute the data revealed that the interviewees were involved in a complex and often shifting process that included fulfilling social, familial and cultural expectations while also negotiating terms for a possible reconciliation. This demonstrates the dilemmas and the conflicts that women's identities as individuals and as members of the family group may give rise to (see Hellum, 1999, p. 88). As discussed in the previous chapter, the plurality of shifting identities for women in South Asian Muslim communities also provides an insight into their complex relations in the home, family and community.

Well initially I told no one because I didn't want my parents to get involved and then you know for things to get worse, the more people that get involved then things can get out of hand. I was a bit scared anyway because I hadn't been married that long and if I say I've got problems, they'd be really, really worried about it ... It was too difficult. I was expected to make it work, so it really had to get bad before I could tell them.

Farhana (Birmingham)

I spoke to one of my uncles but I made him promise me that he wouldn't tell my parents because they'd be really, really upset about it. So I said to him I want you to help me sort out this mess because he had been involved in getting me together with my husband. So they came over and they had a word and they said, 'Well, you know it's not fair that you're doing this.' I was in a real state.

Sabia (London)

Well, not my side of the family but his side of the family did get involved. His eldest sister-in-law did give me a lot of support. She said, 'This is not right, something has to be done', and then she told her husband and they talked within the family and they told me they did speak to him but I don't know what was said.

Shaheen (London)

It was hard for me to go to my parents. They didn't want me to marry this guy, so when things started to go wrong I tried to deal with it myself. But then it got pretty bad; you know, he hit me and stuff, so then I called them. They were really upset at the start but then they were OK. They helped me sort things out.

Mina (London)

The dilemma of preserving the 'family honour' did limit the decision-making abilities of some women within the family and home. The issue of 'exiting' the marriage was neither easily resolved nor uncritically accepted as a final solution and some women grappled with the pressures of maintaining the '*izzat* of the family' (family honour) while others expressed ambivalence about the effects of *izzat* upon their decision to leave.

I couldn't tell my parents straight away because of the *izzat* thing. They were always saying that my marriage had kept the *izzat* of the family, so when things started to go wrong it was difficult for me to explain to them how I was feeling and what I wanted to do about the situation.

Nasima (London)

None of my family wanted me to get divorced but in a way it was easier for them to accept that it was over, that it hadn't worked out but that I had tried to make it work. They blamed my husband for a lot of what was going on, so they didn't talk in terms of *izzat* or *sharam* [shame] when I said I wanted to leave. We spoke about what was right and wrong and what he did was wrong. So no I wasn't worried about losing the family honour.

Shaheen (London)

I never once felt that I was in some way losing the honour of the family, how absurd! Talk to him if you want to know about no honour. It's him and his family who have lost the family honour ... if they ever had any.

Fauzia (London)

My parents aren't educated and we're not middle-class ... But we're Muslims and they understand right from wrong. I wanted their help to sort things out and in Islam they have a duty to support me in my time of need. We discussed things together and only when they came to the conclusion that things wouldn't change did I make up my mind that it was time to go.

Zareena (Bradford)

These findings suggest that some women were able to challenge the notion of family honour as a duty upon women, but in doing so reconceptualize its meaning and reject its wholesale imposition in determining their decision to leave. Instead they were able to transfer this 'responsibility' to their husbands using Islamic principles of fairness and equity. In this way family honour was instead characterized as an obligation to fulfil social and cultural expectations during the process of marriage and, in some cases, this shift challenges the potency of the argument that women are reluctant to leave due to concerns of preserving the family honour. Yet the interview data also revealed the correlation between family intervention and the women's decision to reconcile. The failure of the family to resolve the marital difficulties was then, for some women, a source of regret.

The women engaged in complex negotiations with parents and wider family to either justify their decision to leave or to establish the grounds upon which they would seek a divorce under Islamic law. In addition, for some women, support from female members of the family was of particular importance and for many women this had been a significant factor in their decision to leave. For example, the women were able to create alliances with mothers and sisters, highlighting the importance of interwoven solidarity between them and thus challenging the dynamics of patriarchal power inherent within the family (Bhopal, 1999). Notwithstanding the obvious value of these relationships, at the same time, this 'collective approach' reveals a number of ambiguities and contradictions, as this form of 'strategic essentialism' (Yuval-Davis, 1997) is imbued with both possibilities and limitations. It is true that the women were able to gain support and strength from their female allies but in doing so many women reported they also had to respond to an axiomatic acceptance of arranged marriages. Even though ostensibly opposed to remarrying, some women accepted that a new marriage would be arranged on their behalf by their parents in exchange for leaving their current marriage. Therefore, in what at first seems like a new space of dialogue and autonomy in the family context can in fact rely upon and promote the traditional framework of power embedded within families (Anthias, 2002).

For other women, the experience of family members mediating to resolve the matrimonial dispute was described as a distressing experience. Nabila (London) complained that her parents had been unwilling to accept that her marriage was over and her subsequent refusal to participate in family mediation had been met with stern parental opposition. This had led to a deterioration of relations with her husband and family, culminating in her parents blaming her for the breakdown of the marriage. Pressure to return to the family home for some women therefore led to an increased risk of physical and emotional abuse.

This form of unofficial family mediation most often takes place prior to any formal counselling or mediation. The links between unofficial and official family mediation have been explored by family law scholars. Eekelaar explains, 'there exists within society a network of social norms which is formally independent of the legal system, but which is in constant interaction with it. Formal law sometimes seeks to strengthen the social norms. Sometimes it allows them to serve its purposes without the necessity of direct intervention; sometimes it tries to weaken or destroy them and sometimes it withdraws from enforcement, not in an attempt to subvert them, but because countervailing values make conflicts better resolved outside the legal arena' (2000, p. 8). Feminist scholars have also extensively critiqued this tenuous relationship between family and state intervention in family law disputes (see Wallback, Choudhury and Herring, 2009).

Debates on the criminalization of domestic violence have shaped the nature of state intervention in the private sphere of family and home and over the past decade these private sites continue to be contested in debates on the recognition of cultural autonomy for minority groups. Thornton points to the dangers of the state promoting family intervention as a mechanism for resolving matrimonial disputes, pointing out that such approaches serve merely to ensure that the state is able to abrogate its responsibility for protecting vulnerable members. She explains, 'In mediating interests which appear to be irreconcilable, the task of the liberal state is made easier if there are some areas conceptualized as "private" with which it does not have to grapple' (1991, p. 167). Therefore promoting family mediation can have negative implications for women's equality and 'in a patriarchal society, where men dominate positions of power and authority, women are socialized to play a subservient role' (Sidhu, 2006, p. 11). In addition, due to the inherent nature of women's inequality, societal values and gender role socialization influence how men and women deal with conflict. Men are characterized as being assertive, independent and able to deal with conflict in a rational way whereas women are socialized to act out characteristics such as understanding and compassion (Sidhu, 2006, p. 11). Grillo (1991, p. 160) notes that this socialization 'is reflected in the tendency for women to comply a relational ethic of care in dealing with other people which leads to a negation of any focus on the self'.

Clearly, unofficial family mediation then points to the complicated ways in which power is expressed via the family idiom. There is little mention in official family mediation literature of the ways in which families organize dispute resolution within the private sphere of the family and home and raising the question of why some women may choose not to opt for official mediation. The findings in this study suggest that the interconnected and mutual values of family honour and shame can impose compliance for some women whereas other women embrace this form of family mediation and reformulate it to suit their needs which then provides them with the 'space' upon which to challenge abusive relationships.

Yet it is precisely because of these divergent experiences that proposals to develop official family mediation policies to suit the specific needs of minority ethnic communities must be approached with caution (see Shah-Kazemi, 2000, 2001). There is an inherent danger with such approaches being based upon specific ethnic norms and values and cultural and religious practices with little recognition that all cultural and religious practices are open to change, contestation and interpretation and therefore open to challenge by the very members of the community they wish to serve. It is within this context that some scholars have raised concerns that proposals to promote cross-cultural mediation can lead to delegating rights and protection against abuse to communities in regulating family law matters, effectively a move towards some form of cultural autonomy in family law matters. Undoubtedly in this context formal law provides protection against abuse in the private sphere in which this type of legal ordering operates. As Maclean (2000, p. 137) rightly questions, 'What are the implications for family justice of this move towards private ordering? Is this form of "privatization" safe? Is it dangerous to remove disputes from the legal system with the advantage of due process, plus protection of those at the wrong end of the far from level playing field, and visible negotiation and settlement which takes place if not in court then in the shadow of the law?' At the very least, therefore, mechanisms must be put into place for those who wish not to use these services but may feel compelled to do so due to family and community pressure.

What type of community intervention?

In this study, it was found that unofficial family mediation was also shaped by the involvement of the local community as well as family members and/ or friends. Interview data revealed the intervention of imams as particularly significant. With the perceived weakening of family ties, parents in particular encouraged the intervention of imams based in local mosques to help resolve the marital dispute. Once admitted into this process the extent to which imams may have influenced the outcome raises important questions regarding the influence upon the women's decision-making.

Data revealed that the decision to invest in community resources lay primarily with parents, then the wider family and friends, and finally the women themselves. In defining the marital dispute via the local community and envisaging solutions through various kinds of cultural and religious ADR mechanisms, some women were able to mitigate the effects of divorce both for themselves and their families. By utilizing the local community they were able to ease the pressure of being stigmatized as a divorcee and in some cases even strengthened fragile relationships with family and local community members.

> My Dad is quite well known in the community and the community did know that if I came back there's a good reason for it ... I mean people talk but you can't do anything about it.
>
> Fauzia (London)

> When I came back everyone was looking at me thinking that 'Well, all of us go through hard times, right, but at the end of the day you could have tried a bit harder'. The community were badmouthing me; they were looking at me, looking at me in a degrading way, like I was second class basically. But I just said, 'Well, accept it'. I mean if I had let it get to me it would have mentally affected me.
>
> Zareena (Birmingham)

> It really helped my parents that they were able to talk to their friends. I know they got a lot of support from them and that kind of eased the pressure off me.
>
> Nighat (London)

> Well they went to see our imam and explained everything to him, what I had been through and how my parents had tried to help, tried to talk to his family but were shoved away. So it really helped them to know that under Islam we had done nothing wrong, that it wasn't my fault or their fault and they had nothing to feel ashamed about.
>
> Shabana (London)

> We were really surprised that we got so much support. It was good ... good for my parents. It's been harder for them because they've had a lot to deal with ... especially when no one in our family has ever been divorced before.
>
> Parveen (Birmingham)

In particular the significance of community involvement in the early stages of the marital dispute raises the question of whether these women were then also establishing 'new more inclusive collective ethnic identifications' (Alexander, 2002, p. 560) as a way of strengthening a sense of belonging in the local family and community context. Describing this sense of belonging to a local Muslim community in terms of the community fulfilling a social function, meeting social expectations and familial obligations reflects how some of the women were able to self-consciously reconceptualize constructions of community as fluid and changing. In reality this sense of belonging was contested but many women were able to manipulate both its resources and at times sidestep its obvious constraints and therefore their positioning had to be continually constituted and negotiated.

There's a huge sense of belonging within the community. I've grown up in the Muslim community and it's important for me to feel that I'm part of the community.

Nadia (Birmingham)

If you had a love marriage and it failed, you would have a divorce and then you would be likely to be rejected by the community. You would have nowhere to go.

Mina (London)

I worked very hard at perfecting my community role whether that was as a daughter, as a niece or as a wife or as a mother or as someone who did the *tabliq* [religious work] or whatever it was. I did all of that because I knew how to do it because someone before me had done it.

Yasmin (London)

It took me a long time to get the strength to do what was right. My Dad goes to the mosque a lot and he spoke to one of the maulvis there and he came back to me and said that only my husband could divorce me and that I should stay with him to make it work.

Zareena (Bradford)

The community doesn't particularly care … it just fills up the gaps, so as long as he is seen in the mosque, as long as he is seen fairly respectably because most of the marriages are judged by how the women behave as well and how the children are. So therefore we have this façade.

Parveen (Birmingham)

It was difficult because my family used to say to me, 'Well, you're away from home, you're away from the community so you don't have to listen to this but we do.' I would say to my family ignore them but they can't because they live in the community and that's their life, that's their lifestyle. I felt as though people were judging me and my family. I felt really sad because my parents are basically good people. They're good Muslims that have never hurt anybody, they didn't deserve it.

Rabia (Birmingham)

Hence while the women negotiated the nature of community intervention, many were simply reluctant to opt out and exercise the 'exit option' (see also Phillips, 2003). The point which seems to be crucial, however, is that the women were able to draw upon the community for support while at times remaining critical of its lack of resolve in challenging cultural practices that they deemed oppressive to all Muslim women and ultimately 'un-Islamic'. For some women, therefore, the community acted as an important support mechanism for them and their families, even if this meant they did not always agree with its position. 'Community expectations' were therefore challenged and resisted in different ways.

At times the interviews reveal a protracted and ambivalent relationship between the women and those imams who intervened and helped in resolving the marital dispute. On the one hand the imams were identified as pivotal to the negotiation process, often negotiating the terms upon which a possible reconciliation could be achieved. But on the other hand the data also revealed some women's deep anxiety about the nature of this intervention and concerns about the pressure placed upon them to reconcile and to accept the terms of the reconciliation that had been negotiated by the imams on their behalf. For example, when questioned about why imams had intervened in their cases, eight women described being 'persuaded by family members' to seek the involvement of imams. A further five women described the problems they had encountered in communicating with an imam due to the imam's close relationship with their parents and/or wider family members. Imams had often been appointed by family members (most often parents) and in most cases this had caused some consternation among the women. As Shazia (London) explained, 'The role of the family particularly and the community at large is to make sure that you stay together.' To this end she felt that although her opinion had been taken into account during the negotiation process, her viewpoint rarely prevailed because of her limited input into the reconciliation process. In his research Bunt (1998) found that informal dispute resolution processes are largely based in mosques where the imam plays a critical role in the nature of the advice given. His findings reveal imams as 'conservative' in nature with many of them encouraging Muslim parents to arrange 'quick' marriages for their daughters so as to maintain the stability and honour of the family and community.

However, some of the women in this study found that the intervention of the imam provided a space in which to challenge cultural practices. In the case of Shabana (Bradford), for example, being able to challenge parental pressure to reconcile was of significant importance. She explained:

> He [the imam] was really good. I explained the situation to him and he told me that it's not God's intention that you sit in that unhappiness, you need to have a decent husband and I don't think you'll find it in this relationship. It won't be any shame on you to leave and end it.

She was therefore able to exit the marriage without an accusatory finger of blame pointed towards her. Some women were also able to garner considerable support from imams to convince parents that divorce was permissible in Islam. As Rabia (Birmingham) explained:

> My parents are strict Muslims ... they thought he's a good and decent man [the imam] so it was important for me to explain everything to him so that he could make my parents understand that it was OK to get divorced and also ... you know, how to deal with the community who would definitely be gossiping.

This approach echoed the stance taken by Fauzia (Birmingham) who described the intervention by the imam as crucial to the successful mediation between the two families who were then able to resolve complex matters such as the redistribution of financial assets and the return of the *mahr*. In this case the imam had also acted as a go-between and had travelled from London to Manchester to return monies to her that she had acquired upon marriage. At the very least, this shows that some women were able to use this space and the skills of imams to intervene in such disputes and to produce the particular outcomes which they sought. It is important to note that a woman's relationship to local community maybe predicated upon the multiple ways that they are positioned in families and the household. What the data in this study also points to is how culture is socially constructed, contested and transformed often to suit particular ends (see also Griffiths, 2001, p. 119). So, for example, some women were vocal in their criticism of any type of community intervention and this was reflected in difficult and fraught relationships, yet in specific contexts they were also able to engage with this process primarily to support themselves and their families. In her work on Kwena women, Griffiths points out that women often engage in this process of ADR 'from an understanding of themselves as forming a part of the same society as that of Kwena men. Their primary aim is not to subvert or radically alter the premises of society but seek to transform its practices in a direction more responsive to their needs' (2001, p. 119).

Contact with Shari'ah councils

Interview data with Muslim women using a Shari'ah council to obtain an Islamic divorce highlight the ways in which women are able to participate in complex negotiations and raise the crucial question of whether they are able to achieve their desired outcomes. In doing so, they critically challenge traditional feminist scholarship on women's agency which 'continues to portray Muslim women as incomparably bound by the unbreakable chains of religious and patriarchal oppression' (Mahmood, 2006a, p. 7). In contrast the work of scholars such as Mahmood (2006a) and Hellum (1999) explores the strategic use of alliances and forms of empowerment to better understand how Muslim women might use Shari'ah councils as mediums in which to accept, reject and/or challenge conservative Islamic norms and values in their pursuit of an Islamic divorce.

How and to what extent were the women in this study able to participate in negotiating their matrimonial disputes within institutions and structures that are in essence embedded in patriarchal norms and values? Feminist scholars have long critiqued the concept of patriarchy that continues to underpin state and community infrastructures within Western societies and seeks to affirm the existing status quo of women's subordination, exclusion and inequality (see Hunter, 2008).

With the exception of one interviewee, all the women in this study had sought guidance from family members, friends and/or an imam (based at the local mosque) prior to contacting a Shari'ah council. Interestingly the intervention of family members and in particular a local imam seemed to suggest that the decision as to whether or not to contact a Shari'ah council, and if so which one, may not have been entirely the woman's own. In fact all the respondents in the research explained that prior to seeking a religious divorce they had had little, if any, knowledge of the existence of Shari'ah councils and it was often family members who had recommended contacting a council, often providing an address or telephone number. As one interviewee explained:

> The family got me the address for the Shari'ah council. I didn't know the process. I had an aunt who is like one of the eldest in the family and takes care of these things. She said to me I had to write to them and tell them my case and ask for a *khul*.
>
> Sameena (Birmingham)

In relation to obtaining a Muslim divorce a number of women expressed surprise on discovering that under Islamic law they had the right to instigate divorce proceedings against the wishes of their husbands. One interviewee recalled:

> I remember saying to my uncle, 'Why didn't you ever tell me about this before', and he said, 'Well, you know ... it wasn't really important that a woman can divorce her husband in the first place'. But for me it was.
>
> Yasmin (London)

Viewed in this way the Shari'ah councils were perceived by some women simply as part of a continuing process of dispute management that had been organized by the family. In this way both the councils and the families not only interact but are each underpinned by a mutual set of shared norms and values. For example, families often played a key role in referring the women to the councils and these women were then accompanied to the council meetings by parents and family members. The councils in particular were keen to identify commonalities and alliances with 'Muslim families' with their twin objectives of reconciling the disputing parties and maintaining the stability of marriage, identified as two key shared values. Some councils held traditional ideas about Muslim marriage with parental consent that was deemed crucial and were keen not to undermine the stability of the Muslim marriage framework. However, the women were also able to challenge what can be loosely termed 'culturalized' ideas of marriage as being at odds with Islam and Islamic law. For example, forced marriage was recognized as un-Islamic and cited as an example of a cultural practice rather than a religious one and instead individual choice of marriage partner was identified as the cornerstone of Islamic values of marriage, motherhood and family.

Therefore, in some cases, the women were able to use Shari'ah councils to clarify interpretations of marriage, divorce and the status of women in the family according to Islamic thought and jurisprudence. This was perceived as being not only progressive in promoting the rights of Muslim women but ensuring the Islamic values of fairness and equitable justice being upheld. More often than not, however, the exercise of considerable discretion by the religious scholars in their interpretation of multiple Islamic norms and values (as understood by the families), coupled with the social norms and cultural values that underpin marriage in Pakistani Muslim communities, meant that in practice the councils had only limited effect in promoting the rights of Muslim women in family law matters even if they chose too.

Obtaining a Muslim divorce certificate

Given the importance the women attached to obtaining a Muslim divorce and the fact that the whole issue of divorce can be fraught with difficulties for them, this section draws upon interview data to better understand the strategies and bargaining techniques the women adopted in their quest to obtain a Muslim divorce.[8] It is crucial to understand the use of religious ADR mechanisms from the perspective of female users as it not only challenges the discourse of Muslims women's agency as one that continues to be framed around the binary of subordination versus resistance that underlies liberal feminist theory, but also provides an insight into the administration and process set up by the councils which in turn raise fundamental questions about their legitimacy within local communities and any possible conflicts with state law. The primary intention is therefore to question how women participated in reproducing unofficial social and legal norms and values within this privatized space of religious dispute resolution.

The initial contact

Initial contact with a Shari'ah council was usually made via telephone and/or letter. Of the sample of women, 18 had initially made a telephone inquiry, four had written to the council in question and three women had made an initial visit with no appointment. As discussed in the previous chapter, at this very early stage the scholars were keen to dissuade women from proceeding with the religious divorce. So how did the women respond to the initial advice given to them? One might, for example, anticipate tensions between the objectives of the applicant in her quest to obtain a Muslim divorce and the objectives of the religious scholar in dissuading her from doing so. Indeed differences did emerge between the two parties, albeit in more subtle ways and these varied in relation to the different councils that the women had contacted. For some women, the initial advice they were given was described as 'helpful' and sympathetic to their needs, which enabled them to continue and pursue the divorce. As Sameena (Bradford) explained:

> I rang the number of this Shari'ah council that our Maulvi had given to us. I told them what had happened to me and that I wanted to divorce my husband but that he wasn't happy with it and wouldn't agree to it. They were very helpful, they explained that divorce was wrong but that in Islam in some circumstances it was allowed ... they took my address and contact details and told me they would send me some forms to fill in and then decide whether it would be possible.

Likewise, a further 13 women reported being pleased with the initial advice that had been given to them which had helped them to convince their parents that divorce was permissible under Islamic law. Other women voiced criticism of this initial meeting and in particular the stance taken by the religious scholar. Four women reported that they had been left with the impression that in some way they were at fault for the breakdown of the marriage and were blamed, even when they had not disclosed the facts of the breakdown of marriage to the religious scholar. Yasmin (Birmingham) explained that at one Shari'ah council she had been informed by the scholar that 'they did not represent bad girls' and was refused to even apply for a divorce. She chose simply to contact a different council that was prepared to consider her application. Some Shari'ah councils therefore can adopt a conservative, male-centred approach to resolve matrimonial disputes while others seek to deliver a more 'woman-centred approach'. The women were able to 'shop around' for a council they were happy with, one which they perceived as more flexible and sympathetic to their needs and in doing so challenged conservative interpretations of Islam that often bear very little relevance to their lives as British Muslim women. A theory of forum shopping has been advanced in literature in dispute settlement in international trade. Helfer (1999) for example discusses the ideas as a process of 'choice of forum' and members choice of overlapping institutions. This issue of forum shopping is addressed in the final chapter of this book.

The process of obtaining a divorce certificate

The process of obtaining a Muslim divorce certificate was described as complex, lengthy, protracted and complicated. It was compounded by the reluctance of some religious scholars to accept the applicant's version of events and the insistence some placed upon reconciliation. It is clear from data analysis in this study and as discussed in the previous chapter that compliance with reconciliation and mediation within Shari'ah councils can render some women vulnerable to physical and emotional abuse.

The investigation

As outlined in the previous chapter, the main objective of the investigation stage is to collate all relevant information on the background to the marriage and the reasons for its breakdown. This is done in order to establish and verify the grounds upon which divorce is sought, which is cited by the applicant in the divorce application. Applicants cannot assume that a divorce certificate will be granted unconditionally, and on occasions the councils have rejected applications altogether. Fauzia (Birmingham) explained:

> They sent me some forms to fill in. They wanted to have copies of my marriage certificate, my *nikah* certificate, copies of petition and a copy of the decree absolute and a cheque for £50. I also had to fill in some of their forms which stated why I wanted to have a divorce, what were my reasons.

Proof of marriage is required – for example, a copy of the *nikah* certificate and/or civil marriage certificate. If women are unable to provide these documents, then an affidavit must be produced that confirms that the marriage had taken place. It is important to note that a substantial number of women who had registered their marriages according to civil law did not hold a copy of the *nikah* certificate.

Unsurprisingly the women expected to complete the process with minimal disruption and conflict to their lives. Despite this, a total of 23 women complained that the process was inchoate, time consuming, and at odds with Shari'ah council claims of being speedy and in the best interests of Muslim women.

> They heard his side of the story and then I heard nothing, nothing, months and months passed. And I wrote them reminders but nothing.
>
> Sadia (Birmingham)

> I got a letter back from them saying they were looking into the case and in the meantime I think they had met with my husband and heard his side of the story. But I'm not sure – every time I asked what was going on I never got an answer.
>
> Rabia (Birmingham)

These women understood that the scholars had to verify their account of the marriage breakdown, but even so they complained that the scholars relied too heavily on their husbands' apparent willingness to participate in the process when it was quite obvious to them that they were deliberately creating obstacles and adopting 'delaying tactics' to delay the divorce certificate from being issued.

> It's not as though it's my fault. I know he's making it harder than it has to be. Of course he is; he just didn't want me to get my Muslim divorce and now that he knows I'll get it without him, he's just trying to make things more difficult.
>
> Hina (London)

In this case, as with several other women, the interviewee's husband had simply refused to collaborate and communicate with the council which consequently delayed the divorce certificate from being issued by several months. For the scholars such delays provided a further opportunity to possibly reconcile the parties in the hope of saving the marriage. Others refused to issue a religious divorce certificate until the civil divorce had been pronounced and in some cases this led to delays of up to a year. One interviewee thus complained that the council was simply not taking her case seriously enough.

> I had no sense of what was happening with the case, whether that meant they were proceeding with it or not. Then one day I phoned them and I spoke to someone, I don't know who it was, and they said that they were really not happy with my case because obviously I had behaved very badly, that they weren't there to represent bad women and they were only there to represent good women.
>
> Humeira (London)

Appalled with this response she eventually asked her aunt to intervene.

> My aunt was furious and she told them she knew someone on the committee, she then spoke to someone more senior, she told this guy, 'I'm going to be writing to so and so and speaking to so and so'. And miraculously they find my file and said, 'Oh, we think there's been a misunderstanding, we had seen this case and we had agreed that, yeah obviously she should be divorced and it's all been sorted and you have our blessing and agreement that this has happened.' So it all got sorted in a matter of days and a phone call and I got a letter saying it was all done.

Clearly the important issues here relate to the bureaucratic nature of the process the councils adopt in issuing divorce certificates, leading to lengthy delays which led some women to then question the motives of the council. As summed up by one interviewee,

> I think they were kind of holding out ... hoping that we'd get together and sort things out.
>
> Rubina (Birmingham)

Experiences of reconciliation and mediation

In family law there has been much debate on the 'delegalized family obligations' that has led to 'a retreat from legal intervention into private family arrangements' (Maclean, 2000, p. 156) as discussed in Chapter 1. Indeed one of the key objectives in contemporary social policy thinking is a renewed emphasis on moving the resolution of family disputes away from the public sphere and towards 'private ordering'. Consequently there have been various attempts to redefine this notion, forcing feminists to rethink the concepts of individual autonomy, choice and the public/private spheres. Under the current climate, whereby individuals are encouraged towards informal settlements achieved through negotiation, conciliation or mediation, it becomes imperative to better understand this process from the perspective of women (see O'Donovan and Diduck, 2006). Not only are gender relations central to this process but, and perhaps more importantly, the process is itself contested and resisted by the women participants themselves. For example, as pointed out earlier, it is via this process of dispute resolution that some women were able to challenge cultural practices such as forced marriage as 'un-Islamic' and antithetical to the values of 'being a Muslim'.

This process aims to reconcile the parties principally through establishing a dialogue with the female applicant and her husband. Fieldwork data revealed that in some cases legal practitioners, most often solicitors, did intervene to negotiate more favourable terms on behalf of their male clients in return for a unilateral Muslim divorce, a *talaq*. Observation revealed that in some cases women were encouraged to reconcile even if they wished not to do so. In one case the religious scholar informed the female applicant that her husband had been in touch with the council and wished to reconcile. The extract that follows highlights the dangers of this type of intervention.

Religious scholar: In Islam it is a wife's duty to listen carefully to the needs of her husband, she must respect him and not argue with him ...

Applicant: I understand that but he has to make it work too. He just left, left his children ...

Religious scholar: Well, I've spoken to him on the telephone and he tells me a different story that you would taunt him and belittle him. In Islam women must obey their

	husbands, the relationship must be based on love, understanding and respect ...
Applicant:	He has walked out and just left us because he couldn't cope? How am I to cope by myself?
Religious scholar:	A woman must support her husband and ...
Applicant:	I did support him and I understand there were problems but we have to sort them out together. I've been reading books on Islam and a husband also has duties to his wife.

More worryingly perhaps, the observation found that in one case a religious scholar reported that social workers, under the rubric of 'diversity', had attended such sessions in order to understand 'how Islam works'. Therein lay, at least, the seeds of the argument that the autonomy of the women who use these services may be undermined.

Similarly the language of reconciliation embodies dynamics of power which seeks to place emphasis on what is described as the women's divinely ordained obligations to maintain and stabilize marriage and family relations and thereby the wish to reconcile with husbands. Yet interview data also revealed the women's ambivalence about the reconciliation sessions; opinions ranged from indifference to outrage to one of genuine commitment. The extracts from interview data illustrate this varied experience.

> They wanted me to meet with my husband. In fact they said that I couldn't have a divorce unless we both met with the imam. But it wasn't as bad as I thought. My husband took it very seriously ... what the imam was saying. I think he needed a religious person to explain to him where he was going wrong and why I was leaving him.
>
> Sabia (London)

> I needed to explore the possibility of us getting back together from an Islamic perspective. I'm a Muslim so it helps if you can get advice and assistance from another Muslim. I think a Muslim woman would have been able to understand where I was coming from.
>
> Humeira (London)

> Well at the end of the day we had the responsibility to make it work, so I can't blame those who were trying to help us. Besides, by that stage it was too late to get back together; we'd been through too much and our families weren't even speaking to each other.
>
> Noreen (Birmingham)

> I agreed to three sessions where basically the imam wanted us to discuss everything, just so we understood what divorce meant and also I think

to try and get us back together again. I was OK with that ... only I felt as though he wasn't really listening to what I had to say. My husband spoke and then the imam spoke to me, you know explained to me what I should be doing as a Muslim wife.

Parveen (Birmingham)

Therefore although the reconciliation sessions took place in a space that is preoccupied with reconciling the parties, is male dominated and often imbued with conservative interpretations about the position of women in Islam (as mothers, wives and daughters), some women did find it useful. The study reveals, however, that the process can create discomfort and unease for other women who were regarded by religious scholars as potentially dangerous participants as they were perceived as unwilling to reconcile. For these women the contentious issue related to the lack of space and opportunity they were given to participate in the process in an equal way. Many women, for example, reported that they had been expected to reconcile with their husbands and were encouraged to be more understanding of their husband's 'limitations' because women were presented as nurturers of the Muslim family and therefore in some way more open to compromise. Under this model of reconciliation, husbands were given greater room for negotiation which in some cases had led to better outcomes for them. One interviewee explained:

It was weird but it felt as though I was the one being told off and when I tried to put across what I thought was wrong ... it's as though he [the imam] didn't want to hear it.

Hina (London)

Other extracts reveal how some women felt marginalized by this process.

No, I didn't find it was helpful at all. Just the way it was set up meant that things weren't going to change.

Shabana (London)

They were right from the beginning on his side. They didn't even listen to what I was saying. I mean I do read books. I don't go into it that much but I do know the basics you know, what a husband has to do. I was really disappointed with the maulana because he just wouldn't blame my ex-husband and I was blamed for everything.

Mina (London)

To be honest I didn't understand the point of it. I told the Sheikh that I didn't want to be in the same room as my husband, that he might lash out because that's what he's like, he's unpredictable. But he was insistent, that we had to both be in the same room, that that's how it's done in Islam.

Raheela (London)

Perhaps an even more troubling finding was that ten women reported that they had been 'coaxed' into participating in the reconciliation sessions with their husbands even though they were reluctant to do so. More worrying still, four of these women reported that they had existing injunctions against their husbands on the grounds of violence and yet they were urged to sit only a few feet away from these men during the reconciliation sessions. Again, the next extracts from the interviews reveal how potentially dangerous this may be for women and illustrate how husbands may use this opportunity to negotiate access to children and in some cases financial settlements, matters which are in effect being discussed under the 'shadow of law'.

I told him that I left him because he was violent but he started saying things like, 'Oh how violent was that because in Islam a man is allowed to beat his wife!' I mean I was so shocked. He said it depends on whether he really hurt me! I was really shocked because I thought he was there to understand but he was trying to make me admit that somehow I had done wrong.

Shazia (London)

I was very upset, in tears, holding my friend's hand. It was awful but apparently that's what it says in Islam, the husband and wife have to meet like this. I didn't want to but didn't really have a choice. As a Muslim I wanted to do the right thing, in God's eyes.

Farah (London)

Empirical findings in this study confirm the existence of intra-group inequalities and that Shari'ah councils construct boundaries for group membership that rely upon traditional interpretations of the role of women in Islam, primarily as wives, mothers and daughters. Under such conditions the multicultural accommodation of Muslim family law in Britain can lead to violations of human rights for Muslim women. In effect this privatized form of religious arbitration means the shifting of state regulation to the private domain, thereby giving religious leaders greater power to dictate acceptable patterns of behaviour. The women in this study echoed this caution but in doing so they articulated a wide range of differing opinions from the implications of being governed by a separate legal process to the impracticalities of bodies such as Shari'ah councils administering 'justice' in resolving matrimonial disputes. They were able to explore the contradictions inherent in the dichotomy of protecting group (or community) interests versus individual

choice and freedom, to moving towards creating more nuanced and complex understandings of their 'positioning' and participation in the religious
arbitration process. While acknowledging that their criticism and/or support
of Shari'ah councils remained largely dependent upon their position within
the family, home and community, some women did articulate a notion of
belonging to the Muslim *umma*, although how they did this varied:

> I'm a Muslim. I identify as one, and anything that helps to validate and
> enhance my role as a Muslim in British society obviously I welcome and
> I will support it.
>
> Yasmin (London)

> To be Muslim is to be part of the Muslim *umma*. If they [Shari'ah coun-
> cils] are recognized, I think that's great, an important development for
> all Muslims.
>
> Sadia (Birmingham)

> I don't see it as belonging to the Muslim community. I mean what does
> it mean in practice anyway? Muslims – just like all other groups – are so
> bloody divided! I mean I wasn't aware of Shari'ah councils before I needed
> to get a divorce but that didn't mean I felt any less of a Muslim.
>
> Anisa (London)

Thus for some women it was the distinctiveness of Shari'ah councils from
other community bodies that acted as a focal point of reference to belonging
to a wider Muslim *umma*. Seen in this way, these women defined the role
of Shari'ah councils as bridging the gap between older and younger generations and challenging intra-family inequalities such as forced marriage. It is,
however, also worth noting a general point here that in principle initiatives
that facilitated relations between individuals and their families were welcomed by the women, yet at the same time the women expressed a desire to
choose whether or not to use the services offered by Shari'ah councils:

> They serve a useful purpose but really when people ask for these councils
> to be formally recognized, alarm bells go off in my head. When you start
> bringing in special things I think there are two things that can happen.
> One, I think you can have ghettoization – you have a community within
> a community that is ostracized and marginalized and you then become
> a target for many other things. Secondly I think why? Why would you
> need it?
>
> Anisa (Bradford)

> I do identify myself as both British and Muslim, so I don't want to sup-
> port initiatives that mean that I have to choose between one kind of

legal system and you know choose whether I'm British or not and then which legal system to go to. It's just not feasible and anyway it's not right. Reality is a lot more difficult than choosing between one and the other!

Parveen (Birmingham)

If it's about community control I think they [Shari'ah councils] should be honest about that but I don't know if it is. I mean women want the Islamic divorce and I guess they are providing a service. It's just the way some of them do it that's the problem.

Sabia (London)

Hence the observation is that those bodies may fail to capture the complex realities of women's lives. One consequence of this may be to situate Muslims unfairly on the periphery of British society by reducing their chances of gaining 'access to justice' and being 'equal before the law', thus in effect undermining their citizenship rights. This becomes particularly important in relation to protecting the human rights of women. From this perspective formalizing Shari'ah councils may serve to reinforce the social and legal identities of Muslims as fixed and unchanging while undermining the Islamic precepts of individual autonomy, choice and free will. Perhaps more worrying still are the interview extracts which reveal the confusion a small number of women expressed in relation to the authority, power and jurisdiction of Shari'ah councils in Britain. One interviewee explained:

I couldn't understand ... they wrote me a letter saying that there was issues to be taken into account that was about child custody, which was about the house, which was about possessions, which was about ... all kinds of things. I thought, hold on, what jurisdictions do they have? I've already been through the courts. What do I have to go through a set of Islamic courts for? Do I have to go through them again? It's all been done and what if it means I can't have custody? Who wins, English law or the Islamic Shari'ah council?

Yasmin (London)

As discussed in Chapter 1, feminist scholars have warned of the dangers of resolving marital disputes away from the protection of formal law. This may include situations where 'cultural norms deny women decision-making authority' (Roberts, 1997, p. 129) and where the mediator is not neutral and provides the 'normative framework for discussion' (Roberts, 1983, p. 549) which can transform the nature of the negotiations and curtail the autonomy of the female disputant. Grillo raises concerns about the potential dangers of such negotiations taking place in private 'without the presence of partisan lawyers and without access to appeal' (1991). Numerous studies also point to the fact that state-law mediation practices can place women in a weak bargaining position where they are encouraged to accept a settlement considerably less than they would have received had they gone through the civil law process. In their study of mediation and divorce, Greatbach and Dingwall found that mediators do not act in a neutral way and enter the mediation process guiding the participants to particular outcomes (1993, p. 208). There is, therefore, a strong imbalance of power and the parties are not equal and do not respond in a fair way. Furthermore, Bottomley reminds us that reconciliation 'has not arisen in a vacuum and is not practised in one' and we therefore need to explore the dynamics of power which underpin this process (1984, p. 45).

Hence reconciliation and mediation can promote a particular familial ideology that is based on upholding existing social and patriarchal norms and values underpinned by subliminal pressures of power and coercion. In this context formal law can instead provide better protection against abuse taking place in the private sphere, whereas a move towards private legal ordering can fail to deliver on the key issue of 'justice'.

However, as discussed earlier, during the investigation, all the women had participated in some form of unofficial mediation and reconciliation. Hence there would appear to be no clear and consistent approach to reconciliation with Shari'ah councils. For example, some women reported that mediation involved no discussion of financial matters or issues of custody and access, while other councils were keen to intervene and reconcile parties and if not then contribute to other family law matters such as custody of and access to children.

Retrieving the *mahr*

As discussed in Chapter 4, one of the key elements of the *nikah* contract is the amount of *mahr* stipulated by the parties. In this study it became apparent that, for various reasons, most women had not attached any importance to the *mahr*. However, upon breakdown of marriage and in complicated ways, this situation had radically changed for some women. It prompted a small number of women to concentrate their efforts in retrieving the *mahr* for two reasons. First, for women whose marriages had not been registered according to civil law, the importance of this approach lay in the belief that they were entitled to some kind of financial redress upon breakdown of marriage. Second, where the *nikah* contract had been a focal point of negotiations prior to marriage, the women concentrated their efforts on keeping any monies or goods received upon marriage while also seeking to obtain a Muslim divorce. In this way the Shari'ah councils opened avenues for strategic action within the contested space of 'personal law' and in so doing these women transformed this 'space' of reconciliation into a site of mediation and negotiations for settlement of financial matters.

However, given the fact that the terms '*mahr*' and 'dowry' were used interchangeably, it often meant that such demands were reframed within the context of culture rather than the application of religious personal law. And, given the fact that this site embodies the intermeshing of cultural and religious practices, it is useful to note that when some women were informed by religious scholars that upon receiving the Muslim divorce, the *khul*, they would be required to return the 'dower' to their husbands, they proceeded to then base their claims towards those of culture and identity rather than religion. For example, the terms *'haq mahr'*, *'jahez'* and 'dowry' were articulated to invoke a cultural component of Muslim marriage. To this end for some women invoking cultural or religious practices became a matter of choice warranted by the unfair way they had been treated by husbands during their marriage. And, as discussed in later in the book, most women expressed misgivings about the possibility of retrieving the *'haq mahr'* while questioning the motives of their husbands.

By contrast the religious scholars expressed concern with this quite obvious conflation of religious principles with cultural practice. Interviews revealed that they believed the onus was on Muslim women to educate themselves on the principles of Muslim marriage and divorce. Maulana Mohammed Raza at the MLSC explained, 'Muslim women are simply not aware of their rights at marriage, have little knowledge or understanding of dower and subsequently fail to meet their demands upon breakdown of marriage.'

One interviewee explained:

I wasn't aware that I could demand my rights when I got married. I didn't even know that if the marriage broke down and it wasn't my fault I could demand maintenance under Islamic law. I don't understand that as Muslim women we're not taught this. Why not? We didn't register the marriage and when he walked away I was left with nothing.

Salma (London)

These issues are discussed further in the following chapter.

In this sample, a third of the women awaited a decision on their divorce application while the majority who had contacted a Shari'ah council for a divorce certificate had successfully obtained the *khul*. The women were critical of lengthy delays believed to have been exacerbated by husbands deliberately placing obstacles in order to prevent the divorce certificate from being issued. It was notable that those women who had applied for a divorce at more established Shari'ah councils, such as the BSC, ISC or MLSC, were less critical than those who had gone to smaller Shari'ah councils based at local mosques. One interviewee explained:

When I first tried to find out about getting a Muslim divorce it was awful. I went to six different mosques and they all told me something different. Some said no, it just wasn't possible, that I had to try and make my marriage work, you know, divorce is wrong in Islam. Others explained that it was possible but I had to give back all my dowry. It was so confusing I just didn't know what to think. But then someone told me about Dr Saeeda; they had seen a TV programme on her and what she does and when I went to see her it began to make a lot more sense.

Farhana (Birmingham)

As discussed earlier, a key condition with this type of divorce is for the wife to forego her *mahr*. And, while in practical terms there were slight variations in the amount of *mahr* stipulated in the *nikah* contract, two particular criticisms related to the issue of this type of divorce. First, the women were financially disadvantaged by having to return the *mahr* and wedding gifts when they passionately believed that they had not been at fault for the breakdown of the marriage. Given the deliberate obstacles placed by some husbands to prevent any kind of divorce being issued (by continually challenging the evidence put forward by the applicant) the second criticism related to the religious scholars for failing to challenge their husbands' behaviour and for too readily accepting their version of events.

Just the fact that I'm the one who has instigated the legal proceedings, that goes against me even though it's not my fault. Even though they gave my husband the opportunity to divorce me and he didn't meant that he was holding me in a kind of 'limping marriage', being [in] a twilight zone of being neither here nor there, which I believe was a deliberate ploy.

Rubina (Birmingham)

Men are keen in blackmailing their wives for divorce, you know, 'As long as you give up the jewellery and return the *mahr* I will give you a divorce'. And this is what happened with me, this is what my husband said, that if I returned all of those wedding gifts he would give me a divorce and I refused.

Fauzia (London)

In the majority of cases the women had been involved in negotiations at the Shari'ah council to determine the amount of *mahr* to be returned. The first observation to make of this outcome is the conflation between the *mahr* (dower) and wedding gifts. It seems that in most cases because the dower only reflected the nominal sum stipulated on the *nikah* contract this was largely ignored and, instead, the basis for negotiations moved towards the wedding gifts which involved much larger sums of money, clothing and jewellery. Thus the intermeshing of cultural and religious practices condoned by the religious scholars was met with considerable hostility from the women. Sadia (Bradford) exclaimed, 'I couldn't understand their decision. It wasn't my fault but in effect I was having to pay him to divorce me! That's not right.'

Such outcomes were accepted by the religious scholars as being unsatisfactory but were justified on the grounds that religious practices had to be reformulated to meet the needs of local Muslim communities and this often meant taking into account traditional cultural practices. Dr Suhaib Hasan at ISC explained, 'We do recognize that some women are reluctant to give up their dower and in some cases the dowry [wedding gifts], but this is a precarious situation and we have to think of the welfare of all the parties involved. You see if we keep the proceedings dragging on it affects all the parties, including the children, so it's best to sort things out as quickly and easily as possible. In cases where we feel the husband is not at fault, then the applicant must decide if she wants the *khul* and under Islamic law she has every right to do so.'

An abuse of Muslim women's human rights?

For most scholars the Western human rights framework provides the starting point as a means by which we are able to transform human rights from its Western hegemonic position of power to the more complex picture of rights in relation to culture, community, socio-economic conditions and localized religious practices. The human rights discourse remains problematic for its universalizing approach to understanding cultural and religious difference, but in her study Ali (2000) provides a fascinating legal analysis of women's human rights in Islam on the basis of sources of Islamic law. Drawing upon her extensive work in Pakistan, she illustrates the multiple spaces in law that both restrict and empower women in different contexts. The claim that Islam is antithetical to safeguarding women's human rights is effectively challenged and she draws upon Islamic sources of law and custom to challenge inequalities within the family, home and community which are often based upon localized cultural and religious practice. Other Muslim scholars such as An-Naim (1999) contend that local communities must engage in the process of change and renewal and dispose of oppressive cultural practices. Such an internal process of change can only be achieved via local dialogue within communities where individuals are able to draw on their commonalities and differences, while in the process challenging oppressive cultural practices. An-Naim explains, 'In this way, the combination of all the processes of internal discourse and cross-cultural dialogue will, it is hoped, deepen and broaden universal cultural consensus on the concept and normative content of international human rights' (1999, p. 174).

Yet as data in this study suggest we must recognize that dialogue is often imbued with power relations and is constituted in relation to controlling family and communal boundaries. For example, I found that the relationship between the female users of Shari'ah councils and religious scholars was often predicated on the religious and socio-cultural terms that marginalize women. As Anthias points out, 'Effective dialogue requires an already formulated mutual respect, a common communication language and a common starting point in terms of power' (2002, p. 288). It is the 'common starting point in terms of power' that raises the dilemma of the multicultural question of 'how then can the particular and the universal, the claims of both difference and equality be recognised' (Hall, 2000, p. 235).

These issues need to be discussed in the light of empirical findings rather than based upon abstract theorizing. We need to incorporate debates on complexity, difference and diversity to understand the realities of British Pakistani Muslim women's lives. As this study demonstrates, women feel the contradictory pulls which these forces exert but their narratives must be heard. Some are happy to conform, others are not; some trade identities but for others a Muslim identity is paramount. Many are suspicious of state intervention which challenges cultural norms deemed oppressive because the state has not historically acted as the neutral arbiter of disputes (Hall, 2000, p. 238). Furthermore some women see themselves 'strictly bound to submit to the dictates of Islamic law and the commands of the authorities charged with its execution' (Mayer, 1999, p. 45) and we must recognize this as their lived experience.

The picture painted by legal pluralists and liberal feminists as a dialectical process of Muslim personal law versus state law is also very different from the picture emerging from the data in this study. The real conflicts are over power and how those competing voices for power and representation ignore the internal voices of dissent and change, most often the voices of women. For example, a large number of interviewees argued one way forward was to increase the role and presence of female Muslim scholars in the process of religious arbitration:

> I think that women's organizations should be taken seriously as well, whether they're Muslim women or Asian women. They know the lifestyle of women within Britain today, having been brought up as Asian women and being British themselves; so I think they're more than qualified.
>
> Nasima (Bradford)

> When was the last time a women's organization was invited to contribute to the legal system in order to analyse, for example, the impact of marital breakdown in Shari'ah councils and the courts? I just don't think it happens and yet a British Muslim woman is more of an expert than the imams I can think of.
>
> Naheed (London)

Undoubtedly the site of Shari'ah councils makes gender visible and in this context the women who use its services identify themselves as Muslims and Muslim women. This is particularly significant for Muslim women's organizations such as Muslim Women's Helpline (MWHL) and the An-Nisa Society both of which advocate the development of social policy initiatives to meet the needs of religious communities based upon their religious identities rather than focusing upon the categories of race, gender and cultural differences. These approaches acknowledge the power and presence of Muslim women as actively instigating change within communities. As Parker points out, 'Exploring these experiences in a particular setting demonstrates that an understanding of multiculturalism requires a much closer specification of the perspective from which it is being understood' (2000, p. 93).

A number of Muslim women's organisations such as the Muslim Women's Network have successfully created an interesting space within Muslim communal politics and women's activism, while developing strategies to meet the needs of Muslim women. Such strategies include providing premarital counselling based upon Islamic perspectives, training imams and community leaders to challenge the practice of forced marriage and providing guidelines for Muslim women escaping domestic violence. However, MWHL warns of the dangers of relying on rudimentary Islamic principles[9] and instead advocates education and discussion within Muslim communities with Muslim women being at the forefront of these debates. In terms of challenging the unequal cultural norms inherent within Shari'ah councils, it has produced a guide titled *Marriage and Dissolution of Marriage According to the Principles of Shari'ah*, which draws upon the work of Muslim feminists and scholars.[10] Ms Sheriff (MWHL, co-ordinator) states:

> It is high time that our leadership bodies got to grips with such problems and provided clear and effective leadership and more importantly were seen to publicly support the victims of unscrupulous behaviour at individual and institutional level. But the responsibility lies not just with the establishment and the community. In the middle of these two are the Muslim and civil legal structures which urgently need to talk to each other and ensure that they are better informed so that vulnerable people, particularly women, are at least not misled as to their rights. Awareness and training is one such step that is needed, but there is so much more that needs to be done.

More recent initiatives include the Muslim women's Network guidelines for Muslim women on Islamic marriage and divorce.[11]

8
Shari'ah Councils and Civil Law

Having explored the ways in which Shari'ah councils operate as privatized and alternative dispute resolution (ADR) mechanisms and the experiences of female users, this chapter now examines the extent to which Shari'ah councils interact, complement and/or are in conflict with English civil law in matters of family law. In particular, the chapter draws attention to the emergence of new forms of community and state governance with the Muslim Arbitration Tribunal (MAT), the use of Muslim marriage contracts and some preliminary discussions on the recognition of *mahr* under English law.

The use of legal practitioners

This study found that in cases where a civil marriage had taken place the women sought the use of solicitors to dissolve the civil marriage. The data revealed that at times the relationship with solicitors was fraught with conflicts over client confidentiality, delay and the lack of knowledge of Muslim family law principles and the recognition of religious divorce certificates in the English courts. For solicitors, who work in the best interests of their clients, the question arises of whether they can be sufficiently trained to provide advice on matters of Muslim marriage and divorce. Yet the consequences of solicitors providing inaccurate legal advice can be extremely damaging to clients. In her study Shah-Kazemi found that solicitors often dispensed erroneous legal advice as many were simply unaware of the validity of Islamic marriages in English law and subsequently misunderstood when a civil law divorce was required (2001, p. 53). This finding was confirmed in this study and highlights the fact that some solicitors simply lack the required training to advise on matters of legal validity of transnational marriages, the validity of a religious marriage in England and Wales and the validity of the *nikah* contract under English law. As mentioned earlier, today we have an emerging body of legal practitioners (for example the solicitor Aina Khan and the barrister Ahmad Thompson) specialising in the conflicts-of-law scenario generated by Islamic law and English legal principles both in national and international context.

The data in this study found that solicitors were used in connection with three key issues. The first centres on those marriages that are formally registered according to civil law but then, upon divorce, require one or both parties to instigate legal proceedings and dissolve the marriage under the Matrimonial Causes Act 1973. As noted in previous chapters, in an attempt to avoid a conflict-of-laws scenario religious scholars often demand that applicants first obtain a civil divorce prior to making an application for a religious divorce certificate. The second issue involves women whose marriages had taken place in Pakistan and then England or in England only, but these marriages had not then been registered according to civil law. Advice was then sought from solicitors to determine the validity of a religious marriage conducted overseas (in this case Pakistan) and the validity of religious marriages solemnized outside the formalities of the marriage laws of England and Wales. The third issue concerns the legal validity of those religious marriage ceremonies which had been conducted in an unlicensed building in England, most often a local mosque. And finally a small number of women sought advice on the validity of the *nikah* contract, specifically in the hope of recovering the *mahr* upon divorce.

It was notable that in the majority of cases it was held that religious marriages were valid according to English civil aw. The use of civil law to dissolve religious marriages was therefore deemed possible. However, many interviewees reported feeling hugely disappointed with the advice given to them by solicitors and complaints ranged from their general ignorance of cultural and religious practices (which some women explained drew upon the stereotypical perception of Muslim women as passive and disempowered) to a complete lack of understanding of Islamic law and the conflict-of-laws scenario they experienced if, for example, the marriage had taken place in Pakistan.

I was very disappointed with my solicitor because I rang him time and time again but he just couldn't understand the issues in my case. He just told me my marriage was valid when it wasn't, so he obviously didn't know the law himself.

Salma (London)

I said to my solicitor, 'I want to be paid back every penny that they've done to me', and she said, 'Yeah, fair enough, you do have a case.' I've spent a year in this case and I've got nothing out of it. At the beginning she said everything was OK and then a couple of months later she writes to me and says, 'Well, I'm sorry we're going to have to take the divorce proceedings out of the court because it's not recognized – only some courts recognize Islamic marriages, not all the courts recognize them.'

So I turned around and said, 'Well, why did you say to me they were recognized? This was the only reason I took the case forward.' And she said, 'Well, I have dealt with this case before. I have had a lady who has been through the same thing as you and her marriage was recognized in the courts so I thought that your case was the same thing but when we took it into court they said no, it's not recognized.'

Zareena (Bradford)

I don't think it's fair that I should have to pay my solicitor to have to learn about my religion and its doctrines on divorce. I don't think it's fair that I should have to pay the extra money to him so that he reads something in order to understand where I'm coming from and I don't think I should be obliged to go to a Muslim solicitor and that's one of the reasons why I went to an English one.

Fauzia (London)

Why should I have to pay for solicitors who aren't even able to help me? I had to do all the chasing up, the reading and discussing with my solicitors on what would be the best options. I had to do the work they couldn't do, all because they just didn't know how.

Parveen (Birmingham)

I was really upset and I went to see one of the senior partners and I told her that I was really upset because he had given me the wrong advice. Then he eventually called and I said, 'Look, at the end of the day I came to you for advice. I made a lot of decisions based on what you said. Had I known that my marriage was not valid I would not have made a fool out of myself like doing a petition and all that against him.' I even had to pay for it all.

Nighat (London)

What they were basically trying to say is it's in your community to sort this mess out, you know, it's nothing to do with them. Well, as a Muslim woman I was quite offended with the way that these solicitors were basically badmouthing our religion. And I felt as though they were laughing at my expense which I think is wrong.

Shaheen (London)

Well, what they were basically saying was that if you're not going to learn to stand up for yourself then what do you expect. I was like 'I do stand up for myself and it was my ex-husband that gave me the problems and I did it the way I did out of respect for my parents'. But you know he should try to understand but basically he just didn't want to know.

Farhana (Birmingham)

This analysis reveals the confusion experienced by solicitors as to the validity of Muslim marriage and divorce in Britain. An analysis of case files shows, for example, in Case E the solicitor writes to the Shari'ah council:

> We have consulted by ... concerning the requirements of the Shari'ah Council in respect of the Islamic divorce. We have discussed with our client any potential financial claims that she might have arising from the marriage. Mrs ... has instructed us to inform you that provided a divorce is pronounced by the Shari'ah Council within 21 days of 28th September 1998 then she will make no claims against your client in relation to financial or property matters arising from their marriage under Muslim law.

The Shari'ah council responds:

> We acknowledge the receipt of the letter. Out legal advisers advise us that Ms ... and Mr ... never registered their marriage in the UK. It was only an Islamic religious marriage which is not recognized as equal to a legal/civil marriage. Hence a civil divorce is not required in this case.

Such experiences had left many women in this study feeling both angry and vulnerable. The particular examples of women being advised by solicitors to formally lodge divorce petitions in English courts when no valid marriage had taken place according to English law implies that solicitors need to be better trained on laws pertaining to religious and transnational marriages and religious divorce.

Anecdotal evidence on the role of solicitors intervening in issues of Muslim marriage and divorce was also found in case-file analysis of one Shari'ah council. It was found that of a total of 25 cases, 15 applicants made some form of contact with solicitors that included queries regarding the validity of marriage, and progress on finalising the decree absolute, mediation, access to children for ex-husbands and attempts to retrieve the *mahr*.

File C illustrates the nature of one such interaction. In this case, a young British Pakistani woman married a British Pakistani man and their marriage had been registered in the UK followed by the religious marriage, the *nikah*. Upon breakdown of the marriage the applicant argued that she had been forced into marriage, citing violence and 'neglect' as reasons for seeking a religious divorce and therefore instructed solicitors to instigate civil proceedings to obtain a civil divorce. Her husband was refusing to give her a Muslim divorce and she wrote to the council to inquire about the possibility of obtaining one without his consent. In her letter she states, 'Being a Muslim is important to me, I was married with a *nikah* and now that my marriage has broken down it's important to me that I get an Islamic divorce. My husband is acting unreasonably and I want no further contact with him.' The council responded with a number of notices being sent to the applicant's husband but he failed to respond to any of these. The council then decided that one possible way to contact the husband was via his solicitor, to whom they wrote:

> Dear Sirs
> May we inform your client that according to Shari'ah law, he has to live with his wife and discharge his matrimonial duties and if it is somehow not possible, then he has to divorce her? An option of a legal separation is not approved by Islamic law.

A note dated a few weeks later in the case file states that the council did receive a telephone call from the husband's solicitors stating that their client was prepared to grant his wife an Islamic divorce but only if she first accepted mediation in the hope of reconciliation. In this letter they outlined her husband's demands, which included that she must learn 'to act like a proper Muslim woman'.

A letter was then sent from the council to the applicant outlining her husband's position and to clarify 'whether (she) seeks reconciliation'. The applicant wrote back:

> I have made it clear on several occasions that I do not wish to get back together with my husband.

The council decided it was not worthwhile pursuing mediation and sent a final letter to the solicitor stating:

> Your client's wife claims that the couple have separated for seven months. In our view, after such a long time of separation, reconciliation seems to be a remote possibility. We still wish and pray for the success of any such efforts in this respect. The Council, however, thinks that if your client's wife is adamant for an Islamic divorce, he is expected to act realistically and responsibly and should divorce his wife in the due course of time.

There is no further correspondence in the file and a note describes the case as 'on-going'.

Case D further illustrates the possible dangers of solicitors using this arena for negotiating divorce settlements. In this case a solicitor wrote to the Shari'ah council with the proposition that if the female applicant was willing to opt for mediation and allow his client (her husband) 'access' to the children he would agree to grant her a Muslim divorce. In her application to obtain a Muslim divorce she cites violence and emotional abuse as the two grounds for divorce. This case illustrates some of the dangerous situations that vulnerable female applicants find themselves in.

This case demonstrates how a solicitor may use the Shari'ah council as a forum upon which to negotiate more favourable outcomes of the civil divorce with little actual understanding of how the Shari'ah council ADR process works in practice. In this case the Shari'ah council writes to the female applicant informing her of her husband's wishes:

> Dear Sister,
> May we advise you to confirm to us through your solicitors that you have no objection in allowing regular access to Mr XX to see XX.
> We await to hear from you.

A letter dated a few days later from the female applicant stated:

> Dear Mr XX ...
> I left my husband because of the violence and abuse towards myself and my two children. You can contact my solicitor ... who can let you know why I don't want my husband to have contact with my children.

Case-file analysis also reveals a further six cases that illustrate the dangers of unofficial bodies acting as mediation forums upon which to resolve disputes over access to children. It illustrates and the ways in which some solicitors may use the religious divorce to negotiate more acceptable terms for their clients even though this may put the female applicant into dangerous and vulnerable situations. In the previous case the female applicant had refused all such demands and subsequently was not placed under any immediate threat. Negotiating such settlements in this arena also brings to the fore the issue of custody of and access to children, two issues that Shari'ah councils seek to avoid conflict with civil law. Zaki Badawi (1995, p. 34) explains, 'Under Muslim law a divorced mother has the right to the custody of her children as long as she does not remarry. If she does remarry she loses that automatic right. The children can only remain with her with her ex-husband's consent and he can succeed if he can prove that his mother can therefore look after the children.' A conflict can arise as under English law it is by convention that the mother be awarded the custody of the children and the husband has to prove that she is an '"unfit" mother' (see Herring, 2009). The extent to which the family law courts take into the cultural and religious background of the parties involved in disputes has been addressed by the courts in relation to children and issues of custody and access. Statutory requirements as laid out in the Children's Act 1989 make clear the importance of the welfare principle and the need to ensure the overriding principle of the 'best interests of the child' remains paramount. However, as Justice Marfalane (2011, p. 953) points out, 'within the overall welfare evaluation, when determining what weight to give to one or another feature amongst the issues that go into one side or the other of the balancing scales, the cultural and/or religious context must be taken into account. The court will need to understand how one or other arrangement for the child's care will be received by the family and wider community in accordance to the dictates of the faith and law of that community.'

In relation to negotiating *mahr* settlements, the following extracts from case files reveal the type of intervention made by husbands and solicitors. For many women the issue of returning the *mahr* is central to their being granted a divorce. A number of letters focus on demands made by the husband to return the *mahr*. And disputes often centre on the amount given by the husband and the amount he demands back.

> Dear ...
> Following our recent telephone conversation and a very threatening letter which I received today, to which this is a response. As you mentioned in our conversation it is in my best interest that I write to you and ask it of you to make a little request upon my dearly beloved that this marriage has come to an end due to the single mindedness of the party concerned. So for there to be an end to it all legally and morally she/her family should pay costs of the jewellery and as soon as possible. I will be more than happy to sign anything to get rid of her. So I look forward to receiving her response.

A letter from the council to the wife of the aforesaid stated:

> We refer to your application of an Islamic divorce to the Shari'ah Council. The Council after contacting your husband Mr X has received an assurance from him that he will issue an Islamic divorce to you provided you return the following items of jewellery, which according to his claim, was given to you by him at the time of one year after the marriage.

It also included a list of the goods to be returned to the husband and then goes on:

> If you agree to the above details of items of jewellery then according to Shari'ah law under the terms of the Khul you are required to return these items or its cost to your husband in return of an Islamic divorce. The Council accordingly asks you to accept these terms and co-operate with us to resolve this case. However, if you dispute the details of the above mentioned items or their value, then write to us so that we can negotiate further with your husband and try to achieve an agreed list of items and their value as soon as possible.

Religious arbitration and civil law

The relationship between Shari'ah councils and civil law remains largely undocumented as traditionally these bodies are deemed to operate in the private sphere with little if any state interaction with civil law. Subsequently this relationship has largely been characterized as part of the strict delineation of the public/private spheres whereby Shari'ah councils seek to operate in the private to avoid any conflict with state law and its mechanisms. However, emerging case law in family, contractual and commercial type disputes points to an interesting relationship between these councils and the type of interaction taking place with civil law. In particular the contractual agreements brokered by the councils reveal the nature of such conflicts. For example, in *Al-Midani* v. *Al-Midani* (1999)[1] a dispute over the validity of a will centred on an agreement that had been brokered and reached between the parties with the assistance of a Shari'ah council based in London. The claimant had refused to recognize the terms of the will and argued that the Shari'ah council in question was neither a legitimate judicial body nor recognized in law. The courts held that as the negotiators had not obtained the consent of all the parties involved and as the arbitration agreement was neither based on any statutory authority nor recognized in law the terms of the will were invalid. It is useful to note that such reasoning can also be applied to the divorce certificates issued by Shari'ah councils – certificates which are not recognized under English law. In Sharif, Petitioner (2000)[2] the administration of a particular Shari'ah council illustrated the extent to which internal conflicts of power and dispute can be found among Shari'ah councils and their members. The involvement of such councils in commercial and property-related disputes is of particular interest. For example, in *Bhatti* v. *Bhatti* (2009)[3] the court granted summary judgement on the applicant's claim to the beneficial ownership of certain properties following the determination of the dispute in that party's favour by a quasi-judicial body of the Muslim Ahmadiyya Community acting as an arbitral body for English legal purposes. The *Khan* v. *Khan* (2007)[4] case addressed the issue of a family meeting, as part of a dispute resolution, discussing some of the pre-contractual negotiations that formed the basis of a business agreement. The court stated that evidence of these communications was quite obviously not admissible on a question of the interpretation of the agreement. In her judgement Lady Arden stated, 'They made their agreement, which took place as part of a family gathering within the Muslim culture, or at least within the culture of that part of the Muslim community to which the parties in this action belong ... As I have said, when interpreting an agreement, whether written or oral, the court must look at the matrix of fact as described by Lord Hoffmann.'

In a recent case *Jivraj* v. *Hashwani* (2011),[5] the Supreme Court unanimously held that an Arbitrator is not an employee for the purposes of the Equality Act 2010. An arbitration award which is given under some law other than English law cannot be appealed on the grounds that the arbitrators got that law wrong, but it can be challenged and set aside by an English court under section 68 of the Arbitration Act 1996 on various grounds, including failure by the tribunal to comply with its general duty to act fairly and impartially. Furthermore all agreements made by Arbitration bodies are now subject to the provisions of the European Employment Equality (Religion and Belief) Regulations 2003.[6] This raises the question whether an arbitration agreement requiring any arbitrator to be of a particular religious persuasion is valid and falls under the provisions of the new law. The Jivraj case centred on the legitimacy of an arbiter chosen from a specific religious community, in this case the Ismaili community, and the dispute centred on the breakdown of a joint commercial venture. Three members of the Ismaili community were then appointed to assist in dividing the assets. Unable to do this, one of the parties then appointed an arbiter who was not a member of the Ismaili community. The application made on the requirement that the arbitrators be members of the Ismaili community, although lawful when the agreement was made, had been made rendered unlawful because it contravened the Employment Equality (Religion and Belief) Regulations 2003. The applicant also relied upon the Human Rights Act 1998 and public policy considerations (see Tumbridge, 2011, p. 202). However, at first instance the claim was dismissed by Mr Justice Steel who held that the regulations did not apply to arbitrators as they were not employees and 'that there is nothing in the Human Rights Act or public policy that renders the requirement that the arbitrators should be members of the Ismaili community void or unenforceable' (see Tumbridge, 2011, p. 202).

The application was therefore dismissed. The Court of Appeal overturned this decision on the basis that an arbitrator was an employee of the appointing parties, providing services under a 'contract personally to do any work'. The Court of Appeal also held that no particular religious requirements were necessary for the discharge of the function of an English-seated tribunal determining the dispute in accordance with English law. The Supreme Court unanimously overruled the Court of Appeal decision, holding that an arbitrator's role is not 'naturally described as one of employment at all' and he is in effect a 'quasi-judicial adjudicator'. The Court explained that although an arbitrator may provide services on a personal basis he 'does not perform those services or earn his fees for and under the direction of the parties'; rather an arbitrator is an 'independent provider of services who is not in a relationship of subordination with the parties who receives his services'.

Neil Addison points out, 'Though it was not directly relevant to its decision the Court also went on to consider whether the appointment of a religious arbitrator could be considered to be a Genuine Occupational Requirement and held that because there was a long tradition and an ethos for resolution of disputes within the Ismaili community itself and a stipulation that an arbitrator be of a particular religion or belief can be relevant to the manner in which disputes are resolved it was a GOR for the purposes of the regulations, and hence the Act. The Court did however state that the decision whether any post should be covered by the GOR exemption had to be made by an objective analysis of the evidence.'[7] Matthew Gearing (2011) discusses the importance of this ruling: 'The Court's decision demonstrates an understanding that, besides the functional component in terms of application of a given national law to the dispute, arbitration has a very significant process-based dimension which is largely left to the discretion of the arbitrators by most national arbitration legislations, major institutional rules and other international codes (such as the UNCITRAL Model Law), subject only to certain safeguards necessary in the public interest. The exercise of this discretion and an arbitrator's approach to the resolution of the dispute are bound to be influenced by a number of characteristics linked to his/her nationality, cultural background, ethos, legal training and experience. Indeed, even if, in fact, an arbitrator is not so influenced, the objective perception of the parties would always be otherwise. This point is well illustrated by the different attitudes and practices of arbitrators from diverse legal, cultural and regional backgrounds, which might manifest themselves in a predisposition towards adversarial or inquisitorial or conciliatory approach, or attitude towards confidentiality.'

The use of religious scholars at Shari'ah councils who act as expert witnesses in family law disputes has also been addressed by the courts. In *Uddin v. Choudhury and Ors* (2009)[8] three key questions were raised about the validity of the *nikah* ceremony as a valid marriage, the process of religious divorce and the use of an expert witness in court based at a British Shari'ah council. This case centred on the breakdown of a religious marriage that had been arranged by the families of the parties. A religious ceremony had taken place but the marriage had not been registered according to civil law. The dispute then centred on the amount of *mahr* the bride had retained upon breakdown of the marriage. The ruling stipulated that the gifts made were not returnable even if the marriage had failed as they were not conditional upon the marriage and were not part of the dower (*mahr*) but simply gifts. The judgement has been criticized by the legal anthropologist Roger Ballard who questioned the basis upon which the council had dissolved the *nikah* contract and the over-reliance the judges had placed on the evidence put forward by the council expert. For Ballard (2010, p. 58), 'That both the trial judge and a Lord Justice of Appeal should have been prepared to recognize the enforceability of a *nikah namah* contract in English Law can only be regarded as welcome: one step forward. But as a result of being presented with unreliable evidence, the learned Judge has introduced a new precedent into English Law: namely that Muslim brides are entitled to retain their *mahr* and/or their dowries, regardless of the circumstances in which the marriage breaks down. That certainly makes a nasty pitfall for those who assume that English law is beginning to accept the legitimacy of the principles of Shari'ah when agreements have explicitly been arrived at in those terms.'

Mahr and the *nikah* contract

As discussed in earlier, the contractual use of *mahr* in Muslim marriages among Muslims living in Europe has led to questions of 'whether it is reconcilable with the gender equality principle' (Rutten, 2010, p. 46). In her work Fournier (2010) discusses how Muslim marriage and *mahr* travel from Islamic legal orders to European legal orders and describes these 'legal transplants' as complex, contradictory and at times in flux. Subsequently, as Fredriksen points out, the process of translation itself reveals that 'mahr can be treated in different ways: mahr as an integral and essential part of the Islamic marriage contract; mahr as a substitute for post-divorce maintenance; mahr as the division of the surplus of marital profits, as *mahr al-mithl* and mahr as a gift' (2010, p. 93).

There are very few cases regarding the recognition of *mahr* in English case law and this has led to a somewhat confusing situation. In *Shahnaz* v. *Rizwan* (1964)[9] the parties had contracted their marriage in India with a clause that stipulated deferred *mahr*. In 1959 the husband instigated divorce proceedings against his wife and she in turn brought an action in English law in the hope of recovering £1400, equivalent to the deferred *mahr*. The case revolved around the central issue of whether or not the claim for *mahr* could be heard within the jurisdiction of English law. The matter therefore rested on whether there was a contractual issue to consider. The husband argued that due to the marriage being polygamous or potentially polygamous, English courts had no jurisdiction to consider the claim. Judge Winns concluded it was a contractual rather than a matrimonial issue, 'while it can in the nature of things only arise in connection with a marriage by Mohammedan law (which is ex hypothesi polygamous), it is not a matrimonial right. It is not a right from the marriage but it is a right *in persona*, enforceable by the wife or widow against the husband or his heirs'. The force of this case was largely removed by the Matrimonial Causes Act 1973, which essentially gives the English court a broad discretion in financial provision. This case illustrates that the force of contract law can be used to recognize *mahr* in Muslim marriage contracts. In this case the Muslim marriage itself is deemed a consideration of the contract – in essence Muslim marriage was viewed as a prenuptial agreement.

The second case, *Qureshi* v. *Qureshi* (1972), involved the case of a couple, the wife being an Indian citizen and the husband a Pakistani citizen. They married in Britain at the Kensington Register Office in 1966. A few months after the breakdown of the marriage, a religious divorce was issued to the husband. The principal issue of this case surrounded the wife's argument that the marriage subsists and that her husband should continue maintenance. If, however, the marriage had been dissolved, then she wished to claim the dower as stipulated in the religious marriage contract, plus some maintenance. The question before the courts therefore was where the couple were domiciled to consider the validity of the marriage. The courts concluded that the religious marriage had been valid and thereby the divorce and maintenance payments could continue.

On the question of *mahr*, Rutten (2010, p. 67) summed up the key difference between the two cases: 'A significant difference between the Shahnaz and the Qureshi judgements is that, in Shanaz, the wife was excluded from seeking ancillary relief on the basis that the marriage was considered potentially polygamous, while in the case of Qureshi the marriage was considered monogamous so the wife could seek ancillary relief. As the husband was planning to return to Pakistan, the only realistic way for the wife to get any money after the divorce, as the court saw it, was through *mahr*, as this would be easier to enforce by English courts than any ancillary relief.'

As discussed in chapter 6 the contractural nature of the Muslim marriage as led to interesting discussions by Muslim feminist scholars over the extent to which it allows women to participate in a 'free', 'autonomous' and 'equal' way. In particular the normative values underpinning the male-female relationship also underpin the contractual relations which mean in practice little can effectively be achieved (Barlas, 2006).

In this study a group of women also sought advice on the possibility of claiming back the *mahr* stipulated in the *nikah* contract under English contract law. No further data on this issue was collected but one interviewee explained that although her solicitor was looking into the possibility she had been told 'that the chances of me winning the full amount are limited'.

Reforming religious marriage for Muslims in Britain

Such concern over the non-formalization of religious marriage and the limited use of the *nikah* contract has led to some attempts by religious scholars in Britain to strengthen the *nikah* contract by producing a standard *nikah* contract for all Muslims in Britain. This document was launched in August 2008 by the Muslim Institute to address issues of gender inequalities upon breakdown of marriage.

Marital agreements (including prenuptial, postnuptial and separation agreements) are not binding in England and Wales – even those entered into in jurisdictions where such agreements are fully binding. These issues have been addressed in recent cases, notably *MacLeod* v. *MacLeod* (2008)[10] and *NG* v. *KR* (Pre-Nuptial Contract) (2008),[11] *Radmacher* v. *Granatino* (2008).[12] Marital agreements are, however, being given increasing weight in ancillary relief proceedings – see, for example, *K* v. *K* (Ancillary Relief: Prenuptial Agreement) (2003).[13] Many have called for a review of this area of law,[14] notably Sir Mark Potter in *Charman* v. *Charman* (2007).[15] The Law Commission for England and Wales has now included Marital Property Agreements in its tenth Programme of Law Reform; the Commission's project commenced in September 2009 and a report and draft Bill are expected in Autumn 2012.[16] In many jurisdictions, marital agreements can be binding and this has led to discussions on how such issues can be addressed by the English legal system.

The legal developments have raised the question of the extent to which *nikah* contracts mirror the increasing use of premarital contracts in English law. As previously discussed, marriage in Islamic law is underpinned by a strong contractual relationship and one key element of this contract is an 'agreement between future spouses on the financial consequences of the dissolution of the marriage' (Franck, 2009, p. 236). So what is the relationship between prenuptial agreements in England and religious marriage contracts such as the *nikah* contract? As Franck (2009, p. 237) explains further, 'The debate on the enforceability of pre-marital contracts is embedded in a long-standing dispute on the nature of marriage. Should marriage be regarded as a contract, and therefore the mere result of a bargain by autonomous self-interested parties?'

In Britain mosques are often not registered as religious buildings in order to perform marriages that conform to English law and hence religious marriages are not formalized according to civil law procedure. This new marriage contract, drafted by the Muslim Institute, was launched to provide women with written proof of their marriage under Islamic law,[17] and the reforms of the contract include:

- Removing the requirement for a 'marriage guardian' (*wali*) for the bride, who, as an adult, can make up her own mind about whom to marry
- Enabling the wife to initiate divorce and retain all her financial rights agreed in the marriage contract
- Forbidding polygamy whether formally or informally in the UK or abroad
- Encouraging mosques to register to perform marriages

The author of the proposed contract, Dr Siddiqui, claims that the contract will bring Muslim marriages in Britain in line with positive developments in Muslim family law 'across the Muslim world'. Activist and researcher and Chair of the Muslim Women's Network Cassandra Balchin (2010) points to the usefulness of such contracts in promoting the rights of Muslim women based on the principles of equality, justice and fairness. She explains, 'There have recently been major initiatives around model marriage contracts with a firm commitment to advancing equality within the family. Despite the great diversity of laws and practices across the Muslim world, the conditions women insert into the contract when they get the chance are remarkably similar. They want greater financial autonomy and security, a fairer division of property reflecting their contribution to the family's finances, freedom of mobility and equality in decision-making, a monogamous relationship, and, should mutual understanding break down, then equal access to divorce. In other words, the presumed standard model of Muslim marriage, which regards the male as head of household, just isn't working in women's eyes. This model is an edifice built entirely on the concept of *qiwamah* (translated variously as superiority, guardianship, being in charge of, responsibility) which is derived from one of the most contested Qur'anic verses regarding gender relations (Surah al-Nisa:34).' Such contracts can therefore be viewed as part of the process in reforming Muslim marriage practices. However, critics point to how such initiatives have simply led to the creation of parallel legal systems. Neil Addison (2007, p. 23) argues that it continues 'the unfortunate trend of separating Muslims from the general community in Britain. The Contract will still permit imams to perform Muslim Marriage ceremonies when the couple are not married in accordance with British Law; indeed the existence of such a "model" contract endorsed, as this is, by lawyers and MPs gives the seal of approval for the continuation of marriage ceremonies which have no legal legitimacy under British law. It is in fact an encouragement to illegality.'

The use of religious marriage contracts also raises questions on the extent to which common contract norms are based on gendered assumptions. Traditional feminist scholarship on the position of women in the law of contracts points to the voices of women being sidelined and marginalized and the law of contract being inherently phallocentric (Pateman, 1988). However, as Mulcahy points out, more recently, '[a] considerable amount of work has focused on contract as an alternative to marriage and the use of contract in intimate relationships more generally. It has been argued, for instance, that contract has the potential to foster a non-exploitative conception of "private" relationships, although feminists have also argued that using contracts in this sphere could merely entrench existing bargaining inequalities' (2005, p. 5). Thus for feminist scholars the key question is the extent to which contract law can be used to develop models of contract relationships based on pluralism and diversity. New ways of using and understanding contract law are based on a 'context-sensitive model of contract relationships' (Mulcahy, 2005, p. 16) which offer multiple perspectives and outcomes.

Mediation and civil law

Over the past 40 years the practice of resolving matrimonial disputes outside the sphere of formal legal adjudication has gained renewed impetus among legal practitioners, policymakers and more recently socio-legal scholars. This period has seen the emergence of different forms of ADR mechanisms that both act in opposition to and as part of the state-law processes that aim to resolve civil, commercial and family law disputes.[18] This new trend seeks to provide equal access to justice for all citizens and is underpinned by key human rights values, social justice and based on the lived experiences of the disputants. Susan Daicoff (2006, p. 46) catalogues the emergence of multiple systems of dispute resolution as the:

> result of a synthesis of a number of new disciplines within law and legal practice that have been rapidly gaining visibility, acceptance, and popularity in the last decade and a half. These disciplines represent a number of emerging, new, or alternative forms of law practice, dispute resolution, and criminal justice. The converging main 'vectors' of this movement are (1) collaborative law, (2) creative problem solving, (3) holistic justice, (4) preventive law, (5) problem solving courts, (6) procedural justice, (7) restorative justice, (8) therapeutic jurisprudence, and (9) transformative mediation.

The terms 'mediation', 'reconciliation' and 'arbitration' are often used interchangeably and subsequently give rise to some confusion. The term 'mediation', in general, covers a number of current ADR trends which share the ideological aims of resolving disputes outside the formal civil system of court-based adjudication but which also share in promoting a sense of equity and fair practice for all the parties involved. In very simple terms reconciliation focuses on saving the marriage, whereas mediation accepts the breakdown in marriage and then assists the couple in determining the best outcome. In a White Paper by the Lord Chancellor (1995) *Looking to the Future: Mediation and the Ground for Divorce*, mediation is described as 'a process in which an impartial third person, the mediator, assists couples considering separation or divorce to meet together to deal with the arrangements that need to be made for the future' (paragraph 5.4).

ADR, therefore, occupies an interesting and contested arena in law whereby competing legal discourses interact and overlap to produce a wide array of disputing mechanisms. As a process of resolving disputes it acts both in opposition to state law but is equally supervised and supported by the state. Working in tandem with individuals, state law and local communities, ADR has therefore been perceived for many years as the natural space where conflicts can be amicably resolved. This increase in 'informalism' has generally been perceived as a positive development against the overarching power of state law which in turn can have a social transformative role in 'law' and 'legal relations' in promoting access to justice. Indeed, the relationship between ADR and resolving disputes in the wider community has for many decades generated an interesting array of literature on the limits of law (see Festiner, Abel and Sarat, 1980). For Fitzpatrick, the relationship between ADR and state law must be uncoupled to reveal ADR as 'a mere mask or agent' of the state (1992a, p. 199), where such popular forms of justice can oppose formal law 'even while being identical to them' (1992b, p. 200), thereby revealing little if any contestation between the two approaches to resolving disputes. In this way the literature on ADR and its relationship to community raises a number of interesting issues. For example, in Britain localized ADR/mediation services that specifically cater to the needs of local minority communities have flourished since the mid-1980s. Within Muslim communities, for example, organizations such as the Muslim Mediation Forum, Marlborough Family Services, An-Nisa Society and the Muslim Women's Helpline are just a few such organizations which provide local mediation and counselling services. There is potential for future research to analyse the extent to which these bodies complement/conflict or work in conjunction with Shari'ah councils.

The historical origins of the ADR movement can be traced to the USA where the early Community Boards in San Francisco were based upon notions of 'civic responsibility' and 'local self-governance' and aimed to encourage settlements away from state law (Harrington, 1992, p. 32). So to what extent are communities and community needs represented in ADR mechanisms? In their work Harrington and Yngvesson illustrate how mediation actually creates 'representations and identities for "community" in a legal setting' (1990, p. 178). Communities are therefore given a common identity, voice and representation that in effect translate into legal representation on behalf of community members. For example, in the USA religious bodies acting as conflict resolution mechanisms generated much interest for the ways in which disputes were being resolved. Harrington and Merry points out that prior to the setting up of community boards dispute resolution was organized around religious, cultural and ethnic lines, established 'to maintain cultural values and preserve ethnic and religious identity, often seen as being under attack from the "outside"' (1988). In his early research into the formation of such tribunals during the early twentieth century, Auerbach (1983) describes the role of tribunals within the Chinese community in New York as maintaining close-knit ties within the community and ensuring assimilation was being resisted while tracing the origins of the Jewish Conciliation Board in similar terms. In the 1960s in the USA there were a number of government initiatives supported by various funding programmes that aimed to resolve conflicts within communities. The aim of such programmes was not empowerment within the community but instead the courts were given powers to intervene in local communities via local ADR mechanisms to ensure state control and accountability. During this time private mediation bodies also came into operation: for example, the Ford Foundation[19] set up ADR bodies to resolve racial disputes in order to prevent widespread disobedience. In this way the relationship between community and law can be conceptualized according to the different contexts in which it operates. Much of the literature on the use and practice of ADR therefore originates from North America and scholars document both its evolution in the 1970s to modern day approaches.[20] For these scholars, the impetus for the large-scale use of ADR in the USA also stemmed from individual civic pressure. As Juliano (2005, p. 23) points out, 'The modern ADR field grew from communities' increasing awareness of human rights and dignity, a desire to practice democratic participation and empower themselves to solve local problems affecting their lives, and the desires of the American judicial and legal communities to offer more efficient and satisfactory alternatives to the secular court system.' Law, thus, plays a minimal role in the context of some ADR mechanisms and a greater role in governance in others.

For many scholars, therefore, the issue remains the extent to which the state retains control in the resolution of disputes and whether this control underpins the relationship between ADR and the local community. For example, Abel (1992) points out that although ADR operates under the guise of reducing state control and is often presented as being less coercive and oppressive in its intervention in the lives of private individuals, it can in fact lead to greater forms of state control and intervention. For many ADR scholars the question is whether ADR embodies a social transformative role in law and in the lives of the disputing parties. Abel concludes that although ADR remains a part of the existing legal system it cannot in itself instigate any real social change.[21] Nevertheless he accepts that state-law mediation can offer protection against forms of abuse which informal mediation may fail to protect against. 'Formality', he states, 'can frequently be a useful weapon for the powerless. It can justify the demand for equality across lines of race, religion, gender and even class' (Abel, 1982, p. 10).

Mediation in English family law has often been presented as a dilemma for the liberal state, one that grapples with regulating 'family life' on the one hand and with preserving 'family privacy' on the other (Bottomley, 1984; Maclean, 1997). This relationship between the state and the family[22] is epitomized through family law legislation. Kurczewski explains, 'the duty of the state is to support and protect the authentic institution of the family, respecting its natural shape and natural and inalienable rights' (1997, p. 5). Most commentators accept that the 'authentic' shape of the family is based on the idealized vision of the 'sacred character' of the family underpinned by gender relations where the family is transformed to reflect male interests.[23] McCrory outlines four universal characteristics of family mediation: the impartiality of the mediator, the voluntariness of the process, the confidentiality of the relationship between the mediator and the parties, and finally the procedural flexibility available to the mediator (1981, p. 56). The question that arises is what significance does each of these characteristics have in determining the process of mediation itself. The mediation process is one where the power to make decisions is reconfigured to the parties themselves – where they have the power to make change and take control of their lives. In this way issues of empowerment remain at the heart of mediation. ADR is now a recognized part of legal policy and is embedded in the legal framework: the Access to Justice Act 1999 (incorporating section 11 of the Family Law Act 1986), the Adoption and Children Act 2002, and the Children Act 2004.

More recently the issue of mediation in family law disputes has been addressed by Family Justice Review headed by David Norgrove. The Family Justice Review panel was appointed in 2009 to review the whole of the family justice system in England and Wales, looking at all aspects of the system from court decisions on taking children into care to disputes over contact with children when parents divorce (see review guidelines). The final report was published on 3 November 2011[24] and outlined a number of reforms to public and private law and the family justice system as a whole. In relation to mediation the review found that when couples use mediation first they are more likely to continue to mediate rather than go to court and the report encouraged more couples to use it when working out how best to look after their children. This fits in with government initiatives to reduce matrimonial conflict in the adversarial court process and there is now a renewed emphasis upon mediation and disputing parties taking responsibility for their lives. The cuts in legal aid, however, are seen as a challenge to these recommendations the outcomes of which will be unknown for sometime yet. In Scotland the Arbitration (Scotland) Act 2010 was passed in November 2011 to provide a statutory framework for arbitration to encourage greater use of arbitration domestically and attract more international arbitration to Scotland.[25]

The remit of religious courts under the Arbitration Act 1996

The debate on the emergence of new forms of governance in Britain has recently centred on the establishment of Shari'ah courts under the heading of the MAT under the auspices of the Arbitration Act 1996. The establishment of MAT has been controversial for a number of reasons: first, it has been claimed that Shari'ah courts have been allowed through the back door; and second, they directly challenge the superiority of the English legal system and undermine the principles upon which English family law is based.

As Blackett (2009, p. 13) points out, 'It is important to point out that the Muslim Arbitration Tribunal does not resemble or operate as a court but is an arbitration tribunal that must have the consent of the parties to rule on an issue. MAT has no power of enforcement but decisions can be enforced by the English county or high courts. This process therefore means that the decisions made by these arbitration bodies have to be in line with principles of English law or judges will not enforce them under sovereign rule.' The authority within the law of these courts was outlined by the Parliamentary Under-Secretary of State Bridget Prentice in the House of Commons in October 2008:

If, in a family dispute dealing with money or children, the parties to a judgement in a Shari'ah council wish to have this recognized by English authorities, they are at liberty to draft a consent order embodying the terms of the agreement and submit it to an English court. This allows

English judges to scrutinize it to ensure that it complies with English legal tenets.

However, John Eekelaar (2011, p. 34) has recently questioned this understanding, pointing out: 'There is, however, nothing in the Arbitration Act that so restricts arbitration. It is not clear that the Children Act 1989 would necessarily prevent an arbitral award concerning children being enforced because the court's duty to apply the best interests principle under the Children Act only applies when the court makes a determination about the upbringing of the child, which is arguably not the case when an arbitral award is enforced. It is true that an arbitration agreement is unlikely to prevent a party from invoking the courts jurisdiction in family matters because courts will not permit parties to oust that jurisdiction, but that depends on a party both wishing to escape from the arbitral award and being willing to apply to the court. So it seems that at least theoretically, family arbitrations might be capable of being enforced in the civil courts.' This analysis raises crucial questions in relation to questions of choice, fairness and equality, which are addressed in the final chapter of this book.

Under English law parties cannot agree that a court should apply Shari'ah law but in arbitration the position is different. Section 46 of the Arbitration Act 1996 provides that

> (1) The arbitral tribunal shall decide the disputes (a) in accordance with the law chosen by the parties as applicable to the substance of the dispute, or (b) if the parties so agree, in accordance with such other considerations as are agreed by them or determined by the tribunal. (2) For this purpose the choice of laws of a country shall be understood to refer to the substantive laws of that country and not its conflict of laws rules.

Hence the parties can agree that the arbitrators will decide their dispute according to Shari'ah law. The Arbitration Act 1996 contains a number of safeguards. An agreement to arbitrate is, in a sense, just like any other contract and so it is necessary to show a genuine agreement to arbitrate by both parties. Contracts obtained by duress will not be enforced, neither will contracts with minors or the incompetent. Agreements to arbitrate must be evidenced in writing. An arbitration award is, in itself, of no effect. It is of value only to the extent that a court is prepared to enforce it. Courts may refuse to enforce awards on various grounds, including (a) that a party was under some incapacity, (b) that the agreement was not valid under the applicable law, (c) that a party did not have proper notice of the arbitrator's appointment or of the proceedings or was unable to present their case, (d) if the award deals with a matter which it was not agreed would be submitted to arbitration, and (e) if the award relates to a matter which is not capable of being settled by arbitration, or if it would be contrary to public policy to enforce the award. An arbitration award which is given under some law other than English law cannot be appealed on the grounds that the arbitrators got that law wrong, but it can be challenged and set aside by an English court under Article 68 of the Arbitration Act 1996 on various grounds, including failure by the tribunal to comply with its general duty to act fairly and impartially (12).

The Muslim Arbitration Tribunal

The Muslim Arbitration Tribunal (MAT) was set up June 2007 and aims to settle disputes in accordance with religious Shari'ah law. At present, there are five tribunals operating as part of the MAT across Britain. Apart from addressing issues of religious divorce and other Muslim family law matters (including marriage contracts, wills and inheritance disputes) these tribunals also arbitrate on matters relating to forced marriage and domestic violence. MAT states that all agreements are settled

1. In accordance with Qur'anic injunctions and prophetic practice as determined by the recognized schools of Islamic sacred law
2. As fairly, quickly and efficiently as possible
3. Where appropriate, those members of the Tribunal have responsibility for ensuring this is in the interests of the parties to the proceedings and in the wider public interest

It is held that Islamic decisions can be reached quickly and cheaply, and can be used as evidence before the civil court when seeking other remedies. It does not deal with criminal offences but states that 'where there are criminal charges such as assault within the context of domestic violence, the parties will be able ask MAT to assist in reaching reconciliation which is observed and approved by MAT as an independent organization. The terms of such reconciliation can then be passed by MAT on to the Crown Prosecution Service (CPS) though the local Police Domestic Violence Liaison Officers with a view to reconsidering the criminal charges. Note that the final decision to prosecute always remains with the CPS'[26] (Muslim Arbitration Tribunal, 2008a). On 16 March 2008, *The Sunday Times* reported that the tribunal has 'divided the estate of a Muslim man between his two sons and three daughters. Keeping with Islamic religious law, the sons were awarded twice as much money as the daughters. In six domestic violence cases on which the tribunal met last year, the rulings required no further punishment for the husbands than anger management classes and community mentoring. After these rulings were issued, all six women withdrew their complaints to the UK police' (Madeira, 2010, p. 3).

The authority of this tribunal rests with the Arbitration Act 1996 which permits civil matters to be resolved in accordance with Muslim personal law and within the ambit of state law. For many this process of resolving disputes provides the ideal way to allow the arbitrating parties to resolve disputes according to English law while fulfilling any obligations under Islamic law. The advantages of arbitration, it is argued, allow the parties to achieve some level of autonomy in the decision-making process. This coupled with the informal setting, lower costs, flexibility and time efficiency means that for many it may prove a more attractive alternative to the adversarial courts system in England and Wales. However, there remain real concerns on whether this process could seek to restrict women's equality and issues of fairness and justice in areas of family law, including domestic violence, child custody, divorce, financial support and inheritance.

In 2008, MAT produced a report titled *Liberation from Forced Marriages*, which stated that MAT was the most appropriate forum for the Muslim community to resolve such problems. It put forward the following proposals to combat the practice of forced marriage as a community-driven initiative with emphasis placed upon protecting British citizens marrying abroad who are victims of forced marriage. First, this includes the foreign spouse to voluntarily submit 'an oral deposition to the Judges of MAT, satisfying them that the marriage he/she entered into was neither forced nor coerced'. As a voluntary deposition by the British citizen rather than a legal requirement, the judges of MAT would then produce a written declaration that they were satisfied that the marriage entered into was without any force or coercion. The proposal further states that 'the British citizen can then use this declaration to support the application of the foreign spouse to settle in the UK. If, however, the foreign spouse fails to produce such a declaration from MAT or any other appropriate evidence, then it would be open for the ECO at the entry clearance point, to draw such inferences deemed appropriate as to the status of the marriage' (2008, p. 25).

MAT claims that voluntary submission is the key factor to challenging forced marriages with foreign spouses and that 'a community based court would be better placed to deal with the intricacies of the community issues' as the community would be intolerant of state intervention. The report further states, 'Assessment by professionals and scholars of the Muslim Community within the MAT organization will enable this process to be carried out responsibly. When Muslim professionals and scholars who are from the UK, live in our multi-cultural, multi-ethnic and diverse society review a case before them then they will do so with the scrutiny and compassion it deserves. The team that is recruited by MAT to carry out this service will have extensive experience of dealing with forced marriages because they have been surrounded by examples of this in their families, communities and localities. MAT provides that environment which will give British Muslims the confidence to come forward to utilize the process to its fullest potential.'

The decisions of MAT judges are recorded on tape and the hearings recorded on camera. Evidence may include speaking to family members 'to highlight the wider consequences of participating or being complicit in a coerced or forced marriage'. The use of community elders as a source of social scrutiny to embarrass perpetrators is also proposed as a source of action. So the proposal envisages a scenario where they hope to work closely with both perpetrators and victims of forced marriage.

In addition to tackling forced marriage, MAT also deals with issues of domestic violence within Muslim communities. The MAT website states:

> It is not only the victims of domestic abuse who remain silent on the issue, but also certain imams. It is said that the practice of domestic abuse derives legitimacy from the Islamic scriptures and therefore is a matter which all Muslims believe in and accept. For an imam to preach contrary to this would be sacrilege. However, is this actually factually correct and how far is this legitimacy derived from a distorted interpretation of the scriptures? Furthermore, is the silence of the imams more to do with preserving their own position within their communities than preserving the supposed practices of the Islamic faith?

The Forced Marriage Protection Act and Protection Orders

One of the primary objections in the MAT report is what it describes as the limited nature of the Forced Marriage Protection Orders[27] for the following reasons: no clear support infrastructure for the victim of the marriage; the imposition of the Order upon the wider family will be resented by them and held against the victim, adding to his/her perils; there will be greater reluctance of victims to approach the English court system for assistance; the reference by the third parties to the English courts can easily be obfuscated by the efforts of the wider family; and finally there is no clear pathway for the victim to seek annulment of the marriage directly as a consequence of the Protection Order.

As to the FMPA it can be argued that it is too early to examine the impact of the legislation as it has only been implemented relatively recently. Nevertheless the legislation has been a catalyst for a number of changes within the public sector (such as government, judiciary, police, social services, education, health and immigration) and these can be examined.

A recent policy paper by the Ministry of Justice (MOJ) describes the effectiveness of the statute (see Prentice, 2009). The research underpinning the paper shows that there has been a need for such a statute as it has been used widely. If analysed as a whole, the figures in the MOJ report appear to indicate that more orders were made by the courts than actual applications. This in itself has shown the responsibility the courts have taken in attempting to prevent a potential forced marriage taking place. The report also points to the fact that judges are working hard to learn more about the procedures[28] in order to make a just decision. For example, judges have themselves noted that there needs to be more judicial training in this area[29] which reinforces the view that the Act is still at an early stage of interpretation. Furthermore, there appears to be a relatively high proportion of orders attached with powers of arrest; one can assume that the theoretical arguments about the risk forced marriage victims are facing are in fact realities that are being addressed through legal means. The report states that significantly more children under 16 have been victims of forced marriage in the past year than adults. Now, forced marriages can to an extent be quantified which can lead to appropriate methods of dealing with them.

Perhaps more resources and awareness raising should be invested in local authorities, however, as there has been a suggestion that some local authorities have 'been slow to get involved' and there is 'lack of clarity between boundaries between care proceedings under the Children Act, Court of Protection cases and FM cases. The Act does not sit well with social services working methods'.[30] These issues need to be addressed. Without proper training within social services, education and health, for example, or sufficient 'practical and mainstream support', the Act may become 'a symbolic outlawing of forced marriage' rather than serving to eradicate it.[31] Nevertheless the police appear to have taken a more active and dedicated role since the Act's implementation by promoting awareness as well as being able to take action at any sign of a potential case of forced marriage. Government guidelines distributed in schools and among the National Health Service have also had a positive impact in promoting awareness and encouraging preventative actions. Research has shown that schools and GPs have referred suspected cases of forced marriage to the police (see Prentice, 2009, paragraph 56).

In addition applications have been made for FMPOs outside the England and Wales jurisdiction which has helped a number of individuals who have been taken abroad to be married against their will to be protected legally. For example, in December 2008, Judge Coleridge granted an FMPO to prevent Dr Humayra Abedin[32] from undertaking a wedding ceremony in Bangladesh, where she was being held against her wishes, and secure her return to Britain. This was an important case as it encapsulated the importance of having a specific Act so that the courts are better equipped to tackle forced marriages than trying to mould the laws as they had done previously. Coleridge's view is also supported in the policy paper which indicates that the judges have found it easier to grasp the new law on forced marriage, so the court procedures have been fast enough to provide efficient remedies. As discussed earlier the proposed criminalisation of forced marriage is due to be put forward to Parliament in a draft bill in 2013.

Arbitration and the role of the MAT

So what does formal arbitration entail and how does the MAT fall under the ambit of arbitration? The MAT is modelled on the Jewish Beth Din which has operated under the auspices of the arbitration legislation for many decades. The Beth Din tribunals are used to resolve private disputes ranging from religious divorce to business transactions. It is interesting to note that these tribunals have been operating in Britain for many years with little if any of the publicity and hostility that has been directed towards the MAT. A report on the Beth Din observed that 'civil courts however retain the right to intervene in any case where the award of the Beth Din is considered unreasonable or contrary to public policy'. The report also stressed that 'in neither arbitration cases nor religious judgements is the Beth Din recognized as a legal court nor does it offer a parallel legal system: Beth Din rulings or advice can only be reflected in UK law if both parties freely agree and the decision is approved by the civil courts' (Douglas et al., 2011).

In her work Jarman (2008) points out that arbitration is a jurisdictional hybrid of private and public law. Redfern and Hunter point out that 'it begins as a private agreement between the parties. It continues by way of private proceedings, in which the wishes of the parties are of great importance. Yet it ends with an award which has binding legal force and effect and which, on appropriate conditions being met ... the courts ... will be prepared to recognize and enforce' (2004, p. 3).

More recently the relationship between arbitration and the Human Rights Act has been explored in three judgements.[33] The question in these cases was whether it was possible during the course of the arbitration agreement to forego one of the convention rights, namely Article 6 concerning the right to a fair trial. It was found that the terms of the Arbitration Act 1996 did fulfil the requirements of Article 6 as long as the arbitration agreement was entered into 'freely' or was 'agreed without constraint' and the agreement itself 'did not run counter to any important public interest'. Central to all of this was the need for the tribunal to be impartial and to follow procedural fairness.

So how does the MAT run as an arbitration body and does it fulfil key requirements of the Arbitration Act? At present there is no body of case law to analyse its effectiveness but we can see its institutional structure is parallel to state-law mechanisms and also emanates from social and cultural postulates. In this way the overlap of jurisdictions, the choice of forums and the personal behaviours and decision-making focuses attention to new forms of interlegality and multicultural interlegality. The legitimacy of various legal and social domains mixes up our understandings of law and decision-making. But to what extent does this approach challenge liberal conceptions of equality, human rights, individual choice and undermine gender equality?

Should we mediate in cases of forced marriage?

The approach taken by MAT raises the question of whether we should ever mediate in cases of forced marriage. Forced marriage has been described as 'a marriage without the full and free consent of both parties' and 'where people are coerced into a marriage against their will and under duress' (Home Office, 2005) and it falls under the spectrum of domestic violence according to English law. For many practitioners therefore the idea of mediating on the issue of violence is one to be approached with extreme caution. The MAT emphasizes its basis as a community initiative that encourages and promotes family and community cohesion and individual personal autonomy and empowerment for all individuals who wish to resolve such issues within the framework of family, home and local community.

However, MAT does not sufficiently address the issue of power and power relations within the context of family and home. The issue of control and powerlessness for many female victims of forced marriage has long remained a central issue in the challenge to eradicate its practice. Concepts such as dialogue, discussion, compromise and co-operation may in fact compromise the safety of female victims of forced marriage. Research indicates that many women who are victims of forced marriage do not occupy an equal position in the family and home in terms of the bargaining power, respect and prestige that are often accorded to male members of the same household. The mediation process can therefore increase rather than reduce the level of harm and possible violence directed to women. Penny Booth argues that such tribunals can create a system of coercive control for women: 'The danger is in the development of a parallel system of (any) law where the choice as to which system or principle is used is determined not by the individual or the issue but by the group bullies. In family law this danger could arise where the determination of system and approach is not made by the woman but the men; not through female but through the male dominated system' (2008, p. 936).

Feminist criticisms of arbitration and mediation therefore relate to issues of unequal power relations between men and women that can result in unfair bargaining practices and outcomes for women. The issue of fairness and equity of agreements via the mediation approach underpins any feminist criticisms of mediation. Feminist scholars (see Diduck and O'Donovan, 2006) argue that family law statutes and practices are implicitly biased against women. As Irving and Benjamin (1995) sum up, 'Patriarchal bias inheres in the adversarial system, with male judges and lawyers tending to advance characteristically "male" solutions to the problem of divorce, emphasizing conflict, competition and "winning"; and women are consequently typically rendered passive, dependent observers in their own cases' (p. 203).

For some feminists, therefore, only an alternative to an adversarial system with its inherent male bias can provide a better situation for vulnerable women. Rifkin (1984) argues that mediation reflects what she understands as a feminist analysis, one that stresses cooperation, negotiation, equity and especially participation and ownership. In short mediation would appear to provide one basis for resolving divorce disputes that gives women back their voice (quoted in Irving and Benjamin, 1995, p. 203). However, the feminist position on mediation is mostly critical and as a result the debates have largely stagnated as either in favour of mediation or against. Irving and Benjamin (1995) suggest that the feminist critique of family mediation involves four general arguments – neutrality, equality, rights and practice standards – and that these can be translated into five specific assertions:

1. The failure of neutrality: In practice mediation can never be a process that is objective and value-free and the mediator inevitably brings to the mediation process a set of values and beliefs which influence his role as the mediator. In this way the mediator may replicate existing patriarchal forms of social ordering.
2. Patriarchal power and inequality: The argument that mediation merely reflects the subordinate position that women occupy in wider society.
3. Failure of empowerment: Mediation as a process does not empower women to make better settlements for themselves.
4. Mediation and family violence: Mediation can pose considerable risks to women who have experienced violence. The courts provide better safeguards and protection for women.
5. Mediation as a lesser forum.

Davis and Roberts (1988, p. 306) note that perhaps the main challenge to the feminist critique of mediation as perpetuating a power imbalance between men and women lies in this control over the mediation process by controlling the ebb and flow of negotiation; in some cases, the 'weaker' party does indeed feel empowered. They also note an important gender difference: 'what the man sees as unnecessary interference and control, the woman may have experienced as protection and support' (1989, p. 305). Irving and Benjamin point out that feminist-informed mediation would require two modifications in terms of empowerment: (a) to expand its assessment procedures to routinely explore spousal power balance and (b) to expand current techniques to include measures expressly designed with power balancing in mind (1995, p. 216).

There are other problems with organizations such as MAT mediating on the issue of forced marriage. For example, an enormous amount of trust is placed on MAT judges and they may provide a safe framework that cannot be extended to the family context once the victim returns home. As Hester, Pearson and Radford (1997, p. 45) point out, 'While mediation appears to be a safe, humanitarian, non-adversarial, inexpensive way to intervene in many situations, the best way to protect the rights of victims who are in unequal and dangerous relationships to their abusers is to engage in adversarial proceedings which can punish or deter criminal conduct.' In relation to MAT, despite the recording of mediation sessions, the process is conducted in private and there is little if any accountability of mediators and the way in which cases are handled. The intervention of family members may also hinder the female victim's capacity to make an informed decision. In this way the principles of mediation may actually not be suitable for tackling the issue of forced marriage. As Anitha and Gill point out, 'Women exercise their agency in complex and often contradictory ways, as they assess the options that are open to them, weigh the costs and benefits of their actions, and seek to balance their often competing needs with the expectations and desires. While there remains a need to recognize gendered power imbalances at the same time there also remains a need to respect women's exercise of agency ... We need to give more support to those women who wish to express their subjectivity within the framework of the communities of which they perceive themselves to be such a fundamental part' (2009, p. 34).

At present, there is little if any data that documents the experiences of Muslim women using such ADR mechanisms to challenge the practice of forced marriage. Feminist scholars have, however, pointed to the problems associated with the exit-centred approach and the high emotional and psychological costs this may involve (see Anitha and Gill, 2009). However, as discussed in this chapter, the problems of mediating issues such as forced marriage with vulnerable female victims can be both dangerous and ineffective as relationships between abusers and victims are full of power imbalances that are not sufficiently addressed by MAT. Currently we know very little about how this process actually takes shape and we must therefore remain cautious of understanding both the motivations and the experiences of Muslim women using this forum to challenge the practice of forced marriage. Feminist critiques on the experiences of ethnic minority women and mediation focus on the problems of multiculturalism whereby women are encouraged to resolve disputes in the community and via community mechanisms (Patel, 2008).

Such concerns were more recently raised in a private member's bill, the Arbitration and Mediation Services (Equality) bill, put forward by the Conservative peer Baroness Cox in the House of Lords in June 2011. Although the bill did not explicitly mention Islam, Muslims, Islamic or Shari'ah law, the terminology and language adopted in the bill seemed quite obvious to all those working in this area that it was specifically targeting Muslim communities and addressing concerns on the practice of Shari'ah law in Britain. Although the bill failed to pass the first hurdle of becoming law, it did, however, once again raise the 'spectre' of Shari'ah law operating in Britain. The bill itself sought to amend both the Arbitration Act 1996 and the Equality Act 2010 while seeking to outlaw discrimination on the grounds of sex and to clarify more explicitly the role and limits of an arbitrator in forging civil agreements. For example, it made clear that an arbitrator cannot accept cultural and religious norms values and principles that may, for example, be based on ideas that a woman's evidence is worth less and half of that to a man and to address concerns regarding gender bias against women who maybe entitled to reduced inheritance and property rights under religious laws. Clause 7 of the bill proposes an amendment to the section of the Courts and Legal Services Act 1990 and criminalizes 'falsely claiming legal jurisdiction' to prevent the ousting of jurisdiction in matters of family and criminal law. The focus on mediation while clearly raising serious questions such as concerns previously addressed, namely over the types of pressure that maybe exerted upon Muslim women compelled to use Shari'ah councils (a legitimate and fair concern and one that should neither be underestimated nor easily ignored), however, also failed not only to draw upon the lived experiences of Muslim women using Shari'ah councils (issues of choice and agency simply ignored) but it is a generally accepted fact among all mediators, legal practitioners and scholars working in issues of mediation that valid mediation agreements must involve the full and free consent all of the parties involved in the dispute resolution process. My research found no evidence of such agreements being made by Shari'ah councils but if such agreements are being made by the MAT they must comply with the Arbitration Act 1996 and fulfil all principles of English law. Therefore such agreements cannot simply usurp the principles of English family law or criminal law on the basis of cultural and religious principles that deviate from the principles of fairness, equality before the law and common citizenship and must have the authority and recognition (often as consent orders) of legally adjudicated English courts prior to becoming binding agreements.

This raises the question of why such a bill was put forward in the House of Lords while statutory and common law protections exist. Barrister Neil Addison (2011) argues that the bill serves a useful purpose because '[w]hat seems to have been increasingly happening, however, is that Shariah councils are offering "mediation" services that are in fact laying down Sharia rules, which both parties then sign and present to the family court pretending that it is a mediated agreement. Once a court accepts a mediation agreement it becomes a legally binding court order and so the law does have the right to question whether a mediation agreement is truly the result of "mediation". What the bill proposes is to give courts the legal duty to make sure that any mediation agreement really has been properly and freely negotiated rather than the courts simply "rubber stamping" mediation agreements that are handed to them.'[34]

The issue of mediation at Shari'ah councils cannot be simply ignored nor, however, should it be used to justify the arguments that somehow Muslims are seeking to supplement English law in favour of Islamic law and live their lives according to their own cultural and religious norms, values and laws which are in essence antithetical to the values and principles of English law and what it means to be British. This bill, however, simply failed to engage with the lived reality of Muslims in Britain today and the work of scholars who at the very least highlight the empirical reality that, in actual fact, the vast majority of Muslims are not seeking to undermine principles of English law but instead are simply seeking ways to live their lives as Muslims within the boundaries and framework of English law and their personal religious values and belief systems. Furthermore, as Eekelaar (2011) succinctly points out, 'It is a mistake to think of Shari'a as a monolithic system, impervious to change. In fact the bodies apply it in different ways, and it is subject to internal arguments and contestation. Might it be better to allow it to develop within its communities and responding to its internal critiques and influenced by the culture around it? Alongside this, its adherents could be encouraged to make more use of the civil law, including a greater readiness to enter legally recognized marriages without thereby severing their relationship with their religious norms.' But how can the experiences of British Muslim women and their use of Shari'ah councils help in shaping future debates regarding the accommodation of 'minority legal orders (Malik, 2012) in the UK? And can the law effectively capture their diverse experiences in their quest to obtain a religious divorce certificates? These questions are more addressed in the final chapter of this book.

9
Conclusion: Justice in the 'Shadow of Law'?

This book posed two key questions. First, how do Shari'ah councils constitute as unofficial dispute resolution mechanisms in matters of family law? And second, what are the experiences of British Pakistani Muslim women using such 'privatized' forms of dispute resolution to obtain a Muslim divorce?

As briefly discussed in the introductory chapter of this book, the current war on terror in Western European states has created for many Muslims living in the West a problematic and divisive engagement with the state. In Britain, for example, on the one hand the state continues to pursue its multicultural agenda to ensure the integration of minority communities into British society while also continuously demanding explicit expressions of loyalty and commitment (most vividly illustrated by the various commissions on integration and citizenship tests defining national identity). At the heart of these debates lies the question of the extent to which religious practices should now be accommodated within European legal systems, an issue that has unsurprisingly gained momentum within both socio-legal and sociological scholarship (see Adhar and Aroney, 2010). Modood (2008), for example, argues that a new form of 'practical multiculturalism' must allow for a 'nuanced understanding of the inter-relationship of "secular" and "religious" notions of civic life'. He supports the accommodation of Shari'ah by recognizing Shari'ah councils as official arbitration bodies as long as they are consistent with English law, human rights, gender equality and child-protection legislation. For Malik (2009, p. 3) also 'the accommodation of some Muslim legal and ethical norms can encourage Muslim integration into the European public sphere and strengthen mainstream legal and political institutions'. Her recent report on 'Minority Legal Orders' (Malik, 2012) puts forward a number of proposals on the ways in which the state can manage and accommodation religious difference in family law matters (see below). Yet one of the primary concerns of this book has been to strike a note of caution about calls for the recognition and/or accommodation of Shari'ah into English law. Apart from the significant practical difficulties in giving legitimacy to Shari'ah councils, the narratives of Muslim women must underpin such discussions. Debates on accommodation of Shari'ah must place at their very centre the experience of Muslim women, who are the primary users of Shari'ah councils and the ones most likely to be affected by any form of accommodation.

In Britain, in the context of liberal multiculturalism, unofficial non-statutory bodies such as Shari'ah councils have operated within minority communities for at least the past four decades. Framed as sites upon which family law matters are resolved according to Muslim family law principles and Islamic jurisprudence, such bodies have operated as unofficial community-based dispute resolution fora. Most interestingly they have developed specific frameworks of governance within diasporic Muslim communities which can be characterized by specific cultural, ethnic and religious norms and values. Indeed, the institution of religious, person-oriented legal systems within Western democratic societies constitutes a new and important stage in the establishment of Muslims in the West – one which reflects not only the extent of their presence and settlement in the UK, but which also builds upon the multicultural policies of integration and adaptation designed to accommodate ethnic, cultural and religious difference in Britain.

One of the most important issues confronting social and legal policymak-ing in the UK today is the extent to which the law should accommodate cultural and religious pluralism as part of the wider multicultural project of settlement and integration. For many the primary challenge of integration is evident in demands from Muslim communities to retain autonomy and seek a public space in civic society where they are able to enhance and main-tain their allegiance to specific religious and legal traditions. The outcry in the media provoked by the Archbishop of Canterbury, Dr Rowan Williams', speech on legal and cultural diversity in England lends weight to the argu-ment that in essence, Islam cannot be reconciled with the central features of Western democracy and modernity – features such as pluralism, secularism, democracy, civil social structure, religious tolerance and gender equality are deemed incompatible with Islamic principles of law, governance and justice.

The recognition of these plural legal orders has led to interesting scholarly debate on what is understood as law, legal pluralism and Muslim family law (Hamilton, 1995; Carroll, 1997; Pearl and Menski, 1998; Shah-Kazemi, 2001; Yilmaz, 2002). More interestingly still, the debate in Britain has been closely framed around the idea of a homogeneous 'Muslim identity' that leads to the demands for a parallel legal system, which in turn presupposes a deeply felt cultural and religious conviction, without providing adequate analysis of the complexities that identity entails. As exemplified in this study, the task of exploring the multiple ways in which British Pakistani Muslim women perceive dispute resolution means it is necessary to engage in the analysis of gender and its intersection with culture, rights and 'unofficial law'. Viewing these debates from an interdisciplinary perspective transforms the analytical framework from fairly essentialist terms to much more fluid and contradictory understandings. This gives rise to a pluralism that is neither essentialist nor relativist but also provides a 'stronger grounding in the conversation between theory and method' (Cowan, Dembour and Wilson, 2001, p. 20). Taking into account these specificities, does this research provide us with any new understandings of Shari'ah councils and the experiences of British Muslim women?

Shari'ah councils and power

The fear of Muslim extremism (see Allen, 2010) has not only transformed the relationship between local and national Muslim organizations and the state but has also been accompanied by the narrative of the British national identity and its representation of the 'good Muslim' (one who seeks integration, is identified as moderate and promotes 'British values') versus the 'bad Muslim' (one who is essentially anti-British and in support of extremist Islam). Rather than a collapse in these dichotomies, it is with regret that today we see a resurgence of representations of Muslims as the 'other', accompanied with the rising tide of the racialization of Muslims. As Vakil (2010, p. 276) points out, 'Where Islam is integral to Muslim identities, the denigration of Islam impacts on Muslim respect and self-worth, but what is primarily and fundamentally at stake in this is not a matter of the protection of belief *per se*, but rather of unequal relations of power, legal protection and institutional clout, in the context of entrenched social inequalities and capabilities.' The rise of anti-Muslim sentiment and Islamophobia therefore masks the very real issues of poverty, discrimination and disempowerment (and the disengagement from local politics) that many Muslims experience in British society today. And at the heart of this rise of Islamophobia lies an increased spotlight on the role of Shari'ah councils and what is perceived as their desire to introduce Islamic law into British society, harking back to traditional, tribal and patriarchal ways. For example, in his report for the think tank Civitas, Denis MacEoin (2009), critical of Shari'ah councils and the Muslim Arbitration Tribunal, argues, 'It is a challenge to what we believe to be the rights and freedoms of the individual to our concept of a legal system based on what Parliament enacts, and to the right of all of us to live in a society as free as possible from ethnic-religious division or communal claims to superiority and a special status that puts them in some respects above the law to which we are all bound' (p. 76). Yet this argument is flawed in multiple ways, not least because it fails to recognize the plural nature of ADR and law and fails to recognise that in practice law evolves, develops and to some extent seeks to accommodate the needs of all its citizens from multiple and diverse backgrounds. It also ignores the lived experiences of Muslim women as primary users of Shari'ah councils.

As discussed in Chapter 4, Shari'ah councils form part of the local, religious and socio-political communities in which they are situated. They represent multiple religious and ideological viewpoints and often produce multiple narratives of what it means to be a Muslim in British society today. Simultaneously this type of Muslim belonging also takes shape around structures of localized power that define who belongs to the wider 'Muslim community'. So some Shari'ah councils seek to produce exclusionary boundaries of the Muslim insider versus the non-Muslim/Muslim 'outsider' where individual Muslim identities and dissent may also be perceived as a threat to this model of 'community dispute resolution'. In this respect, the 'Muslim community' is defined by some councils by its specific focus on group membership and consensus to common Islamic norms and values, a manifestation of 'Muslim identity politics'.

The emphasis on discrete categories of 'Islam' and 'Muslim' means that such bodies can therefore 'reinscribe and rigidify boundaries between social groups that in everyday lived practice could be "fuzzy" and across which individuals might negotiate their multiple group affiliations' (Bennett, 1998, p. 12). The normative framework of these bodies is based upon a specific set of cultural and religious norms and values that can exclude alternative interpretations and discourse on 'Muslim disputing'. The data in this study, for example, illustrate the ways in which women can be both represented in and excluded from this process of dispute resolution. For example, the insistence that all women seeking divorce should participate in reconciliation sessions may serve to reinforce inequality and disadvantage for some women who may already be disempowered in the family and community (Grillo, 1991). In this context, feminist and Muslim feminist concerns about negotiating settlements in such privatized spaces where women may have no access to the protection of state law must be seriously addressed. Such concerns cannot be simply understood nor framed as part of debates on 'community rights' under the liberal multiculturalist framework but instead be understood in relation to debates on agency, power and decision-making both in minority communities and as citizens within public civic spaces (Yuval-Davis, 2011).

The councils are also imbued with patriarchal relations of power (see Walby, 1999) in which gendered power relations are produced and enacted in these community participation processes. But we know that power does not run evenly in a uniform or homogeneous way. A Foucauldian understanding of power for example points to power relations and sites of resistance: 'Power relationships ... depend on a multiplicity of points of resistance: these play the role of adversary, target, support or handle in power relations. The points of resistance are present everywhere in the power network' (1980, p. 95). For example, data from this study suggests that there are sites of resistance within the councils on occasions when, for example, a female counsellor may challenge the authority of a particular religious scholar and seek to promote alternative interpretations, albeit in subtle ways. Yet the data also found that such resistance could also be controlled and maintained within the boundaries of the council. Hence, the female counsellor may be consigned to the periphery of the disputing process, her role reduced to one of observer rather than an active participant in the decision-making process. By contrast, the position of male religious scholars in the councils is both strategic and negotiated to produce gendered narratives on the role of women in Islam (as mothers, wives and daughters). Such gendered cultural practices are endemic in the councils and promote the idea that women cannot occupy positions of local community power or as voices of authority in local Muslim communities.

This is not to suggest that such culturalized interpretations of Islam and what it means to be a Muslim woman in British society are neither contested nor unchallenged. However, the space within which women are able to engage in a transformative dialogue within the councils remains limited and tightly controlled.

The evidence suggests that power within Shari'ah councils is conceptualized in multiple and different ways, from controlling the boundaries of the 'Muslim community', homogenizing Muslim identity to sustaining the ideology of the essentialized construction of the Muslim family. Empirical data about Shari'ah councils thus reveal how these bodies continually seek to reorganize their *administrative* processes to respond to local pressures and the dominant state legal culture while seeking to remain loyal to the specific 'normative underpinnings' of Islamic jurisprudence that underpin these models of dispute resolution. What this means in practice is that these bodies model dispute resolution processes on state-law mechanisms of governance, emulating processes of rules, procedures and oversight and promoting 'personal choice' as a key component in resolving marital disputes in this space, while staying committed to the ethos and principles of Islamic law and jurisprudence. Nagel and Snipp (1993, p. 2004) describe this process as 'ethnic reorganization' which 'occurs when an ethnic minority undergoes a reorganization of its social structure, redefinition of ethnic group boundaries, or some other change in response to pressures or demands imposed by the dominant culture'.

Shari'ah council verdicts serve primarily to uphold the 'moral authority' of the Muslim community and evidence of the enforceability of divorce certificates was not found. The scholars reported that there were no community mechanisms or sanctions in place to enforce the terms of the divorce they issued and this was left to the goodwill of the parties concerned. English case law suggests, however, that at the same time this process of dispute resolution is also able to cross-cut domains of family law, private international law and the use of divorce certificates in Muslim countries for evidential purposes. This has not been explored in this book but remains an important issue in discussions over the legitimacy of such divorce certificates in both foreign and English jurisdictions.

Furthermore, the choice of legal mechanisms available to and utilized by individuals reflects a complex process on the part of individuals who adopt personal strategies in order to achieve specific ends, pointing to the diversity of legal orders in operation in different social fields and how these may converge in the minds of individuals (Santos, 1987). However, the councils actively sought to avoid any conflict with civil law procedure in matters of family law and the respondents explained that the divorce certificates were issued for the personal use of applicants and not viewed as legal documents to be recognized under English law.

The discursive legal spaces where formal and informal law meet provide the opportunity to conceptualize the emergence of such forms of 'informalism' as part of the 'semi-autonomous social field' (Moore, 1972). This strategy of drawing upon different theoretical paradigms provides insights into the 'interpenetrations' (Santos, 1987, p. 67) between the different arenas of disputing approaches and locating these debates within the specific lived realities of women's lives (Griffiths, 2002, p. 120). In this book I have argued that recent claims for cultural autonomy and the accommodation of personal laws in English law must be understood as part of a broader system of meaning and lived experience of law and as part of the wider socio-historical process of migration, belonging and settlement of minority communities.

In Islam, resolving disputes via informal methods of mediation and arbitration exists, among other reasons, in a bid to establish societal order. The development of 'local informal courts' in Islamic states demonstrates how these processes are presented as discrete, clearly bounded entities rivalling the structure of state law (see Rosen, 2000, p. 14). It is clear from discussion in Chapter 4 that the 'discourse of disputing' (Hirsch, 1998, p. 18) is central to the emergence and development of Shari'ah councils in Britain. Without doubt these bodies challenge the cognisance of state law with respect to resolving marital disputes and intervening in the process of divorce. Yet unsurprisingly this process of dispute resolution in Britain has been disrupted and reformulated by the 'diasporic experience' to suit the needs of local Muslim communities (see Werbner, 2000). Rather than embodying a singular set of shared cultural and religious norms, the Shari'ah councils in this study were imbued with differing power relations revealing internal contestation, conflict and change. In this context legal discourse reconfigures as 'different levels of legality' (Santos, 1987, p. 113) and raises our attention to the paradox of there being new 'interdisciplinary dialogues around questions of state power, cultural domination, resistance and hybridity' (Greenhouse and Kheshti, 1998, p. 8).

As discussed in this book, the ways in which Shari'ah councils constitute as unofficial dispute resolution mechanisms reflect how they are situated within local Muslim communities. Hence simply focusing on the paradigm of legal pluralism or dispute resolution obscures the complex contestation within the 'community' over its 'identity' in multicultural Britain. And, by positing these processes in terms of either assimilating into majority society or exercising their choice not to 'belong', leaves unaddressed the issue of the internal dynamics of power. This is not, of course, to deny that these bodies share a set of 'common characteristics' based on religious norms and values as clearly they do and, in doing so, they identify their unity of belonging to a universal Muslim community. In this way their mark of 'otherness' derives from a shared set of understandings with little need or desire for state recognition. Instead the private sphere provides the space and opportunity for them to develop forms of communal autonomy and the regulation of communities, away from state interference. From this perspective Shari'ah councils do fit the model of the 'semi-autonomous social field' (Moore, 1978) since this approach places very little demands on the state and remains autonomous but also recognizes the power of state law. However, as fieldwork data suggest, given the strong desire to ground and establish these unofficial legal processes within the framework of state law, some Shari'ah councils do seek the establishment of a parallel legal system in Britain. For this to be met, the universal language of rights, autonomy and choice are reformulated within particularistic claims for recognition (based on religious specificity) as the basis for differential treatment.

The data reveal that the duality of law and unofficial law is misleading and fails to capture the complex ways in which these 'legal processes' shape the patterns of dispute resolution for Muslims in Britain. This study revealed how gender relations are introduced, redefined and appropriated in a social field of power constituted by the Shari'ah council. The important question about gender relations and power relates to 'how particular cultural conceptions and practices become embedded' (Merry, 1988, p. 46) into these bodies. For example, the data reveal that the process of dispute resolution is 'gendered' to produce particular outcomes. The contradiction of a traditional interpretation of the role of women in Islam with the complex realities of these women's lives is neither explored nor challenged by the religious scholars, as the meanings of culture and religion are understood as homogeneous and fixed. At the same time, these bodies do provide the normative framework for disputes to be resolved from particular Islamic perspectives.

A second finding relates to the internal contestation of power within these bodies. As discussed in Chapter 2, Yilmaz argues, 'Muslims do not only wish to be regulated by the principles of Islamic law when they are living in a non-Muslim state; they also seek to formalize such an arrangement within the state's own legal system' (Yilmaz, 2001b, p. 299). Yet empirical data in this study found little support or enthusiasm for such a development. The apparent unity of Muslims presented in such literature bears little resemblance to the diversity on the ground. For example, there are conflicts over the different approaches to dispute resolution and differences over the interpretation of Islamic principles relating to divorce and interpersonal conflicts within these bodies. In his study, Geaves reports on conflicts between imams based at Shari'ah councils and those who have attempted to resolve and conciliate in conflicts between different groups fighting for control of mosques in Birmingham, Bradford and Manchester (1996b, p. 175).[1] The fact that a Shari'ah council may provide space for Muslims to resolve marital disputes away from the context of a Western secular framework does not imply that these local settings predetermine a more suitable outcome.

This is not of course to deny that Muslims adhere to a complex set of unofficial Muslim laws as clearly many do. However, empirical research suggests this process is multifaceted and complex as different levels of adherence are not only contextual upon factors of time, social context and the specific branches of Muslim law but also in relation to gender and identity. Identities must be understood as dynamic, fluid and contested within Muslim communities, especially relating to women and the laws of marriage and divorce. The dichotomous approach that posits 'law' and 'unofficial law' as opposite and in conflict consequently fails to explore the spaces in between, the sites of resistance and change. Undoubtedly, as empirical data suggests, this is a dynamic process, but one which is also contested. This, of course, takes us back to the normative frameworks upon which Shari'ah councils are based and the cultural norms of the group. Using Foucault's conception of 'power relations', we can see how such bodies create specific self-identities that fit into the system of law in operation. Empirical data suggest that in this context, the specific forms of power serve the function of maintaining the boundaries of the organization. The religious scholar exercises this power with his decision-making capacities premised upon certain forms of knowledge, in this case 'Muslim family law'. Foucault (1980, p. 65) points out, 'Power is not possessed, it acts in the very body and over the whole surface of the social field according to a system of relays, modes of connection, transmission, distribution, etc.' In this way, we can see how power is exercised within Shari'ah councils and in particular, the ways it is exercised over women. The role of religious scholars as bearers of this power raises issues on the ways in which unofficial mediators may influence particular outcomes. In their study of official mediators, Greatbatch and Dingwall (1993) found that mediators do not act in an objective neutral way and instead disputants are encouraged to follow a specific set of procedures, which guide them to outcomes acceptable to them. This illustrates the use of covert coercion and as Mulcahy points out, 'Viewed in this way, mediation substitutes the mystification of law and is more pernicious because its sources are less obvious and points of resistance concealed' (2000, p. 141).

Shari'ah councils: New fora for mediation?

In this study a second finding relates to the way in which these bodies, working as unofficial dispute resolution mechanisms, actually fit into existing 'frameworks' of community and family mediation. Early literature on legal pluralism and community mediation embraced a rigid definition of what we understand as 'law', 'mediation' and 'community' and subsequently failed to take into account differences in communities in relation to gender, age, sexuality, and notions of identity and belonging. Thus official community mediation programmes envisaged communities as homogeneous rather than heterogeneous. As the data analysis in this study suggests, Shari'ah councils challenge this traditional definition of community mediation and have in a sense occupied a new space in these debates. Interestingly, all four Shari'ah councils studied reported little, if any, direct contact with official agencies but observation research and data analysis of case files suggest that there was contact (albeit limited) between the two 'spheres'. Harrington (1992) points out that contact between the formal and informal agencies are complex. In her study, she found that community mediation cases were often referred from state agencies such as police and prosecutors to informal bodies to offload work from the official agencies to the unofficial. What we see happening with Shari'ah councils in Britain is an interesting development. This form of multiculturalism can reinforce inequality. Furthermore, this inevitably raises the question of what interest the state may have in allowing some issues to be resolved in the private, while the state intervenes in others. And as Bhatt (2006) asks, how tolerant of diversity are those who seek recognition in the name of equality in diversity?

As discussed in Chapter 1 the 'politics of multiculturalism' are based upon uncontested notions of identity while simultaneously recognizing 'cultural difference' as fixed and bounded. Black feminists point to the dangers of delegating communal responsibility to community leaders under the multiculturalist rubric of 'communal autonomy' (Patel, 2008). As Mulcahy explains, 'These concerns are exacerbated by the fact that many forms of informal resolution, community mediation included, discourage legal representation' (2000, p. 140). In this study data revealed that although the Shari'ah councils did not discourage the use of state-law mechanisms to resolve marital disputes, they did all seek to develop methods of dispute resolution consistent with 'Islamic' norms and values.

Official family mediation occupies an intermediate legal and social space at the boundary of state law and non-state forms of ordering (Santos, 1987). This conceptual space between state law and personal law is contested whereupon state law and personal law struggle to establish control (see Abel, 1982; Fitzpatrick, 1992a). This is a process whereby unofficial mediation marks the site upon which to resolve marital disputes from the perspective of Muslim personal law. Because of the centrality of gender relations in Muslim family law and in particular the position of women in relation to marriage and divorce, attempts to strengthen or develop unofficial mediation bodies raise questions on the position and autonomy of women using these bodies to resolve marital disputes.

Empirical data points to some key differences between official and unofficial mediation[2] but the key question remains whether state law is moving from a position of formalism towards 'informalism' whereby power is in effect transferred from the private sphere to 'informal bodies' as represented by Shari'ah councils. At one level it is legitimate to argue that this debate is redundant, as under existing family law provisions couples are not required to seek mediation prior to the formal dissolution of marriage. More recently social policy initiatives are being developed to encourage resolution of marital disputes via mediation as discussed in recent Family Justice Review led by David Norgrove a move welcomed by some members of the judiciary. As Justice MacFarlane (2011, p. 952) argued, 'Resort, or at least exposure, to mediation or other forms of dispute resolution is to be encouraged before a dispute may be permitted to move into the family court. In this regard, the potential for the various faith communities to provide assistance in dispute resolution, either within their formal council or tribunal structure or more informally is not to be ignored.'

This raises the two key questions: first whether the state may implicitly recognize religious bodies as suitable arenas for mediation, and second whether this will lead to religious bodies taking up the role of mediation bodies to resolve family law disputes.

In this study fieldwork data found no evidence of a formal, intertwined relationship between formal mediation and unofficial mediation which takes place in the private and it is to be noted that Shari'ah councils are often keen to avoid any conflict with state law.

Yet it is also accepted that the large number of women using these bodies testifies to the argument that 'cross-cultural mediation' must also be addressed. In her study Shah-Kazemi argues that 'negotiations within the domain of marital disputes assume a very particular complexity as the dynamics of both gender and identity-defining normative ethics shape the setting in which the negotiations take place' (2000, p. 304). This approach challenges the very basis upon which this study is based as Shah-Kazemi argues that a Western human rights approach to notions of justice, equality, choice and rights for Muslim women inevitably obscures the normative orders upon which this form of dispute resolution is based. She explains, 'members of the community who consider themselves to be practising Muslims (and the degrees of adherence vary considerably) are keen to involve the intervention of outsiders with religious authority in their marital disputes in an attempt to ensure that the dispute be resolved within a common normative framework' (2000, p. 307). Critical of adopting a neutral approach to mediation she argues that 'the insistence upon "neutrality" as a notion in mediation parlance, even when that is contrary to the common ethical framework shared by the parties, results in the imposition of outsiders as mediators to the exclusion of community members, at the expense of achieving the ideal of genuine community mediation' (2000, p. 319). This study is invaluable for its insights into the complex dynamics of power within families and communities (see Witty, 1980). Women are involved in the process of dispute resolution and the participation of family members does indeed challenge the assumed hegemonic position of the mediator. For this we are given a unique insight into the dynamics of dispute resolution within minority ethnic communities. Yet this community 'self-definition' can quite easily fall into the 'charybdis of cultural relativism' (Anthias, 2002, p. 275). Clearly this argument is also premised upon fixed understandings of culture, identity and religion. It embraces Shari'ah councils as creating a new discursive legal space constructed by community members but fails to engage in debates on how they may sanction power within their boundaries of community, personal law and individual decision-making.

A better understanding of this process of unofficial dispute resolution can challenge the binary oppositions of multiculturalism versus feminism, secular versus religious practice and universalism versus cultural relativism. Current multicultural literature has been extensively critiqued by feminist political theorists who point to the unresolved tensions and inequalities multiculturalism imposes upon women and which, it is argued, ultimately preserves cultural and religious expression within the framework of cultural relativism, essentialism and identity politics leading to the disadvantage of women. For many these tensions are most clearly visible in relation to Islam and its 'subordinating' effects upon Muslim women (see Okin, 1999). While Western women are presented as 'enlightened' and bearers of liberal ideals such as equality and non-discrimination, the Muslim female subject is presented as the 'other', a victim of cultural and religious practices and thus unable to realize her human rights. Yet such understandings of Islam and Islamic family practice in the West and the so-called demands Islam imposes upon the individual, the group and the state have been challenged from several different directions (Wadud, 1999; Ramadan, 2004; Modood, 2005; Ali, 2007; Naim, 2008). One such argument is that Muslim women have been able to negotiate within Muslim families and communities, and thus group membership of the Muslim community/*umma* does not in itself violate their autonomy or undermine their citizenship rights as individuals within Western societies (Purkayastha, 2009b). Indeed the very real potential for Muslim women to renegotiate their positions within family, home, local community and wider society has now led to a growing recognition among some feminist liberal theorists that to posit feminism and multiculturalism as oppositional and in conflict is a false and misleading dichotomy. The evident inadequacy of understanding Islamic practice as insider/outsider not only relegates the experience of women within minority cultural/religious communities to the position of victims but most importantly denies them agency, autonomy and choice as subjects of their own communities. Thus the experience of women from minority cultural/religious communities is objectified in pursuance of a liberal political agenda (see Razack, 2004).

Traditional legal pluralist scholarship continues to present the practice of minority religious personal law systems as a 'cultural clash' whereby the dominant legal system proves irreconcilable to the demands generated by minority communities living in the West. Such arguments are largely understood as a continuum of conflict and accommodation or a 'conflict-oriented spectrum' whereby the complicated balance between law, religious belief and personal autonomy is consistently at odds. This type of scholarship recognizes the plurality of law and dispute resolution processes but equally defines cultural and religious practice as fixed, unchanging and homogeneous. This discourse of conflict and incompatibility insufficiently engages with processes of change and transformation which open up the ways for new contestations and developments. As Estin (2008, p. 8) points outs, 'Beyond the work that all families carry out, the multicultural family navigates a complicated balance of tradition and change, home and diaspora, community and autonomy. These families absorb many tensions born of transformation, and pose in turn new challenges for legal orders premised on more stable community membership and identity.' Thus communities symbolize the transformation of change, settlement and diaspora and they cannot be viewed as 'fixed', 'natural' social entities, rather they emerge in specific historical conditions and usually have shifting and contested boundaries, depending on different political projects which include and exclude different categories of people (Soyal, 2000). Moreover, one cannot assume that the members of any community are homogenous, have the same attachment to the community and its culture, religion and tradition or even understand them in the same way; and we must take into account unequal intracommunal as well as intercommunal power relations and competing political projects. Finally the notions of 'faith' and 'religion' have to be understood in an inclusive way as faith is a syncretic as well as a multilayered construct (see Yuval-Davis, 2006).

In this way the concepts of interlegality and multicultural interlegality, to describe legal experience and the use of law, are useful as they point to the fluid and permeable characters of legal orders in Western societies. In the case of Muslim legal pluralism we can see in evidence different forms of mobilizations with underlying cultural and religious meanings which interact, conflict and reorder themselves according to state law and the different communities in which they are located. The decision-making processes produce an internal legal structure – a process of mixing-up, overlapping and at times in conflict. For example, Shari'ah councils and the MAT are evidence of the operation of interlegality where the adaptation of Muslim family law into English civil law principles means there are overlapping identities/conflicts where boundaries are drawn but dialogue continues between users and those in power as to what constitutes the process of dispute resolution.

Interestingly this mobilization of community and 'community laws' not only challenges the hegemonic power of state law but also unsettles the multicultural project (in particular its management of ethnic and cultural diversity) in its attempt to reconfigure social and legal discourse in matters of private family law. In other words state legal pluralism develops to what Woodman (1998) refers to as the 'institutional recognition' of minority religious practices particularly in matters of family law. Today we see new forms of state legal pluralism in the form of MATs which encapsulate new forms of legalist accommodative solutions regarding family law matters and raises a number of important questions. Where is this all leading? How can we better understand this kind of legal multiplicity? How do social and legal actors engage with multiple social and legal orders? What do we understand by the terms 'legal pluralism' and 'hybrid legal cultures'? What are the social and legal techniques adopted by these unofficial ADR mechanisms to resolve matrimonial disputes? How are legal norms interpreted and reinterpreted in such contexts? And what of the feminist concerns that the toleration or accommodation of minority family law regulation might be bad for women in that such diverse regimes are said to perpetuate (and sometimes even mark a return to) patriarchal systems of social ordering? Interestingly, the issue of gender remains central to these debates. One of the salient features that defines the perceived incompatibility of Islam with Western ideas is its supposed ill treatment of women. From a liberal perspective, Muslim women are often presented as dominated, controlled and subordinate to archaic religious traditions and, within this discourse, it is the gendered construction of the Muslim family that is perceived to be the barrier that denies Muslim women access to the rights, equality and degree of empowerment bestowed upon other women in the West (see Nussbaum, 1999). Conspicuously absent from these debates, however, are the voices of Muslim women themselves, and in particular those of Muslim women living in the West. This is surprising if we bear in mind the great diversity that exists among the generations of British Muslims, Muslims who form local, national and transnational networks and communities which in themselves generate immense differences (see Razack, 2008).

For many legal scholars the primary challenge for state law remains the extent to which it opens up a 'public space' for other legal traditions. In recent years the renewed visibility of Muslim communities in Britain has led to increased discussion on questions of identity, belonging and citizenship in multicultural societies. For example report titled *Living Apart Together: British Muslims and the Paradox of Multiculturalism*[3] suggests that 37 per cent of all British Muslims are in favour of being governed by some form of Shari'ah law in the UK. Although the methodological framework of this report has been heavily criticized, especially for the authors' presumption that the findings accurately reflect the views of *all* Muslims in Britain, this statistic does raise interesting questions about the relations between Muslims, law, religious legal practice and – perhaps most importantly – loyalty to the state. And recognition of the cultural and religious diversity of the Muslim communities has led for calls for a better understanding of multiculturalism. For example, there is now a burgeoning body of literature on multiculturalism from the disciplines of political theory, philosophy, sociology and anthropology which questions the limits of cultural and religious pluralism, conflicts generated by individual rights versus community rights and the supposed universality of human rights norms in Western legal orders. As Estin (2008, p. 10) points out, 'Some of the most interesting and important questions ... concern the extent to which multicultural approaches can and should be permitted to shift or expand the normative boundaries of particular legal traditions.' Thus Western commentators and scholars now discuss at length the limits of religious practice and belief and many query the need to accommodate and respect cultural and religious diversity in Western societies. For some the politics of multiculturalism and the recognition of cultural difference have led to a politics of cultural separatism, but for others the liberal principles of justice, equality and human rights justify the protection of all cultural and religious minority communities.

Yet the ways in which multiculturalist policies have successfully ensured the integration of minority ethnic communities into British society to produce a multi-faith pluralism, which recognizes both cultural and faith identities, have of late come under sustained attack and critique. Critics argue that there must be a set of irreducible minimum standards to protect the fundamental human rights of all individuals that at times may conflict with the cultural and religious practices of some minority ethnic groups. In particular it has been argued that multiculturalism has itself been disruptive to the cohesion of multiple and disparate groups into majority society (see Mirza, 2011). Goodhart (2004) argues that multiculturalism has led to increasing segregation, mutual distrust and intolerance between communities and 'the difference now in a developed country such as Britain is that we not only live among stranger citizens but we must share with them ... Immigrants from the same place are bound to want to congregate together but policy should try to prevent that consolidating into segregation across all the main areas of life: residence, school, workplace, church'. Other commentators such as Malik (2006) argue that multiculturalism 'has not simply entrenched the divisions created by racism, but made cross-cultural interaction more difficult by encouraging people to assert their cultural differences'. The combination of migration and globalization in the West has therefore presented new challenges for Western legal orders where scholars increasingly document how social and cultural practices and norms interact and conflict with legal orders (see Buchler, 2011; Nichols, 2012).

Yet in practice a different picture also emerges with fieldwork finding evidence of the multiple legal processes interacting and at times intermeshed. Anecdotal evidence found some solicitors negotiating settlements at Shari'ah councils, a space that provides no formal protection for those who may feel compelled to use the mediation or reconciliation services in order to obtain a Muslim divorce. Thus the complex relationship between individual and community, informal and formal law can dynamically interact in the area of mediation and reconciliation. The relationship between these four interlinked areas increasingly raises important yet complex questions on the relationship between gender disadvantage, the public/private divide, the sphere of regulation and a sphere of non-regulation (Fletcher, 2002, p. 145). As fieldwork reveals, some of these councils do eschew gender equality in favour of religious and communal homogeneity.

Some religious scholars call for the official establishment of a single Shari'ah council in Britain, a form of state legal pluralism (Woodman, 1998). However, such voices are rare and remain outside general development of councils in Britain. Dr Badawi, the late director of the Muslim Law Shari'ah Council and the Muslim College, during interview explained that '[u]niformity of the law is central in ensuring that justice is served to all members of society' and 'there should be just one legal system which should be applied to all'. Similarly, Sheikh Abdullah (Shari'ah Court of the UK) stated, 'I do understand why some people want this development but it's a small minority, more of a political slogan than anything else. You cannot incorporate two systems into one especially when they are based on two very different ideas, one is secular and the other divine.' This cautious approach was further echoed by Dr Nasim (Birmingham Shari'ah Council) who emphasized that the 'legitimacy' of Shari'ah must remain in the private sphere. There was also concern that the establishment of a single Shari'ah council could undermine the autonomy and independence of the Muslim community. For Dr Badawi 'the responsibility of the community is to live up to the Shari'ah because it is part of our *"ikeeda"*'.

While these scholars emphasize the need for all Muslims to abide by Shari'ah, they argued that the ethics of Muslim law permitted these processes to remain within the private spheres of family, home and community. In this scenario conflicts of law may arise but their resolution would take place without the intervention of state law. Dr Badawi explains: 'What we are doing now is trying to resolve issues, to keep the identity of our community, to keep its laws, to keep it whole, while at the same time not breaking the law of the state ... to use our own private language while speaking the common language' (1996, p. 80). In fact to implement and set up Shari'ah would be 'un-Islamic' as Shari'ah law can only be implemented in a Muslim country. Whether these disputes are resolved within a local, national or international context, these debates are constructed in fairly essentialist terms. For example, all the councils reported that diversity within and between Shari'ah councils means that Muslims have the option to choose between the various councils available. Muslim communities, they say, should be allowed to compete and establish their authorities individually. Maulana Mohammed Raza (Muslim Law Shari'ah Council) explained: 'It is impossible to bring and wait for a unified opinion on any of these issues and I think that the attitude towards resolving these issues should always be of flexibility.'

Yet this model of Muslim unity is exemplified with the emergence of more recent European initiatives such as the 'Islamic Council of Europe' (see Nielsen, 1989) lobbying on behalf of the interests of Muslims at a European-wide level (see Modood, 2008). The emphasis here is upon the language of community, 'difference' and human rights guaranteeing the freedoms necessary for the full realization of the demands of the Muslim community. Freedom of religious belief and practice in the context of personal laws are thus transformed from the private realm into the civil jurisdiction and accommodation is premised on identification with the Muslim *umma* (community) and Muslim identity (see Sarat and Berkowitz, 1994, p. 95). In fact the very emergence of such a force reflects the fact that the reality of plurality may prove a constraint for those deemed outside this idea of a unified Muslim *umma*.

At present a three-pronged approach to Muslim disputes in matters of family law exists. First, Muslim women use state civil law under English family principles; second, they choose to use Shari'ah councils to obtain a Muslim divorce certificate only; and finally, they use both systems, including resolving disputes in the private arenas of family and home with no state or local community intervention.

The emergence of the MAT in 2007 represents a new phase of Muslim legal pluralism in Britain which builds upon existing cross-cultural mechanisms of dispute resolution. And more recently as discussed in Chapter 8 we have had the introduction of the Muslim marriage contract which seeks to promote and protect the rights of Muslim women. The contract stipulates the rights of the Muslim woman within an Islamic framework but allows flexibility of a woman to 'divorce herself if there is a need' (Badawi 1995, p. 112). Dr Badawi concedes, however, that 'we are now trying to make it a standard marriage certificate all over Britain but I don't know whether we will be successful or not. We have in this country Shari'ah councils and groups of scholars who are very conservative and who are not really ready to embrace ... any change.' There have also been developments in curbing the use of *talaq* where the presence of two reliable witnesses is needed.

For many religious scholars Jewish rabbinical courts serve as a useful benchmark. As discussed in Chapter 5, in Britain, non-state dispute resolution mechanisms must operate within the ambit of the law as they are subject to civil or criminal action but are able to use state law, making their decisions subject to a binding contract in the case of for example the Jewish Beth Din. This court was established under Jewish religious law and stipulates that all those who wish to use its services must accept the provisions of the Arbitration Act 1979:

> In Jewish Law, Jewish parties are forbidden to take their civil disputes to a secular court and are required to have those disputes adjudicated by a Beth Din. The LBD sits as an arbitral tribunal in respect of civil disputes and the parties to any such dispute are required to sign an Arbitration

Agreement prior to a Hearing taking place. The effect of this is that the award given by the Beth Din has the full force of the Arbitration Award and may be enforced (with prior permission of the Beth Din) by the civil courts.

Cownie and Bradney point out that the issue of choice over whether or not the individual wishes to use these alternative bodies is crucial because 'in the case of state courts the state itself can compel the presence of one of the parties to an action but in this context it seems that parties are obliged to take part in the proceedings whether they want to or not' (1996, p. 7). The parallels with the Muslim community are twofold. First, Jewish women have had similar problems in obtaining a religious divorce, the *get*. And second, some Muslim scholars advocate a complementary approach whereby the state intervenes to resolve disputes generated by personal religious laws. For example, the Divorce (Religious Marriages) Act 2002 introduced s10 A into the Matrimonial Causes Act 1973 to ensure that Jewish women were able to obtain a religious divorce from their husbands. Under this provision either spouse may apply to the court for an order that a decree absolute may not be granted 'until a declaration made by both parties that they have taken such steps as are required to dissolve the marriage in accordance with (the usages of the Jews or any other prescribed religious usages) is produced to the court'. Furthermore, the court has discretion whether or not to grant such an order and will only grant it if it is 'satisfied that in all the circumstances of the case it is just and reasonable to do so' and the court can cancel the order at any time (see Faith and Levine, 2003, p. 13).

Religious scholars such as Dr Nasim and Dr Badawi are in favour of such developments rather than a strict parallel legal system for Muslims. Dr Nasim explained: 'The Beth Din is just like us; there is no difference at all. They are local just like we are and they function in the community just like we do. We are not really courts of law in the sense that we cannot enforce our decisions but we have a moral authority and position within the community and in the sense that our people would listen to us. I mean a woman, for example, would never go and remarry without a certificate from a Shari'ah council to say that she is eligible for remarriage.'

The problem of Muslim women 'forum shopping'

The degree of interaction and co-operation between the councils raises interesting questions about the competing 'cultural logics rooted in particular structures of power' (Merry, 1988, p. 44). In short the ways in which such bodies engage in dialogue with each other can illustrate the ways in which they are constituted within local communities. Although Muslim women are not compelled to use this forum to resolve disputes, Badawi explains that there is 'a *duty* upon all Muslims to abide by the requirements of the Shari'ah'

(1996, p. 12) and Muslims are therefore expected to utilize community frameworks and resolve disputes according to Islamic principles. The scholars reported the problems they encountered with women 'forum shopping' between the councils. It was argued that if women continued to 'pick and choose' the councils they preferred, this can have the effect of undermining the divorce certificate and creating tensions between the councils. Hoekema (2005) points out, 'Individuals are not the prisoners of their own supposedly integrated and homogeneous culture, but shop for forums, choose among legal orders, pressure their own leaders and authorities to take legal elements into consideration and also, vice versa, challenge national authorities to take local legal sensibilities into consideration.' This notion of 'forum shopping' has been developed by international law scholars where they trace the ways in which international disputes are often resolved by plaintiffs using forums and jurisdictions deemed to have more favourable outcomes. This literature also develops fascinating critiques on studying institutions and institutional dispute resolution forums (see Busch, 2007).

Empirical data revealed little contact between the four Shari'ah councils in this study and, on occasions when contact was made, it was to clarify whether a client/applicant had previously approached a different council and if so the reasons why the application for a divorce certificate had been refused by the particular council in question. The councils all reported their reluctance to issue a divorce certificate if they found evidence that the applicants had been 'forum shopping'. Mohammed Raza at MLSC explained: 'I cannot speak on behalf of other Shari'ah councils but our Shari'ah council has some rules to which we are trying to self-regulate ourselves. Like in our application we clearly say that if you have already applied to another Shari'ah council we cannot entertain your application. If other Shari'ah council complaints are lodged with us we do not entertain that at all so we do not wish to create any conflict among these Shari'ah councils … they have every right to work as we have.' He went on, 'Although we are all independent from each other we are working for the same purpose. But definitely we don't have any regular link with each other.'

This viewpoint was confirmed by the scholars in the other Shari'ah councils. Dr Nasim at BSC was concerned with the emergence of multiple Shari'ah councils that can lead to confusion for applicants and undermine the work of all councils. He explained, 'I know of a few cases where women have come to us because other Shari'ah councils have been unsympathetic to them and refused to grant them a divorce. This leads to confusion and our authority is undermined.' This was unquestionably a concern for all the religious scholars but it was reported that most were reluctant to unify the different councils into one central body. For Dr Badawi, adjudicating responsibility to one body would merely serve to concretize the inherent diversity in Islam. He explained, 'We are not one community but several communities and we should be left to compete individually and to establish our authorities individually ... that would be a better and healthier approach for us.' In particular Dr Badawi was critical of shifting responsibility of such bodies to a state-regulated body which, he argued, would undermine both the autonomy and authority of the councils in the local communities in which they operate.

A number of scholars expressed criticism of divorce certificates being issued by imams based at local mosques. Maulana Mohammed Raza, explained, '[W]e have reported that in some cases where a single imam in a mosque is claiming to be the judge of the Muslim Supreme Court in this country ... things like that are happening and perhaps the community needs to be educated about that. These things should not be handled in such a way where just one individual is doing everything because he may or maybe not be biased. It is quite easy to influence one single individual. I do not suspect the integrity of any of the imams but it is a more exposed situation whereas a board of scholars coming from all over the world seems to me a safe sort of institution.' As Dr Badawi explained the solution to such problems lay within the Muslim community itself, 'We need time to educate ourselves and apply it for ourselves and that is the responsibility of the community. The responsibility of the community is to live up to Shari'ah because it is part of *ikeeda*. So if we are going to live up to the Shari'ah voluntarily, not by the force of law, we have to resolve issues as part of the community. The function of Shari'ah councils must remain within the private sphere, under the control and auspices of the Muslim community.'

Demands for legal autonomy?

Demands by some Muslim leaders for the establishment of a single Shari'ah council with state recognition seek to legitimize the group's autonomy in matters of family law. The growth of these demands attests to increasing attempts by some individuals and groups to unify the 'Muslim community'. In this context communal autonomy takes the form of decision-making power, which maintains the group's membership boundaries vis-à-vis the larger society. An integral aspect of this project is the preservation of Muslim identity and it is the unique position of women within these groups as 'cultural conduits' that gives rise to the problem of gender-biased norms and practices which often subordinate women (Shachar, 2001, p. 50). As discussed in Chapter 1, for liberal feminists this raises a clash-of-values scenario which undermines the liberal principles of justice, common citizenship and equality before the law. Okin (1999) questions, 'What should be done when the claims of minority cultures or religions clash with the norm of gender equality that is at least formally endorsed by liberal states (however much they continue to violate it in their practices)?' She lists a number of possible clashes with Islam that include Muslim children wearing the headscarf, polygamy and clitoridectomy among others.

Yet it is precisely this dichotomous approach that posits feminism and multiculturalism as oppositional and assumes women are victims of their cultures and religions (Volp, 2001, p. 181) that renders this argument problematic. Moreover, this obscures the complexities in the realities of women's lives and privileges one form of discrimination over others (Crenshaw, 1989). For example, race and economic inequality are given little if any consideration and 'race' and 'gender' are perceived as oppositional and mutually exclusive (Yuval-Davis, 1997; Volp, 2001; Anthias, 2002). As Volp points out, 'The tension believed to exist between feminism and multiculturalism, or universalism and cultural relativism, not only relies upon the assumption that minority cultures are more sexist, but also assumes that those cultures are considered traditional, and made up of unchanging and long practices that warrant submission to cultural dictates. Non-western people are assumed to be governed by cultural dictates, whereas the capacity to reason is thought to characterize the west' (2001, p. 192). Again, as discussed in earlier chapters other feminist scholars have developed a more complex, nuanced approach to understanding these 'dilemmas'. The 'intersectionality' approach points to the complex embeddedness in the social life of race and class from patterns of gender discrimination that are construed as cumulative and intersecting (see Crenshaw, 1994; Yuval-Davis, 1997). And the concept of 'translocational positionality' (Anthias, 2002) allows us to challenge the dichotomous approach based on the fixed categories of insider/outsider in understanding the relationship between Asian Muslim women, family and community but allows us to introduce a more nuanced approach to the interplay of power, complexity and difference in the lived realities of women's lives.

The emergence of anti-essentialism in scholarly debate has therefore led to a greater analysis of the relationship between community, identity and claims for recognition. Indeed, it seems that one of the most pressing questions today is whether Muslims have become a politically effective diaspora that challenges the national polity (Werbner, 2000). More recently multicultural debates have focused on the relationship between state intervention, non-intervention, a dialogue between majority and minority communities and the right to exit a group in cases of forced marriage (Phillips, 2007).

Drawing upon this approach, I found that some sections of the Muslim community in Britain would like to claim legal autonomy in matters of family law, to enable Muslim law to be applied in the 'private' sphere of family relations. If this claim were accepted in Britain, a different system of personal laws would govern Muslim citizens from those applied to the community at large. But this would raise the issue of how to deal with those individuals who do not wish to conform to the traditional customs of their communities. Clearly, such a group right is problematic if it is based on the exclusive recognition of a single common identity for all the members of the cultural and religious minority. As Montgomery points out, support for such a right rests on a number of assumptions. First, the group must have some discrete identity, which enables its members to be distinguished from outsiders. Second, the group must be essentially homogeneous in respect of its desire for special treatment. Third, not only must the group generally want special treatment, but also the treatment must be of a nature which creates liberties that can be exercised by all (1992, p. 123). The claim for an exclusive or territorially based separate personal law system remains problematic since the cultural boundaries of groups is rarely unambiguous. This is because, as Verman points out, 'Individual people are likely to feel part of one group in some contexts and of another in relation to different issues' (1982, p. 32). Boundaries are more easily defined when minorities are concentrated territorially, as is the case with indigenous minorities. A further option, the one adopted in India, is to create two parallel systems of personal law – customary/religious and civil and allow all citizens the right to choose between them (see Ahmed, 2010).

The debate as to whether Britain should adopt a pluralist legal system to accommodate the practice of South Asian religious personal laws must be approached with great caution. Within the English legal system the rights of minority groups have been defined through anti-discrimination legislation. At present the cultural rights of minority groups are recognized and protected in English law as long as they do not violate national and international human rights law. We have seen that this may present problems in the case of South Asian personal laws. The law must also take into account the heterogeneity of South Asian and Muslim settlers in the UK and the many different varieties of religions they practise. Clearly, no single authority can define Muslim personal law, and individuals in line with liberal principles would have to be able to opt for a court of their choosing. The danger of a rigid pluralism is evident: it would encourage the creation of separatist politics, ghettoizing minority communities outside the mainstream legal system and thus defining them as the 'other'. As a result, instead of enhancing the rights of South Asians or Muslims in Britain, it would serve to curtail their rights and to segregate groups from one another. This would lead to a reduction of cultural and religious diversity, dynamism and pluralism, rather than enhanced integration. Thus we must move away from dealing with questions of citizenship in terms of community versus individualism, solidarity versus diversity, continuity versus change, and responsibility versus duty and obligations.

Shari'ah councils may therefore emanate an emancipatory aura in resolving matrimonial disputes; the consequences for those who use them and for those asked to recognize them are more difficult and contradictory.

Analysis of Shari'ah councils as official mediation bodies must take into account unequal intracommunal as well as intercommunal power relations and competing political projects. Moreover, this intersectional analysis should include consideration of the fact that mere recognition by the state of particular people as 'community leaders' introduces a new element of power that affects intracommunal as well as intercommunal relations. This might create a tendency to perceive the views of some unelected 'representatives' and 'leaders' of a community as reflecting the views of most of its members, or at least the 'authentic' way members of such a community should view things (Patel, 2008).

In fact the growth of typologies that allocate individuals within a theoretical space presupposes the categories of 'sameness and difference' (Anthias, 2002, p. 283) and fails to recognize the dynamics of power by which individuals from one social group may exclude others.

It recognizes that 'communities' should not be viewed as 'fixed', 'natural' social entities but rather that they emerge in specific historical conditions and usually have shifting and contested boundaries, depending on different political projects which include and exclude different categories of people. Moreover, one should never assume that the members of any community are homogenous, have the same attachment to the community and its culture, religion and tradition or even understand them in the same way. Yet it is precisely this dichotomous approach that inevitably utilizes the primacy of one approach as opposed to the other and, subsequently, fails to problematize the very grounds upon which these arguments are based. More precisely still, they fail to explore the active engagement of women in developing strategies, negotiations and interrogating spaces that challenge the hegemonic power inherent within both official and unofficial law. These spaces can act as sites of resistance, struggle and change.

Muslim identities are complex, negotiated, contested and historically unstable. Purdam points out that 'Muslims themselves are debating and contesting exactly what it means to be a Muslim, what Islam means and how it should be constructed and reproduced both in the west and in the rest of the world' (1996, p. 130). That empirical data suggest that these non-state legalities do not emerge from a community that is necessarily resistant to the state but in fact is also part of a community that constitutes the state and actively structures it as well, challenging the idea popular among theories of legal pluralism that it is only state law that structures other legalities. These various legalities are in fact intertwined with each other, constituting each other dialectically and in this way the plurality of laws and legal systems are constantly mixing up with each other, overlapping and in flux, and in this way revealing a multiplicity of hybrid legal situations (Santos, 1987). Cultural and legal diversity must instead be understood as complex, negotiated, contested and historically unstable. In light of this reality, dispute resolution for women within Muslim communities must also be understood in the context of change, complexity and ambiguity.

More recent scholarship puts forward some 'concrete' solutions to claims for legal autonomy from religious communities in matters of family law. In his recent work Eekelaar (2012, p. 45) puts forward an approach he describes as 'cultural voluntarism' which would allow individuals to follow group norms as long as they comply with civil law norms. He explains: '[F]amily courts could make orders based on agreements reached under religious law but only if the agreement was genuine and followed independent advice, and was consistent with overriding policy goals (for example the best interests of the child). State law would be available at all times to anyone who chose to invoke it and access to it should be safeguarded and encouraged.' And in her report, *Minority Legal Systems in the UK: Multiculturalism, Minorities and the Law*, Maleiha Malik (2012) proposes that the Equalities and Human Rights Commission can have a specific role in playing a 'regulatory function in those circumstances where religious courts (arbitration; alternative dispute resolution) is causing harm to women users'. For these scholars the importance of 'inter-cultural dialogue' is crucial to promote normative differences between the groups. For example, Gover (2008) argues that the recognition of non-state legal orders should include the recognition of 'practices of normative deliberation and decision-making – the processes by which normative claims are discussed, disagreement adjudicated (in the largest sense of 'adjudicate', including all means of settling disputed norms), and the resultant norms interpreted and elaborated'.

The twin issues of autonomy and choice and the state monitoring of religious bodies underpin the proposals put forward. The former is discussed in more depth further but in relation to the question of state monitoring of Shari'ah councils it is important to note that this presupposes that the community would itself recognize the 'state-backed' Shari'ah council, also presupposes some kind of unity within the community in question and fails to consider the fact that the council in question could be rejected by the community precisely because of 'state recognition'. Regulation would also inevitably mean these bodies would need the capacity and resources for training and many Shari'ah councils simply lack this capacity. As Justice McFarlane (2011, p. 952) points out, 'in terms of the secular courts "recognising" the impact of Sharia law on a particular family law issue, the potential for there being different and separately valid utterances on the point, dependant upon choice of council, needs to be borne in mind.'

The process of 'reform' and change within communities can be a long and fractured one for multiple reasons and often contextual and dependent upon state support and subsidy (see Abbas, 2005). To better understand the complex ways in which Muslims live their lives in Britain and utilize Muslim family law, the focus cannot simply be upon debates of cultural and religious diversity versus secular systems of civil law and the claims for legal recognition of Muslim family law. This is simply not enough. Narratives from Muslim women using religious mechanisms of dispute resolution reveal both their strategic and the complex use of these bodies. But this use cannot then simply translate into calls for 'recognition' or accommodation (albeit limited in various ways) of religious norms in family disputes – the context upon this use is made must be closely understood.

Shari'ah councils and the question of gender oppression

The traditional tension presented by individuals who simultaneously belong to both civic and religious communities has more recently focused on the possibility of mutual recognition and the 'transformative accommodation' of both law and religious communities into state-law mechanisms of dispute resolution. In her work Ayelet Shachar (2008, p. 578) puts forward the idea of 'regulated interaction' between religious and secular sources as long as the baseline of citizenship-guaranteed rights remain firmly in place. Under this model of citizenship she points out that the multiple affiliations and multiple identities of individuals can generate positive value for all communities and society as a whole but this process of transforming cultural and legal practices to accommodate difference must also protect vulnerable members of the communities in question – most often women. She explains, 'These overlapping "belongings" offer religious women a significant source of meaning and value; at the same time, they may also make them vulnerable to a double or triple disadvantage, especially in a legal and governance system that categorically denies cooperation between their overlapping sources of obligation' (2008, p. 575).

As previously discussed, throughout Europe today gender equality has become a critical means to differentiate the liberated European and the oppressive non-European religious models of family and community life (Roggeband and Verloo, 2007). And this vision of privatized diversity can be applied to the new MAT if we understand privatized diversity as a model in which to achieve and possibly separate the secular from the religious in the public space, in effect encouraging individuals to contract out of state involvement and into a traditional non-state forum when resolving family disputes. This would include religious tribunals arbitrating according to a different set of principles than those enshrined in English law. This approach was recently advocated by the Archbishop of Canterbury, Dr Rowan Williams, as discussed earlier in the book who stated that 'there are ways at looking at marital disputes, for example, which provide an alternative to the divorce courts as we understand them. In some cultural and religious settings they would seem more appropriate.' He also suggested that the recognition of Shari'ah in Britain seems 'unavoidable' and advised that we need to find a 'constructive accommodation' of Shari'ah in the law (2008, p. 2).

For Shachar (2008, p. 580) there are real concerns of individuals being expected to live 'as undifferentiated citizens in the public sphere, but remain free to express our distinct cultural or religious identities in the private domain of family and communal life'. For her and other liberal scholars (See

Eeeklaar, 2012; Malik, 2012), the issue surrounds the contentious question of where private identity and life ends and public identity begins. Shachar quite rightly points out – if we are expected to express personal identities in the private, at which point in the public sphere do they cease to be so? She also discusses the fact that the vision of privatized diversity will evoke different feelings for different people. For those who want to establish a pluralistic system of law that recognizes claims of culture and religion, this would not be so terrifying, but those who are 'blind' to these needs will see it as challenging the superiority of universal laws that apply to all: 'for others who endorse a strict separationist approach, or "blindness" towards religious or cultural affiliation, the idea that we might find unregulated "religious islands of binding jurisdiction" mushrooming on the terrain of state law is seen as evidence of the dangers of accommodating diversity, potentially chipping away, however slightly as the foundational, modernist citizenship formula of "one law for all' (Shachar, 2008). Such arguments are echoed by Parkinson (1996, p. 24), who remarks: 'Acceptance of cultural diversity, and recognition of cultural issues in the application of the law, are especially important in relation to family law, for families play such an important role in the development of a person's cultural identity.' Therefore the intimate relations between the individual, family and community must to some extent be recognized by a legal system that increasingly serves plural and multicultural Western societies. In her work Ahmed (2010) applies normative legal theory and analyses the Indian system of personal laws as a test case to consider the 'extent to which these modes of accommodation undermine personal autonomy' in the West. She concludes that '(i) many people do not enjoy a meaningful right to exit from the personal laws because of community pressure to conform to the personal laws and (ii) the limited legal power of individuals to choose the law that applies to them is enough neither to remove other objections to the system nor to support the claim that the system enhances personal autonomy' (2010, p. 230).

Prior to this study there was very little empirical evidence documenting the experience of British Muslim women using Shari'ah councils to resolve matrimonial disputes (see Shah-Kazemi, 2001; Bano, 2007). Furthermore, issues of choice and autonomy are often based upon fixed and prescriptive understandings. For example, Justice McFarlane (2011, p. 951) argues, 'This is not a truly voluntary process in the sense that once adherents have become members of the faith community and wish to remain so, they must use the religious court and are bound, within their faith community by its results. To opt out of the court's jurisdiction, may therefore carry the high price of having at the same time to opt out of the community of those who strictly adhere to the faith. It is not therefore to be seen strictly as a form of alternative dispute resolution.'

However, this research also points to the diversity of women's experiences and the strategic and complex ways in which they utilize such ADR mechanisms. The lived social realities of Muslim women challenge the boundaries of secularity and the 'religious' and the distinction of public and private. Muslim women's engagement with Shari'ah councils cannot be understood in relation to being insiders or outsiders of their communities. Many do view the use of such bodies to obtain a divorce certificate as an important aspect of their religious identity although this is neither fixed nor universal. We must bear in mind that Muslim women constitute a heterogeneous group of individuals who belong to many different families and communities and who are part and parcel of the struggle of cultural and religious contestations. The liberal position on equality is often imbued with simplified and unqualified understandings of culture, religion, identity and community that fail to adequately engage with the multiple positions that women occupy in relation to race, ethnicity, class, religion, family and community. Indeed Western culture is posited against 'other cultures' (the preoccupation mostly with Islam and its 'subordinating' effects upon Muslim women) and loses sight of the fact that women are social agents and 'occupy positions in other categories of difference and location' (Anthias, 2002, p. 276). Furthermore, the postcolonial presupposition that only a Western framework of 'human rights' can provide Muslim women with access to equality, justice and autonomy is false and misleading. We should not lose sight of the fact that Muslim women are active agents within their families and communities and, furthermore, Muslim feminists and scholars are currently engaged in exploring the relationship between human rights, Islam and gender equality from an Islamic perspective, some of which renders such simplistic analyses virtually meaningless in relation to the complex lived realities of Muslim women's lives (see Wadud, 1999; Barlas, 2006). At the outset of the twenty-first century and with the emergence of the third and fourth generations of South Asian Muslims in Britain, we must embrace this complexity, difference and transformation in an attempt to challenge oppressive cultural norms and values rather than seek to produce a common language of homogeneity from both a secular feminist or religious position. Difference is an integral part of being a British Pakistani Muslim woman. Furthermore, difference as well as the difference that conflict generates is also part of the Muslim tradition as Muslim feminists point out (see Mernissi, 1992; Ahmed, 1992; El Saadawi, 1997; Haeri, 1990; Siddiqui, 1996). Liberalism therefore develops its position on equality and tolerance committed to an ahistorical abstraction that affords individuals little agency and autonomy in relation to their lived realities.

Trying to understand these socio-legal processes also therefore requires a critique of the underlying power relations within family, community and state. The concept of 'translocational positionality' (Anthias, 2002, p. 275) addresses the potential conflicts and tensions that arise in different and at times conflicting social contexts, including intra-family relations. This study found that women's experiences of marriage, divorce, family and community relationships were messy, fragmented and complex. These findings suggest that during the process of marital disputes women cannot be stereotyped as requesting no family support or going down the road of nothing but family support. Instead they are themselves negotiating the outcomes of their marital disputes. British Pakistani Muslim women have complex views about who they are and thus their identity cannot be understood as a dichotomous variable of insider/outsider, Muslim/non-Muslim or resistance versus victim. Instead the narratives produced by the women themselves justify attention to their participation, interaction and outcomes with these 'unofficial' bodies.

This study demonstrates the ambivalent relationship between British Muslim women and Shari'ah councils. While on the one hand the women identified themselves as Muslims and recognized the importance of Shari'ah councils in helping them to obtain a Muslim divorce, they were also critical of these bodies as mediation fora and critical of the consistent attempts by the scholars to reconcile them with their husbands. Yet in transcending the ethnocentric construction of Muslim female identity as 'victims' they were able to redefine what it means to be a Muslim woman and adjust their participation with these bodies according to the social contexts in which they were situated. This research thus reveals the dynamism of these women and in particular their capacity to shift, change and develop in response to new needs and situations. This draws upon the work of legal pluralists who have incorporated an understanding of gender relations and the dynamics of power in their work. Griffiths (2001) calls for a non-essentializing pluralism which is grounded in the reality of women's lives and which is neither universalist nor pluralist and Hellum advocates an understanding based on the 'processual' approach that takes into account 'perceptions and values in complex chains of human relationships' (1999, p. 96).

Probably the most common criticism of Shari'ah councils is that they refuse to allow Muslim women to act as religious scholars on par with male scholars when issuing Muslim divorce certificates. For example, it is widely assumed within the councils that Muslim women are simply forbidden under Islamic law and jurisprudence to act as religious scholars in family law matters and this then acts as a widely accepted norm. As discussed in previous chapters the councils very much operate against a background of widely accepted norms few of which are challenged within the context of the councils themselves whereupon disputes are resolved. Despite this, such concerns are being addressed by some of these councils: for example, the Birmingham Shariah Council (BSC) and the MAT now have Muslim women who act as religious scholars in family law disputes and have the ability to issue Muslim divorce certificates. Feminists, however, remain concerned about the continuing restrictions placed upon Muslim women using these services and/or working within them and it is useful to remember that simply adopting 'rights-based strategies can over simplify complex power relationships'

(Wallback, Choudhury and Herring, 2009). The gendered dimension and these implications that form part of the institutional framework and nature of these councils cannot simply be ignored and I recognize that the use of one female scholar at the BSC cannot simply be characterized in itself and put forward as an example of new forms of empowerment for Muslim women when power relationships underpinning their interdependence can be so unequal (see Lister, 2003). Furthermore, the option of using Shari'ah councils does not necessarily translate into choice. Women may simply lack the autonomy to exercise other. Sezgin (2008) questions the extent to which the exit option can help promote ideas of freedom, choice and autonomy for women actually comprises. She quite rightly points out unless there is a liberal community on the 'outside' that can provide support and advice the exit option is simply too ineffective and problematic.

Therefore the very notion of difference as a site of struggle involving the contestation of meanings often imbued with internal contradictions, leads us to briefly consider how we can develop strategies that challenge intra-family inequalities and community regulation of women, while recognizing identities as complex and fluid. As data in this study suggest, dialogue is often imbued with power relations and is constituted in relation to controlling family and communal boundaries. For example, I found that the relationship between the female users of Shari'ah councils and religious scholars were often predicated on the religious and sociocultural terms that marginalize women (which included the female counsellor based at a Shari'ah council). As Anthias points out 'effective dialogue requires an already formulated mutual respect, a common communication language and a common starting point in terms of power' (2002, p. 288). It is the 'common starting point in terms of power' that raises the dilemma of the multicultural question of 'how then can the particular and the universal, the claims of both difference and equality be recognized' (Hall, 2000, p. 235).

Undoubtedly, these issues need to be addressed in the light of empirical findings rather than to devise solutions based upon abstract theoretical discussions which focus on the need to accommodate Islamic law into the English legal framework. Instead there is a need to incorporate new debates on complexity, difference and diversity to better understand the complex realities of British Pakistani Muslim women's lives. As this study demonstrates, women feel the contradictory pulls which these forces exert but their narratives must be heard. Some are happy to conform, others are not; some trade identities, but for others there is a primacy of a Muslim identity. Many are reluctant to see state intervention challenging cultural norms deemed oppressive because the state has not historically acted as the neutral arbiter of disputes (Hall, 2000, p. 238). Furthermore, some women see 'themselves strictly bound to submit to the dictates of Islamic law and the commands of the authorities charged with its execution' (Mayer, 1999, p. 45) and we must recognize this as their lived experience.

More importantly the argument that all Muslim cultural and religious norms inherently render women powerless and insubordinate is simply wrong and reflects today a rigid understanding of culture and religion that endorses the idea that formal mediation is problematic and informal mediation is either acceptable or dangerous. As discussed in Chapter 7, such a dichotomous approach obscures how norms are challenged by female members within a cultural and religious group. Clearly to impose a blanket ban on informal mediation would prove difficult to implement and deny women their agency in resolving their personal disputes. Muslim women are actively engaging in these spaces and their voices must be heard. Findings in this study suggest that some women are in favour of using Shari'ah councils as reconciliation bodies but others clearly are not. To judge the women in the latter category as in some way any less 'Islamic' than their counterparts is simply wrong. To judge the women in the former category as fundamentalist or traditional is also inaccurate. Yet the problem with current literature on legal pluralism, multiculturalism and feminism is that it employs a culturally relativist approach to challenging state power and oppressive cultural norms. The danger of this approach is that there is a growing polarity in the ways in which each of these approaches inhabits a social space that operates on the fixed constructions of insider/outsider, those who belong and those who do not, a space that in reality bears little resemblance to the complex realities of women's lives.

For some Muslim women's organizations, multiculturalism is understood as a strategically useful process with which to challenge state power but also the secular narratives that claim to speak on behalf of all women. In interview Ms Sheriff, co-ordinator of MWHL (Muslim Women's Helpline), explained:

> By recognizing our needs as Muslim women does not mean that we delegate our space and power to men inside or outside of our communities. We work with young Muslim women so they are able to use Islamic principles, to be empowered to stand up and say no. It is not us who are fundamentalists but the secularists; they are fundamentalist in the way that they deny us our voice, our experience as Muslim women.

In this way the ideological differences and practical approaches espoused by Muslim women's organizations in challenging intra-family inequalities such as forced marriage or domestic violence has inevitably led to conflicts with secular women's organizations such as Southall Black Sisters (SBS). Rahila Gupta, a long-serving management committee member of SBS, states:

> We are suspicious of developments such as the setting up of refuges for particular religious denominations like those for Muslim women. Do their experiences vary greatly from other women or other women's organisations? Or is the real reason for setting up such refuges an

attempt to contain the issue of domestic violence, to ensure that women return to the marriage after a period of respite without challenging the status quo?

(2003, p. 270)

In an apparent attempt to unify women's experiences it seems that such approaches fall into the trap of 'identity politics' that liberal feminists demarcate as the space that symbolizes and brings to the fore tensions between multiculturalism and feminism and the moral frameworks of universal rights and the politics of cultural relativism. Yuval-Davis observes that in feminist identity politics, women are usually 'perceived to constitute a basically homogeneous social grouping with the same interests' and 'women's individual identities have become equated with women's collective identity'. Differences are either ignored or perceived as 'reflections on different stages of raised consciousness' and thus such differences appear as expressions of a deficit that will, and has to, disappear (1997, p. 119). Accommodating the principle of equality to reflect the experiences of women means going beyond these distinctions.

Empirical research in this study reveals that the management of marital disputes in the sphere of privatized religious arbitration gives rise to a different set of responsibilities and obligations. Women who participated in the Shari'ah councils' process viewed themselves as not only individuals but also as members of families and communities. In a situation where notions of religious identity, belonging and familial norms and values interact with the values of individual choice and consent, some women were successfully able to negotiate between the plurality of norms and values that exist within the context of family, home and Shari'ah councils. An important aspect of such findings, therefore, is to challenge the perceived inherent marginality of Muslim women in this process of dispute resolution. For example, it is interesting to note that several women reported that they were aware that the meanings and interpretations of some Islamic perspectives put forward by religious scholars were contested and therefore open to change. In this way they were able to disregard them and were fully aware of the need to utilize state law for their protection and entitlement to rights. For this reason they were able to challenge their weak bargaining position in the marriage within the family context, to occupy a more 'open' space at the Shari'ah council as a basis for entering into negotiation, dialogue and possible change. In such a situation some women participated in the reconciliation process as a strategic manoeuvre to challenge conflicting interests. Yet this shift of dispute resolution from the public to the private sphere also raises serious concerns on how power is effectively reconfigured from the state to the family and community. From such a perspective the differential treatment of women in the process of marriage and divorce can lead to a conflict between equality and autonomy and the conflicting interests of the protection of family, culture and religion as enshrined by the norms and values of Shari'ah councils.

As discussed in this book the recognition of these plural legal orders in Britain has led to interesting scholarly debate on what is understood as law, legal pluralism and Muslim family law. While most literature presents these developments as a reflection of cultural and religious life, we are also drawn to the conclusion that understandings of culture and religion are to be understood as fixed, bounded and indeterminate. This is particularly clear from the work of legal pluralists who present the duality of culture and religion as the underlying premise upon which this presupposed framework of dispute resolution must be understood. In turn state law is presented as overarching and universalist with the power to annihilate or accommodate difference at its whim. More interestingly still, the debate in Britain has been closely framed around the construction of a homogeneous 'Muslim identity' that leads to the demands of a parallel legal system, which presupposes a deeply felt cultural and religious conviction, without providing adequate analysis of the complexities that identity entails. Two recent studies on religious systems of dispute resolution and minority communities have challenged such fixed notions of law and identity. The first report, titled *Social Cohesion and Civil Law: Marriage, Divorce and Religious Courts* by Douglas et al. (2011), explored how religious law functions alongside civil law in the area of marriage and divorce and examined the workings of three religious courts in detail: a Jewish Beth Din, a matrimonial tribunal of the Roman Catholic Church and a Muslim 'Shari'ah Council'. This fascinating comparative study found that 'these tribunals provide an important service for their users in enabling them to remarry within their faith, which serves both to enable them to remain within their faith community and to regularize their position with the religious authorities. None of the tribunals sought greater autonomy and all recognized the supremacy of state law' – a finding confirmed in my study of Shari'ah councils in Britain. The second report, titled *Minority Legal Systems in the UK: Multiculturalism, Minorities and the Law* (Malik, 2012) raises theoretical and practical questions about the proper balance between the state and minorities, as well as a fundamental choice about whether the liberal state will be 'muscular' (require all minorities to conform to liberal values) or pluralist (allow some non-liberal or illiberal forms of life to flourish).

As exemplified in this study, the task of exploring the multiple ways in which British Pakistani Muslim women perceive dispute resolution means it is necessary to engage in the analysis of gender and its intersection with culture, human rights, official and unofficial law. Viewing these debates from an interdisciplinary perspective transforms the analytical framework from fairly essentialist terms prevalent in existing literature to much more fluid and contradictory understandings. This gives rise to a pluralism that is neither essentialist nor relativist but as argued earlier provides a 'stronger grounding in the conversation between theory and method' (Cowan, Dembour and Wilson, 2001, p. 20).

The space inhabited by the Shari'ah council is neither distinct from local communities nor in totality separate from state law; instead it is a space that intersects with contested sites of local communal power and in this way is a unique formation of a British diaspora. As Soysal (1994) points out, this space draws upon local and transnational networks for legitimacy connecting with the global Muslim *umma* while developing strategies to fulfil the needs of specific local Muslims. This study demonstrates the ambivalent relationship between British Muslim women and Shari'ah councils. While on the one hand the women identified themselves as Muslims and recognized the importance of the councils in helping them to obtain a Muslim divorce, they were also critical of these bodies as mediation fora and the consistent attempts to reconcile them with their husbands. Yet, in transcending the ethnocentric construction of Muslim female identity as 'victims', they were able to redefine what it means to be a Muslim woman and adjust their participation with these bodies according to the social contexts in which they were situated. This research reveals the dynamism of these women and in particular their capacity to shift, change and develop in response to new needs and situations.

This research demonstrates how identities are fluid, multiple and changing. The women in this study identified themselves variously as Muslims, as British and as Pakistani in different contexts. Cultural, religious and legal diversity must therefore be understood to be in flux, contested and open to change. As Hall points out, 'The temptation to essentialize community has to be resisted – it is fantasy of plenitude in circumstances of imagined loss. Migrant communities bear the imprint of diaspora, "hybridization" and difference in their very constitution. Their vertical integration into their traditions of origin exists side by side with their lateral linkages to other "communities" of interest, practice and aspiration, real and symbolic' (2000, p. 209).

Central to the resolution of disputes is the way in which bodies such as Shari'ah councils engage with Muslim women. Scholars such as Hayes and Acton (2006) point to the fact that minority communities reformulate their ways of being over time which can stress the relevance of the individual actors' definitions and behaviours – a continual process of renewal and adaptation. The picture painted by legal pluralists on understanding this process as structured by the dialectic of Muslim personal law and state law is also very different from the picture emerging from the data in this study. Instead we can see how difference is constituted in multiple ways in between these differing social and legal processes (Santos, 1987). This process, moreover, is interactional, negotiated and shaped by the specificities of the complex realities of the women's lives. The real conflicts are not so much the theoretical debates on multiculturalism and feminism or state law versus unofficial law but between power and how the competing voices for power and representation ignore the internal voices of dissent and change, most often the voices of women. And we should not forget that complexity, difference and ambiguity open up the conceptual spaces for us to explore the entanglements of law, gender, community, diaspora and identity, and the contestation over cultural and religious meanings. As Bauman points out, 'From whatever side you look at it, difference is today an asset rather than a liability and those different from the dominant majority may reasonably expect to gain rather than lose' (1999, p. 13).

Notes

1 Multiculturalism and Secularism in the British Context

1. Most Pakistanis are drawn from just a few areas in Pakistan: mainly from Faisalabad and Jhelum Districts in Punjab, Mirpur District in Azad Kashmir and the Attock District in the North-West Frontier Province (see Shaw, 1994 and Werbner, 1988).
2. In June 2012, The Home Secretary, Theresa May announced the introduction of a new part of the Citizenship test with a closer focus on 'Britishness'. See Travis, A, 'UK Migrants to face 'patriotic' citizenship test, The Guardian, 1st July 2012. A copy of this article can be accessed via www.guardian.co.uk
3. Hall argues that it has now become so discursively entangled that the term can only be used 'under erasure' (2000, p. 234).
4. For example, see Lord Goldsmith (2008). A summary of the issues may be found in Kostakopoulou (2006).
5. The debate on multiculturalism has been accompanied with critiques on what is understood as 'British' and 'Britishness' (see Gilroy, 1987; Rattansi, 1992; Hall, 1997). Also Hall (1997) has challenged the popular misconception that prior to post-war migration to Britain, the country symbolized a fixed, unified nation state. In fact, the presence of 'black' and Asian communities in Britain has been documented as early as the sixteenth and eighteenth centuries (see Ballard, 1997).
6. Cited in Dunleavy and O'Leary (1987, p. 30).
7. For example, in *R* v. *Bibi* (1980) the Court of Appeal reduced the imprisonment of a Muslim widow, found guilty of importing cannabis, from three years to six months. The grounds for this were, inter alia, that 'she was totally dependent on her brother-in-law and was socialized by her religion into subservience to the male members of her household'. In *R* v. *Bailey* (1964) and *R* v. *Byfield* (1982) the moral codes of men brought up in the West Indies were taken into consideration in sentencing them for having sexual intercourse with girls under the age of 16. Again in *Malik* v. *British Home Stores* (1980) the Court ruled that in appropriate circumstances Asian women might wear trousers at work, even though other women might not.

2 South Asian Muslims and State-Law Relations

1. In his study Ballard (1994) points out that South Asian migration in Britain began as early as the seventeenth century.
2. The last Census was conducted in April 2001. For full breakdown of the Census data, visit the Office for National Statistics (ONS) website at http://www.ons.gov. uk. In 2011 a new census was completed and the statistical data is currently being compiled (see http://www.ons.gov.uk/ons/guide-method/census/2011/the-2011-census/index.html).
3. Most Pakistanis are drawn from just a few areas in Pakistan: mainly from Faisalabad and Jhelum Districts in Punjab, Mirpur District in Azad Kashmir, and the Attock District in the North West Frontier Province (see Shaw, 1994 and Werbner, 1988).

4. Again settlement patterns of Pakistanis in Britain have been extensively documented. For an overview see Ballard (1994).
5. For a fascinating study on the processes of 'gift-exchange', marriage and affluent Pakistani businessmen in Manchester, see Werbner (1989).
6. And recognizing a distinction in group identity between a 'mode of oppression' and 'mode of being' (see Modood, 2006, p. 56).
7. The term 'active citizenship' has been used by a number of theorists to analyse the organizational dimensions of 'diasporas' (see Modood, 2000; Werbner, 2002b).
8. According to Ballard corporate families originate from 'the swath of territory which runs from North Africa through the Eastern Mediterranean and the Middle East to South Asia' (2008, p. 38). South Asia remains the largest source of marriage migration (although not of child migration) to the UK. See *Control of Immigration Statistics UK 2007* (Home Office 10/08, 2008, p. 28).
9. See European Monitoring Centre on Racism and Xenophobia (EUMC), *Muslims in the European Union: Discrimination and Islamophobia* (2006, pp. 44–59), available at http://www.eumc.Europa.eu/eumc/material/pub/muslim/Manifestations_EN.pdf
10. Hazel Blears announced that she was suspending engagement due to the views of its deputy secretary general.
11. In Britain, for example, efforts to ensure the successful integration of minority groups into mainstream society (described more generally as multiculturalism) have been accompanied by ill-defined conceptions of what is understood as British identity most vividly illustrated by the various commissions on integration and citizenship tests introduced to define national identity. Yet it remains unclear what values nationality should include (see Jacobson, 1997).
12. See Adrian Michaels, 'Muslim Europe: The demographic time bomb transforming our continent', *The Telegraph*, 8 August 2009. A copy of this article can be obtained at www.thetelegraphy.co.uk/news
13. See 'Burka ban: Why must I cast off the veil?' *The Telegraph*, 17 July 2010. A copy of this article can be accessed at http://www.telegraph.co.uk/comment/personal-view/7896536/Burka-ban-Why-must-I-cast-off-the-veil.html
14. *Refah Partisi (The Welfare Party) and Others* v. *Turkey*, Judgement of the European Court of Human Rights, Strasbourg, 13 February 2003.
15. 21 s. 1 6 Domicile and Matrimonial Proceedings Act 1973. This laid down that no extra-judicial divorce obtained anywhere in the British Isles should be recognized in England. This has now been re-enacted in the Family Law Act, 1986.
16. *Shanoz* v. *Rizwan* (1962) 1 Q.B 390; *Qureshi* v. *Qureshi* (1972) Fam 173.
17. Aina Khan is a senior consultant solicitor at Russell, Jones & Walker Solicitors (see www.rjw.co.uk). Ahmad Thompson is a barrister at Wynne chambers, specializing in Islamic law (see wynnechambers.co.uk).
18. A copy of this lecture can be found at *Archbishop – UK law needs to find accommodation with religious law codes*, www.archbishopofcanterbury.org/1580, posted on 7 February 2008.
19. Other issues such as polygamy also remain of public policy concern. On 20 February 2009 a senior conservative peer, Baroness Warsi, criticized the government for failing to tackle the issue of polygamy due to cultural sensitivity and argues that it was a 'failure' of policymakers not to take the issue seriously. Source, Radio 4 Today Programme *news.bbc.co.uk/2/hi/7900779.stm*
20. An overview of existing equalities legislation can be found at www.equalities.gov.uk

21. 1 A C 100 (2006) UKHL 15HL.
22. 19 BHRC 590.
23. (2008) EWCA Crim 1450.
24. Early scholarship drew upon a 'cultural image' of Pakistani women who were assigned to the role of carriers of traditional 'cultural patterns' within the family and home. These explanations focused on the 'conflict model' with young Asian women being presented as being caught between two conflicting cultures represented by the home and the school. Largely disempowered within the family and home, their lives were perceived as incompatible with the outside world. These ideas were later replaced with the idea of 'best of both worlds' where women were deemed more successful in synthesizing their lives in both the public/private spheres and were acceded more control and initiative (see Knott and Khokker, 1993).
25. The concept of agency is often understood in relation to concepts of the individual, the person and the self; discussion of these questions falls outside the scope of this book.

3 Background to the Study

1. See, for example, Harding (1987). Such issues are central to the research. It allows the researcher to structure an interview schedule in such a way that the researcher is in a position to ask probing questions which may elicit fuller answers. The respondent may also feel that they are in a position to think about their responses and they are given the time and the space to do so. They may answer a question, move on and later decide they want to return to that particular question and they are able to do so.
2. MacEoin (2009).

4 Shari'ah Councils in Britain

1. There are three key principles: *Istihan* – the principle of juristic preference that comes into play when analogical reasoning seems too rigid to ensure equity; *Istislan* – the principle of public interest that comes into play in cases where public interest is not 'textually specified'; and *Istishab* – the principle of presumed continuity that bases rulings on antecedents deemed valid unless proven otherwise (see Nasir, 1986).
2. The codification of Shari'ah in different countries has led to extensive discussion among scholars on the interpretive methodologies used to develop Shari'ah (see An-Naim, 1990).
3. Yilmaz (2001b, p. 3) describes *ijtihad* as an activity, a struggle and a process to discover the law from texts and apply them to a new set of facts. In this way Muslim legal pluralism in Britain is an indication of new *ijtihad*.
4. In Pakistan, for example, the relationship between divorce and mediation is one enshrined in law. In cases of divorce the contending parties have to nominate their representative while the 'Umpire' shall be the Chairman of the Local Council. Under section 7 of the Muslim Family Laws Ordinance (MFLO 1961) once a husband pronounces a *talaq* it must be registered with the Chairman of the Union Committee or Arbitration Council and a copy of this notice must be supplied to his wife. This notice remains valid for 90 days and during this time

the couple are encouraged to resolve the marital dispute outside of the legal framework. Thus section 7 sub-section 4 states, 'Within thirty days of the receipt of notice under sub-section (1), the Chairman shall constitute an Arbitration Council for the purpose of bringing about reconciliation between the parties, and the Arbitration Council shall take all steps necessary to bring about such reconciliation' (see Nasir, 1986).

5. A report in *The Telegraph* on 2 April 2008 headlined, 'No more mosques, says senior Synod member'. The article explained that a prominent evangelical member of the Church of England general synod called for a ban on building any more mosques in Britain. Copy of the report can be found at http://www.telegraph. co.uk/news/uknews/1583666/No-more-mosques-says-senior-Synod-member.html

6. These bodies include The Muslim College in London, Darul Uloom al-Arabiya al-Islamia in Lancashire, Institute of Islamic Education in Dewsbury and the Al-Mahdi Institute in Birmingham (see FAIR, 2002).

7. Analysis of these newspapers reveals that most objections are raised against the mosque committees that are seen to be run by an older generation which has little understanding of the needs of young British Muslims (see Bunt, 2006).

8. For the example the Birmingham Central Mosque runs a Marriage Bureau. See www.birmingham central mosque for details.

9. For example the issue of *khul* and *mubara't* has led to interesting discussion on its form and validity (see Bharatiya, 1996).

10. Pearl and Menski (1998) draw upon cases of verbal *nikah* where the husband had pronounced a unilateral *talaq* to explore the nature of the intervention of state law to regulate this area.

11. One effect might be that the couple is considered to be divorced in one jurisdiction but married in another. The costs upon Muslim women are particularly high as men may use their powerful position to make greater demands such as favourable financial settlements (see Hamilton, 1995; Carroll, 1997; Badawi, 1996).

12. Shari'ah councils also issue *fatwas* which can simply be translated as a ruling from a religious scholar to members of the Muslim community over a contested issue. Observation research in this study revealed that at some Shari'ah councils the scholars spend considerable time deliberating on issuing *fatwas*. The outcomes of these *fatwas* are not known but raise interesting questions on the ways the community attempts to deal with local conflicts within the boundaries of the 'Muslim community' and the extent to which these processes may conflict with state law.

5 Shari'ah Councils and the Practice of Law-Making

1. The role of the Prophet as an arbitrator has been traced back to the episode in reconstruction of the *Ka'ba*. There was a dispute over the placing of the Black Stone (*Hajr al-Aswad*) into the building between tribes of the *Quraysh* who wanted to have the honour of placing the stone. The Prophet asked each of the tribes to introduce a representative. He then placed the stone in a sheet of cloth, asking all representatives to hold it and raise it together. The Prophet Muhammad had taken action as an arbitrator over several disputes. Another incidence reported in *Sahih al-Bukhari* is that Prophet Muhammad had conciliated between litigants on dispute of debt. He was reported to have cut the claim of a creditor in half in order to reach a rapid settlement (see *Sahih al-Bukhari*, vol. 3 by Muhammad Muhsin Khan).

2. The principles of *adl, ihsan* and *hikmah* also have been referred as core values of the Islamic peacemaking framework: 'Islam yields a set of peace building values that if consistently and systematically applied can transcend and govern all types and levels of conflict, values such as justice (*adl*) beneficence (*ihsan*) and wisdom (*hikmah*) which constitute core principles of peacemaking strategies and framework' (see Abu-Nimer, 2001).
3. Khadduri (1984, pp. 236–37).
4. Ibid.
5. Since the completion of this project the BSC now includes a female member in the council panel (see Douglas et al., 2011).
6. This may include copies of certain documents – for example, marriage certificates and any civil divorce proceedings documentation.
7. Each scholar reported that although they were prepared to meet with clients who made unscheduled visits to the councils they were reluctant to introduce a drop-in service due to the financial and time constraints they faced.
8. These costs ranged from £50 for ISC, £60 for BSC, £75 for MLSC but no charge for SCUK.
9. By contrast, the SCUK did not provide application forms or any other forms of written documentation. Instead the onus rested upon the applicants to attend scheduled meetings to discuss the breakdown of the marriage. In this instance access to case files was refused, but observation revealed that family members often accompanied clients to meetings and were permitted to contribute to all discussions.
10. For the purposes of this study, the overarching term 'religious scholar' is being used.
11. In this way a number of scholars reported they were able to mediate between parents and young women who were being forced into marriage and prevent such marriages.
12. Again access to observe these sessions was withheld on the grounds of confidentiality.
13. These comprised London Central Mosque and Islamic Cultural Centre, London; Muslim World League, Matkazi Jamiat Ahl-e-hadith, UK; UK Islamic Mission; Dawatul Islam, UK; Jamia Mosque and Islamic Centre, Birmingham; Islamic Centre, Glasgow; Islamic Centre, Manchester; Jamia Masjid Hanafiya, Bradford; and Muslim Welfare, London. For a complete outline of the aims and objectives of the Council see The Islamic Shari'a Council of Great Britain and Northern Ireland (1982, p. 3).

6 Personal Experiences of Marriage

1. Given the complexities involved in the marriage process these categories are used with caution while recognising that categorizing marriages in this way does not allow an understanding of the subtle interconnections and differences between the categories being employed.
2. Forced marriage has become the subject of public concern in most European countries and increasingly the terms 'arranged marriage' and 'forced marriage' are used interchangeably. The definitions of force are wide. For a comprehensive discussion on the use and limits of such definitions, see Welchman and Hossain (2005).
3. The requirement to comply restricts the terms upon which women are able to develop strategies to challenge parental authority and limits the space upon which they are able to instigate change within the process.

4. This study draws upon interviews to elicit Asian women's views on arranged marriages, including their definitions of arranged marriage, their importance within South Asian communities and, in cases where the women themselves were involved in arranged marriages, the type of contact they had with their prospective husbands. It also examines whether women would want their own daughters to have arranged marriages and their views towards women who do not have arranged marriages.

5. In 1999 CIMEL (Centre for Islamic and Middle Eastern Law) and INTERIGHTS (International Centre for the Legal Protection of Human Rights) began a three-year project on 'honour crimes' which worked closely with national and international organizations to explore ways in which to develop strategies to combat the practice of honour crimes. See *Roundtable on Strategies to Address 'Crimes of Honour'* (2002) which can be accessed at http://www.soas.ac.uk/honourcrimes/resources/ Last accessed 22nd August 2012.

6. In January 2004, the Metropolitan Police set up a Taskforce to deal with the practice of 'honour crimes'.

7. These cases include the murder of Rukhsana Naz (1999), Heshu Yones (2003) and Shafilea Ahmed (2004). On 2 August 2012 the parents of Shafilea Ahmed were sentenced to life imprisonment with a minimum term of 25 years after being found guilty of murdering their 17-year-old daughter (see http://www.guardian. co.uk/uk/shafilea-ahmed, accessed on 22 August 2012). A further concern is the extent to which cultural and religious beliefs are used as partial defences in law against the charge of murder. In her extensive analysis of English case law and the use of cultural defences, Phillips concludes that 'cultural arguments only have an effect when they resonate with mainstream views' and are rarely utilized to effect (see Phillips, 2003, p. 531).

8. This interpretation of duress can also be found in the following cases *P* v. *R* (Forced marriage: Annulment procedure, 2003) 1 FLR 661 (with short comment in [2003] *Fam Law* 162); *Singh* v. *Singh* (1971) P 226; *Kaur* v. *Singh* (1972) 1 WLR 105; *NS* v. *MI* (2006) EWHC 1646 (Fam); *Re E (An alleged patient)*; *Sheffield City Council* v. *E and S* (2004) EWHC 2808 (Fam); *A Local Authority* v. *N, Y and K* (2005) EWHC 2956 (Fam); *NS* v. *MI* (2006) EWHC 1646 (Fam).

9. There are also public order offences according to the Public Order Act 1986 and protection against harassment according to section 2 of the Protection from Harassment Act 1997.

10. For more details see www.homeoffice.gov.uk/forcedmarriage

11. For example, the women's organization, Southall Black Sisters, resigned from the working group on forced marriage protesting the recommendation of mediation to reconcile victims of forced marriage with their families.

12. There is wide-ranging literature that documents the emergence and development of the Muslim marriage contract, the *nikah*, in Muslim and non-Muslim societies (see Doi, 2008; Esposito, 1988; Nasir, 1990; Engineer, 2005; Welchman, 2004).

13. See Fournier (2010).

14. For example, a refusal or abstention to the marriage may constitute as consent (see Welchman, 2000).

15. This takes into account six considerations: descent, Islam, profession, freedom, good character and wealth. It effectively means that a Muslim woman may only marry someone her equal and not of lower status (see Siddiqui, 1996).

16. EWCA Civ 198.

17. For some Islamic scholars, such as Badawi, these practices are simply customary ceremonials and in reality have no place within Islamic law (1995, p. 57).

18. See White Paper (1992) *Civil Registration: Vital Change – Birth, Marriage and Death Registration in the Twenty-First Century* (Cm5355, 2002).
19. See Marriage Act s.41(1).
20. These statistics have been taken from ONS (2000) *Marriage, Divorce and Adoption Statistics 1998*, London: Stationery Office, Tables 3.43 and 3.42.
21. Probert (2002) provides a fascinating historical account of the British institution of marriage and how it continues to be deeply influenced by English history to maintain its privileged status.
22. 1 FLR8.
23. 2 FLR 6.
24. 1 FLR 603.
25. EWHC 2651.
26. See Matrimonial Causes Act 1973, s.11 and s.12.
27. English civil marriages are recognized as valid in Pakistan (see Pearl and Menski, 1998).
28. This raises a different set of questions on utilizing national and international legal remedies that are not addressed in this book.
29. According to Islamic legal principles, this payment can be paid promptly at the point of marriage or deferred and paid after the breakdown of marriage (see Engineer, 1992).
30. See *Shanaz v. Rizwan* (1964) 2 All ER 993.

7 Muslim Women, Divorce and Shari'ah Councils

1. Pearl and Menski (1998) draw upon cases of verbal *nikah* where the husband has pronounced a unilateral *talaq* to explore the nature of the intervention of state law to regulate this area.
2. One effect might be that the couple are considered to be divorced in one jurisdiction but married in another. The costs upon Muslim women are particularly high as men may use their powerful position to make greater demands such as favourable financial settlements (see Hamilton, 1995; Carroll, 1997).
3. For example, training on ethnic minority customs for the judiciary. For an interesting discussion on the limitations of such training, see Ballard (2006).
4. Southall Black Sisters was set up in 1979 to meet the needs of Asian and African-Caribbean women (see Gupta, 2003).
5. Newham Asian Women's Project was set up in 1983 to meet the needs of Asian women in East London.
6. HC 395, para 281 (iii) Related provisions apply to spouses wishing to join a refugee (HC 395, para 352A (iii), to fiancé(e)s (para 290(iii) and to spouses of students (para 76(ii)). See MacDonald, MacDonald and Webber (2001).
7. For a study on the Hindu Gujerati community in Leicester, see Goodwin et al. (1997).
8. There has been some discussion on the similar problems experienced by Jewish women in Britain and the recent passage of the Divorce (Religious Marriages) Act 2002 (see Barnett (2000)). The fundamental difference between Muslim and Jewish women is that Muslim women do not need the express consent of their husbands to divorce religiously and can obtain a divorce certificate from religious scholars at Shari'ah councils.
9. For more discussion on this, see Shah-Kazemi (2001).

10. The MWHL has been actively engaged in calling for the regulation of Shari'ah councils and consultation between Shari'ah bodies and civil legal authorities. See 'Islamic and civil legal structures need to interface', *Muslim News*, 19 December 2003.
11. See www.MMN.ac.uk/marriage

8 Shari'ah Councils and Civil Law

1. 1 Lloyds Rep 923 (1999) C.L.R 904.
2. SLT 294.
3. EWHC 3506.
4. EWCA Civ 399.
5. UKSC 40.
6. *Jivraj* v. *Hashwani* (2010) EWCA Civ 712.
7. Analysis and details of the cases discussed here are based on the summaries provided by the barrister Neil Addison, a scholar specializing in Criminal and Family Law, and can be found at http://www.religionlaw.co.uk/
8. EWCA Civ 1205.
9. 3 WLR 1506.
10. UKPC 64.
11. EWHC 1532 (Fam).
12. EWCA Civ 1304.
13. 1 FLR 120.
14. See Resolution in *A More Certain Future*. www.resolution.org.uk/site_content_files/files/a_more_certain_future__resolution.pdf
15. EWCA Civ 503.
16. A copy can be accessed at www.lawcom.gov.uk/marital_property.htm
17. The contract is the work of Dr Ghayasuddin Siddiqui, Founder Director of the south London-based Muslim Institute.
18. There is now an expansive body of scholarship that has contributed to our understanding of mediation, ADR and the best available services. For an overview, see Roberts (2008).
19. For a brief outline on the role of the Ford Foundation, see http://www.fordfoundation.org/
20. See Moore (2003).
21. Adopting a dialectical approach to the relationship between law and community justice, Abel (1982) illustrates the contradictions in law. He argues that to understand the dialectical relationship between formal law and informal justice we must focus on the intersection between law, justice and power.
22. Sociological accounts of the family vary. Functionalist writers such as Talcott Parsons argue that the family serves a particular purpose to ensure the stability of all individuals and hence the stability of the existing social system. Marxist and feminist accounts of the relationship between state and family is based 'on the notion that state activity is not simply family-relevant but presupposes, reinforces and perpetuates, as the appropriate unit for personal care and for the regulation of sexual and parental relationships, a privatized nuclear family based on the sexual division of labour and the subordination of women' (see Smart, 1992).
23. In particular the role and position of women within the family serve to reflect male interests. In her work MacKinnon argues that as the law itself is patriarchal, family law merely reflects this. She writes, 'If objectivity is the epistemological

stance of which women's sexual objectification is the social process, its imposition the paradigm of power in the male form, then the state will appear most relentless in imposing the male point of view' (1983, p. 447).

24. A copy of this report can be accessed at http://www.justice.gov.uk/about/moj/independent-reviews/family-justice-review/
25. For a copy, see www.legislation.gov.uk/asp/2010
26. Go to http://www.matribunal.com/cases_faimly.html.
27. The Forced Marriage (Civil) Protection Act 2007 s63B(1); Family Law Act 1966 Part 4.
28. Ibid., p. 22, para 40.
29. Ibid., p. 22, para 40.
30. Ibid., p. 33.
31. *Hansard, Lords Debates*, vol. 688, col. 1326 (26 January 2007).
32. Judge Coleridge granted further orders to continue her protection and to prevent her being removed from the country without her consent (see Walsh, 2009).
33. *Stretford* v. *Football Association* (2007) All ER (D) 346; *Sumukan Ltd* v. *The Commonwealth Secretariat* (2007) EWCA Civ 243; and *Shuttari* v. *The Solicitors Indemnity Fund* (2007) EWCA Civ 244.
34. The views of Neil Addison can be found at http://www.religionlaw.co.uk/

9 Conclusion: Justice in the 'Shadow of Law'?

1. For a fascinating account of the different Barelwi traditions practised in three different mosques in Birmingham, see Geaves (1996a).
2. Critical legal literature on community justice has focused on whether these movements can have a social transformative effect on the legal system (Henry, 1983). It is argued that these movements are not completely autonomous and independent from the state nor are they completely dependent upon the state; thus there is a state of ambiguity and this ambiguity gives the potential for a social transformative effect on the wider structure of the legal system (Merry, 1988; Harrington and Merry, 1988).
3. The report was produced by the Conservation think tank Policy Exchange and was published in May 2007. For a copy of the report, go to http://www.policyexchange.org.uk/Publications

Bibliography

Abbas, T. (2001) 'Media capital and the representation of South Asian Muslims in the British press: an ideological analysis', *Journal of Muslim Minority Affairs*, 21(2): 245–57.

Abbas, T. (2005) *Muslim Britain: Communities Under Pressure*, London and New York: Zed Books.

Abel, R. L. (1982) *The Politics of Informal Justice. The American Experience*, New York: Academic Press.

Abel, F. (1992) 'Popular justice, populist politics: Law in community organizing', *Social and Legal Studies*, 1(2): 177–98.

Abou El Fadl, K. (1994) 'Legal debates on Muslim minorities between rejection and accommodation', *Journal of Religion and Ethics*, 22(1): 127–62.

Abou El Fadl, K. (2010) *Speaking in God's Name: Islamic Law, Authority and Women*, London: Oneworld.

Abu-Odeh, L., 'Crimes of Honour and the Construction of Gender in Arab Societies in M. Yamani (ed.) *Feminism and Islam, Legal and Literary Perspectives*, Ithaca Press, pp. 141–195.

Abu-Lughod, L. (2002) 'Do Muslim women need saving? Reflections on cultural relativism and its others', *American Anthropologist*, 104(3): 783–90.

Abu-Nimer, M. (2001) 'Conflict resolution in an Islamic context: Some conceptual questions', in A. A. Said, N. C. Funk and A. S. Kadayifci (eds) *Peace and Conflict Resolution in Islam*, New York: University Press of America, pp. 165–190.

Addison, N. (2007) *Religious Discrimination and Hatred Law*, Routledge-Cavendish London: Routledge.

Addison, N. (2011) 'Lady Cox's bill is not so controversial', *The Guardian*, 23 June, available at www.theguardian.co.uk.

Afshar, H. (1994) 'Muslim women in West Yorkshire: Growing up with Real and imaginary values amidst conflicting views of self and society', in H. Afshar and M. Maynard (eds) *The Dynamics of 'Race' and 'Gender'*, London: Taylor and Francis, pp. 127–50.

Afshar, H. (2005) 'Behind the veil', in H. Moghissi (ed.) *Women and Islam: Critical Concepts in Sociology*, Routledge, 56–72.

Afshar, H. (2007) 'Muslim women and feminisms: Illustrations from the Iranian experience', *Social Compass*, 54(3): 419–34.

Afshar, H. (2008) 'Can I see your hair? Choice, agency and attitudes: The dilemma of faith and feminism for Muslim women who cover', *Ethnic and Racial Studies*, 31(2): 411–27.

Ahdar, R. and Aroney, N. (2010), *Shari'a in the West*, Oxford: Oxford University Press.

Ahearn, L. (2001) 'Language and agency', *Annual Review of Anthropology*, 30: 109–37.

Ahmed, A. and Donnan, H. (eds) (1994) *Islam, Globalization and Modernity*, London: Routledge.

Ahmad, F. (2006) 'The scandal of "arranged marriages" and the pathologization of BrAsian Families', in N. Ali, V. Kalra and S. Sayyid, (eds), *A Postcolonial People: South Asians in Britain*, London: Hurst, pp. 272–88.

Ahmed, F. (2010) 'Personal autonomy and the option of religious law', *International Journal of Law, Policy and the Family*, 24(2): pp. 222–35.

Ahmad, F., Modood, T. and Lissenburgh, S. (2003) *South Asian Women and Employment in Britain*. London: Policy Studies Institute, Report No. 891.

Ahmed, F. and Luk, S. (2011) 'Religious arbitration: A study of legal safeguards', *Arbitration*, 77: pp. 1–22.

Ahmed, L. (1992) *Women and Gender in Islam*, New Haven: Yale University Press.

Ahsan, M. (1995) 'The Muslim family in Britain,' in M. King (ed.) *Gods Law versus State law. The Construction of Islamic identity in Western Europe*, GreySeal, pp. 21–30.

Alam, S., Kalra, V. and Fieldhouse, E. A. (2002) 'Towards Equality: Experience of the New Deal amongst young people from minority ethnic communities', *Journal of Ethnic & Migration Studies*, 28(3): 499–514.

Al-Hibri, A. (1999) 'Is Western patriarchal feminism good for Third World/minority women?' in J. Cohen, M. Howard and M. C. Nussbaum (eds) *Is Multiculturalism Bad for Women?* Princeton, NJ: Princeton University Press, pp. 41–6.

Alexander, C. (2002) 'Beyond Black: Rethinking the Colour/Culture Divide', *Ethnic and Racial Studies*, 25(4): 552–71.

Ali, S. S. (2000) *Gender and Human Rights in Islam and International Law: Equal Before Allah? Equal Before Man?* The Hague: Kluwer Law International.

Ali, S. S and Rehman, J. (2003) 'Freedom of Religion versus Equality in International Human Rights Law: Conflicting Norms of Hierarchical Human Rights (A case study of Pakistan)', *Nordic Journal of Human Rights*, No. 4 pp. 330–45.

Ali, S. S. (2002) 'Women's Rights, CEDAW, and International Human Rights Debates: Toward Empowerment?', in S. Rai, J. Parpart and Staudt (eds) *Gender and Empowerment in a Local Global World*, CEDAW, pp. 61–78.

Ali, S. S. (2007) 'Religious pluralism, human rights and citizenship in Europe: Some preliminary reflections on an evolving methodology for consensus', in T. Loenen and J. Goldschmidt (eds) *Religious Pluralism and Human Rights in Europe: Where to Draw the Line*, Utrecht: Intersentia, pp. 57–79.

Ali, S. S. (2010) 'Cyberspace as emerging Muslim discursive space? Online fatawa on women and gender relations and its impact on Muslim family law norms', *International Journal of Law, Policy and the Family*, 24(3): 338–60.

Ali, S.-S., Shahid, S., Lawan, M., Akhtar, R. and Abubakar, M. (2009) Islamic Law and the Muslim Diaspora: A Teaching Manual. A copy of this manual can be accessed at www.warwick.ukcle/islamiclaw

Ali, K. (2010) *Islam and English Law*, Roundtable discussion at Grays Inn Chambers, London (unpublished paper).

Allen, C. (2001) 'Mentioning the unmentionable: Islamophobia in Britain', *Q-News*, 334: 16–18.

Allen, C. (2002) 'Righting Bradford's wrongs', *Q-News*, 345–6: 16–17.

Allen, C. (2003) 'Emerging from the Fog: Islamaphobia in the Wake of 9/11', *Islamica Magazine*, 10: 25–31.

Allen, C. (2010) *Islamophobia*, New York: Ashgate Publishing Ltd.

Alleyne, B. (2002) 'An idea of community and its discontents: Towards a more reflexive sense of belonging in multicultural Britain', *Ethnic and Racial Studies*, 25(4): 607–27.

Allott, A. and Woodman, G. (1985) *People's Law and State Law: The Bellagio Papers*, Dordrecht and Cinnaminson: Foris Publications.

Aluffi, P. R. and Zincone, G. (eds) (2004) *The Legal Treatment of Islamic Minorities in Europe*, USA: Peeters.

Anand, D. (2010) 'Generating Islamaphobia in India', in S. Sayyid and A. K. Vakil (eds) *Thinking through Islamophobia: Global Perspectives*, London: Hurst.

An-Naim, A. (1990) *Toward an Islamic Reformation: Civil Liberties, Human Rights and International Law*, New York: Syracuse University Press.

An-Naim, A. (1999) *Universal Rights, Local Remedies: Legal Protection of Human Rights under the Constitutions of African Countries*, London: Interights.

An-Naim, A. (2008) *Islam and the Secular State: Negotiating the Future of Shari'a*, Cambridge, MA and London, England: Harvard University Press.

Andersen, L. M. (1993) 'Studying across difference: Race, class, and gender in qualitative research', in H. J. Stanfield and M. D. Rurledge (eds) *Race and Ethnicity in Research Methods*, Newbury Park, CA: Sage, pp. 127–38.

Anderson, B. (1983) 'Imagined Communities', *Reflections on the Origin and Spread of Nationalism*, London: Verso Books.

Anderson, B. (1992) *Long Distance Nationalism: World Capitalism and the Rise of Identity Politics*, Amsterdam: Amsterdam Centre for South Asian Studies.

Andrews, A. (1996) 'Muslim attitudes towards political activity in the United Kingdom: A case study of Leicester', in W. Shadid and V. S. Koningsveld (eds) *Political Participation and Identities of Muslims in Non-Muslim States*, Kampen, the Netherlands: Kok Pharos, pp. 115–28.

Ansari, H. (2004) *The Infidel Within: Muslims in Britain since 1800*, London: C. Hurst & Co.

Anitha, S. and Gill, A. (2009) 'Coercion, consent and the forced marriage debate in the UK', *Feminist Legal Studies*, 17(2): 165–84.

Anthias, F. (1992) Ethnicity, Class, Gender and Migration, London: MacMillan Press.

Anthias, F. (1998) 'Evaluating "diaspora": Beyond ethnicity?' *Sociology*, 32(3): 557–80.

Anthias, F. (2001) 'The material and the symbolic in theorizing social stratification: Issues of gender, ethnicity and class', *British Journal of Sociology*, 52(3): 367–90.

Anthias, F. (2002) 'Beyond feminism and multiculturalism: Locating difference and the politics of location', *Women's Studies International Forum*, 25(3): 275–86.

Anthias, F. (2011) 'Intersections and Translocations: new paradigms for thinking about cultural diversity and social identities', *European Educational Research Journal*, 10(2): 204–17.

Anthias, F. and Yuval-Davis, N. (1989) 'Introduction', in F. Anthias and N. Yuval-Davis (eds) *Woman-Nation-State*, London: Macmillan, pp. 1–15.

Anthias, F. and Yuval-Davis, N. (1992) *Racialized Boundaries: Race, Nation, Gender, Colour and Class and the Anti-Racist Struggle*, London: Routledge.

Anwar, M. (1979) *The Myth of Return*, London: Heinemann Educational Books.

Anwar, M. (1985) *Pakistanis in Britain: A Sociological Study*, London: New Century.

Anwar, M. (1992) 'Muslims in Western Europe', in J. Nielsen (ed.) *Religion and Citizenship in Europe and the Arab World*, London: Grey Seal, pp. 37–48.

Anwar M. (1998) *Between cultures: continuity and change in the lives of young Asians*, Routledge.

Anwar, M. (2008) 'Muslims in Western states: the British experience and the way forward', *Journal of Muslim Minority Affairs,* 28(1): 125–37.

Anwar, M. and Bakhsh, Q. (2003) *British Muslims and State Policies*, University of Warwick: Centre for Research in Ethnic Relations.

Anwar, M. and Firsila, S. (2004) 'Muslim women and experiences of discrimination in Britain', in J. Blaschke (ed.) *Multi-Level Discrimination of Muslim Women in Europe* (second edition), Berlin: Parabolis, pp. 217–64.

Airaksinen, T. (1988) 'An analysis of coercion', *Journal of Peace Research*, 25(3): 213–27.

Arthurs, H. W. (1985) *'Without the Law': Administrative Justice and Legal Pluralism in Nineteenth-Century England*, Toronto: University of Toronto Press.

Asad, T. (2003) *Foundations of the Secular. Christianity, Islam, Modernity*, Stanford: Stanford University.

Atkinson, P. and Silverman, D. (1997) 'Kundera's immortality: The interview society and the invention of the self', *Qualitative Inquiry*, 3(1): 304–25.

Auerbach, J. S. (1983) *Justice without Law*, New York: Oxford University Press.

Austin, J. (1995 [1832]) *The Province of Jurisprudence Determined*, W. Rumble (ed.) Cambridge: Cambridge University Press (first published 1832).

Badawi, Z. (1995) 'Muslim justice in a secular state', in M. King (ed.) *God's Law Versus State Law*, London: Grey Seal, pp. 73–80.

Badawi, Z. (1996) 'Muslim Justice in a secular state', in M. King (ed.) *God's law versus state law: the construction of an Islamic identity in western Europe*, Michigan: University of Michigan, Grey Seal, pp. 73–89.

Bader, V. (2009) 'Secularism, public reason or moderately agonistic democracy?' in B. G. Levey and T. Modood (eds) *Secularism, Religion and Multicultural Citizenship*, Cambridge: Cambridge University Press.

Baderin, M. A. (2003) *International Human Rights and Islamic Law*, Oxford and London: Oxford University Press.

Badr, G. M. (1978) 'Islamic Law: Its relation to other legal systems', *American Journal of Comparative Law*, pp. 187–209.

Badran, M. (2009) *Feminism in Islam, Secular and Religious Convergences*, London: Oneworld.

Bagguley, P. and Hussain, Y. (2008) *Riotous Citizens: Ethnic Conflict in Multicultural Britain*, Aldershot: Ashgate.

Bakht, N. (2004) 'Family arbitration using Sharia Law: Examining Ontario's Arbitration Act and its impact on women', *Muslim World Journal of Human Rights*, 1(1): pp. 30–45.

Bakht, N. (March 2005) 'Arbitration, religion and family law: Private justice on the backs of women', *National Association of Women and the Law*, available at http://www.nawl.ca/ns/en/publications.html, accessed on 30 July 2012.

Bakht, N. (2006) 'Were Muslim barbarians really knocking on the gates of Ontario? The religious arbitration controversy – another perspective', *Ottawa Law Review*, 40th anniversary volume: 67–82.

Bainham, A. (1995) 'Family law in a pluralistic society', *Journal of Law and Society*, 22(4): 234–47.

Baker, C. (1998) 'Membership categorization and interview accounts', in D. Silverman (ed.) *Qualitative Research – Theory, Method, and Practice*, London: Sage, pp. 12–24.

Balchin, C. (2009) *Plural Legal Orders and Human Rights*, New York: International Council on Human Rights.

Balchin, C. (2010) 'Negotiating bliss', *openDemocracy*, 8 March, available at http://www.opendemocracy.net/5050/cassandra-balchin/negotiating-bliss.

Ballard, R. (1994) 'The emergence of Desh Pardesh', in R. Ballard (ed.) *Desh Pardesh: The South Asian Presence in Britain*, London: C. Hurst & Co. Ltd.

Ballard, R. (1996) 'Islam and the construction of Europe', in W. A. R. Shadid and P. S. van Koningsveld (eds) *Muslims in the Margin: Political Responses to the Presence of Islam in Western Europe*, Kampen: Kok Pharos Publishers, pp. 15–51.

Ballard, R. (2005) 'Popular Islam in Northern Pakistan and its reconstruction in urban Britain', in J. Malik and J. Hinnels (eds) *Sufism in the West*, London: Routledge Curzon, pp. 160–86.

Ballard, R. (2006) 'Ethnic diversity and the delivery of justice: The challenge of plurality', in P. Shah and W. Menski (eds) *Migration, Diasporas and Legal Systems in Europe*, London: Routledge.

Ballard, R. (2008) 'Inside and outside: Contrasting perspectives on the dynamics of kinship and marriage in contemporary South Asian transnational networks', in R. Grillo (ed.) *The Family in Question: Immigrants and Minorities in Multicultural Europe*, Amsterdam: University of Amsterdam Press, pp. 37–70.

Ballard, R. (2010) 'Did Arden, LJ's conclusions with respect to the facts in Khan v Khan (2007) EWCA Civ 399 actually live up to the principles of her own dicta'. A copy of can be obtained at www.casas/commentary-on-pluri-legal-issues.com. Last accessed on 20th August 2012.

Banda, F. (2003) 'Global standards: Local values', *International Journal of Law, Policy and the Family*, 17(1): 1–27.

Banakar, R. (2000) 'Reflections on the methodological issues of the sociology of law', *Journal of Law and Society*, 27(2): 273–95.

Banakar, R. (2008) 'The politics of legal cultures', *Retfaerd Argang*, 31 NR. 4/123.

Bano, S. (2007) 'Muslim family justice and human rights: The experience of British Muslim women', *Journal of Comparative Law*, 2(2): 35–68.

Bano, S. (2008) 'In pursuit of Religious and Legal Diversity: A Response to the Archbishop of Canterbury and the Sharia Debate in Britain,' *Ecclesiastical Law Journal*, 10: 283–309.

Bano, S. (2010) 'Asking the Law questions: Agency and Muslim women in', in S. Sayyid and A. K. Vakil (eds) *Thinking through Islamaphobia: Global Perspectives*, Hurst, pp. 135–56.

Bano, S. (2012) *An Exploratory Study of Shariah Councils in England with respect to Family Law*, University of Reading and the Ministry of Justice: University of Reading.

Banton, M. (1991) 'The race relations problematic', *British Journal of Sociology*, 42(1): 115–30.

Barker, R. (1991) 'Citizenship, legitimacy and cultural pluralism in Britain', in R. Nile (ed.) *Immigration and the Politics of Ethnicity and Race in Australia and Britain*, London: Institute of Commonwealth Studies, pp. 17–43.

Barlas, A. (2006) *Believing Women in Islam: Unreading Patriarchal Interpretations of the Qu'ran*, Austin: University of Texas Press.

Barnes, B. (1994) 'Conflict resolution across cultures: A Hawaii perspective and a Pacific mediation model', *Mediation Quarterly*, 12(2), Winter, pp. 14–24.

Barnett, A. (2000) Getting a 'Get' – the limits of law's authority? *N v. N* (Jurisdiction: Pre-nuptial agreement) [1999] 2 F.L.R. 745', *Feminist Legal Studies*, 8(2): 241–54.

Basdevant-Gaudemet, B. (2000) 'The legal status of Islam in France', in S. Ferrari and A. Bradney (eds) *Islam and European Legal Systems*, Aldershot: Dartmouth Publishing Company, pp. 52–67.

Basit, T. (1996) '"Obviously I'll have an arranged marriage": Muslim marriage in the British context', *Muslim Education Quarterly*, 13(2): 4–19.

Baszanger, I. and Dodier, N. (1998) 'Ethnography: Relating the part to the whole', in D. Silverman (ed.) *Qualitative Research – Theory, Method, and Practice*, London: Sage, pp. 67–88.

Bauman, Z. (1991) *Modernity and Ambivalence*, Cambridge: Polity.

Bauman, Z. (1999) 'On universal morality and the morality of universalism', in C. Lund (ed.) *Development and Human Rights: Negotiating Justice in Changing Societies*, London: Frank Cass Publishers, pp. 82–102.

Bay, C. (1978) 'From contract to community: Thoughts on liberalism and postindustrial society', in F. R. Dallymar (ed.) *From Contract to Community*, New York: Marcel Inc., pp. 78–92.

Benda-Beckmann, v F., Benda-Beckmann, K. and Griffiths, A. (2005) *Mobile People, Mobile Law: Expanding Legal Relations in a Contracting World*, Great Britain: Asgate.

Benhabib, S. (1986) *Critique, Norm and Utopia: A Study of the Foundations of Critical Theory*, New York: Columbia University Press.

Benhabib, S. (2002) *The Claims of Culture: Equality and Diversity in the Global Age*, Princeton, New Jersey: Princeton University Press.

Bennett, D. (1998) 'Introduction', in D. Bennett (ed.) *Multicultural States: Rethinking Difference and Identity*, London: Routledge, pp. 2–18.

Bennett, D. and Bhabha, H. (1998) 'Liberalism and minority culture: Reflections on "cultures in between"', in D. Bennet (ed) *Multicultural States: Rethinking Difference and Identity*, London: Routledge, pp. 37–44.

Bentham, J. (1996 [1798]) 'The principles of morals and legislation', in J. H. Burns and H. L. A. Hart (eds) *The Collected Works of Jeremy Bentham*, New York: Oxford University Press.

Benton, L. (1994) 'Beyond legal pluralism: Towards a new approach to law in the informal sector', *Social and Legal Studies*, 3(2): 223–42.

Berg, J. (1994) 'The Jewish family mediation service – lessons for the future', *Family Mediation*, 4(2): 10–14.

Berger, N. (2002) 'Putting gender and sexuality on the agenda: Queer theory and legal politics', in R. Banakar and M. Travers (eds) *Introduction to Law and Social Theory*, Oxford: Hart Publishing, pp. 173–88.

Bernard, L. (1994) 'Legal and historical reflections on the position of Muslim populations under non-Muslim rule', in L. Bernard and D. Schnapper (eds) *Muslims in Europe*, London and New York: Pinter, pp. 68–82.

Bhabba, J. and Shutter, S. (1994) *Women's Movement: Women under Immigration, Nationality and Refugee Law*, Stoke-on-Trent: Trentham Books.

Bhabha, H. (1994) *The Location of Culture*, London: Routledge.

Bhabha, H. (1998) 'Cultures in between', in D. Bennet (ed.) *Multicultural States: Rethinking Difference and Identity*, London: Routledge, pp. 29–36.

Bhachu, P. (1985) *Twice Migrants: East African Sikh Settlers in Britain*, Routledge.

Bhachu, P. (1999) 'Multiple-Migrants and Multiple Diasporas: Cultural Reproduction and Transformations among British South Asian Women in 1990s Britain,' in C. Peteivich (ed.) *The Expanding Landscape: South Asians in the Diaspora*. Association of Asian Studies Monograph Series, University of Michigan Press, pp. 34–67.

Bhandar, B. (2009) 'The Ties that Bind: multiculturalism and secularism reconsidered', *Journal of Law and Society*, 36(2): 301–26.

Bharatiya, V. P. (1996) *Syed Khalid Rasheed's Muslim Law*, Lucknow: Eastern Book Company.

Bhatt, C. (2006) 'The fetish of the margins: Religious absolutism, anti-racism and postcolonial silence', *New Formations*, 59: 98–115.

Bhimji, F. (2009) 'Identities and Agency in Religious Spheres: A Study of British Muslim Women's Experience', *Gender, Place, and Culture: A Journal of Feminist Geography*, 16(4): 365–80.

Bhopal, K. (1998) 'How Gender and Ethnicity Intersect: The Significance of Education, Employment and Marital Status' *Sociological Research Online*, 3(3), http://www.socresonline.org.uk/3/3/6.html

Bhopal, K. (1999) 'South Asian women and arranged marriages in East London', in R. Barrot, H. Bradley and S. Fenton (eds) *Ethnicity, Gender and Social Change*, New York: St Martin's Press, pp. 36–45.

Bilgrami, A. (2004) 'Secularism and relativism', *Boundary*, 31(2): 173–96.

Binion, G. (1991) 'On women, marriage, family, and the traditions of political thought', *Law and Society Review*, 25(2): 445–61.

Birt, Y. (2010) 'Governing Muslims after 9/11', in S. Sayyid and A. K. Vakil (eds) *Thinking through Islamaphobia: Global Perspectives*, London: Hurst, pp. 117–28.

Blackett, R. (2009) 'The status of "religious courts" in English law', *Decisions, Decisions: Disputes and International Arbitration Newsletter*, 11–19.

Bloor, M. (1998) 'Addressing social problems through qualitative research', in D. Silverman (ed.) *Qualitative Research – Theory, Method, and Practice*, London: Sage, pp. 305–25.

Bock, G. and James, S. (1992) *Beyond Equality and Difference: Citizenship, Feminist Politics and Female Subjectivity*, London: Routledge.

Booth, P. (2008) 'Judging Sharia', *Family Law*, 38: 935–39.

Bonnell, V. and Hunt, L. (1999) *Beyond the Cultural Turn: New Directions in the Study of Society and Culture*, Berkeley: University of California Press.

Boshoff, A. (2007) 'Woman as the subject of (family) law', in R. Hunter and S. Cowan (eds) *Choice and Consent, Feminist Engagements with Law and Subjectivity*, New York: Routledge-Cavendish.

Bottomley, A. (1984) 'Resolving family disputes: A critical view', in M. D. A. Freeman (ed.) *State, Law and the Family: Critical Perspective*, Oxford: Sweet & Maxwell, pp. 13–22.

Bottomley, A. and Conaghan, J. (1993) *Feminist Legal Theory and Legal Strategy*, Oxford: Blackwell.

Bowen, J. (2004) 'Muslims and citizens: France's headscarf controversy', *Boston Review*, 29(February/March): 31–5.

Bowen, J. (2011) 'How could English courts recognize Shariah?' *St Thomas Law Review*, 7(3): 411–35.

Boyd, S. (1997) *Challenging the Public/Private Divide: Feminism, Law and Public Policy*, Toronto: University of Toronto Press.

Boyd, S. (2004) *Dispute Resolution in Family Law: Protecting Choice, Promoting Inclusion*, Ministry of the Attorney General.

Bradby, B. (1999) 'Negotiating marriage: Young Punjabi women's assessments of their individual and family interests' in R. Barrot, H. Bradley and S. Fenton (eds) *Ethnicity, Gender and Social Change*, New York: St. Martin's Press, pp. 152–66.

Brah, A. (1993) '"Race" and "culture" in the gendering of the labour markets: South Asian young Muslim women and the labour market', *New Community*, 19(3): 441–58.

Brah, A. (1996) *Cartographies of Diaspora and Contesting Identities*, New York: Routledge.

Brah, A. (2005) 'Empirical interrogations', *Feminist Review*, Issue 78.

Brannen, J. (1988) *New Mothers at Work: Employment and Childcare*, London: Unwin Hyman.

Braude, B. and Lewis, B. (1982) *Christians and Jews in the Ottoman Empire: The Functioning of a Plural Society*, New York: Holmes and Meier Publishers.

Bredal, A. (2005) 'Arranged marriages as a multicultural battle field', in M. Andersson, Y. Lithman and O. Sernhede (eds) *Youth, Otherness, and the Plural City: Modes of Belonging and Social Life*, Gothenburg: Daidalos, pp. 67–89.

Breton, S. (1991) *The Governance of Ethnic Communities*, New York: Greenwich Press.

Brewer, J. D. (1990) 'Sensitivity as a problem in field research: A study of routine policing in Northern Ireland', *American Behavioral Scientist*, 33(5): 578–93.

British Muslims Monthly Survey (1998) 'Youths riot in Bradford', 6(11): 7–8.

Brunt, R. (1989) 'The politics of identity', in S. Hall and M. Jacques (eds) *New Times*, London: Lawrence & Wishart, pp. 150–59.

Buchler, A. (2011) *Islamic Law in Europe? Legal Pluralism and its Limits in European Family Laws*, England: Ashgate.

Bulmer, M. (1982) 'Ethical problems in social research: The case of covert participant observation', in M. Bulmer (ed.) *Social Research Ethics*, London: Macmillan, p. 3012.

Bunt, G. (1998) 'Decision-making concerns in British Islamic environments', *Islam and Christian–Muslim Relations*, 19(1): 103–13.

Bunt, G. (2006) 'Towards an Islamic Information Revolution?', in L. Poole and J. Richardson (eds) *Muslims in the News Media*, London: IB Tauris, pp. 153–64.

Burlet, S. and Reid, H. (1996) 'Riots, representation and responsibilities: the role of young men in Pakistani-heritage Muslim communities', in W. A. R. Shahid and P. S. v. Koninsveld (eds) *Political Participation and Identities of Muslims in non-Muslim States, Kampen*, Netherlands: Kok Pahros, pp. 144–57.

Burlet, S. and Reid, H. (1998) 'A gendered uprising: Political representation and minority ethnic communities', *Ethnic and Racial Studies*, 21(2): 271–87.

Busch, M. L. (2007) 'Overlapping institutions, forum shopping and dispute settlement in international trade', *International Organisation*, 61(4): 735–61.

Butler, C. (1999) 'Cultural diversity and religious conformity: Dimension of social change among second-generation Muslim Women' in R. Barrot, H. Bradley and S. Fenton (eds) *Ethnicity, Gender and Social Change*, New York: St. Martin's Press, pp. 134–56.

Cantle, T. (2001) *Community Cohesion: A Report of the Independent Review Team*, London: Home Office.

Carroll, L. (1997) 'Muslim women and "Islamic divorce" in England', *Journal of Muslim Minority Affairs*, 17(1): 97–115.

Castells, M. (1997) *The Rise of the Network Society*, Oxford: Basil Blackwell.

Castells, M. and Michalak, L. (eds) (2004) *Islam and the Changing Identity of Europe*, New York: University Press of America, Lexington Books.

Cesari, J. and McLoughlin, S. (eds) (2005) *European Muslims and the Secular State*, Aldershot: Ashgate.

Charity Commission (2009) *Survey of Mosques in England and Wales*, Birmingham: BMG Research.

Charsley, K. (2005a) 'Unhappy husbands: Masculinity and migration in transnational Pakistani marriages', *Journal of the Royal Anthropological Institute*, 11(1): 85–105.

Charsley, K. (2005b) 'Vulnerable brides and transnational Ghar Damads, gender, risk and "adjustment" among Pakistani marriage migrants to Britain', *Indian Journal of Gender Studies*, 12(2–3): 381–406.

Charsley, K. (2007) 'Risk, trust, gender and transnational cousin marriage among British Pakistanis', *Ethnic and Racial Studies*, 30(6): 1117–31.

Charsley, K. and Shaw, A. (2006) 'South Asian transnational marriages in comparative perspective', *Global Networks*, 6(4): 34–48.

Charusheela, S. (2004) 'Postcolonial Thought, Postmodernism, and Economics: Questions of Ontology and Ethics,' in Zein-Elabdin and Charusheela (eds) *Postcolonialism meets Economics*, Routledge, pp. 40–58.

Chetkovich, C. (2004) 'Women's agency in a context of oppression: Assessing strategies for personal action and public policy', *Hypatia*, 19(4): 12–141.

Chiba, M. (1986) *Asian Indigenous Law*, London: Kegan Paul.

Coffey, A. (1999) *The Ethnographic Self: Fieldwork and the Representation of Identity*, London: Sage.

Cohen, J., Howard, M. and Nussbaum, C. M. (1999) 'Introduction: Feminism, multiculturalism, and human equality', in J. Cohen, M. Howard and C. M. Nussbaum (eds) *Is Multiculturalism Bad for Women?* Princeton, NJ: Princeton University Press, pp. 3–5.

Collier, F. J. and Starr, J. (1989) *History and Power in the Study of Law: New Directions in Legal Anthropology*, Ithaca and London: Cornell University Press.

Collins, P. (1986) 'Learning from the outsider within: The sociological significance of Black feminist thought', *Social Problems*, 33(6): 14–32.

Collins, P. H. (1990) *Black Feminist Thought: Knowledge, Consciousness and the Politics of Empowerment*, London: HarperCollins.

Collins, P. H. (2000) *Black Feminist Thought: Knowledge, Consciousness, and the Politics of Empowerment*, New York: Routledge.

Comaroff, L. J. and Roberts, A. S. (1981) *Rules and Processes: The Cultural Logic of Dispute in an African Context*, Chicago and London: University of Chicago Press.

Commission on British Muslims and Islamophobia (1997) *Islamophobia: A Challenge for Us All*, Runnymede Trust.

Council of Europe (2005) *Forced Marriages in Council of Europe Member States*, http://www.coe.int/T/E/Human_Rights/Equality/PDF_CDEG%282005%291_E.pdf

Cooper, D. (2000) 'And you can't find me nowhere: Relocating identity and structure within equality jurisprudence', *Journal of Law and Society*, 27(2): 249–72.

Cooper, D. (2004) *Challenging Diversity, Rethinking Equality and the Value of Difference*, Cambridge: Cambridge University Press.

Cotterrell, R. (1995) *Law's Community: Legal Theory in Sociological Perspective*, Oxford: Clarendon Press.

Cotterrell, R. (1998) 'Why must legal ideas be interpreted sociologically', *Journal of Law and Society*, 25(2): 171–95.

Cowan, K. J., Dembour, M. and Wilson, R. (eds) (2001) *Culture and Rights: Anthropological Perspectives*, Cambridge: Cambridge University Press.

Cownie, F. and Bradney, A. (1996) *English Legal System in Context*, London: Butterworths.

Crenshaw, K. (1989) 'Demarginalizing the intersection of race and sex: A black feminist critique of antidiscrimination doctrine', *Feminist Theory and Antiracist Politics*, University of Chicago Forum, 139.

Crenshaw, K. (1991) 'Mapping the margins: Intersectionality, identity politics, and violence against women of color', *Stanford Law Review*, 43(6): 1241–99.

Dahl, T. S. (1987) *Women's Law: An Introduction to Feminist Jurisprudence*, Osli: Norwegian University Press.

Daicoff, S. (2006) 'Law as a healing profession: The comprehensive law movement', *Pepperdine Dispute Resolution Law Journal*, 6(1): 21–30.

Dale, A. Shaheen, N. Kalra, V. and Fieldhouse, E. (2002) 'Routes into education and employment for young Pakistanis and Bangladeshi women in the UK', *Ethnic and Racial Studies*, 25(6): 942–68.

Dale, A. and Ahmed, S. (2008) Migration, marriage and employment amongst Indian, Pakistani and Bangladeshi residents in the UK – CCSR Paper 2008–02.

Davies, M. (2002) *Asking the Law Question: The Dissolution Of Legal Theory*, Sydney: Lawbook Co.

Davis, G. and Roberts, M. (1988) *Access to Agreement: A Consumer Study of Mediation in Family Disputes*, Milton Keynes: Open University Press.

Derrida, J. (1990) 'Force of law: The "mystical foundation of authority"', *Cardozo Law Review*, 11: 919–35.

Drakopoulou, M. (2007) 'Feminism and consent: A genealogical inquiry', in R. Hunter and S. Cowan (eds) *Choice and Consent: Feminist Engagements with Law and Subjectivity*, London: Routledge, pp. 9–39.

Dobash, E. and Dobash, R. (1992) *Women, Violence and Social Change*, London: Routledge.

Diduck, A. and Kaganas, F. (1999) *Family Law, Gender and the State*, Oxford and Portland, OR: Hart Publishing.

Diduck, A. and O'Donovan, K. (eds.) (2006) *Feminist Perspectives on Family Law*, New York and London: Routledge-Cavendish.

Dien, I. (2004) *Islamic Law, From Historical foundation to contemporary practice*, Edinburgh: Edinburgh University Press.

Dingwall, R. and Eekelaar, J. (eds) (1988) *Divorce, Mediation and the Legal Process*, Oxford: Clarendon Press.

Doi, A. R. (1984) *Shariah: The Islamic Law*, London: Ta-Ha Publishers.

Doi, A. R. (2008) *Shariah: Islamic Law*, London: Ta-Ha Publishers.

Douglas, G. F., Gilliat-Ray, S., Doe, N., Sandberg, R. and Khan, A. (2011) *Social Cohesion and Civil Law: Marriage, Divorce and Religious Courts*, Cardiff University.

Dunleavy, P. and O'Leary, B. (1987) *Theories of the State*, London: Macmillan.

Dworkin, R. (1986) *Law's Empire*, London: Fontana.

Dwyer, C. (2000) 'Negotiating diasporic identities: Young British South Asian Muslim Women', *Women's Studies International Forum*, 23(4): 475–86.

Dwyer, C. and Meyer, A. (1995) 'Institutionalisation of Islam in the Netherlands and in the UK: the case of Islamic schools', *New Community*, 21(1): 37–54.

Eade, J. (1996) 'Nationalism, community and the Islamization of space in London', in D. B. Metcalf (ed.) *Making Muslim Space in North America and Europe*, Berkeley: University of California Press, pp. 217–34.

Edwards, D. (1990) *Discourse and Cognition*, London: Sage.

Eekelaar, J. (2000) 'Uncovering social obligations: Family law and the responsible citizen', in M. Maclean (ed.) *Making Law for Families*, Oxford: Hart Publishing, pp. 45–60.

Eekelaar, J. (2011) 'The Arbitration and Mediation Services (Equality) Bill 2011', 41 *Family Law* 1209.

Eekelaar, J. (2012) 'Family law – what family law?' in R. Probert and C. Barton (eds) *Fifty Years in Family Law: Essays for Stephen Cretney*, Cambridge: Intersentia, pp. 221–36.

Eekelaar, J. and Maclean, M. (2004) 'Marriage and the moral bases of personal relationships', *Journal of Law and Society*, 31(4): 510–38.

Ehrlich, E. (1936) *Fundamental Principles of the Sociology of Law*, trans by W. L. Moll, Cambridge, MA: Harvard University Press.

El-Nimr, (1996) 'Women in Islamic Law', in M. Yamani (ed.) *Feminism and Islam, Legal and Literary Perspectives*, Ithaca Press, pp. 87–102.

El Saadawi, N. (1997) *Women At Point Zero*, New York: Zed Books.

Engineer, A. A. (1992) *Rights of Women in Islam*, London: Sterling Publishers.

Engineer, A. (1995) *The Rights of Women in Islam*, New Delhi: Sterling.

Engineer, A. (2005) *The Qu'ran, Women and Modern Society*, Slough Berkshire, New Dawn Press Group.

Engle, M. S. (2005) 'Human Rights and Gender Violence: Translating International Law Into Local Justice', Chicago: The University of Chicago Press.

Enright, M. (2009) 'Choice, culture and the politics of belonging: The emerging law of forced and arranged marriage', *The Modern Law Review*, 72(3): 331–59.

Eriksen, T. (2009) *Paradoxes of Cultural Recognition*, London: Ashgate.

Esposito, J. L. (1982) *Women in Muslim Family Law*, New York: Syracuse University Press.

Esposito, J. L. (1988) *Islam: The Straight Path*, New York: Oxford University Press.

Esposito, J. L. (2002) *Unholy War: Terror in the Name of Islam*, Oxford: Oxford University Press.

Estin, A. (2008) 'Toward a multicultural family law', in A. L. Estin (ed.) *The Multi-Cultural Family*, England: Ashgate, pp. 5–33.

Evans, S. and Bowlby, S. (2000) 'Crossing boundaries: Racialised gendering and the labour market experiences of Pakistani migrant women in Britain', *Women's Studies International Forum*, 23(4): 461–74.

Fadl, K. A. E. (1994) 'Islamic law and Muslim minorities: The juristic discourse on Muslim minorities from the 2nd/8th to the 11th/17th centuries', *Islamic Law and Society*, 1(2): 141–87.

FAIR (2002) *Employment Status in Relation to Statutory Employment Rights*, Muslim College, Al-Khoei Foundation.

Faith, S. and Levine, D. (2003) *Getting Your Get*, London: Cissanell Publications.

Ferrari, S. and Bradney, A. (eds) (2000) *Islam and European Legal Systems*, Aldershot: Ashgate.

Festiner, W., Abel, R. L. and Sarat, A. (1980) 'The Emergence and Transformation of Disputes: Naming, Blaming, Claiming', *Law and Society Review*, 15(3): 627–55.

Festzer, J. S. and Soper, J. C. (2004) *Muslims and the State in Britain, France and Germany*, Cambridge University Press.

Fineman, M. A. and Thomsaden, N. S. (1991) *At the Boundaries of Law: Feminism and Legal Theory*, London: Routledge.

Finnis, J. (1986) *Natural Law and Natural Rights*, Oxford: Clarendon Press.

Fiss, O. (1996) *Liberalism Divided*, USA: Westview Press.

Fishman, S. (2006) *Fiqh al-Aqualliyyat- Current Trends in Islamist Ideology*, Center on Islam, Democracy and the Future of the Muslim World, Series No.1. Paper No. 2.

Fitzpatrick, P. (1984) 'Law and societies', *Osgoode Hall Law Journal*, 22: 115–38.

Fitzpatrick, P. (1992a) 'The impossibility of popular justice', *Social and Legal Studies*, 1(2): 199–215.

Fitzpatrick, P. (1992b) *The Mythology of Modern Law*, London: Routledge.

Fitzpatrick, P. (1994) 'Being social in socio-legal studies', *Journal of Law and Society*, 21: 105–12.

Fitzpatrick, P. (2009) 'Law as theory: Constitutive thought in the formation of (legal) practice', *Socio-Legal Review*, 5(2): 1–20.

Fletcher, R. (2002) 'Feminist legal theory', in R. Banakar and M. Travers (eds) *An Introduction to Law and Social Theory*, Oxford: Hart Publishing, pp. 135–54.

Foblets, M. C. (ed.) (2008) *Islam and Europe: Challenges and Opportunities*, Leuven: Leuven University Press.

Foblets, M. C. and Carlier, J. (eds) (2009) *Islam and Europe: Crises are Challenges*, Leuven: Leuven University Press.

Foucault, M. (1977) *Discipline and Punish: The Birth of the Prison*, London: Penguin.

Foucault, M. (1997 [1980]) 'On the government of the living', in P. Rabinow (ed.) *Essential Works of Foucault, Volume 1, Ethics, Subjectivity and Truth*, New York: New Press, pp. 81–5.

Foucault, M. (1990) *The History of Sexuality: An Introduction, Volume I*, London: Penguin.

Fournier, P. (2010) *Muslim Marriage in Western Courts: Lost in Transplantation*, England: Ashgate.

Franck, J. (2009) '"So hedge therefore, who join forever": Understanding the interrelation of no-fault divorce and premarital contracts', *International Journal of Law, Policy and the Family*, 23(3): 235–76.

Frank, K. (2006) 'Agency', *Anthropological Theory*, 6(3): 281–302.

Fraser, N. (1989) *Unruly Discourses: Power, Discourse and Gender in Contemporary Social Theory*, Cambridge: Polity Press.

Frazer, N. and Lacey, N. (1993) *Politics of the Community*, London: Harvester Wheatsheaf.

Fredriksen, K. J. (2010) 'Mahr (dower) as a bargaining tool in a European context: A comparison of Dutch and Norwegian judicial decisions', in R. A. Mehdi and J. S. Nielsen (eds) *Embedding Mahr in the European Legal System*, Copenhagen: DJOF Publishing, pp. 65–78.

Freeman, M. (1985) 'Towards a critical theory of family law', *Current Legal Problems*, 38(4): 144–53.

Frow, J. (1995) *Cultural Studies and Cultural Value*, Oxford: Oxford University Press.

Fyzee, A. (1963) *A Modern Approach to Islam*, Bombay: Asia Publishing House.

Galanter, M. (1981) 'Justice in many rooms: Courts, private ordering and indigenous law', *Journal of Legal Pluralism and Unofficial Law*, 19(1): 69–83.

Gale, R. (2004) 'The multicultural city and the politics of religious architecture: Urban planning, mosques and meaning-making in Birmingham, UK', *Built Environment*, 30(1): 18–32.

Gardner, K. and Grillo, R. (2002) *Transnational Migration and Household Ritual*, Global Networks, 2(1).

Gearing, M. (2011) *Jivraj v Hashwani: A Pro-Choice, Corrective Ruling from the Supreme Court*, Kluwer Arbitration Blog, available at http://kluwerarbitrationblog.com/, accessed on 26 October 2011.

Geaves, R. (1996a) 'Cult, charisma, community: The arrival of Sufi Pirs and their impact on muslims in Britain', *Journal of Muslim Minority Affairs*, 16(2): 169–92.

Geaves, R. (1996b) *Sectarian Influences within Islam in Britain with Reference to the Concepts of 'Ummah' and 'Community'*, Leeds: Department of Theology and Religious Studies, University of Leeds.

Geertz, C. (1973) *The Interpretation of Culture: Selected Essays*, New York: Basic Books.

Gellner, E. (1983) *Nations and Nationalism*, Ithaca, New York: Cornell University Press.

Genn, H. (1999) *What People Do and Think about Going to Law*, Oxford: Hart Publishing.

Gilbert, N. (2001) *Researching Social Life*, Oxford: Sage.

Giles, K. (1997) *Allah in the West: Islamic Movements in America and Europe*, Cambridge: Polity Press.

Gilroy, P. (1987) *There Ain't No Black in the Union Jack*, London: Verso.

Gillessen, J. (1989) 'Return to legal pluralism: Twenty years later', *Journal of Legal Pluralism and Unofficial Law*, 28: 149–57.

Gilliat-Ray, S. (1998) 'Multiculturalism and identity: Their relationship for British Muslims', *Journal of Muslim Minority Affairs*, 18(2): 347–54.

Gilliat-Ray, S. (2010) *Muslims in Britain: An Introduction*, Cambridge University Press.

Glaser, B. G. and Strauss, A. L. (1967) *The Discovery of Grounded Theory*, Chicago: Aldine.

Goddard, V. (ed.) (2000) *Gender, Agency and Change: Anthropological Perspectives*, New York: Routledge.

Goodhart, D. (2004) 'Discomfort strangers', *The Guardian*, Tuesday, February 24.

Goodwin, R., Adatia, K., Sinhal, H., Cramer, D. and Elus, P. (1997) *Social Support and Marital Well-Being in an Asian Community*, London: Joseph Rowntree Foundation.

Goolam, H. (2001) 'Gender equality in Islamic family law: Dispelling common misconceptions and misunderstandings', *International Family Law*, pp. 182–90.

Gopin, M. (2002) *Holy War, Holy Peace: How Religion Can Bring Peace to the Middle East*, Oxford: Oxford University Press.

Greatbatch, D. and Dingwall, R. (1993) 'Who is in charge? Rhetoric and evidence in the study of mediation', *Journal of Social Welfare and Family Law*, 17: 199–206.

Greenhouse, C. (1998) 'Legal pluralism and cultural difference: What is the difference? A Response to Professor Woodman', *Journal of Legal Pluralism and Unofficial Law*, 42: 61–71.

Greenhouse, C. J. and Kheshti, R. (1998) 'Introduction: The Ethnography of Democracy and Difference', in C. J. Greenhouse and R. Khesti (eds.) *Democracy and Ethnography: Constructing Identities in Multicultural Liberal States*, New York: State University of New York Press, pp. 1–25.

Greenhouse, C. and Strijbosch, F. (1993) 'Legal pluralism in industrialized societies', *Journal of Legal Pluralism and Unofficial Law*, 33.

Griffin, G. (2007) 'What mode marriage? Women's partner choice in British Asian cultural representation', *Women: A Cultural Review*, 18(1): 1–18.

Griffiths, A. (1997) *In the Shadow of Marriage: Gender and Justice in an African Community* (University of Chicago Press).

Griffiths, A. (1999) 'In the shadow of marriage: Gender and justice in an African community', Book review in *Feminist Legal Studies*, 7(3): 351–3.

Griffiths, A. (2001) 'Gendering culture: Towards a plural perspective on Kwena women's rights', in J. K. Cowan, M.-B. Dembour and R. A. Wilson (eds) *Culture and Rights: Anthropological Perspectives*, Cambridge: Cambridge University Press, pp. 102–27.

Griffiths, A. (2002) 'Remaking law: Gender, ethnography and legal discourse' (Review article of 'Pronouncing and persevering: Gender and the discourses of disputing in an African Islamic court', by S. Hirsh, University of Chicago Press, 1998), *Law and Society Review*, 35(2): 101–14.

Griffiths, A. (2003) '*Writing Women's World's: An Anthropological Perspective on Legal Research*', Paper for workshop on Socio-Legal Research Methods, 3–4 April, Onati International Institute for the Sociology of Law, unpublished paper.

Griffiths, A. (2005) 'Using Ethnography as a Tool in Legal Research: An Anthropological Perspective', in Reza Banakar and Max Travers (eds) *Theory and Method in Socio-Legal Research* (Hart Publishing) pp. 113–131.

Griffiths, J. (1986) 'What is legal pluralism?' *Journal of Legal Pluralism and Unofficial Law*, 24: 1–56.

Grillo, T. (1991) 'The mediation alternative: Process dangers for women', *The Yale Law Journal*, 100(6): 1545–610.

Gover, K. (2008) *Legal Pluralism and State-Indigenous Relations in Western Settler Societies*, Geneva: ICHRP.

Gulliver, P. H. (1963) *Social Control in an African Society*, London: Routledge and Kegan Paul.

Gulliver, P. H. (1979) *Disputes and Negotiations: A Cross-Cultural Perspective*, New York: Academic Press.

Gupta, R. (2003) 'Some recurring themes: Southall Black Sisters, 1979–2003 – and still going strong', in R. Gupta (ed.) *From Homebreakers to Jailbreakers: Southall Black Sisters*, London: Zed Books, pp. 1–27.

Habermas, J. (1996) *Between Facts and Norms: Contributions to a Discourse Theory of Law and Democracy* (trans. W. Rehg), Cambridge, MA: MIT Press.

Haeri, S. (1990) 'Divorce in contemporary Iran: A male prerogative in self-will', in C. Mallat and J. Connors (eds) *Islamic Family Law*, Kluwer International: Graham and Trotman, pp. 215–25.

Hale, B. (2004) 'Unmarried couples in family law', *Family Law*, 34: 391–474.
Hall, S. (1992) 'The West and the rest: Discourse and power', in S. Hall and B. Gieben (eds) *Formations of Modernity*, Cambridge: Polity Press, pp. 105–22.
Hall, S. (1996a) 'When was the "post-colonial" thinking at the limit', in I. Chambers and L. Curti (ed.) *The Post-Colonial Question*, London: Routledge, pp. 116–33.
Hall, S. (1996b) 'Politics of identity', in T. Ranger, Y. Samad and O. Stuart (eds) *Culture, Identity and Politics*, Aldershot: Avebury, pp. 1–18.
Hall, S. (1997) *Representation: Cultural Representations and Signifying Practices*. London: SAGE Publications Ltd.
Hall, S. (2000) 'The multi-cultural question', in B. Hesse (ed.) *Un/settled Multiculturalisms: Diasporas, Entanglements, Transruptions*, Zed Books, pp. 209–36.
Hallaq, W. (1999) *A History of Islamic Law Thought*, Cambridge: Cambridge University Press.
Hallaq, W. (2001) *Authority, Continuity and Change in Islamic Law*, Cambridge University Press.
Hamilton, C. (1995) *Family, Law and Religion*, Oxford: Sweet & Maxwell.
Hammersley, M. and Atkinson, P. (1983) *Ethnography: Principles in Practice*, London: Tavistock.
Handler, J. (1990) *Law and the Search for Community*, Philadelphia: University of Pennsylvania Press.
Harding, S. (1987) *Feminism and Methodology*, Bloomington and Indianapolis: Indiana University Press; Milton Keynes: Open University Press.
Harrington, C. B. and Merry, S. E. (1988) 'Ideological Production: The Making of Community Mediation', *Law and Society Review*, 22(4): 709–35.
Harrington, C. (1992) Popular Justice, Popular Politics: Law in Community Organizing, 1 Social & Legal Studies 177.
Harrington, C. B. and Yngvesson, B. (1990). 'Interpretive Sociological Research', *Law & Social Inquiry*, 15(1): 135–48.
Harris, A. (1990) 'Race and essentialism in feminist legal theory', *Stanford Law Review*, 42(3): 581–616.
Hart, H. L. A (1994) *The Concept of Law*, Second edition, Oxford: Clarendon Press.
Hayes, M. and Acton, T. (eds.), (2006) *Counter-Hegemony and the Post-Colonial 'Other'*, Cambridge: Cambridge Scholars Press.
Helfer, L. R. (1999) 'Forum Shopping for Human Rights', *University of Pennsylvania Law Review*, 148: 285–315.
Hellum, A. (1999) 'Women's human rights and African customary laws: Between universalism and relativism – individualism and communitarism', in C. Lund (ed.) *Development and Rights: Negotiating Justice in Changing Societies*, Portland, Oregon: Frank Cass Publishers, pp. 88–105.
Hennink, M., Diamond, I. and Cooper, P. (1999) 'Young Asian women and relationships: Traditional or transitional?' *Ethnic and Racial Studies*, 22(5): 867–91.
Henry, S. (1983) *Private Justice: Towards Integrated Theorising in the Sociology of Law*, London: Routledge and Kegan Paul.
Herring, J. (2009) *Family Law*, Fourth edition, London: Pearson Longman.
Hesse, B. (2000) 'Introduction: Un/settled multiculturalisms,' in B. Hesse (ed.), *Un/settled Multiculturalisms: Diasporas, Entanglements, Transruptions*, London: Zed Books.
Hester, M., Pearson, C. and Radford, L. (1997) *Domestic Violence: A National Survey of Court Welfare and Voluntary Sector Mediation Practice*, Cambridge: Policy Press.
Hirsch, F. S. (1998) *Pronouncing and Persevering: Gender and the Discourses of Disputing in an African Islamic Court*, USA: University of Chicago Press.

Hirsch, H. N. (1986) 'Liberalism: Constitutional liberty and the renewal of community', *Political Theory*, 7(2): 16–25.

Hoekema, A. J. (2005) 'European Legal Encounters between Minority and Majority Culture: Cases of Interlegality', *Journal of Legal Pluralism*, 51: 1–26.

Home Office (2000) *A Choice by Right: The Report of the Working Group on Forced Marriage*, London: Home Office Communications Directorate, available at http://www.fco.gov.uk/Files/KFile/AChoiceByRightJune2000.pdf.

Home Office (2005) *Forced Marriage: A Wrong Not a Right*, Consultation paper, available at http://www.fco.gov.uk/en/publications-and-documents/publications1/consultations1/closed-consultations/

Holstein, A. J. and Gubrium, F. J. (1998) 'Active interviewing', in D. Silverman (ed.) *Qualitative Research – Theory, Method, and Practice*, London: Sage, pp. 140–62.

Hooker, M. (1975) *Legal Pluralism: An Introduction to Colonial and Neo-Colonial Laws*, Oxford: Oxford University Press.

Hossain, S. (1994) 'Equality in the home: Women's rights and personal laws in South Asia', in R. J. Cook (ed.) *Human Rights of Women: National and International Perspectives*, New York: University of Pennsylvania Press.

Humphrey, M. (1984) 'Community disputes, violence and dispute processing in a Lebanese Muslim immigrant community', *Journal of Legal Pluralism*, 22: 53–88.

Hunt, A. (1978) *The Sociological Movement in Law*, London: Macmillan.

Hunt, A. and Wickham, G. (1994) *Foucault and Law: Towards a Sociology of Governance*, London: Pluto.

Hunter, R. (2008) 'Alternatives to equality', in R. Hunter (ed.) *Rethinking Equality Projects in Law: Feminist Challenges*, Onati International Series in Law & Society, Oxford: Hart Publishing, pp. 81–101.

Hunter, R. and Cowan, S. (2007) 'Introduction', in R. Hunter and S. Cowan (eds) *Choice and Consent: Feminist Engagements with Law and Subjectivity*, Abingdon, Oxon: Routledge, pp. 1–7.

Huntington, S. (1996) *The Clash of Civilizations and the Remaking of World Order*, New York: Simon and Schuster.

Hussaini, M. (2010) *Marriage and Family in Islam*, London, Ta-Ha Publishers.

Idriss, M. (2005) 'Laïcité and the banning of the "hijab" in France', *Legal Studies*, 25(2): 260–95.

Idriss, M. and Abbas, T. (eds) (2010) *Honour, Violence, Women and Islam*, Abingdon, Oxon: Routledge.

Inglehart, R. and Norris, P. (2004) *Sacred and Secular: Religion and Politics Worldwide*, Cambridge, UK: Cambridge University Press.

Irving, H. H. and Benjamin, M. (1995) *Family Mediation, Contemporary Issues*, California: Sage Publications.

Islam, Y., Ahmed, N., Uddin, P., Bunglawala, I., Abdul Aziz, M., Majid, N. and Ullah, A. (2005) *Working Together to Prevent Extremism*, Home Office Paper. A copy is available at www.communities.gov.uk/documents/communities/pdf/152164.pdf, accessed on 22 August 2012.

Jacobson, J. (1997) 'Religion and ethnicity: Dual and alternative sources of identity among young British Pakistanis', *Ethnic and Racial Studies*, 20(2): 239–54.

Jacobson, J. (1998) *Islam in Transition: Religion and Identity among British Pakistani Youth*. London: LSE/Routledge.

Jamal, N. (1990) *The Islamic Law of Personal Status*, London: Graham and Trotman.

Jarman, A. (2008) *The Limits of Legal Pluralism*, CRONEM conference, University of Surrey, unpublished paper.

Joly, D. (1995) *Britannia's Crescent: Making a Place for Muslims in British Society*, Aldershot: Avebury.

Jones, R. and Welhengama, G. (2000) *Ethnic Minorities in English Law*, Stoke-on-Trent: Trentham Books.

Judicial Studies Board (1999) 'Equal treatment bench book', 305.

Juliano, J. (2005) 'Muslim dispute resolution in America: A challenge of religious pluralism', *World Religion 201: World Religions as a Resource*. A copy of this paper is available at http:www.scribd.com./doc/911

Kabbani, R. (1986) *Europe's Myths of Orient*, London: Pandora.

Kahani-Hopkins, V. and Hopkins, N. (2002) '"Representing" British Muslims: The strategic dimension to identity construction', *Ethnic and Racial Studies*, 25(2): 288–309.

Kandiyoti, D. (2007) 'Between the Hammer and the Anvil: Post-Conflict Reconstruction, Islam and Women's Rights,' *Third World Quarterly*, 28(3): 503–17.

Kapur, R. (2005) *Erotic Justice: Law and the New Politics of Postcolonialism: Postcolonial Feminism Law Sexuality*, London: Glass House Press.

Kelly, J. M. (1992) *A Short History of Western Legal Theory*, Oxford: Clarendon Press.

Kelman, M. (1987) *A Guide to Critical Legal Studies*, Boston, USA: Harvard University Press.

Keshavjee, M. (2007) 'Alternative dispute resolution in a diasporic Muslim community in Britain', in P. Shah (ed.) *Law and Ethnic Plurality: Socio-Legal Perspectives*, Leiden: Martinus Nijhoff, pp. 145–75.

Kettani, A. M. (1996) 'Challenges to the organization of Muslim communities in Western Europe: The political dimension', in W. Shadid and V. S. Koningsveld (eds) *Political Participation and Identities of Muslims in Non-Muslim States*, Kampen, the Netherlands: Kok Pharos, pp. 15–35.

Kleinhams, M. Marie and Macdonald, R. (1997) 'What Is a Critical Legal Pluralism A 12 Can', *Journal of Law & Society*, 25: 25–56.

Kline, M. (1989) 'Race, racism and feminist legal theory', *Harvard Women's Law Journal*, 12: 115–50.

Knott, K. and Khoker, S. (1993) 'Religious and ethnic identity among young Muslim women in Bradford', *New Community*, 19(4): 593–610.

Khadduri, M. (1984) *The Islamic Concept of Justice*, Baltimore: John Hopkins University Press.

Knights, S. (2007) *Freedom of Religion, Minorities and the Law*, Oxford: Oxford University Press.

Kostakopoulou, D. (2006) 'Thick, thin and thinner patriotisms: Is this all there is?' *OJLS*, 26(1): 73–106.

Kurczewski, J. (1997) '"Family" in politics and law: In search of theory', in J. Kurczewski and M. Maclean (eds) *Family Law and Family Policy in the New Europe*, The Onati International Institute for the Sociology of Law, Portland, Oregon: Dartmouth Publishing, pp. 3–26.

Kundnani, A. (2007) *The End of Tolerance: Racism in 21st Century Britain*, London: Pluto Press.

Kymlicka, W. (1995) *The Rights of Minority Cultures*, Oxford: Oxford University Press.

Kymlicka, W. (2005) *Multicultural Citizenship: A Liberal Theory of Minority Rights*, New York: Oxford University Press.

Lacey, N. (1992) 'From individual to group?' in B. Hepple and E. M. Szyszczak (eds) *Discrimination: The Limits of Law*, London: Mansell, pp. 235–56.

Lacey, N. (1993) 'Theory into practice: Pornography and the public/private dichotomy', *Journal of Law and Society*, 20(1): 93–113.

Lacey, N. (1995) 'Feminist legal theory beyond neutrality', *Current Legal Problems*, 48(2): 1–38.

Lee, M. R. (1999) *Doing Research on Sensitive Topics*, Thousand Oaks, California: Sage.

Lester, A. and Bindman, G. (1972) *Race and Law*, Harmondsworth: Penguin.

Levey, B. G. (2009) 'Secularism and religion in a multicultural age', in B. G. Levey and T. Modood (eds) *Secularism, Religion and Multicultural Citizenship*, Cambridge, UK: Cambridge University Press, pp. 216–42.

Levey, B. G. and Modood, T. (eds) (2009) *Secularism, Religion and Multicultural Citizenship*, Cambridge, UK: Cambridge University Press.

Lewis, L. and Schnapper, D. (1994) *Muslims in Europe*, London and New York: Pinter.

Lewis, P. (1994) 'Being Muslim and being British: The dynamics of Islamic reconstruction in Bradford', in R. Ballard (eds) *Desh Pardesh: The South Asian Presence in Britain*, London: C. Hurst & Co. Ltd, pp. 58–88.

Lewis, P. (2002) *'Islamic Britain: Religion, Politics and Identity among British Muslims*, London: I. B. Tauris.

Lister, R. (2003) *Citizenship: Feminist Perspectives*, London: Palgrave MacMillan.

Lofland, J. and Lofland, L. (1994) *Analyzing Social Settings*, Belmont, CA: Wadsworth.

Lord Chancellor's Department (1995) *Looking to the Future: Mediation and the Ground for Divorce: The Government's Proposals*, White Paper, London: HMSO, Cm 2799.

Lord Chancellor's Department (1996) 'Introduction', *Marriage and Family Law Act 1996: The New Legislation Explained*, London: LCD.

Lord Goldsmith (2008) *Our Common Bond* and a series of articles published in *Prospect* between 2004 and 2006, London: Ministry of Justice.

MacKinnon, C. (1987) *Feminism Unmodified*, Cambridge, MA: Harvard University Press.

MacKinnon, C. (1993) 'Toward feminist jurisprudence', in K. D. Weisberg (ed.) *Feminist Legal Theory Foundations*, Philadelphia: Temple University Press, pp. 276–88.

MacKinnon, C. (2005) *Women's Lives, Men's Law*, Boston, Harvard University Press.

MacEoin, D. (2009) *Sharia Law or 'One Law for All'?* London: Civitas, Institute for the Study of Civil Society.

Maclean, M. (1997) 'Delegalized family obligations', in J. Kurczewski and M. Maclean (eds) *Family Law and Family Policy in the New Europe*, The Onati International Institute for the Sociology of Law, Oxford: Dartmouth Publishing, pp. 121–34.

Maclean, M. (ed.) (2000) *Making Law for Families*, Onati International Series in Law and Society, Oxford and Portland, OR: Hart Publishing.

MacLean, M. and Kurczewski, J. (2011) *Making Family Law: A Socio-Legal Account of Legislative Process in England and Wales*, Oxford: Hart Publishing.

Maclean, M. and Kurczewski, J. (eds) (1994) *Families, Politics and the Law*, Oxford: Clarendon Press.

Macdonald, I. A. and Webber, F. (2005) *Macdonald's immigration law and practice*, London: LexisNexis Butterworths.

Madeira, M. A. (2010) *Shari'a or the State? Islamic Law Tribunals in Western Democracies*, unpublished paper for International Sociological Association Conference, 12 February.

Mahmood, S. (2006a) *Politics of Piety, The Islamic Revival and the Feminist Subject*, Princeton: Princeton University Press.

Mahmood, S. (2006b) 'Secularism, hermeneutics, empire: The politics of Islamic reformation', *Public Culture*, 18(2): 323–47.

Malik, M. (2000a) 'Minorities and the Human Rights Act,' in *Sceptical Approaches to the Human Rights Act*, T. Campbell, K. D. Ewing and A. Tomkins (eds), Oxford: Oxford University Press, pp. 277–97.

Malik, M. (2000b) 'Faith and the State of Jurisprudence,' in *Faith in Law: Essays in Legal Theory*, P. Oliver et al. (eds), Oxford: Hart, pp. 12–34.

Malik, M. (2006) 'Feminism, Multiculturalism and Minority Women' in *Feminist Perspectives on Family Law*, Alison Diduick and Katherine O'Donovan (eds), Routledge: London, pp. 211–31.

Malik, M. (2008) *From Conflict to Cohesion: Competing Interests in Equality Law and Policy*, Equality and Diversity Forum, available at http://www.edf.org.uk/, accessed on 21 August 2012.

Malik, M. (2009) *Muslim Legal Norms and the integration of European Muslims*. EUI Working Papers, Robert Schuman Centre for Advanced Studies.

Malik, M. (2012) *Minority Legal Systems in the UK: Multiculturalism, Minorities and the Law*, British Academy Policy Papers.

Malik, N. (2004) 'Equality? The treatment of Muslims under the English legal system', in M. S. Seddon, D. Hussain and N. Malik (eds) *British Muslims between Assimilation and Segregation: Historical, Legal and Social Realities*, Markfield, Leicestershire: The Islamic Foundation, pp. 43–81.

Malinowski, B. (1948) *Magic, Science and Religion and Other Essays*, Glencoe, Illinois: The Free Press.

Manfield, N. (2000) *Subjectivity: Theories of the Self from Freud to Haraway*, New York: New York University Press.

Marinetto, M. (2003) 'Who wants to be an active citizen? The politics and practice of community involvement', *Sociology*, 37(1): 103–20.

Mason, J. (1996) *Qualitative Researching*, London: Sage.

Masood, M. (2003) 'Untangling the complex web of Islamic Law: Revolutionazing the Sharia', *The Fletcher School On-line Journal for Issues related to Southwest Asia and Islamic Civilization*, Fall 2003 Articles 4, pp. 1–7.

Massey, D. (1994) *Space, Place and Gender*, New York, USA: Cambridge Polity Press.

Maussen, M. (2005) 'Making Muslim presence meaningful: Studies on Islam and mosques in Western Europe', *ASSR Working Papers Series*, May.

May, S. (1999) *Critical Multiculturalism: Rethinking Multicultural and Anti-Racist Education*, Brighton: Falmer Press.

Mayer, E. (1990) 'The Shari'ah: A methodology or a body of substantive rules?' in N. Heer (ed.) *Islamic Law and Jurisprudence*, Washington: University of Washington Press, pp. 177–98.

Mayer, E. (1994) 'Universal versus Islamic Human Rights: A clash of cultures or a clash with construct?' *Michigan Journal of International Law*, 15: 307–404.

Mayer, E. (1999) *Islam and Human Rights*, Boulder, Colorado: Westview Press.

Maynard, M. and Purvis, J. (1994) 'Doing feminist research', in M. Maynard and J. Purvis (eds) *Researching Women's Lives from a Feminist Perspective*, London: Taylor & Francis, pp. 10–26.

McCarthy, R. J., Holland, J. and Gillies, V. (2003) 'Multiple perspectives on the "family" lives of young people: Methodological and theoretical issues in case study research', *International Journal of Social Research Methodology*, 6(1): 1–23.

McCorkel, A. J. (2003) 'What difference does difference make? Position and privilege in the field', *Qualitative Sociology*, 26(2): 199–231.

McCrory, J. P. (1981) 'Environmental mediation – another piece for the puzzle', *Vermont Law Review*, 6(1): 49–84.

McFarlane, J. (2011) '"Am I bothered?" The relevance of religious courts to a civil judge', *Family Law Journal*, 41, September: 946–55.

McGoldrick, D. (2005) 'Multiculturalism and its discontents', *Human Rights Law Review*, 5(1): 27–56.

McIntyre, G. (1981) *The Limits of Freedom*, London: Blackwells.

Mclennan, G. (1995) 'Feminism, epistemology and postmodernism: Reflections on current ambivalence', *Sociology*, 29(2): 391–409.

McLoughlin, S. (1996) 'In the name of the umma: Globalization, "race" relations and Muslim identity politics in Bradford', in W. Shadid and V. S. Koningsveld (eds) *Political Participation and Identities of Muslims in Non-Muslim States*, Kampen, the Netherlands: Kok Pharos, pp. 206–28.

Mehdi, R. (2003) 'Danish law and the practice of *mahr* among Muslim Pakistanis in Denmark', *International Journal of the Sociology of Law*, 31(2): 115–29.

Mehdi, R. and Jorgen, S. N. (2011) *Mahr in the European Legal System*, Denmark: DJOF Publishing.

Mehmood, T. (1995) *Mulla's Mohamedan Law (Urdu Translation Of Principles Of Mahomedan Law)*, London, Butterworths.

Menski, W. (1993) 'Asians in Britain and the question of adaptation to a new legal order: Asian laws in Britain?' in M. Israel and N. Wagle (eds) *Ethnicity, Identity, Migration: The South Asian Context*, Toronto: University of Toronto Press, pp. 238–68.

Menski, W. (1994) 'Plural arrangements in family law by Muslims in Britain', *Angrezi Shari'a*, unpublished paper, SOAS, University of London.

Menski, W. (1997) 'South Asian Muslim law today: An overview', *Sharqiyyat*, 9(1): 16–36.

Menski, W. (2001) 'Muslim law in Britain', *Journal of Asian and African Studies*, 62: 202–36.

Menski, W. (2006) 'Rethinking legal theory in the light of South–North migration', in P. Shah and W. Menski (eds) *Migration, Diasporas and Legal Systems in Europe*, Abingdon, Oxon: Routledge-Cavendish.

Menski, W. (2008) 'Law, religion and culture in multicultural Britain', in R. Mehdi, H. Petersen, E. Reenberg Sand and G. R. Woodman (eds) *Law and Religion in Multicultural Societies*, Copenhagen: DJOF Publishing, pp. 43–62.

Menzies, R. and Palys, T. (1987) *Transcarceration*, Farnborough: Gower.

Mernissi, F. (1992) *Women and Islam, an Historical and Theological Enquiry*, Oxford: Blackwells.

Mernissi, F. (1993) *Islam and Democracy, Fear of the Modern World*, London: Virago Press.

Merry, E. S. (1988) 'Legal pluralism', *Law and Society Review*, 22(5): 869–96.

Merry, E. S. (2001) 'Changing rights, changing culture', in K. J. Cowan, M. Dembour and R. Wilson (eds) *Culture and Rights: Anthropological Perspectives*, Cambridge: Cambridge University Press, pp. 31–56.

Merry, E. S. (2006) *Human Rights and Gender Violence, Translating International Law into Local Justice*, Chicago: Chicago University Press.

Metcalf, D. B. (1996) 'Introduction: Sacred words, sanctioned practice, new communities', in D. B. Metcalf (ed.) *Making Muslim Space in North America and Europe*, Berkeley: University of California Press, pp. 1–31.

Mies, M. (1983) 'Towards a methodology for feminist research', in G. Bowles and D. Klein (eds) *Theories of Women's studies*, London: Routledge and Kegan Paul, pp. 117–40.

Miller, J. and Glassner, B. (1998) 'The 'inside' and the 'outside', finding realities in interviews', in D. Silverman (ed.) *Qualitative Research – Theory, Method, and Practice*, London: Sage, pp. 125–40.

Mirza, Q. (2000) 'Islam, hybridity and the laws of marriage', *Australian Feminist Law Journal*, 14(1): 1–22.

Mirza, M. (2010) 'Beyond race and multiculturalism', *Prospect Magazine*, October, pp. 1–6.

Mirza, M. (2011) *The Politics of Culture: The case for universalism*, New York and London: Palgrave MacMillan.

Mir-Hosseini, Z. (2006) 'Muslim women's quest for equality: Between Islamic law and feminism', *Critical Inquiry*, 32(4): 629–45.

Modood, T. (1993) 'Muslim views on religious identity and racial equality', *New Community*, April, 19(3): 513–19.

Modood, T. (2000) 'The place of Muslims in British secular multiculturalism', in N. Alsayyad, M. Castells and L. Michalak (eds) *Islam and the Changing Identity of Europe*, USA: University Press of America, Lexington Books.

Modood, T. (2005) *Multicultural Politics: Racism, Ethnicity and Muslims in Britain*, Edinburgh: Edinburgh University Press.

Modood, T. (2006) 'British Muslims and the politics of multiculturalism' in T. Modood, A. Triandafyllidou and R. Zapata-Barrero (eds) *Multiculturalism, Muslims and Citizenship*, New York: Routledge, pp. 37–57.

Modood, T. (2007) *Multiculturalism: A Civic Idea*, Cambridge: Polity Press.

Modood, T. (2008) 'Is multiculturalism dead?' *Public Policy Research*, 15(2): 84–8.

Modood, T. (2009) 'Muslims, Religious Equality and Secularism', in G. Levery and T. Modood (eds) *Secularism, Religion and Multicultural Citizenship*, Cambridge: Cambridge University Press, pp. 164–86.

Modood, T., Berthoud, R., Lakey, J., Nazroo, J., Smith, P., Virdee, S. and Beishon, S. (eds.) (1997) *Ethnic Minorities in Britain: Diversity and Disadvantage*, London: Policy Studies Institute.

Mohammed, J. (1992) *Race Relations and Muslims in Great Britain*, Muslim Parliament of Great Britain.

Mohanty, C. (1997) *Feminist Genealogies, Colonial Legacies, Democratic Futures*, New York: Routledge.

Mohanty, C. (1991) 'Under Western eyes: Feminist scholarship and colonial discourse', in C. T. Mohanty, A. Russo and L. Torres (eds) *Third World Women and the Politics of Feminism*, Indianapolis: Indiana University Press, pp. 51–80.

Mojab, S. (2006) 'In the quagmires of ethnicity: A Marxist critique of liberal "exit" strategies', *Journal of Ethnicities*, 5(3): 341–61.

Montgomery, M. (1992) 'Legislating for a multi-faith society', in B. Hepple and M. E. Sczyrack (eds) *Discrimination: The Limits of Law*, London: Mansell, pp. 237–71.

Moore, C. W. (2003) *The Mediation Process: Practical Strategies for Resolving Conflict*, Third edition, San Francisco: John Wiley & Sons, Inc.

Moore, S. F. (1972) 'Law and social change: The semi-autonomous social field as an appropriate subject of study', *Law & Society Review*, 7(1): 719–46.

Moore, S. F. (1978) *Law As Process: An Anthropological Approach*, London, Boston: Routledge & K. Paul.

Morgan, K. (1991) 'Women and the knife: Cosmetic surgery and the colonization of women's bodies', *Hypatia*, 6(3): 25–53.

Morrill, C., Buller, D. B., Buller, M. K. and Larkey, L. L. (1999) 'Toward an organizational perspective on identifying and managing formal gatekeepers', *Qualitative Sociology*, 22(1): 51–72.

Motha, S. (2007) 'Veiled women and the affect of religion in democracy', *Journal of Law and Society*, 34(1): 138–61.

Mouffe, C. (2000) *The Democratic Paradox*, London: Verso.

Mulcahy, L. (2000) 'The devil and the deep blue sea? A critique of the ability of community mediation to suppress and facilitate participation in civil life', *Journal of Law and Society*, 27(1): 133–50.

Mulcahy, L. (2005) 'The limitations of love and altruism – Feminist perspectives on contract law', in L. Mulcahy and S. Wheeler (eds) *Feminist Perspectives on Contract Law*, New York and London: The GlassHouse Press, pp. 1–20.

Muslim Arbitration Tribunal (2008a) *Family Dispute Cases*, available at http://www.matribunal.com/cases_faimly.html.

Muslim Arbitration Tribunal (2008b) *Liberation from Forced Marriages*, Report, London.

Muslim Council of Britain (2006) *Voices from the Minarets: A Study of UK Imams and Mosques*, London: The Muslim Council of Britain.

Muslim News (2002) 'Muslim council of Britain: Its history, structure and workings', 157: 8.

Nader, L. and Todd, F. H. (1978) *The Disputing Process: Law in Ten Societies*, New York: Columbia Press.

Naffine, N. (2003) 'Who are law's persons? From Cheshire cats to responsible subjects', *Modern Law Review*, 66(3): 346–67.

Nagel, J. and Snipp, C. (1993) 'Ethnic reorganisation: American Indian social, economic, political and cultural strategies for survival', *Ethnic and Racial Studies*, 16(2): 203–35.

Narayan, U. (1997) *Dislocating Cultures. Identities, Traditions and Third World Feminism*, New York: Routledge.

Nasir, J. (1986) *The Islamic Law of Personal Status*, London: Graham and Trotman.

Nasir, J. J. (1990) *The Islamic Law of Personal Status (Arab & Islamic Laws)*, London: Graham and Trotman.

Nelken, D. (1984) 'Law in action or living law? Back to the beginning in sociology of law', *Legal Studies*, 4.

Nichols, J. A. (2012) *Marriage and Divorce in a Multicultural Context: Multi-Tiered Marriage and the Boundaries of Civil Law and Religion*, New York: Cambridge University Press.

Nielsen, J. S. (1987) 'Islamic law and its significance for the situation of Muslim minorities in Europe: Report of a study project', *Research Papers: Muslims in Europe*, 35.

Nielsen, J. S. (1989) 'Emerging claims of Muslim populations in matters of family law in Europe', *Journal of Muslim Affairs*, 15: 120–42.

Nielsen, J. S. (1991) 'A Muslim agenda for Britain: Some reflections', *New Community*, 17(3): 467–75.

Nielsen, J. S. (1992) *Islam, Muslims, and British Local and Central Government*, Selly Oak, Birmingham: Centre for the Study of Islam and Christian–Muslim Relations.

Nielsen, J. S. (1997) 'Muslims in Europe: History revisited or a way forward?' *Islam and Christian–Muslim Relations*, 8(2): 135–43.

Nielsen, J. (2004) *Muslims in Western Europe*, Third edition, Edinburgh: Edinburgh University Press.

Nielsen, J. S. and Christoffersen, L. (2010) *Shari'a as Discourse: Legal Traditions and the Encounter with Europe*, England: Ashgate Press.

Norrie, A. (2005) *Law & the Beautiful Soul*, London: The GlassHouse Press.

Nozick, R. (1969) 'Coercion', in S. Morgenbesser, P. Suppes and M. White (eds) *Philosophy, Science, and Method: Essays in Honor of Ernest Nagel*, New York: St Martin's Press, pp. 440–72.

Nussbaum, M. C. (1999) *Sex and Social Justice*, Oxford: Oxford University Press.

Oakley, A. (1998) 'Gender, methodology and people's ways of knowing: Some problems with feminism and the paradigm debate in social science', *Sociology*, 32(4): 707–31.

Oboler, R. (1986) 'For better or for worse: Anthropologists and husbands in the field', in T. Whitehead and M. Conway (ed.) *Self, Sex and Gender in Cross-Cultural Fieldwork*, Urbana, IL: University of Illinois Press.

O'Donovan, K. (1985) *Sexual Divisions in Law*, London: Weidenfeld and Nicolson.

O'Donovan, K. (1993) *Family Law Matters*, London: Pluto Press.

O'Donovan, K. and Diduck, A. (2006) *Feminist Perspectives on Family Law*, London: Glasshouse Press.

ONS (2000) *Marriage, Divorce and Adoption Statistics 1998*, London: Stationery Office.

Okin, S. M. (1979) *Women in Western Political Thought*, Princeton: Princeton University Press.

Okin, S. (1999) *Is Multiculturalism Bad for Women?* Princeton, NJ: Princeton University Press.

Olen, F. (1983) 'The family and the market: A study of ideology and legal reform', *Harvard Law Review*, 96: 1497–1578.

Oliver, P., Douglas-Scott, S. and Tadros, V. (2000) *Faith in Law: Essays in Legal Theory*, Oxford: Hart Publishing.

Parekh, B. (1990) 'Britain and the social logic of pluralism', in *Britain: A Plural Society*, London: CRE.

Parekh, B. (1994) 'Equality, fairness and the limits of diversity', *Innovation*, 7(3): 289–308.

Parekh, B (1995) 'The Rushdie Affair: Research Agenda for Political Philosophy,' in W. Kymlicka (ed.) *The Rights of Minority Cultures*, Oxford: Oxford University Press, pp. 303–21.

Parekh, B. (1997) 'Dielmmas of a Multicultural Theory of Citizenship, *Constellations*, 4(11): 54–62.

Parekh, B. (2000) *Rethinking Multiculturalism: Cultural Diversity and Political Theory*, New York: Macmillan Press.

Parekh, B. (2002) *The Future of Multi-Ethnic Britain. The Parekh Report*, London: The Runnymede Trust.

Parekh, B. (2006) 'Europe, liberalism and the "Muslim question"', in T. Modood, A. Triandafyllidou and R. Zapata-Barrero (eds) *Multiculturalism, Muslims and Citizenship: A European Approach*, Oxford: Routledge, pp. 199–200.

Parker, D. (2000) 'The Chinese takeaway and the diasporic habitus: Space, time and power geometries', in B. Hesse (ed.) *Un/settled Multiculturalisms: Diasporas, Entanglements, Transruptions*, London and New York: Zed Books, pp. 73–96.

Parkinson, P. (1996) 'Multiculturalism and the recognition of marital status in Australia', in G. Douglas and N. Lowe (eds) *Families Across Frontiers*, London: Kluwer, pp. 45–67.

Patel, P. (2003) 'Shifting terrains, old struggles for new?' in R. Gupta (ed.) *From Housebreakers to Jailbreakers*, New York: Southall Black Sisters, Zed Books, pp. 1–28.

Patel, P. (2008) 'Faith in the state? Asian women's struggles for human rights in the UK', *Feminist Legal Studies*, 16(1): 9–36.

Pateman, C. (1988) *The Sexual Contract*, Stanford: Stanford University Press.

Patton, Q. M. (1980) 'The nature of qualitative inquiry', in Q. M. Patton (ed.) *Qualitative Evaluation and Research Methods*, Newbury Park: Sage, pp. 23–36.

Pearl, A. (1987) 'South Asian immigrant communities and English family law 1971–1987', *New Community*, 14(1/2): 84–105.

Pearl, D. and Menski, W. (1998) *Muslim Family Law*, Sweet & Maxwell.

Perakyla, A. (1998) 'Reliability and validity in research based on tapes and transcripts', in D. Silverman (ed.) *Qualitative Research – Theory, Method, and Practice*, London: Sage, pp. 234–45.

Petersen, H. and Zahle, H. (1995) *Legal Polycentricity: Consequences and Pluralism in Law*, Aldershot: Dartmouth.

Phillips, A. (1993) *Democracy and Difference*, Philadelphia: Pennsylvania University Press.

Phillips, A. (2003) 'When culture means gender: Issues of cultural defence in the English courts', *Modern Law Review*, 66(4): 510–31.

Phillips, A. (2007) *Multiculturalism without Culture*, Princeton, New Jersey: Princeton University Press.

Phillips, A. and Dustin, M. (2004) 'UK initiatives on forced marriage: Regulation, dialogue and exit', *Political Studies*, 52(3): 531–51.

Phillips, Lord Justice (2008) 'Equality before the law', Speech at East London Muslim Centre, 3 July.

Phillipson, C., Ahmed, N. and Latimer, J. (2003) *Women in Transition: A Study of the Experinces of Bangladeshi Women in Tower Hamlets*, Bristol: The Policy Press.

Phoenix, A. (1994) 'Practising feminist research: The intersection of gender and "race" in the research process', in M. Maynard and J. Purvis (ed.) *Researching Women's Lives from a Feminist Perspective*, London: Taylor & Francis, pp. 49–72.

Pierce, L. J. (2003) 'Feminist methods and methodologies: Personal narratives and theorizing women's agency in context', Paper presented to the *Socio-Legal Research Methods Workshop*, Onati, Spain.

Pieterse, J. N. (1997) 'Travelling Islam: Mosques without Minarets', in A. Oncii and P. Weyland (eds) *Space Culture and Power*, London: Zed Books, pp. 65–76.

Poulter, S. M. (1986) *English Law and Ethnic Minority Customs*, London: Butterworth & Co.

Poulter, S. M. (1990) 'The claim to a separate Islamic system of personal law for British Muslims', in C. Mallat and J. Connors (eds) *Islamic Family Law*, London: Graham and Trotman, pp. 147–66.

Poulter, S. M. (1992) 'The limits of legal, cultural and religious pluralism', in B. Hepple and M. E. Sczyrack (ed.) *Discrimination: The Limits of Law*, London: Mansell, pp. 77–90.

Poulter, S. M. (1994) 'Minority rights', in C. McCrudden and G. Chambers (eds) *Individual Rights and the Law in Britain*, Oxford: Clarendon Press, pp. 457–89.

Poulter, S. M. (1995) 'Multiculturalism and human rights for Muslim families in Britain', in M. King (ed.) *God's Law Versus State Law*, London: Grey Seal, pp. 81–7.

Poulter, S. M. (1998) *Ethnicity, Law and Human Rights*, Oxford: Clarendon Press.

Prentice, B. (2009) *One Year On: The Initial Impact of the Forced Marriage (Civil Protection) Act 2007 in its First Year of Operation*, Policy Paper, Ministry of Justice.

Probert, R. J. (2002) 'When are we married? Void, non-existent and presumed marriages', *Legal Studies*, 22(3): 398–419.

Probert, R. (2003) 'The right to marry and the impact of the Human Rights Act 1998', *International Family Law*, 1(54): 29–32.

Probert, R. (2004) 'Regulating Marriage and Cohabitation: Changing Family Values and Policies in Europe and North America – An Introductory Critiqu', Warwick SSRN Working Paper.

Punch, M. (1986) *The Politics and Ethics of Fieldwork*, California: Sage Publications.

Purkayastha, B. (2009a) 'Transgressing the sacred–secular, public–private debate', in A. Narayan and B. Purkayastha (eds) *Living Our Religions: Hindu and Muslim South Asian American Women Narrate Their Experiences*, USA: Kumarian Press, pp. 1–23.

Purkayastha, B. (2009b) 'Conclusion: Human rights, religions, gender', in A. Narayan and B. Purkayastha (eds) *Living Our Religions: Hindu and Muslim South Asian American Women Narrate Their Experiences*, USA: Kumarian Press, pp. 285–97.

Purdam, K. (1996) 'Settler political participation: Muslim local councillors', in W. Shadid and V. S. Koningsveld (eds) *Political Participation and Identities of Muslims in Non-Muslim States*, Kampen, the Netherlands: Kok Pharos, pp. 129–43.

Purdam, K. (2000) 'The Political Identities of Muslim Local Councillors,' *Local Government Studies*, 26(1): 47–64. eScholarID:1b1543.

Purvis, J. (ed.) (1994) *Researching Women's Lives from a Feminist Perspective*, London: Taylor & Francis.

Purvis, T. and Hunt, A. (1999) 'Identity versus citizenship: Transformations in the discourses and practices of citizenship', Social and Legal Studies, 8(4): 470–88.

Ralson, H. (1997) 'Arranged, "semi-arranged" and "love" marriages among South Asian immigrant women in the diaspora and their non-migrant sisters in India and Fiji: A comparative study', *International Journal of Sociology of the Family*, 27(2): 43–68.

Ramadan, T. (1999) *To be a European Muslim*, Markfield, Leicestershire: The Islamic Foundation.

Ramadan, T. (2002) 'Europeanisation of Islam or Islamisation of Europe?' in S. T. Hunter (ed.) *Islam, Europe's Second Religion: The New Social, Cultural and Political Landscape*, Westport, CT and London: Praeger, pp. 207–18.

Ramadan, T. (2004) *Western Muslims and the Future of Islam*, Oxford et al.: Oxford University Press.

Rattansi, A. (1992) 'Changing the subject? Racism, culture and education', in J. Donald and A. Rattansi (eds) *'Race', Culture and Difference*, London: Sage, pp. 11–49.

Rawls, J. (1999) *A Theory of Justice*, Cambridge, MA: Harvard University Press.

Rawls, J. (2005) *Political Liberalism*, New York: Columbia University Press.

Raz, J. (1986) *The Morality of Freedom*, Oxford: Clarendon Press.

Raz, J. (1994) 'Multiculturalism: A liberal perspective', *Dissent*, 67(2): 96–105.

Raza, M. (1991) *Islam in Britain, Past Present and Future*, Leceister: Volcano Press Ltd.

Razack, S. (2004) 'Imperilled Muslim women, dangerous Muslim men and civilised Europeans: Legal and social responses to forced marriages', *Feminist Legal Studies*, 12(2): 129–74.

Razack, S. (2008) *Casting Out: The Eviction of Muslims from Western Law and Politics*, Canada: University of Toronto Press.

Redfern, A. and Hunter, M. (2004) *International Commercial Arbitration*, Cambridge: Cambridge University Press.

Reinharz, S. (1992) *Feminist Methods in Social Research*, Oxford: Oxford University Press.

Rex, J. (1996) 'National Identity in the Democratic Multi-Cultural State', *Sociological Research Online*, 1(2), http://www.socresonline.org.uk/1/2/1.html

Rhijn, J. (2003) 'First steps taken towards Sharia law in Canada', *Law Times*, November.

Rifkin, J. (1984) 'Mediation from a feminist perspective: Promise and Problems', 2(1): 21–45.

Roberts, A. S. (1979) *Order and Dispute*, New York: St Martin's Press.

Roberts, A. S. (1998) 'Against legal pluralism: Some reflections on the contemporary enlargement of the legal domain', *Journal of Legal Pluralism and Unofficial Law*, 42: 95–106.

Roberts, M. (1997) *Mediation in Family Disputes: Principles of Practice*, Arena.

Roberts, M. (2008) *Mediation in Family Disputes: Principles of Practice*, Fourth edition, Farnham: Ashgate.

Roberts, S. (1983) 'Mediation in family disputes', *Modern Law Review*, 46(2): 537–57.

Roberts, S. (1993) 'Alternative mediation and civil justice: An unresolved relationship', *Modern Law Review*, 56(4): 452–70.

Rohe, M. (2004) 'The formation of a European Shari'a', in J. Malik (ed.) *Muslims in Europe: From the Margin to the Centre*, Münster: LIT Verlag, pp. 161–84.

Rohe, M. (2006) 'The migration and settlement of Muslims: The challenges for European legal systems', in P. Shah and W. F. Menski (eds) *Migration, Diasporas and Legal Systems in Europe*, London: Routledge-Cavendish, pp. 57–72.

Rohe, M. (2007) *Muslim Minorities and the Law in Europe: Chances and Challenges*, New Delhi: Global Media.

Rohe, M. (2008) 'Islamic norms in Germany and Europe', in A. Al-Hamarneh and J. Thielmann (eds), *Islam and Muslims in Germany, Muslim Minorities*, Vol. 7, Leiden, the Netherlands: Brill, pp. 49–81.

Rohe, M. (2009) 'Shari'a in a European context', in R. Grillo, R. Ballard, A. Ferrari, A. J. Hoekema, M. Maussen and P. Shah (eds) *Legal Practice and Cultural Diversity*, Farnham: Ashgate, pp. 93–114.

Roggeband, C. and Verloo, M. (2007) 'Dutch women are liberated, migrant women are a problem: The evolution of policy frames on gender and migration in the Netherlands 1995–2005', *Social Policy and Administration*, 41(3): 271–88.

Rose, N. (1987) 'Beyond the public/private division: Law, power and the family', *Journal of Law and Society*, 14(1): 61–75.

Rosen, L. (1989) *The Anthropology of Justice: Law as Culture in Islamic Society*, Cambridge University Press.

Rosen, L. (2000) *The Justice of Islam*, Oxford: Oxford University Press.

Roundtable on Strategies to Address 'Crimes of Honour' (2002) available at http://www.honourcrimesproject.ac.uk, accessed on August 2012.

Roy, O. (2007) *Secularism Confronts Islam*, Columbia University Press.

Rt. Hon Lord Justice MacFarlane (2011) '"Am I bothered?" The relevance of religious courts to a civil judge', *Family Law*, 41: 946–55.

Rutten, S. (2010) 'Prtoection of spouses in informal marriages by human rights', *Utrecht Law Review*, 6(2)(June): 77–92.

Ryan, L. (2011) 'Muslim women. negotiating collective stigmatization: We're just normal people', *Sociology*, 45(6), December: 1045–60.

Saeed, A. (2009) 'Muslims in the West and their attitudes to full participation in western societies: Some reflections', in G. Levey and T. Modood (eds) *Secularism, Religion and Multicultural Citizenship*, Cambridge: Cambridge University Press, pp. 200–16.

Said, E. (1985) *Orientalism*, Harmondsworth: Penguin.

Saghal, G. and Yuval-Davis, N. (eds) (1992) *Refusing Holy Orders: Women and Fundamentalism in Britain*, London: Virago Press.

Samad, Y. and Eade, J. (2002) *Community Perceptions of Forced Marriage*, London: Foreign and Commonwealth Office.

Samad, Y. (2010) Muslims and Community cohesion in Bradford, The Joseph Rowntree Foundation.

Sandberg, R. (2011) *Law and Religion*, Cambridge: Cambridge University Press.

Sandel, M. (1982) *Liberalism and the Limits of Justice*, Cambridge: Cambridge University Press.

Santos, B. de Sousa (1982) 'Law in community: The changing nature of state power in late capitalism', in R. Abel (ed.) *The Politics of Informal Justice*, New York: Academic Press, pp. 345–55.

Santos, B. de Sousa (1987) 'A map of misreading – Toward a postmodern conception of law', *Journal of Law and Society*, 14(93): 279–302.

Santos, B. de Sousa (2002) *Toward a New Legal Common Sense*, London: Butterworths.

Santos, B. de Sousa (2005) *Law and Globalization from Below: Towards a Cosmopolitan Legality*, Cambridge: Cambridge UP.

Sarat, A. and Berkowitz, R. (1994) 'Disorderly differences, recognition, accommodation, and American Law', *Yale Journal of Law & the Humanities*, 6: 285–316.

Savage, T. M. (2004) 'Europe and Islam: Crescent waxing, cultures clashing', *Washington Quarterly*, 27, Summer: 25–50.

Sayyid, S. (1997) *A Fundamental Fear: Eurocentrism and the Emergence of Islamism*, London: Zed Books.

Sayyid, S. (2000) 'Beyond Westphalia: Nations and diasporas – the case of the Muslim umma', in B. Hesse (ed.) *Un/settled Multiculturalisms: Diasporas, Entanglements, Transruptions*, London: Zed Books, pp. 33–51.

Sayyid, S. (2009) 'Contemporary Politics of Secularism', in G. Levery and T. Modood (eds) *Secularism, Religion and Multicultural Citizenship*, Cambridge: Cambridge University Press, pp. 186–200.

Sayyid, S. and Vakil, A. K. (eds) (2010) *Thinking Through Islamaphobia*, New York: Columbia University Press.

Sayyid, S. (2010) 'Out of the devils dictionary', in S. Sayyid and A. K. Vakil (eds) *Thinking through Islamaphobia: Global Perspectives*, Hurst, pp. 1–5.

Scott, J. W. (2007) *The Politics of the Veil*, Princeton, New Jersey: Princeton University Press.

Sezgin, Y. (2008) *A Comparative Study of Personal Status Systems in Israel, Egypt and India*, Geneva: ICHRP.

Shabani, O. (2007) 'Introduction: The practice of law-making and the problem of difference', in O. P. Shabani (ed.) *Multiculturalism and Law*, Cardiff: University of Wales Press, pp. 1–19.

Shachar, A. (1999) *The Paradox of Multicultural Vulnerability: Individual Groups, Identity Groups and the State*, Oxford: Oxford University Press.

Shachar, A. (2001) Multicultural Jurisdictions: Cultural Differences and Women's Rights, New York: Cambridge University Press.

Shachar, A. (2005) 'Religion, state and the problem of gender: New modes of citizenship and governance in diverse societies, *McGill Law Journal*, 50(1): 49–88.

Shachar, A. (2008) 'Privatizing diversity: A cautionary tale from religious arbitration in family law', *Theoretical Inquiries in Law*, 9(2): 573–607.

Shadid, W. A. R. and van Koningsveld, P. S. (1995) *Religious Freedom and the Position of Islam in Western Europe*, Kampen, the Netherlands: Kok Pharos.

Shadid, W. and Koningsveld, V. S. (1996a) 'Islam in the Netherlands: Constitutional law and Islamic organisations', *Journal of Muslim Minority Affairs*, 16(1): 111–28.

Shadid, W. and Koningsveld, V. S. (1996b) 'Loyalty to a non-Muslim government: An analysis of Islamic normative discussions and of the views of some contemporary Islamicists', in W. Shadid and V. S. Koningsveld (eds) *Political Participation and Identities of Muslims in Non-Muslim States*, Kampen, the Netherlands: Kok Pharos, pp. 84–114.

Shah, P. (2005) *Legal Pluralism in Conflict: Coping with Cultural Diversity in Law*, London: Glass House Press.

Shah, P. and Menski, W. (2006) 'Introduction: Migration, diasporas and legal systems in Europe', in P. Shah and W. Menski (eds) *Migration, Diasporas and Legal Systems in Europe*, London: Routledge.

Shah-Kazemi, N. S. (2000) 'Cross-cultural mediation: A critical view of the dynamics of culture in family disputes', *International Journal of Law, Policy and Family*, 14(3): 302–25.

Shah-Kazemi, N. S. (2001) *Untying the Knot: Muslim Women, Divorce and the Shariah*, Oxford: The Nuffield Foundation.

Shaw, A. (1988) *A Pakistani Community in Britain*, Oxford: Blackwell.

Shaw, A. (1994) 'The Pakistani community in Oxford', in R. Ballard (ed.) *Desh Pardesh: The South Asian Presence in Britain*, London: C. Hurst & Co. Ltd.

Sheleff, L. (2000) *The Future of Tradition: Customary Law, Common Law and Legal Pluralism*, London and Portland: Frank Cass.

Sheriff, S. (2001) 'Mosques fire bombed, Muslims assaulted: British Muslims under seige', *Muslim News*, 149: 1 & 8.

Siddiqui, M. (1996) 'Law and the Desire for Social Control: An Insight into the Hanafi Concept of Kafa'a with Reference to the Fatawa 'Alamagiri (1664–1672),' in M. Yamani (ed.) *Feminism and Islam, Legal and Literary Perspectives*, Ithaca Press, pp. 49–68.

Sidhu, S. (2006) *Perspectives on Conflict Resolution in South Asian Families: Examining the Role of Family Mediation*, Clearinghouse, Canada.

Sieber, J. and Stanley, B. (1988) 'Ethical and Professional Dimensions of Socially Sensitive Research', *American Psychologist*, 42: 49–55.

Silverman, D. (1993) *Interpreting Qualitative Data: Methods for Analysing Talk, Text and Interaction*, London: Sage.

Silverman, D. (1998) 'Introducing qualitative research', in D. Silverman (ed.) *Qualitative Research – Theory, Method, and Practice*, London: Sage, pp. 1–14.

Skeggs, B. (1994) 'Situating the production of feminist ethnography', in M. Maynard and J. Purvis (eds) *Researching Women's Lives from a Feminist Perspective*, London: Taylor & Francis, pp. 99–110.

Smart, C. (1984) *The Ties that Bind: Law, Marriage and the Reproduction of Patriarchal Relations*, London: Routledge and Kegan Paul.

Smart, C. (1992) 'The woman of legal discourse', *Social Legal Studies*, 1(1): 29–44.

Song, M. and Parker, D. (1998) 'Commonality, difference and the dynamics of disclosure in in-depth interviewing', in A. Bryman and R. Burgess (eds) *Qualitative Research*, 6: 112–26.

Southall Black Sisters (1990) *Against the Grain: Southall Black Sisters 1979–1989, A Celebration of Struggle and Survival*, London: Southall Black Sisters.

Soyal, N. Y. (2000) 'Citizenship and identity: Living in diasporas in post-war Europe?' *Ethnic and Racial Studies*, 23(1): 1–15.

Soysal, Y. N. (1994) *Limits of Citizenship: Migrants and Postnational Membership in Europe*, The University of Chicago Press Books.

Spivak, G. (1988) 'Can the subaltern speak?', in C. Nelson and L. Grossberg (eds) *Marxism and the Interpretation of Culture*, Illinois: University of Illinois Press, pp. 271–313.

Spivak, G. (1990) *The Postcolonial Critic: Interviews, Strategies, Dialogues*, New York: Routledge.

Squires, J. (2001) 'Representing groups, deconstructing identities', *Feminist Theory*, 2(1): 7–27.

Squires, J. (2002) 'Culture, equality and diversity', in P. Kelly (ed.) *Multiculturalism Reconsidered*, London: Polity Press.

Stanley, L. and Wise, S. (1988) *Breaking Out Again*, London: Routledge.

Stanley, L. and Wise, S. (1990) 'Method, methodology and epistemology in feminist research processes', in L. Stanley (ed.) *Feminist Praxis: Research, Theory and Epistemology in Feminist Sociology*, London: Routledge, pp. 34–49.

Stewart, A. (2000) 'The contribution of feminist legal scholarship', in A. Stewart (ed.) *Gender, Law and Social Justice*, London: Blackstone Press.

Stooler, G. (2007) 'Contextualising multiculturalism: A three dimensional examination of multicultural claims', *Law and Ethics of Human Rights* 1(1), Art. 10: 310–53.

Stopes-Roe, M. and Cochrane, R. (1990a) 'The child-rearing values of Asian and British parents and young people: An inter-ethnic and inter-generational comparison in the evaluation of Kohn's 13 qualities', *British Journal of Social Psychology*, 29(2): 149–60.

Stopes-Roe, M. and Cochrane, R. (1990b) *Citizens of this country: The Asian-Britain*, Multilingual Matters Ltd.

Sunder, M. (2005) 'Enlightened constitutionalism', *Connecticut Law Review*, 37(3).

Surty, M. (1991) 'The Shariah family courts of Britain and the protection of women's rights in Muslim family law', *Muslim Education Quarterly*, 9: 59–63.

Synder, G. F. (1981) 'Anthropology, dispute processes and law: A critical introduction', *British Journal of Law & Society*, 8(2): 141–80.

Taher, A. (2008) 'Revealed: UK's first official Sharia courts', *The Sunday Times*, 14 September.

Tamahana, Z. B. (1997) *Realistic Socio-Legal Theory: Pragmatism and a Social Theory of Law*, Oxford: Clarendon Press.

Tamahana, Z. B. (2001) *A General Jurisprudence of Law and Society*, London: Oxford University Press.

Taylor, C. (1994) 'Examining the politics of recognition', in A. Gutmann (ed.) *Multiculturalism*, Princeton: Princeton University Press, pp. 25–74.

Taylor, C. (2007) *A Secular Age*, Boston: Harvard University Press.

Taylor, C. (2009) 'What is Secularism', in G. Levery and T. Modood (eds) *Secularism, Religion and Multicultural Citizenship*, Cambridge: Cambridge University Press, pp. xi–xxx.

Taylor, J. S. (1998) 'Leaving the field: Research, relationships and responsibilities', in D. Silverman (ed.) *Qualitative Research – Theory, Method, and Practice*, London: Sage, pp. 67–93.

The Islamic Shari'a Council of Great Britain and Northern Ireland (1982) *An Introduction*, Leyton, London.

Thiara, R. and Gill, A. (2010) *Violence Against Women in South Asian Communities: Issues for Policy and Practice*, London: Jessica Kingsley Publishers.

Thornton, M. (1991) 'The public/private dichotomy: Gendered and discriminatory', *Journal of Law and Society*, 18(4): 38–52.

Thornton, M. (1995) *Public and Private: Feminist Legal Debates*, Melbourne: Oxford University Press.

Tie, W. (1999) *Legal Pluralism: Toward a Multicultural Conception of Law*, Aldershot and Brookfield: Dartmouth and Ashgate.

Tilley, S. (2007) 'ADR professional: Recognising gender differences in all issues mediation', *Family Law*, 37, 1 April.

Tully, J. (2007) 'The practice of lawmaking and the problem of difference', in O. P. Shabani (ed.) *Multiculturalism and Law: Critical Debates*, Cardiff: University of Wales Press, pp. 19–41.

Tumbridge, J. (2011) 'Arbitration: Can you choose your arbitrator or not? Jivraj v Hashwani Case comment', *International Company and Commercial Law Review*, 22(6): 201–3.

Turam, B. (2004) 'The politics of engagement between Islam and the secular state: Ambivalences of "civil society"', *The British Journal of Sociology*, 55(2): 259–81.

Twining, W. (2000) *Globalisation and Legal Theory*, Cambridge University Press.

Unger, M. R. (1983) *The Critical Legal Studies Movement*, Cambridge, MA: Harvard University Press.

Vakil, A. K. (2010) 'Is the Islam in Islamophobia the same as in the Islam in Anti-Islam: Or when is it Islamophobia Time in', in S. Sayyid and A. K. Vakil (eds) *Thinking through Islamaphobia: Global Perspectives*, Hurst, pp. 23–45.

Van Dyke, V. (1995) 'The individual, the state, and ethnic communities in political theory', in W. Kymlicka (ed.) *The Rights of Minority Cultures*, Oxford: Oxford University Press, pp. 31–57.

Varenne, H. (1998) 'Diversity as American cultural category', in Greenhouse J. C. and Roshanak Kheshti (eds), *Democracy and Ethnography: Constructing Identities in Multicultural Liberal States*, pp. 35–55.

Verman, F. (1982) *Education for All: A Landmark in Pluralism*, London: The Falmer Press.

Vertovec, S. (1996) 'Multiculturalism, culturalism and public incorporation', *Ethnic and Racial Studies*, 19(1): 48–69.

Vertovec, S. (2002) 'Islamophobia and Muslim recognition in Britain', in Y. Yazbeck Haddad (ed.) *Muslims in the West: From Sojourners to Citizens*, Oxford and New York: Oxford University Press, pp. 19–35.

Vertovec, S. and Peach, C. (eds) (1997) *Islam in Europe: The Politics of Religion and Community*, Basingstoke: Palgrave Macmillan.

Vickers, L. (2008) *Religious freedom, religious discrimination and the workplace.* Hart Publishing.

Volp, L. (2001) 'Feminism versus multiculturalism', *Columbia Law Review*.

Volpp, L. (2007) 'The culture of citizenship', *Theoretical Inquiries in Law*, 8(2): 571: 1181–218.

Wadud, A. (1999) *Qur'an and Woman, Rereading the Sacred Text from a Woman's Perspective*, Oxford University Press.

Waggoner, M. (2005) 'Irony, embodiment and the critical attitude: Engaging Saba Mahmood's critique of secular', *Culture and Religion*, pp. 237–61.

Wallback, J., Choudhury, S. and Herring, J. (eds) (2009), *Rights, Gender and Family Law*, London: Routledge.

Walby, S. (1990) *Theorizing Patriarchy*, Wiley-Blackwell, Oxford.

Walsh, E. (2008) 'ADR professional: Publicly funded family mediation: the Way Forward, *Family Law*, 1144.

Walsh, E. (2009) 'Forced marriage action', *Family Law*, 81(2).

Warraich, S. (2001) *Migrant South Asian Muslims and Family Laws in England: An Unending Conflict*, unpublished MA thesis, University of Warwick.

Warraich, S. and Balchin, C. (2006) *Recognizing the Un-Recognized: Inter-Country Cases and Muslim Marriages and Divorces in Britain*, Women Living Under Muslim Laws (WLUML) publications, Nottingham: The Russell Press.

Warren, C. (2003) 'After the interview', *Qualitative Sociology*, 26(1): 93–110.

Webber, J. (2007) 'A judicial ethic for a pluralistic age', in O. P. Shabani (eds) *Multiculturalism and Law: Critical Debates*, Cradiff: University of Wales Press, pp. 67–100.

Weinstock, D. M. (2005) 'Beyond exit rights: Reframing the debate', in A. Eisenberg and J. Spinner-Halev (eds) *Minorities within Minorities: Equality, Rights and Diversity*, Cambridge: Cambridge University Press, pp. 227–46.

Welchman, L. (2004) *Women's Rights and Islamic Family Law: Perspectives on Reform*, London: Zed Books.

Welchman, L. and Hossain, S. (2005) 'Introduction: 'Honour', rights and wrongs', in L. Welchman and S. Hossain (eds) *'Honour': Crimes, Paradigms and Violence Against Women*, New York: Zed Books, pp. 1–22.

Wendell, S. (1990) 'Oppression and victimization; choice and responsibility', *Hypatia*, 5(3): 15–46.

Werbner, P. (1988) 'The fiction of unity in ethnic politics: Aspects of representation and the state among British Pakistanis', in P. Werbner and M. Anwar (eds) *Black and Ethnic Leadership in Britain*, London: Routledge, pp. 62–73.

Werbner, P. (1989) *The Migration Process: Capital, Gifts and Offerings among British Pakistanis*, Oxford: Berg.

Werbner, P. (1990) *Capitals, Gifts and Offerings among British Pakistanis*, London, Berg Publishers.

Werbner, P. (1996) 'Public spaces, political voices: Gender, feminism and aspects of British Muslim participation in the public sphere', in W. Shadid and V. S. Koningsveld (eds) *Political Participation and Identities of Muslims in Non-Muslim States*, Kampen, the Netherlands: Kok Pharos, pp. 206–28.

Werbner, P. (2000) 'Divided loyalties, empowered citizenship? Muslims in Britain', *Citizenship Studies*, 4(3): 307–24.

Werbner, P. (2001) *Imagined Diasporas among Manchester Muslims: The Public Performance of Pakistani Transnational Identity Politics*, James Currey Publishers: Oxford.

Werbner, P. (2002a) 'The place which is diaspora: Citizenship, religion and gender in the making of chaordic transnationalism', *Journal of Ethnic and Migration Studies*, 28(1): 119–33.

Werbner, P. (2002b) *Imagined Diasporas among Manchester Muslims: The Public Performance of Pakistani Transnational Identity Politics*, Oxford: James Currey; Santa Fe, NM: School of American Research Press.

Werbner, P. and Modood, T. (1997) (eds) *Debating Cultural Hybridity*, London: Zed Books.

Werbner, P. and Yuval-Davis, N. (1999) *Women, Citizenship and Difference*, London: Zed Books.

Wheeler, B. M. (1996) *Applying the Canon in Islam: The Authorization and Maintenance of Interpretive Reasoning in Hanafi Scholarship*, Albany: State University of New York Press.

White Paper (1987) *Looking to the Future – Mediation and the Ground for Divorce* CM 2799. A copy of the report can be accessed at www.official-documents.gov.uk/document/cm27/2799/2799.pdf last accessed 20th August 2012.

White Paper (1992) *Civil Registration: Vital Change – Birth, Marriage and Death Registration in the Twenty-First Century* (Cm5355, 2002).

Williams, P. (1988) 'On being the object of property', *Signs*, 14(1): 5–24.

Williams, R. (2008) 'Civil and religious law in England: A religious perspective', *Ecclesiastical Law Journal*, 10(3): 262–82.

Wilson, A. (1978) *Finding a Voice, Asian Women in Britain*, Virago Press.

Wilson, A. (2006) *Dreams, Questions, Struggles: South Asian Women in Britain*, London: Pluto Press.

Witty, C. J. (1980) *Mediation and Society, Conflict Management in Lebanon*, New York: London Academic Press.

Wolf, N. (1991) *The Beauty Myth: How Images of Beauty are Used Against Women*, New York: Doubleday.

Woodman, G. (1998) 'Ideological combat and social observation: Recent debate about legal pluralism', *Journal of Legal Pluralism and Unofficial Law*, 42: 21–59.

Woodman, G. R. (2008) 'The possibilities of co-existence of religious laws with other laws', in R. Mehdi, H. Petersen, E. Reenberg Sand and G. R. Woodman (eds) *Law and Religion in Multicultural Societies*, Copenhagen: DJOF Publishing, pp. 23–43.

Woodward, K. (1997) 'Concepts of identity and difference', in K. Woodward (ed.) *Identity and Difference*, New York: Sage and Milton Keynes, Open University Press.

Wray, H. (2006) 'Hidden purpose: ethnic minority international marriages and intention to live together', in P. Shah and W. Menski (eds) *Migration, Diasporas and Legal Systems in Europe*, London and New York: Routledge-Cavendish, pp. 163–184.

Wray, H. (2011) *Regulating Marriage Migration into the UK*, New York, Ashgate: Ashgate.

Yamani, M. (1996) *Feminism and Islam: Legal and Literacy Perspectives*, Reading, Berkshire: Ithaca Press.

Yilmaz, I. (2001a) 'Muslim law in Britain: Reflections in the socio-legal sphere and differential legal treatment', *Journal of Muslim Minority Affairs*, 20(2): 353–60.

Yilmaz, I. (2001b) 'Law as chameleon: The question of incorporation of Muslim personal law into English law', *Journal of Muslim Minority Affairs*, 21(2): 297–308.

Yilmaz, I. (2002) 'Challenge of post-modern legality and Muslim legal pluralism in England', *Journal of Ethnic and Migration Studies*, 28(2): 343–54.

Yilmaz, I. (2003) 'Muslim alternative dispute resolution and neo-Ijtihad in England', *Alternative, Turkish Journal of International Relations*, 2(1), available at http://www. alternativesjournal.net/volume2/number1/yilmaz.htm, accessed on 22 August 2012.

Yilmaz, I. (2005) *Muslim Law, Politics and Society in Modern Nation States*, Aldershot: Ashgate.

Young, I. (1990) *Justice and the Politics of Difference*, Princeton: Princeton University Press.

Yuval-Davis, N. (1997) *Gender and Nation*, London: Sage.

Yuval-Davis, N. (2006) 'Intersectionality and feminist politics', *European Journal of Women's Studies*, 13(3): 193–209.

Yuval-Davis, N. (2011) *The Politics of Belonging: Intersectional Contestations*, London: Sage.

Index